# Power and Policy in Western European Democracies

# Power and Policy in Western European Democracies

*Fourth Edition*

DAVID M. WOOD

*University of Missouri—Columbia*

Macmillan Publishing Company

NEW YORK

Editor: Bruce Nichols
Production Supervisor: Lisa G. M. Chuck
Production Manager: Richard C. Fischer
Text Designer: Patrice Fodero
Cover Designer: Brian Sheridan
Photo Researcher: Barbara Schultz
Illustrations: Hadel Studio

This book was set in Palatino by C. L. Hutson, Inc., and printed and bound by Halliday Lithographers. The cover was printed by New England Book Components.



Printed in the United States of America



Macmillan Publishing Company
866 Third Avenue, New York, New York 10022

Collier Macmillan Canada, Inc.
1200 Eglinton Avenue East
Suite 200
Don Mills, Ontario M3C 3N1

LIBRARY OF CONGRESS CATALOGING-IN-PUBLICATION DATA

Wood, David Michael, 1934–
Power and policy in Western European democracies / David M. Wood.
—4th ed.
p. cm.
"Also forms part one of a three-part hardback text entitled Comparing political systems"—Pref.
Includes bibliographical references and index.
ISBN 0-02-429575-2
1. Europe—Politics and government—1945–2. Comparative government. I. Title.
JN94.A2W66 1991
306.2'094—dc20 90-37471
CIP

Printing: 1 2 3 4 5 6 7 Year: 1 2 3 4 5 6 7

# PREFACE

*Power and Policy in Western European Democracies*, 4th Edition, is a textbook that introduces undergraduates to the politics of Western Europe's larger democracies: Great Britain, France, West Germany, and Italy. More generally, it treats the similarities and differences between major countries of the First World, a term that is applied to the 24 industrially advanced countries that have competitive political and economic systems. In so doing, it makes frequent comparisons of these countries of Western Europe with the two most populous First World countries, the United States and Japan. A special effort is made in this edition systematically to include Japan in the comparisons that are made. The book places the systems of government and politics of these countries in their socioeconomic contexts and accounts for their political similarities and differences in terms of historical and contemporary economic, social, cultural, and political factors.

An additional feature of the book is that it serves to introduce the student to general concepts and themes that are encountered in courses in political science generally and in comparative politics particularly. Certain values that are central to the attainment of human dignity as it is understood in the First World are applied to the comparisons made in the first six chapters. These values are used in the seventh chapter as measuring devices to evaluate comparatively the performances of First World political systems. Also in that final chapter is a "Postscript" that outlines the process of German reunification that has been going on while this edition has reached its final stages.

*Power and Policy in Western European Democracies*, 4th Edition, also forms Part One of a three-part hardback textbook entitled *Comparing Political Systems: Power and Policy in Three Worlds*, 4th Edition. My co-authors in this work are Professor Gary K. Bertsch of the University of Georgia and Professor Robert P. Clark of George Mason University. Part Two of the larger textbook, written by Professor Bertsch, treats the Communist, or Second World countries as they have undergone a period of dramatic political change since the time the last edition of the text was written. Part Three, by Professor Clark, compares the wide array of Third World political systems found in Asia, the Middle East, Africa, and Latin America. (The parts by Professors Bertsch and Clark have also been published separately by Macmillan as *Reform and Revolution in Communist Systems* and *Power and Policy in the Third World*, 4th Edition, respectively.) In all three parts, the approach is an analytical rather than a country-by-country one; that is, political systems are compared within common analytical categories in all three parts rather than each part being subdivided with country-specific subparts. In the combined volume, this approach makes possible a general conclusion that compares the three worlds with one another.

I wish to acknowledge the invaluable cooperation of Gary Bertsch and Robert Clark in working on a common framework, in providing helpful ideas for approaching the material, and in making innumerable decisions in the course of the project. Eben Ludlow and Bruce Nichols, editors in Macmillan's College Division, deserve special thanks for their roles in easing the transition involved in moving the text from John Wiley & Sons. All of the editors and editorial staff at Wiley and Macmillan who have assisted in improving my work over the past fifteen years are hereby wholeheartedly thanked. For whatever deficiencies the book contains, I take full responsibility.

David M. Wood

# CONTENTS

# Power and Policy in Western European Democracies

# INTRODUCTION: STUDYING POLITICS IN WESTERN EUROPEAN DEMOCRACIES

For the past twenty-five years or so, approximately two dozen countries in the world have occupied most of the top ranks in the world league standings for economic indicators and have shared a characteristic found among few other countries in the world: They are, by the consensus of the most knowledgeable observers, democracies. These are the countries of what we shall call "the First World." Most of them are in the region of the world known as Western Europe. In this book, which has "Western European Democracies" in its title, the central topic is the domestic politics of these two dozen countries, including those, such as the United States, Japan, Australia, and Israel, that are not in Western Europe, but that are advanced industrial countries—and democracies. The four countries that are given principal attention—Great Britain, France, West Germany, and Italy—are Western European countries. A fifth country, Japan, is discussed at length at appropriate points, although Japan is an Asian country and does not share the cultural heritage of the others. Yet, like the others, it is an advanced industrial democracy—in fact, probably the most successful of the two dozen in economic terms. Next to the United States, which is another point of reference, although less systematically treated, Japan is the largest of the advanced industrial democracies, both in population and in the size of its economy. Japan is well ahead of the four Western European countries on both of those measures. The inclusion of Japan is intended to make it possible to test whether certain generalizations about advanced industrial democracies that are made on the basis of the Western European cases are more universally applicable. Will they hold up even when Western cultural influences are set aside? But the text is still fundamentally about advanced industrial democracies in Western Europe.

Why learn about Western Europe? First of all, this area of the world is vital to U.S. security, economic well-being, and sense of identity. Through the North Atlantic Treaty Organization (NATO), we have committed ourselves irrevocably to the joint defense of the West. We now assert forcefully what we only accepted rather reluctantly during the two world wars: Our own fate is tied to that of Western Europe.

Although true in a military sense, it is even more true economically because the First World countries are one another's largest trading partners. We export inflation and unemployment to one another as well as goods and services. Slight economic tremors cause reverberations on both sides of the Atlantic. As for our identity, culturally we *are* European. Even those Americans whose ethnic origins are non-European share in a culture, including many of our religions, that has its roots—and some of its most ancient roots—in Europe. Within that cultural heritage is a *political culture* derived in considerable part from Western Europe as well. Whether we have such thoughts at the back or the front of our minds, we are materially and spiritually dependent on Western Europe to a greater extent than on any other part of the world outside of North America.

Beyond these obvious aspects of mutual interdependence, Western Europe and the United States can also be instructive to one another as each attempts to solve its own domestic problems, such as environmental protection or the regeneration of inner cities. A truism that underlies this entire volume is that the countries of the First World are more like one another than any one of them is like other countries elsewhere, at the very least in the fact that they are all relatively advanced industrially and have many similar problems that arise therefrom. Moreover, these countries are organized in a similar way to deal with these as public policy problems, particularly when compared with the political organization of non–First World countries. Thus, we are able to hold a great deal constant. If, say, Sweden comes up with a better way of disposing industrial wastes than we do, can we really suppose it is because Sweden as an industrial democracy does not have the problems we do? Is it not more likely that Sweden has simply found a better solution, one that we might do well to consider ourselves? Admittedly, things are not quite that simple, as we shall see. But, if we look on the First World as a gigantic laboratory in which experimental solutions are simultaneously being sought for similar problems in two dozen countries, the value of paying considerable attention to this part of the world becomes obvious. We employ such reasoning in the field of medicine; why not in politics?

In this textbook, the student is introduced to the rich and variegated field of Western European politics. The purpose of the book is to give an overview and to ask and answer some broad-gauged questions that stem from basic values held by the author. An attempt is not made to discuss in depth the politics of particular countries although, as noted above, five countries are emphasized. In this introduction, I explain what my underlying values are and how they guide me in the comparative analysis of Western European political systems. This textbook accompanies two similar textbooks on the politics of communist regimes and the politics of Third World countries.[1] The authors of those works have collaborated with me in bringing the three studies together into a single, three-part introduction to comparative politics.[2] Although each of the three worlds—First, Second, and Third—is treated separately in that volume, all have a common framework, which is used herein as well. The framework's most important element is a commitment to certain basic values in the study of comparative politics. Because of the collective nature of this work, from this point on the author refers to himself in the first person plural.

## Politics and Human Values

A purpose of this textbook is to evaluate the performance of Western European political systems. One of the main ways of doing this is the comparative method, through which we roughly measure the similarities and differences among the various political systems. Such measurements will enable us to evaluate our findings. Thus, if we find that Western European countries devote a larger proportion of their government budgets to health care than does the United States, we can make evaluative statements about two different types of resource allocation. The key question is: By what set of values will we be making these judgments? It is our intention to answer this question explicitly.

The range of human values that concern political scientists is potentially large. One leading political scientist, Harold Lasswell, has listed eight values that, in one fashion or another, are distributed among people in all political systems.[3] Few political scientists have followed Lasswell in adopting exactly the same list. Some have used different terms for essentially the same values. Some have made shorter lists; others have made longer ones. Some emphasize just one or two values. The point is that no political scientist can claim obvious superiority for any one list of values or assignment of priorities among values. Each political scientist may devise his or her own list. The political scientist has a responsibility to the student to define clearly what he or she means by each value and to state why each is important. In our three-part textbook, we adapt Lasswell's list by reducing his eight values to four: *power*, *well-being*, *enlightenment*, and *respect*. Each of these values is distributed in a certain way in each country, and each can be redistributed as a result of events within the political system.

In the ways these four values are interpreted, the bias of the author in favor of modern values rather than values usually thought of as traditional should become apparent. They reflect two philosophical commitments that are products of the Western experience of modernization: individualism and egalitarianism. Each of the four values is interpreted in the sense that the value is maximized if each individual has the capacity to seek a share of the value equal to that of every other individual in society, without restraints discriminating in favor of others. This would mean, for example, that each individual should be free to pursue whatever share of material well-being he or she wishes, as long as in so doing, he or she does not use the resources available or the resources gained in the process in such a way as to deprive others of the opportunity to do likewise. This is, of course, an unattainable ideal, but it is also a standard against which to measure real-world conditions. It is accompanied by a rejection of either pure selfishness or pure altruism as the valued motivation of persons in society.[4] To pursue a maximum of any particular value can be considered selfish from one perspective, but if in pursuing private ends one is likewise concerned that social and political conditions will be maintained in which everyone has the right to do likewise, then one's behavior will be motivated by a measure of altruism. Yet, the orientation of this modern person to a larger collectivity will be of a kind that enables individuality to be maintained, and not to be submerged into the collective interest of a larger, preexisting group, whether this be a family, locality, community, or nation. All of the values discussed in the following paragraphs are stated as containing elements of both selfishness and altruism, but the preference is for individualism over collectivism, as it is for Western versions of modernity. However, the contrast between individualism and collectivism and between Western and non-Western forms of modernity will be useful when we compare Japan with the major Western European countries.

It is sometimes suggested that modernity itself is a strictly Western phenomenon, and that Japan, as an "Eastern" country, could at most borrow the "modern" things that the West has created. Japan is credited with having effectively adapted Western modernity to its own traditions in order to be able to compete effectively with the West at the West's game. But the Japanese see the technology and many of the cultural artifacts that originated in the West as being the property of the world at large, not of any single part of it. As we shall see, the Japanese reinterpretation of Western technological and cultural imports has produced some unique features, such as the Japanese style of management, that are now being copied by the West in an effort to meet the "Eastern" competition of Japan and some of her neighbors in East Asia. The particular mix of values that we attribute to Japan in the chapters to come is not really exportable. But it is a *Japanese*, not an "Eastern," mix as opposed to some imagined "Western" mix, because, as we shall also see, each of the Western European countries we deal with has its own particular mix of cultural attributes as well.

## Power

Although the three other values may be regarded as ends in themselves, power can also be an instrumental value, a means to the achievement of the other values. As used in this textbook, *power* means the capacity to determine what public policy will be. Public policy consists of sets of government decisions made over time that affect human lives with respect to problems faced by people in a given society, for example, welfare policy, environmental policy, energy policy, and foreign policy. Those who make these decisions have power in this sense. Likewise, others who do not have formal decision-making responsibility may nevertheless have power in certain areas because those who make policy decisions defer to their judgment. Examples of formal power holders are prime ministers, legislators, and judges. Examples of those who might hold a more informal type of power are leaders of industry, the trade unions, or the church. Those who hold power have the instruments in their hands to make decisions affecting many human lives.

In this textbook we study the distribution of power. So far as formal power is concerned, its distribution can be studied by analyzing the various units of government, the powers held by each, and the relations between units. For example, we analyze the differences between presidential systems of government and parliamentary systems, observing the roles of the executive and legislative branches of government in both systems and how they relate to one another. When we turn to the informal distribution of power, we assess the weight of power holders who have no formal decision-making power. These include government officials (such as high-ranking civil servants) who are formally subordinate to executive leaders (such as presidents, prime ministers, and department heads) but whose command of information makes them indispensable to the formal decision makers and, thus, gives them informal power. Extragovernmental power holders who also possess valuable information include leaders of important interest groups, especially those serving as spokespersons for important economic sectors. One question to ask about the distribution of informal power in Western European countries is: What are the relative weights of business, agriculture, and labor?

More generally, we ask about the distribution of both formal and informal power between government, on the one hand, and ordinary citizens, on the other hand. The countries we look at are all regarded as democratic both in form and in actual practice, at least by most Western political scientists who attempt to classify political systems. But to what extent can the average citizen actually influence the public policymaking process? In all of the so-called democracies, a relatively small number of political elites have the lion's share of power, whereas the mass of ordinary citizens (as individuals, at any rate) are in a very weak position. Collectively, through organizing for political purposes and through exercising its right to vote, the populace has its impact, which is why First World countries come closer than other countries to meeting the standards for democracy. But the impact of the populace is more likely to be felt in choosing between broad value alternatives, not in making specific government decisions.

## Well-Being

We are using the term *well-being* in the material sense, by which we mean (1) the wealth of a nation and (2) the shares of this wealth that are held by different groups in society. An apt analogy often made is to liken wealth to the whole pie and the varying size of its slices. Those who are preoccupied with the overall size of the pie are often indifferent to the way it is sliced, or they assume that a larger pie will automatically mean larger slices for everyone. Those who are interested in the distributive question—how the pie is sliced—may focus on that problem without any concern for the pie's total size. When we talk about economic or material well-being of a given country, we must clarify whether we are talking about the total national wealth and growth or about the way in which wealth is distributed among different groups and how it could be redistributed. In this textbook, we discuss both types of well-being.

From the standpoint of overall national wealth, there are several ways in which governments can stimulate economic growth—through investment policies and through fiscal and monetary policies designed to stimulate economic activity. But a nation's economic potential depends on its capacity to market its goods and services abroad so that, in turn, it is able to afford goods and services from abroad that are in short supply at home. Governments must foster balanced economic policies that provide enough stimulus to ensure continued domestic growth at high levels of employment and at the same time protect the value of their nation's money so as not to jeopardize its own capacity to acquire goods and services in the international market. Levels of unemployment and inflation point to a government's success or failure in these areas, as do the gross national product (GNP) and import–export balances.

There is another sense in which the value of well-being is held by increasing numbers of people. This is what may be called "long-term" well-being, or the preservation of an acceptable standard of well-being for future generations, a matter over which the present generations have some control. The concern for environmental protection and conservation of resources can, at times, conflict with other economic policy goals, especially the goals of economic growth and high levels of industrial employment. Environmentalists argue that advanced industrial economies have so polluted, destroyed, and otherwise threatened the natural environment, while depleting vital mineral and vegetable resources, that there is serious question whether these economies can continue to produce manufactured goods, raw materials, or even foodstuffs at present levels. The clash of "productionism" and environmentalism can also be seen as a conflict between two different conceptions of modernity, the former a conception with which the West became familiar during the Industrial Revolution, the second a late twentieth-century concept of modernity in which future-oriented "altruism" takes precedence over materialistic individualism. We return to this conflict in Chapter 3.

## Enlightenment

The term *enlightenment* has a rather specific meaning in the Western cultural tradition. With a capital *E* it refers to the period in the eighteenth century preceding the French Revolution when, in France and other European countries, educated people awakened to ideas of the dignity of human beings and of their capacity to elevate their condition by manipulating the forces of nature for the good of humanity. All four of the values considered here can be viewed as having stemmed, directly or indirectly, from this heritage. What we have in mind, however, is enlightenment in the sense of the quantity and quality of formal education, bearing in mind that formal education may not always be very enlightening. We have borrowed the term from Lasswell, but we acknowledge full responsibility for its particular application.

In most countries, governments assume a major role in the education of their young people. Countries can be compared according to how many of their citizens are being educated (entirely or in part) at government expense, and up to what levels. Such quantitative indicators will not, of course, tell us much about the quality of the education or whether it is really adequate to the society's needs. Indeed, it is possible that, beyond a certain level at least, a quantitative increase is likely to mean a qualitative decline. High-quality education is often elitist education. In elitist educational systems, resources are highly concentrated in a few schools and universities to give the best possible education to the few who are destined to be the nation's leaders. If enlightenment is to be more widely distributed, greater quantity may have to be chosen at the expense of quality. In Western Europe, where, relative to the United States, quality has traditionally been given priority over quantity, a very serious reassessment of priorities is taking place today.

Enlightenment can also be taken to mean the role of the press and the electronic media in communicating information and ideas about politics to adult citizens who enjoy varying degrees of sophistication about the subject. We take a look in Chapter 7 at the extent to which the press and media in our five countries provide readers, viewers, and listeners with a thorough and balanced coverage of political events.

## Respect

We also use the term *respect* in a rather specialized sense to refer to what Americans often mean by civil rights and civil liberties. Respect is accorded to the individual if (1) he or she is able to exercise and enjoy all the rights that are available to every other citizen in the society, and (2) these rights are those that ought to be available to all members of all societies, according to the highest standards of justice and equity. Governments may enhance the value of respect in several ways.

1. Through the judicial system, governments can act to protect the individual when other individuals or other branches of government threaten individual rights.
2. The more active branches of government—the legislative and the executive—can deliberately restrain themselves from taking actions restricting human rights.
3. The more active branches of government can take forthright action to protect in-

dividuals and groups whose rights are threatened by other individuals or groups.

It is important to point out that violations of individual rights are often specific instances of systematic violations of the rights of particular groups in society. Thus, Mary Smith's rights may have been violated not so much because she is Mary Smith per se, but because she is a woman, or a black, or a Catholic, or speaks a minority language. If the rights of women, for example, have been systematically violated in the past in a particular country and the government of that country begins acting in such a way as to uphold these long-neglected rights, then it may be said that government is acting in a redistributive way in the matter of respect. It may not be as easy to measure respect as it is to measure well-being or enlightenment, but we can at least gauge the direction in which the government is moving. In cases where the government resists the claims of deprived groups that their rights are being violated, or where the government actively promotes their violation, then we can say the government has consciously opted for the status quo regarding the way respect is distributed.

### Human Dignity

From time to time, we substitute the term *human dignity* for our four values. If, in a given country, power, well-being, enlightenment, and respect are widely and equitably distributed among the various groups, then we can say that human dignity is well served in that country. Needless to say, this is an ideal that is nowhere realized in practice. Therefore, it can serve as a measuring device not only for characterizing particular countries but also for our central purpose—comparing various countries. In the final chapter of the textbook we evaluate countries with respect to all four of the values that make up human dignity. Again, the definition of human dignity is our own. It is hoped that the student now has a clear understanding of what it means in this particular textbook.

## *An Analytical Model*

There are several possible ways to proceed in undertaking comparative political study. Most political scientists would agree, however, that before beginning their inquiry, they must specify (1) what kinds of questions they are asking and (2) what steps they will be taking in answering them. In the preceding section on Politics and Human Values, we presented the questions. Now what we need is a sort of road map alerting the student to the route we will be taking. The analytical model presented provides the basis for the chapter outline, or itinerary, that follows. Many political scientists use an analytical model to help them look for information and to convert this information into answers to important questions. An analytical model can be simple, offering only the most significant categories of information as to what kinds of phenomena we should examine. Other analytical models can be quite complex, specifying not only the categories of information needed but also the anticipated causal relationships among them. Because this is an introductory textbook, we take the simpler approach.

As noted, in this textbook we are asking how and to what extent the various Western European political systems enhance the values that constitute human dignity. We also want to know why certain countries go farther than others in this direction. In other words, we are interested in comparison for the purpose of explanation as well as for gaining a broader perspective on the politics of given countries. Ultimately, we seek answers to the following question: Does it make a difference what type of political system a country has, or could the same level of human dignity be achieved in a given country regardless of the political system? In the broadest terms, we are assessing the relative importance of two very general, multifaceted explanations for levels of human dignity—the political system and its environment. Figure I.1 shows what we have in mind.

By *political system* we mean a process that involves structured interaction among actors. These actors are directing themselves toward particular goals that produce certain intended or unintended outcomes that will either promote or detract from human dignity as we have defined it. The binding decisions of government are the actions that will bring about such outcomes, but the decisions themselves are due to the interactions of goal-seeking actors, including the decision makers themselves. For example, the proponents of nuclear energy and the environmentalists both want to promote the value of well-being. The former believe that nuclear energy can solve the energy shortages that threaten our present standard of living. On the other hand, the environmentalists fear the possible consequences of nuclear energy for the biological environment and even for the future of life itself. Each group calls on the government to adopt its own conception of well-being exclusively. Government decision makers must choose between the competing goals. The choices will undoubtedly reflect the values of those holding decision-making power as well as those of the contending groups. The decisions will then be implemented with consequences for both energy supply and environmental quality. These consequences are what political scientists call the "outcomes." The total impact of all actions taken in the political system will, then, lead us to reassess the extent to which human dignity is being promoted in that society.

However, events may occur outside the political system that will also have consequences for the level of human dignity. In fact, the political system itself does not exist in a vacuum. Political actors seek to realize their goals through government action because they find certain aspects of their daily lives unsatisfactory. In the beginning, at least, most of these aspects are not political in nature. Economic uncertainty, racial conflict, and external threats to the national security originate in various ways outside the political system itself, owing to dislocations in other systems: the economy, the ecology, the social structure, the general culture, the international political arena. The sum total of these other systems constitutes what we call the "environment" of the political system. It is a broader

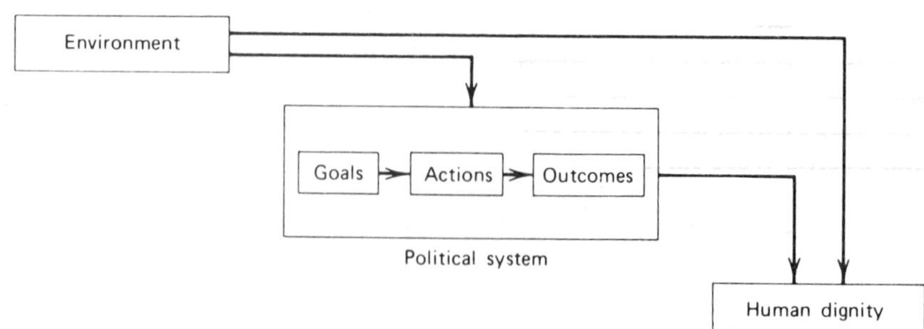


*Figure I.1* Diagram of the analytical model.

meaning of environment than what is currently popular, that is, our ecological environment. Many aspects of human life itself may be politically relevant although they are not political aspects in their own right. A strike by automobile workers against the car manufacturers is not at the outset a political action. But it is bound to have political consequences, for example, when representatives of the Department of Labor get together with representatives of the automobile companies and the automobile workers' union to try to help them iron out differences, or when new legislation is introduced in Congress to give the federal government greater authority to deal with such situations in the future.

Sometimes events occur in the environment of a political system that significantly alter the level of human dignity, before the political system can be called into effective play, for example, the influx of black- and brown-skinned peoples into Great Britain during the 1950s and 1960s. In some areas of the country, the racial composition of the population was visibly altered, and many of the indigenous whites became anxious about racial intermingling and the economic threat of new groups. There were occasional race riots, and there was large-scale private discrimination. In the 1960s, the political parties began to focus on the problem. They tried both to limit immigration of the so-called coloureds and to discourage private discrimination, thus facilitating integration of the existing "coloured" population into society at large. Until the political system responded, one could say that environmental events were having a negative impact on human dignity in Great Britain. Although the eventual response of the political system was mixed, some of the worst threats to human dignity were alleviated. This example also indicates that raising such problems from the subpolitical to the political level usually means that they become semipermanent political problems and that the government will be called on again and again to raise the level of human dignity yet another notch while making every effort to see that the situation does not deteriorate. In the late twentieth century, it is unlikely that a serious threat to human dignity will sustain itself for very long in the political systems of Western Europe or Japan before important societal groups will begin to turn to government and formulate goals for remedial action. Yet, to examine the actions taken and their outcomes without referring to the environmental conditions that produced them would be to tell only half the story—probably the less interesting half.

## *Chapter Organization*

This textbook is organized to take the political system/environment distinction into account. The first three chapters deal with the environment, and the following three with the political system itself; the last chapter presents an evaluation of the five political systems in terms of how well they have attained the four values making up human dignity. It also tries to answer the question posed above: Does it make a difference what kinds of policies a government undertakes? In each chapter there is a discussion of similarities and differences between the four Western European countries and Japan with respect to the characteristics examined in the chapter.

The first two chapters discuss the social and economic environmental characteristics that impinge directly on the political system. Chapter 1 shows the historical interrelationship among social, economic, and political factors that have been common to Western European countries at similar stages in their industrial development.

In Chapter 2, the contemporary economic and social structures of the five countries being examined are described. These countries face a wide variety of recurring economic problems today, including unemployment, inflation, scarcity of raw materials, cyclical fluctuations, and regional disparities in economic development. Some of the countries are also noted for deep-set social cleavages with respect to social class, religion, or ethnicity. These frequently have important political consequences.

Chapter 3 discusses a link between the political system and its environment—the political culture. This may be viewed as the pattern of attitudes and beliefs people hold toward their political system, orientations that are acquired through the process of political socialization. One important aspect of political culture is what the ordinary citizen believes he or she can do to influence the political process.

Chapters 4, 5, and 6 deal directly with the political system. Chapter 4 examines the structures and processes by which broad goals are formulated (including choices among competing values) and then presented to the voters to decide among groups of would-be decision makers representing different sets of value commitments. This refers to political party systems and the electoral process. In Chapters 5 and 6, the structures and processes of government are considered. Chapter 5 focuses on the formal holders of government decision-making power and the ways in which that power is distributed among units of government. Chapter 6 emphasizes certain informal power holders—those who play important roles in making economic policy by deciding the overall size of the pie and the way it will be sliced. Case studies are employed to show how the various economic sectors interact in the economic policymaking process.

Finally, Chapter 7 evaluates the performances of the four major Western European political systems and Japan with respect to our four values. The value of well-being is singled out for special treatment and an attempt is made to explain differences among the political systems regarding the attainment of well-being.

## *Notes*

1. Gary K. Bertsch, *Power and Policy in Communist Systems*, 4th ed. (New York: Macmillan, 1991); and Robert P. Clark, *Power and Policy in the Third World*, 4th ed. (New York: Macmillan, 1991).
2. Gary K. Bertsch, Robert P. Clark, and David M. Wood, *Comparing Political Systems: Power and Policy in Three Worlds*, 4th ed. (New York: Macmillan, 1991).
3. Harold Lasswell, *Politics: Who Gets What, When, How* (Cleveland: World, 1958), p. 202.
4. Howard Margolis, *Selfishness, Altruism, and Rationality: A Theory of Social Choice* (Chicago and London: University of Chicago Press, 1984).

CHAPTER 1

# HISTORICAL BACKGROUND

Since World War II, most of the countries of Western Europe have consistently been classified by their own standards as democracies. The extent to which the reality has approached the Western ideal of democracy, considered as an equal distribution of power, has, however, varied. It is true that democracy is a goal toward which Western countries strive. Political scientists seldom claim that the ideal concept of democracy can be used as a descriptive term, that is, as a category to which Western political systems, in fact, belong.[1] American political scientist Robert A. Dahl has suggested that, instead of the word *democracy*, we use the term *polyarchy* to characterize the type of political system that predominates in the First World countries of Western Europe, in North America, and in parts of the western rim of the Pacific Ocean.[2] Polyarchies are political systems in which the many rule, not just in the formal sense of universal or near-universal suffrage but in the sense that there is a meaningful degree of competition among groups contending for power. The many who choose among these contenders have meaningful choices to make, and in making them they determine who will be making the decisions of goverment. But when we look at the distribution of power within the polyarchy, we see that, as individuals, the few who make the decisions of government have considerably more power than have the many, again as individuals, even though the many choose the few. Hence, unlike the ideal of democracy, power is not distributed equally, although it has also been argued that power is more equally distributed in the polyarchies of the First World than it is, or ever has been, anywhere else. Peter L. Berger suggests that, not only does the polyarchy maximize the power of ordinary people in fact, if not in ideal terms, but it also attains a wider distribution of respect than can be found in other forms.[3] This is in part because the competition for power is sufficiently equal to ensure that power will remain fairly equally distributed, and in part because temporary majorities will not be strong enough to diminish the amount of respect enjoyed by individuals and groups that are temporarily, or even permanently, in the minority. In comparison with most other countries of the world, the polyarchies examined share these advantages, but, as we shall see, they differ from one another in the degrees and the ways in which the advantages are realized.

It will be noted that most polyarchies are rather advanced economically and socially. Indeed, they compete economically with one another and are also their own principal trading partners. It is characteristic of polyarchies that they rank high on the various indexes of socioeconomic strength. Actually, most of the more advanced industrial countries of the world are polyarchies, with the notable exceptions of the Soviet Union, East Germany, and Czechoslovakia, which are communist (Second World) countries. But recent changes have moved these countries toward the status of polyarchies as well.

Another characteristic of most polyarchies is that they have parliamentary systems of government. Indeed, almost all of the Western European polyarchies currently have parliamentary systems or, as in the case of France, parliamentary traditions. Furthermore, more polyarchies have multiparty systems (that is, more than two major political parties) than have two-party systems, as in the United States. Again, this is particularly true of Western Europe. Even Great Britain, traditionally regarded as a two-party country, has some of the characteristics of a multiparty system. (See Table 1.1.)

The five political systems we compare are the five most populous polyarchies in the world other than the United States, and they include the four most populous polyarchies in Western Europe. All are advanced industrially. Although the range is wide, the gap between the most and least prosperous of these five countries, West Germany and Italy, has been narrowing in the past decade. All except France have parliamentary systems of government; France has a difficult-to-classify mixture of parliamentary and presidential elements. All, including Great Britain, have multiparty systems by the definition employed here. (See Chapter 4.)

In this fourth edition of the textbook, we have decided to include Japan among the major First World polyarchies that are systematically compared. This is in part because Japan is, after all, a First World polyarchy and, although the principal geographical focus is on Western Europe, Japan can scarcely be ignored when we attempt to generalize from the Western European examples to the First World polyarchies as a type. Japan has enjoyed the highest rates of economic growth and has experienced rates of unemployment and inflation that are among the lowest in the First World. But Japan does not share a deep commitment to Western cultural values, having selectively borrowed elements of the values of power, well-being, enlightenment, and respect that the West has to offer. Particularly, in this volume we call attention to certain cultural and institutional elements relevant to Japanese politics that are distinct from those typically found in Western Europe. This raises the question of whether Japan's economic success has been because of or in spite of the ways in which she differs from the West. Should we look to the cultural and structural ways in which Japan differs from Great Britain, France, West Germany, and Italy for the reasons that Japan has had a better economic record than the four other countries in the past decade or so, or should we expect to find the reasons in the borrowings Japan has made from the West? The student may be moved, in fact, to ask whether the success that Japan has shown in adapting to the value requirements of capitalism as an economic system and of polyarchy as a political system points the way to future successes by other non-Western countries, particularly those of East Asia, which share certain cultural characteristics with Japan. The case of

**Table 1.1 First World Polyarchies**

| *Country* | *Type of Government* | *Area* 1,000s of sq km | *Population (in millions)* | *Urban Population (% of total population)* | *GNP* per capita (1987)* |
|---|---|---|---|---|---|
| Australia | Parliamentary | 7,687 | 16.2 | 86 | $11,100 |
| Austria | Parliamentary | 84 | 7.6 | 57 | 11,980 |
| Belgium | Parliamentary | 31 | 9.9 | 97 | 11,480 |
| Canada | Parliamentary | 9,976 | 25.9 | 76 | 15,160 |
| Denmark | Parliamentary | 43 | 5.1 | 86 | 14,930 |
| Finland | Mixed presidential/ parliamentary | 337 | 4.9 | 60 | 14,470 |
| *France* | Mixed presidential/ parliamentary | 547 | 55.6 | 74 | 12,790 |
| *Germany, Fed. Republic of* | Parliamentary | 249 | 61.2 | 86 | 14,400 |
| Greece | Parliamentary | 132 | 10.0 | 61 | 4,020 |
| Iceland | Parliamentary | 103 | 0.2 | — | 16,600 |
| Ireland | Parliamentary | 70 | 3.6 | 58 | 6,120 |
| Israel | Parliamentary | 21 | 4.4 | 91 | 6,800 |
| *Italy* | Parliamentary | 301 | 57.4 | 68 | 10,350 |
| *Japan* | Parliamentary | 372 | 122.1 | 77 | 15,750 |
| Luxembourg | Parliamentary | 3 | 0.4 | — | 18,550 |
| Netherlands | Parliamentary | 41 | 14.7 | 88 | 11,860 |
| New Zealand | Parliamentary | 269 | 3.3 | 84 | 7,750 |
| Norway | Parliamentary | 324 | 4.2 | 74 | 17,190 |
| Portugal | Mixed presidential/ parliamentary | 92 | 10.2 | 32 | 2,830 |
| Spain | Parliamentary | 505 | 38.8 | 77 | 6,010 |
| Sweden | Parliamentary | 450 | 8.4 | 84 | 15,550 |
| Switzerland | Parliamentary | 41 | 6.5 | 61 | 21,330 |
| *United Kingdom* | Parliamentary | 245 | 56.9 | 92 | 10,420 |
| United States | Presidential | 9,363 | 243.8 | 74 | 18,530 |

(*Source*) The list of polyarchies is adapted and updated from Robert A. Dahl, *Polyarchy: Participation and Opposition* (New Haven: Yale University Press, 1971), pp. 84, 232. Data in the columns are taken from the World Bank, *World Development Report 1989* (Oxford: Oxford University Press, 1989), pp. 165, 225, 230. Population figures are from the latest census data available in 1987.

* GNP = gross national product.

France, West Germany, Italy, Japan, and the United Kingdom are in italics in all figures and tables to emphasize their use as comparative cases.

South Korea, which has registered even more spectacular economic success than Japan of late and has been moving by degrees toward polyarchy, may be particularly worth watching in the years immediately to come.

In this chapter, we discuss the history of the Western European polyarchies and Japan in an attempt to answer some of the questions just raised as well as such questions as these: How have the political systems of these countries (and those of other polyarchies) developed? What are the historical reasons for the similarities and differences between them? Why have they been able to develop economies that are generally more advanced than those of most other countries in the world? Are there historical reasons for these differences among them with respect to economic success? Although we cannot answer these questions fully in this introductory textbook, we can point to certain major developments in the history of advanced industrial societies generally and in particular of the four major Western European countries that are partially responsible. We also emphasize the development of Europe's social structure since the beginning of the Industrial Revolution in the eighteenth century. Our assumption is that the major political upheavals and economic changes during the past two centuries in Europe have been closely related to the conflicts among various social groups for larger shares of power, respect, well-being, and enlightenment.

The discussion is divided into four parts, each taking a stage in the path of Western Europe and Japan toward modernity: (1) the preindustrial social, economic, and political structures of Western Europe as found in the early eighteenth century just before the Industrial Revolution and in Japan before the middle of the nineteenth century; (2) the early industrialization period—an era of rapid change and great upheavals—that began about 1750 in Western Europe and a century later in Japan and lasted until around 1870 in northwestern Europe and perhaps until World War I in northern Italy and Japan; (3) the era of mature industrialization, beginning in the 1870s and 1880s and lasting until World War II; and (4) the post–World War II era in which Western Europe and Japan were developing the characteristics of *postindustrial society*.

## *Preindustrial Western Europe*

At the outset, it should be noted that what we are describing is the process of *modernization* as it took place initially in Western Europe. Modernization in Western Europe followed a different path from what took, or is taking, place in most other countries of the world. For the most part, the industrialization of Western Europe was self-generated; whereas other countries have relied extensively on external stimuli for their industrialization, Western Europe already had certain factors that helped to facilitate self-generated industrialization.

### Preindustrial Economies

Of prime importance in understanding the beginnings of industrialization is the fact that the economic system known as *capitalism* was already well established in Western Europe, and had been developing there for about three centuries before the advent of industrialization. During the period from around the middle of the fifteenth century until the middle of the eighteenth century, a transition took place from agrarian feudalism to industrial capitalism. It was a period in which the economic basis of social standing and political power was shifting from landed wealth to financial capital accumulated particularly in the growth of commerce among European cities, and between Europe and its expanding colonial empires. Capitalism is a dynamic economic system, in which a circular process occurs in the conversion of financial means that are at least in part in private hands, into the manufacture of goods and the provision of services. The realization of financial gain from these activities is then accumulated and put back into the cycle in the form of further investment. Wealth accumulates both in the form of liquid capital that can be reinvested and in the concrete material means of goods production and service provision, such as buildings, machines, and ships and wagons for conveying goods from place to place. The process can at any time be in a phase of expansion or of contraction, but over time, capitalism has produced an immense growth of both the financial and the material means for gains in human well-being. Capitalism is distinguished from *socialism*, the alternative method of accumulating wealth for a society, in that at least part of the financial resources provided and a large portion of the gain realized are by *private* entrepreneurs, who provide inspiration and take the risks for new industrial and commercial ventures. Under socialism, the state spreads the risk across society, and the inspiration is likely to come from state officials. During the three transitional centuries before the beginning of industrialization, capitalism moved from being a rather peripheral feature to becoming the central reality of economic life in Western Europe. In its earliest stages, as more recently elsewhere in the world, capitalism received considerable impetus from the state, which had first to accumulate power in its hands before it could use this power to assist in the development of capitalism and eventually industrialization.

Western Europe in this 300-year period was primarily agrarian, as are most of the Third World countries today. This means that the vast majority of the working population was engaged in agriculture. Many worked as agricultural laborers on large aristocratically owned estates; others divided their time between working for such landowners and working for themselves on their own small plots of land. Many people were independent small landowners able to subsist as such, but probably finding it impossible to accumulate wealth because of the heavy state taxes or manorial dues owed to a local lord. Other impediments were the seasonal uncertainties and the rather primitive state of agricultural technology.

In the smaller towns, the economy was dependent on the nearby countryside. These were market towns where farmers sold their produce and where goods that the farmer might buy were manufactured and sold. Itinerant merchants supplied farmers and townspeople with other goods that were not produced locally; this was about the extent of the economic intercourse between the town and the outside world. Only in the larger cities were goods produced for wider distribution. Because such manufacturing and its marketing often required substantial amounts of capital, the cities became financial centers. At that time (before industrialization), manufacturing existed only on a small scale. The factory system had not yet been introduced. The main source of energy was still the workers themselves.

## Social Structure

The cities had grown sufficiently large by the seventeenth and eighteenth centuries that there was a distinctive urban social class structure. It was based essentially on the ownership of property, which had not yet come into much conflict with the traditional social hierarchy of feudal times. At the top of the social scale was the aristocracy, whose economic and social position was based on the ownership of land and the possession of political power. The leading families of England and France, as well as those of the smaller political units in Germany and Italy, owned land but were also firmly established socially in the leading cities, especially Paris, London, and the other political capitals. Thus, they were found at the pinnacles of both the rural and the urban social hierarchies.

The urban middle class constituted a mixture of elements that was not yet too complex. Ownership of property conferred status within the middle class, and those with the most substantial fortunes were at the top of the social hierarchy, just below the aristocracy. During the century or so before industrialization, upward mobility, at least within the middle class, was becoming increasingly possible. It was this class that was accumulating the wealth necessary to capitalize the coming industrialization. The conservative influence of the aristocracy and of established craftspersons in the towns was giving way to ambitious entrepreneurship. Markets were opening up in the New World and in the European cities for goods, such as clothing and housewares, that could be produced inexpensively on a large scale by using rural laborers. Although such workers were less skilled than urban artisans, they could produce qualitatively by specializing in particular operations—a foreshadowing of the soon-to-emerge factory system.

Rural society was more hierarchical and had fewer class distinctions than urban society. Below the landed gentry on the rural social scale came the various gradations of peasants. The relative number of independent farmers and agricultural laborers varied widely from one part of Europe to another and from region to region within a given country. There were proportionately more independent farmers in northwestern Europe, but more agricultural laborers toward the south and east.

## Preindustrial Political Systems

The politics of the preindustrial period in Western Europe were dominated by the aristocracy or at least by those aristocrats who were concerned with national political matters. Attention focused on monarchs, whether their titles were emperor or empress, king or queen, grand duke, or elector. Aristocratic factions would vie with one another for the monarch's ear, and one measure of the monarch's personal power was the ability to keep factions divided and to maintain alternative sources of support, such as the church or the urban middle class.

Within the towns and cities, the middle class and artisans were rather formidable forces in their own right. In Western Europe, including parts of western Germany and northern Italy, they generally controlled their own local affairs and resisted monarchical intrusion. The development of parliamentary bodies in such countries as England and the Netherlands represented the determined effort of the urban middle class to resist arbitrary monarchical taxes. As the transitional 300-year period proceeded, in the larger and more powerful states of Western Europe—particularly in France, Prussia, and Sweden—monarchs were able to consolidate their own power territorially and to reduce the independent power bases of both the aristocracy and the towns. This was accomplished in part because of the skill employed by monarchs, or more accurately their chief ministers and advisers, in playing on the conflicts between the two principal estates of town and countryside, but also through a tacit alliance between the court and the leading financial and commercial interests.[4]

The system of mercantilism was developed in conjunction with the overseas expansion of European state power in the Americas and into areas bounded by the Indian Ocean. This was a method of accumulation of both wealth and power by the monarchical state through the achievement of surpluses in external trade, and through the plundering of conquered peoples. It enabled the powerful states to provide financial support for capitalist ventures, just as the enhanced power of the state to control internal affairs provided budding capitalists with the security to pursue risk-taking ventures. Part of the wealth accumulated in private hands returned to the state in the form of tax revenues, which funded the intra- and extra-European military endeavors of the state. As the wealth and power of the state expanded, that of a new class, the *bourgeoisie*, did as well. But its arrival to full political status in most countries had to await the explosion of privately held wealth that was the consequence of industrialization.

## Early Industrialization

### Industrialization Defined

The Industrial Revolution as a general European phenomenon began in the middle of the eighteenth century and ran its course in a little more than a century. As a localized phenomenon, however, it occurred at different times in different places and is still taking place today in many parts of the world. In Europe, it began in Great Britain and then spread to the northwestern part of the continent—to France, Belgium, and the Netherlands—by the late eighteenth century. Several decades later, it began to take hold in Germany and Sweden and still later in the Austro-Hungarian Empire; but it did not spread to much of Italy or elsewhere in southern Europe, or to the Russian Empire until the end of the nineteenth century. By the early nineteenth century, industrialization was under way in North America, and it started in Japan toward the end of that century. In the earliest countries to industrialize, about 100 years were needed to complete what is often called the rapid industrialization stage. But early industrialization took longer in France because of factors that are discussed later in this chapter. By contrast, in some of the later industrialized countries—notably Germany, Sweden, and Japan—the early phase of industrialization was telescoped to about half the time, undoubtedly in part owing to the fact that the groundwork had been laid in other countries and, thus, the learning period could be greatly shortened.

We can define *industrialization* as the shift in the manufacturing industries from primary dependence on human energy to dependence on inanimate energy sources, thereby dramatically increasing productivity, or output rate per worker. This shift is accompanied by a reorganization of production so that larger numbers of workers are using machines driven by inanimate power to produce a substantially larger volume of goods for a much wider market than before industrialization. The factory system, an aspect of industrialization, means narrowing the tasks assigned each worker. Artisan production usually meant that each worker was responsible for the entire production process—from the raw material to the finished product. Now, each stage was assigned to a worker who specialized in only one or a few of the operations for producing the goods. The work hours were long and the work itself tended to be tedious and dehumanizing. The earliest decades of industrialization entailed the greatest human suffering. In every country when it occurred, at least one generation was sacrificed so that future generations could enjoy the fruits of its efforts.

## The Origins of Industrialization

Scholars disagree as to why the Industrial Revolution started when and where it did.[5] Before the dawn of industrialization, there was a class of fledgling industrial capitalists in Western Europe who were already experimenting with more efficient forms of production, discovering far-flung markets, and accumulating wealth. The ability of this class to break away from traditional patterns of production and marketing, especially in Great Britain, enabled it to experiment with still newer forms. As for the development of the requisite technology, it meant a pragmatic fitting of means to specific ends. According to the great German social scientist Max Weber,[6] there emerged a certain "spirit of capitalism," a spirit that blossomed more easily in Protestant northwestern Europe than elsewhere. Protestant culture had freed itself from the inhibitions imposed on the individual by Roman Catholicism, thereby developing a greater faith in the human capacity to create and improve, and a belief in something like the modern concept of progress.

French economic historian Fernand Braudel acknowledges that there is a geographic correlation between Protestantism and the advancement of capitalism in Europe after about 1600. But he refuses to accept that Protestantism was the fundamental cause for that development. Capitalism had begun in southern Europe with the development of the Italian banking system over a century earlier, at a time when the countries of northern Europe were virtual colonial outposts of the South, according to Braudel.[7] The Protestant Reformation could thus be seen as providing the ideology supporting a "war of liberation" in which the poorer northern countries established first their political, economic, and cultural independence from the South and later their economic supremacy. In strictly economic terms, an analogy can be drawn with mid-twentieth-century Japan and with today's newly industrial countries on the eastern fringe of Asia, which are successfully penetrating the markets of advanced industrial countries with products that can be manufactured more cheaply by societies that have less developed material needs. From this perspective, Protestantism in northern Europe, in its strictures against lavish consumption and its glorification of the work ethic, made a virtue out of harsh economic necessity and justified turning it to the advantage of societies adopting that ethic. A similar ethic seems to prevail in East Asia today.[8]

By the eighteenth century, certain factors characterized British society that made it unique, even in northwestern Europe. At that time, the population of Great Britain was growing about twice as fast as that of France and approximating the growth rate of Prussia. This helped create a domestic market for new industrial products. More important, the rigid social structure that prevailed in central Europe was less pronounced in Great Britain. Workers' wages were higher, they ate better, and they spent a smaller portion of their income on food than did their counterparts on the Continent. The percentage of small businessmen, artisans, and independent farmers in the active population was higher than in most other countries. Both in the cities and in rural areas, the gradations between the upper, middle, and lower classes were more gentle; upward mobility was easier; and social barriers were more relaxed. There was a strong tradition of entrepreneurial initiative that went back to the Middle Ages. Aggressive entrepreneurship could emerge from almost any social class or geographical area within the kingdom. Like the innovative Dutch, the British were experimenters, tinkerers; they were less afraid to take risks than most of their continental counterparts; and they were less bound to traditional ways of doing things.[9]

It is not coincidental that industrialization got its start in a country in which absolutism never quite took hold. The Tudor monarchs of the sixteenth century—Henry VII, Henry VIII, and Elizabeth I—had succeeded in bringing order out of the chaos that England had experienced during the fifteenth-century War of the Roses, but they had not attempted to overturn the powers and privileges of the medieval Houses of Parliament. By contrast, the Estates General, the French version of Parliament, lapsed into nonexistence during the long seventeenth-, and eighteenth-century Bourbon reigns of Louis XIII, Louis XIV, and Louis XV. The Tudors had been successful in accomplishing their political aims without confronting Parliament, preferring to wield influence through skillful coalition building. But their seventeenth-century successors, the Stuarts, sought to establish the principle that the monarch ruled by Divine Right, the claim to absolute power unfettered by countervailing bodies such as the Houses of Parliament or the courts. In other words, the Stuarts were asserting what the French monarchs were able to establish—absolute rule over a large territorial domain, or absolutism for short. But in England, Parliament rebelled and mounted sufficient military force to overturn two Stuart monarchs during the seventeenth century. In the eighteenth century the British[10] monarch was considered a coequal of the two Houses of Parliament, rather than an absolute ruler, in the enactment of legislation, largely because Parliament had demonstrated a healthy capacity to challenge the king's will—a possibility that was hardly conceivable in absolutist continental systems, even where some sort of representative body still existed.

It is arguable, along the lines of Adam Smith, the great Scottish political economist of the period, that, despite the accumulation of great wealth in France during the period of absolutism before the French Revolution of 1789, industrialization could not have begun there, because, unlike England, the monarch held the power to expropriate private wealth for noneconomic undertakings, creating an atmosphere of uncertainty as to whether even the most promising ventures into untested manufacturing realms could succeed. The earliest industrial experiments were more likely to be attempted in countries like Britain and Holland, where the power of the monarch was curtailed by the countervailing power of bodies representing the interests of private holders of wealth, secure in their belief that the capitalist flow of resources into risky undertakings would only fail to bring private gain if the undertakings themselves were ill conceived, not because of unpredictable diversions of potential gains into the state treasury. This is not to say that early industrial initiatives were not taken in France; indeed, the earliest centers of modern textile manufacturing developed there. But it was in Britain that the "critical mass" of venture capital and practical know-how was accumulated and deployed the most effectively.

By the early nineteenth century, Great Britain had established a half-century lead over her nearest rivals. France found she could not overcome this lead in the nineteenth century. French economic growth was sluggish and fitful throughout the century, even though the French Revolution of 1789 removed absolutism and many of the feudal restrictions and impositions that had previously hindered the budding capitalist class. For the most part, the French bourgeoisie preferred the safety of the small family firm with its assured but nonexpanding market and its handful of loyal workers, who could be protected from economic hazards by the patronizing policies of their employers. During the nineteenth century, the French people shifted from rural to urban life much more gradually than the British. Whereas 50 percent of the British population was urbanized by 1850, the same had not occurred in France even by 1900.

During the early nineteenth century, Germany and Italy were not yet unified nations. Both were still divided into a number of small and medium-sized political units that remained largely agrarian. By the 1840s, German entrepreneurs were beginning to exploit the vast mineral resources of the lower Rhineland. Encouraged by a change in state policy and able to take advantage of technological advances achieved elsewhere, German industry was soon expanding. By 1870, German technology had pulled alongside that of other leading countries in Europe. As for Italy, its unification in 1859–60 did not facilitate immediate industrial development. Like other southern and eastern European countries, Italy lacked indigenous capital and central state financial support, and would have to wait for an infusion from outside. Given Italy's poor resource potential, relatively little capital was invested throughout the nineteenth century. On the other hand, its population growth was rapid, especially in the cities, which were overcrowded in the nineteenth century, not unlike those of Third World countries today.

## Early Industrial Societies

Observing British society in the mid–nineteenth century, Karl Marx came to the conclusion that industrialization was bringing about a simplification of the class structure, reducing the number of relevant social groups to essentially two: the capitalist class and the proletariat, that is, the owners of the dominant means of production and the workers whom they employed. Although the other classes were certainly not disappearing, it is true that these were the two most dynamic classes during early industrialization, in terms both of their growing numbers and of their growing importance to the smooth functioning of the economic order. Although these classes could be found before 1750, they really burst onto the scene during the next 100 years, growing rapidly in numbers and transforming the social structure of every industrial country. Each took a place alongside the older classes, thereby threatening their status, political power, and economic security. Politically as well as economically, these new classes were to be the instruments of change. More often than not, the older classes became the resisters of change, the reactionaries and conservatives.

The capitalist class is not as easy to distinguish from its neighbors in the upper echelons of society as is the proletariat in the lower reaches. Capitalists are distinguishable from other segments of the middle class in terms of their psychological makeup and style of action as much, perhaps, as in terms of their economic activities. During the period of early industrialization, the true capitalist was probably in a minority among business owners. Peter N. Stearns makes a useful distinction between the middle class and what he calls "the middling class."[11] The former was made up of adventuresome, risk-taking capitalists; those in the latter group were content simply to maintain their positions. There appear to have been proportionately more of the dynamic capitalists in Great Britain than in France (at least until the late nineteenth century) and more in Germany than in Italy. The French term for the middling class is *petite bourgeoisie*, meaning, perhaps, small-time middle class. It has often been used as a term of contempt in the twentieth century, but only because capitalism as a value system has taken firmer root. Typical nineteenth-century French business family heads could defend their conservatism in a way most of their contemporaries would understand.

At the lower levels of the social hierarchy, we see a common development everywhere with industrialization: the rapid increase in the size of the industrial proletariat—a class that scarcely existed before industrialization, indeed, whose very definition arises from industrialization. In part, the industrial working class was created through the *déclassement* of artisans in the manufacturing sectors that turned to the factory system. Small artisan shops could not compete with mass-production techniques, and many journeymen (and even some master artisans) found themselves with no alternative but to adapt to the machines and become what are termed skilled workers. But most of the new proletarian ranks were made up of uprooted peasants, those who had lost their means of making a living owing to the growing commercialization of agriculture. During early industrialization, a phenomenon began that later became increasingly common—people moving across political or ethnic borders from the less economically advanced countries to the industrial centers of Western Europe. One of the earliest migrations was of Irish workers to the new industrial cites of the English northwest.

Also during early industrialization, there began a commercialization of agriculture. Independent peasants were assuming the status of modern farm owners in parts of France and Germany. By controlling the political system, the landed aristocracy was able to secure protective tariffs to shore up their domestic markets, which were also expanding because of the growth of the railroad. In Great Britain, however, earlier tariff legislation was repealed in 1846, representing a victory for industrial capital over agricultural interests and reflecting the degree to which Great Britain had already become an industrial nation. It was an acknowledgment that the country could not be self-sufficient in food production. Other European countries, lacking Great Britain's industrial advantage, did not follow suit, and their farmers remained protected. Although it can be said that industrialization led eventually to the decline of agricultural employment, this was not yet a massive phenomenon in Europe during early industrialization.

## Political Changes

Early industrialization was the stage in which the political power of the capitalist class made the most rapid gains. However, these were not as striking as the economic gains. The aristocracy was edged a little to one side, but it certainly had not lost its grip on political power. Although the House of Lords lost ground to the House of Commons after the Reform Act of 1832, individual members of the British aristocracy took note of the fact and managed to retain positions of power for the next few decades. British capitalism probably did not reach equal political stature with the aristocracy until about 1870. By then, Great Britain was a mature industrial nation.

The German aristocracy was even more successful in retaining its power; it continued to dominate politics after unification in 1871 as it had done before in the separate German states.[12] The position of the monarchs and their aristocratic supporters was shaken momentarily by the Revolution of 1848, but when the dust had settled, the monarchs were once again secure on their thrones and the newly introduced legislative bodies were firmly controlled by aristocrats. Some of the states of southwestern Germany had emerged from the period of constitution writing with relatively liberal regimes, giving the middle class an opportunity to share in political power; but with unification, these states became subordinate to the Imperial government, where power was concentrated in the hands of the emperor, his hand-picked chancellor, and a coterie of aristocratic advisers and officials. The legislative body, the Reichstag, was a forum in which middle-class spokesmen could vent their political frustrations, but it was little more than that—at least in the early years of the Empire. German capitalists remained content with their sizable economic rewards during the period of early industrialization; they usually went along with aristocratic initiatives in foreign and domestic policies.

Paradoxically, it was in France that the middle classes, which had been relatively sluggish economically, registered the most evident gains over the aristocracy in the nineteenth century. Formally, at least, the French political system had gone further in removing aristocratic privileges, beginning with the Revolution of 1789 and continuing with a series of political upheavals thereafter—in 1830, 1848, and the 1870s. The power of the Bourbon aristocracy was seriously undermined when the Revolution of 1789 abolished feudal privileges and when Napoleon Bonaparte created an administrative career service that was open to all, regardless of the accident of birth. After Napoleon's fall in 1815, there was an effort to restore the position of the old aristocracy, but this ended with the Revolution of 1830. Universal manhood suffrage was adopted with the Revolution of 1848, and the principle of executive subordination to the legislature became established under the Third Republic in the 1870s.

Although the political star of the middle class was on the rise in early industrial Europe, that of the working class was just beginning to appear on the horizon. By the end of the early industrial period, as artisans began to reconcile themselves to becoming skilled workers, they began to turn from unorganized, spontaneous expressions of anger and anxiety to better-organized, focused industrial action. It was the artisans who sparked much of the development of organized trade unionism around the middle of the nineteenth century. Artisans were coming to realize that industrial workers were their natural allies in the struggle against the common enemy, the capitalist. Even so, the road upward was steep. Universal manhood suffrage, first extended in some countries in 1848, was maintained in France but withdrawn in Germany, to be restored on a limited basis with the establishment of the unified German Empire in 1871. In Great Britain, it was extended gradually to different groups of people but was not fully established until 1918; however, skilled workers enjoyed the right to vote by the 1880s. Universal manhood suffrage was not established in Italy until 1913. But this was before the extension of the suffrage to women in any of our countries, in all of which women's suffrage was attained at least a generation after the early period of industrialization had run its course. In Britain it occurred on a limited basis (middle-class women over thirty) in 1918; and in Germany all women acquired the right to vote in 1919. But in France and Italy women did not gain the right to vote until the end of World War II. The two world wars (1914–18 and 1939–45) were both instrumental in removing opposition to suffrage expansion.

Whenever the right to vote was extended to a new social group, there was usually a time lapse before the results of the suffrage expansion would be manifested in new forms of political organization. In France, workers remained largely alienated from the political system until the socialist movement began to turn its attention to action within the political system late in the century. Less alienated politically, British workers divided their votes between the aristocratic Conservative Party and the capitalist Liberal Party. The powerful Labour Party of the twentieth century dates back only to 1900. In Germany, the response was swifter. The Marxist Social Democratic Party was already entrenching itself within the German working class before 1871. Thereafter, it quickly became the most powerful socialist party in Europe, although, owing to government repression and manipulation, it did not become a potent electoral force until after 1890. In general, one could say that during the later years of the early industrialization period, the groundwork was being laid for the members of the working class to enter the political systems of Europe. They were arriving economically in terms of their significance to the new forms of production and in terms of their growing ability to organize for industrial action, but they had not yet arrived politically.

## Preindustrial and Early Industrial Japan

It is customary to begin the history of modern Japan with what is called the "Meiji Restoration," which began with a palace coup in 1868. The feudalistic Tokugawa Shogunate was overthrown by a group of provincial leaders, bureaucrats, and scholars who were bent on ending Japan's isolation from the rest of the world. The Japan of the mid–nineteenth century had for 250 years been ruled as a "centralized feudal regime," while the island country was forcefully closed to outside influences, including nearby China. Although Japan was formally an empire with a reigning emperor, the real rulers were the heads of the aristocratic Tokugawa family, who had seized power in 1600, assuming the ancient title of shogun, and moving the effective seat of government from Kyoto, where the emperor resided, to the city of Edo, today known as Tokyo. Strong feudal lords (*daimyo*), resembling the dukes and barons of medieval Europe, held extensive land and ruled their areas of the country, but they were dependent on the shogun for military protection. By closing the country to foreign influence, the Tokugawa rulers prevented Japan from falling into the status of a colonial dependency of a stronger European state. This fierce determination of her rulers to retain independence did not die with the Tokugawa regime, but was continued by its successors after 1868.

Isolation also meant that Japan shared only very marginally in the economic growth associated in parts of Western Europe with the preindustrial and early industrial development of capitalism during the same period. However, although Japan retained many features that were similar to the earlier Western feudal system, the cities and towns were spawning a merchant class that was gaining in economic strength, accumulating wealth that would serve as an important source of indigenous capital once industrialization began. Isolation from the rest of East Asia also meant that, by and large, Japan was passed over by the military events of the region during the seventeenth to nineteenth centuries. The long era of peace and stability meant that a significant portion of the warrior class (*samurai*) could give up their weapons for scholarly pursuits, emerging by the late 1700s (the period of Enlightenment in Western Europe) as a sort of window to the West, acquiring what knowledge they could of Western scientific achievements and gradually constituting themselves as a critical intelligentsia preparing the way for the revolutionary transformation of Japan that took place after 1868.

The Meiji Restoration, named for the fifteen-year-old emperor who came to the Imperial throne at that time, reunited the emperor with the effective government of the state; but the real rulers were a coalition of lower-ranking *samurai* based mainly in two of the outlying provinces of Japan. These "oligarchs" wanted to modernize Japan so that the economic dependency that had been forced on her through the naval might of the Western powers could be overcome and Japan could take her place among the self-sufficient and militarily secure nations of the world. The leading figures of the government traveled to the West, visiting the United States, England, France, and Germany, borrowing technology and legal–political ideas. The latter then served as the basis for selection of elements of the Japanese Constitution of 1889. It was based on a new legal system patterned after the French and German code law systems, and it incorporated a set of governmental institutions borrowed selectively from wherever the leaders saw something of merit. For example, the bicameral Parliament was patterned in form after the British House of Commons and House of Lords. But the British system of ministerial responsibility to Parliament was not borrowed. Instead, the German system with a chancellor and cabinet responsible to the emperor, rather than to the Parliament (called the Diet in both Germany and Japan), served as the preferred model. Indeed, the Japanese constitution makers saw the situation of their country as very similar to that of Germany, whose leaders in the later nineteenth century similarly regarded democracy as a premature luxury during a time when priority was assigned to catching up industrially with the most advanced nations of the world. Accordingly, this first Japanese constitution gave only 1 percent of the adult population the right to vote. This was extended further by periodic relaxations of the property requirement until universal male suffrage was adopted in 1925. As in France and Italy, women were not given the right to vote until after World War II.

During the period of constitution building of the 1870s and 1880s, the groundwork was being laid for rapid industrialization of the following twenty-five years. At the time of the Meiji Restoration, the adult literacy rate of Japan stood at more than 40 percent, already as high as that in most contemporary Western countries. Thereafter, educational expansion in Japan kept pace with or even exceeded that in the more advanced European countries, which meant that the new skills for an industrial economy could be rapidly acquired by an educated, literate, intelligent population. This factor should be kept in mind when one asks how Japan could industrialize much sooner than could other Asian countries. Also important is the success of the Meiji leaders in centralizing government and creating an efficient bureaucracy, enabling the state finances to be brought into order and a single currency to be created.

In the 1870s Japan began the development of her railroad, telegraph, and postal systems. In the agricultural sector, tax reform and modernization of property holding brought about a new class of self-sufficient farmers, ending forever the system of serfdom and, for that matter, the feudal landowning class. Agricultural production grew rapidly in the late nineteenth century, so that, unlike that other island nation, Great Britain, emphasis on industrialization did not mean growing dependency on overseas agricultural production to feed the population.

The "take-off" period of early industrialization began around 1886 and lasted until the eve of World War I, or about a twenty-five-year period. Extensive government initiative characterized the early establishment of heavy industry, including steel and shipbuilding. Although Japan was dependent on imports of machinery from the more advanced West, she was able to achieve a cotton textile industry that substituted for imports from abroad, largely through rapid mechanization of production, bringing Japanese textile production up to world competitive standards. During this period, partly as a result of the development of a Japanese armaments industry, Japan became one of the primary military powers in East Asia, defeating China and Russia in brief wars in 1894–95 and 1904–05, respectively, and acquiring the beginnings of her colonial empire in the process. By World War I Japan was entering the mature stage of industrial development, approximately a half-century behind Britain, perhaps a quarter-century behind Germany and the United States, but arguably not much more than a decade behind France.

## *Industrial Maturity*

### Organized Capitalism

The next stage in industrialization—industrial maturity—differs from early industrialization not so much because of any overwhelming technological revolution, such as had occurred in England in the late eighteenth century, but because of a rapid acceleration of trends that had already started. During this period, Great Britain's industrial lead diminished and finally came to an end. Germany reached Great Britain's level and then fell back, although only momentarily, with its defeat in World War I. The United States emerged as the world's new industrial giant, and Japan moved into the second echelon of industrial countries through the rapid industrialization just discussed. France finally experienced an industrial upsurge at the end of the century; Italy began her industrialization around 1900, reaching industrial maturity after World War II. But, despite great differences in levels of economic development, there were certain similarities among them that permit developmental comparisons *from the 1880s until just after World War II*, the period we are labeling "industrial maturity."

The most striking economic change during this period was the emergence of massive monopolistic or oligopolistic corporations in vital economic sectors, which replaced the smaller competitive firms of the preceding period. Anti-combination laws were sometimes relaxed to permit this development; large corporations could acquire a much greater amount of capital and thus could promote the technological advances of the era. Joint stock corporations in Britain and the United States accumulated large amounts of capital through the purchase of stock by a multitude of small investors. In other countries, notably Germany, large investment banks capitalized companies in different industrial sectors, assuming an important role in steering the direction of investment through occupation of strategic positions on company boards of directors. Businesses grew into giant bureaucracies, employing thousands of workers and generating an intermediate supervisory and clerical staff. The latter became the truly new social element of the period—the white-collar workers. Women entered the workforce in large numbers as part of this new social category. The lives of most people were becoming more highly organized. Mass-production and assembly line techniques accelerated, and the distance between employer and employee became much greater. In the larger corporations, the employer became virtually invisible, screened from blue-collar and white-collar personnel by layers of managerial staff.

The development of giant corporations stimulated trade unions to organize on a larger scale as independent craft unions joined together to form large federations. Late in the period, unskilled and semiskilled workers in mass-production fields, such as the automotive industry, were becoming organized as well. In response, the capitalists attempted to organize the industrial sectors. Where laws prohibited the formation of trusts or the combination of competing firms for purposes of market control, trade associations formed to exchange information across a sector. Furthermore, huge industrial cartels began to emerge, representing vertical (rather than horizontal) integration, so that industrialists could better control the supply and cost of needed raw materials and capital goods as well as the markets for their products within industry itself. By the 1920s, industrial concentration and trade union organization had reached the point where serious industrial conflict was a significant concern. Capitalists in the European countries enjoyed varying degrees of success in dealing with the trade union challenge, but in all of our countries before World War I and until after World War II, the state curbed the power of the working class on behalf of employers' interests. Although socialist parties were achieving political power in Scandinavia, and although they secured a tantalizing share of power once or twice in Great Britain, Germany, and France, capitalism was able to retain its hold in most of Europe between the wars. This was even reinforced by fascism in Italy and Germany.

Karl Marx had predicted that class conflict in advanced capitalism would assume revolutionary dimensions. Nevertheless, despite the sharpness of class conflict during this period, it is clear that the conditions for life for the vast majority of people were improving dramatically and that the social structure was experiencing profound changes. Wages were rising during the entire period, whereas prices continued to decline at least until about 1900 and to rise slowly enough most of the time thereafter to allow real wages to rise each decade, with the exception of the 1930s, the decade of the Great Depression. The resulting rise in purchasing power stimulated the perfection of mass-production techniques and the mass distribution of new commodities such as household appliances and bicycles, then automobiles. This certainly helps account for the increased willingness of socialist parties to work within the system toward the end of the century. The parties of the working class were beginning to compete with the middle-class parties for votes and seats in Parliament, hoping gradually to attain majority strength and to enact reforms rather than trying to replace capitalism with socialism through violent means.

Other trends were making it less likely that the transition to parliamentary socialism would be a smooth one. The four decades before World War I were marked by recurrent economic recessions that affected all countries more or less simultaneously. Each recession meant significant unemployment. Financial sources would dry up mysteriously for awhile and then just as mysteriously would begin to flow again. Whatever the state of the market, industrialists could not expand their operations without the needed capital. What was happening was that the pace of industrialization had increased so much that people were losing confidence in its ability to sustain itself. Despite the growth of the domestic market, increases in productivity were even greater, especially because new industrial nations had entered the field. Colonialism, which had once supplemented the domestic market as an outlet for goods, was no longer adequate because the most recently colonized areas, especially those in Africa, although valuable as sources of raw materials, were too primitive to be able to use the sophisticated products of Western Europe. Still, the imperialistic quest forged ahead.

By the time of the Great Depression, capitalists and their political allies were beginning to recognize the advantages of turning to the state to ameliorate industrial conflict. After World War II, a much more enlightened capitalism was to see the advantages of trying to eradicate the sources of social unrest, poverty, and economic insecurity. Such insights were relatively few and far between among the pre–World War I ruling classes. Some of the social reforms that had been undertaken had been instigated by aristocratic conservatives who sought to outflank their liberal rivals and win working-class votes as well as keeping workers from turning out of frustration in a more radical direction. Before World War I, it was often difficult to distinguish between liberals and conservatives on socioeconomic matters. Actually, in each country there had emerged a ruling class made up of aristocrats and businessmen who controlled the powerful leverage points of the private sector, especially the banks. Political leaders, whether liberals or conservatives, radicals or moderates, were essentially extensions of the ruling class. The real political conflicts were between this combined ruling class on the inside and the socialist parties and trade unions on the outside.

The century beginning around 1870, which roughly corresponds to what is here called industrial maturity, is also the time in which there emerged what Scott Lash and John Urry have labeled "organized capitalism."[13] Industrial capital was sufficiently concentrated and the units in which it was concentrated sufficiently well organized that the rapid technological changes of the period could be managed through a combination of private- and public-sector guidance. Although the prevailing rhetoric emphasized the necessity that the state play only a minimal role in the economy, in fact that role was growing. Also growing was the power of organized groups in society, including the trade unions. Capitalism was becoming organized "both at the top and at the bottom."[14]

## World War I and Its Aftermath

Much of the blame for the events leading up to World War I can be placed on political leaders whose perspective on the world focused too narrowly on such balance-of-power factors as the number of armed divisions, battleships, and square miles of territory held. The desire for peace as a value in itself seems to have been virtually beyond their range of vision, perhaps because no one could yet foresee the devastation that mature industrial powers were capable of inflicting on one another.

The loudest calls for peace were coming from those to whom the ruling circles had turned a deaf ear—the socialists. The generation in command of Europe's socialist parties at the turn of the century—leaders such as Jean Jaures in France and Karl Kautsky in Germany—were committed internationalists as well as socialists. They saw socialism, and, indeed, the working-class movement generally, as an international phenomenon. The class conflict knew no national boundaries; the struggle between nations was simply an in-house fight among different branches of the capitalist class. Thus, it certainly was not in the interest of the proletariat to participate in it. National conscription was a way in which the capitalists of one country recruited the workers of that country to fight the workers of other countries on behalf of capitalist objectives. Therefore, true socialists should fight war and militarism just as they should fight capitalism. To these socialists, it was quite logical that a socialist should be a pacifist.

As war became more and more likely, the European socialists found themselves forced to decide what approach they would adopt if it should come about. Many followed the example of the French Marxist Jules Guesde in supporting the war effort in their own countries, whereas others, like Vladimir Ilyich Lenin and Rosa Luxembourg, saw this as a sellout of the workers to capitalism. In short, the war had a devastating effect on European socialism. Because both the leaders and the followers were already uncertain where socialism stood in the era of mature industrialism, the commitment of many to its fundamentals turned out to be rather superficial in the face of the much stronger pull of nationalism.

World War I brought about a profound transformation in the distribution of power, both in Europe and worldwide. Temporarily, the defeat of Germany and the Revolution in Russia left France as the most powerful nation on the continent. On a worldwide scale, it appeared at first that the decline of Germany and Russia had removed the principal threats to the supremacy of the British Empire. But new rivals were coming forth, in the Pacific at least. Both the United States and Japan had emerged from the war considerably strengthened as naval powers. Moreover, Great Britain was finding that her far-flung empire constituted an enormous financial drain, leaving the mother country weakened in the face of postwar inflationary pressures and monetary crises.

It now is clear that World War I left the world divided into two types of powers—the relatively contented and the relatively discontented. In the former category were the principal victors—Great Britain, France, and the United States. In the latter category were Germany, the principal loser; Russia, seriously weakened by revolution and civil war but, as the new Soviet Union, the possessor of enormous potential for development into a stronger power than the old Russian Empire; Italy, technically a victor as a result of her switching sides during the war, but dissatisfied with her meager gains in the peace settlement; and Japan, gradually expanding her power base in the western Pacific, but acutely aware of her dependence for raw materials on islands and East Asian rimland areas to the south that were controlled by other powers. This division between the satisfied and the dissatisfied powers was to become the basis for a new alliance system, foreshadowing a second, even more devastating, worldwide conflagration.

## Totalitarian Dictatorship

In the meantime, developments within the discontented nations were leading toward a new kind of division—between the democracies and the "totalitarian dictatorships."[15] One by one the discontented powers as well as some of the smaller countries of Europe were abandoning the form or the substance of democracy for various types of autocratic rule designed to achieve a unity of purpose in the quest for a stronger position in the world. The first major country to move in this direction was Russia. In late 1917, the Bolsheviks had already converted a budding constitutional democracy into a one-party dictatorship. During the ensuing civil war and even during the period of relaxation that followed in the early 1920s, the power of the Communist Party bureaucracy and the state police was steadily expanding. Following Lenin's death in 1924, the party secretary, Joseph Stalin, drew the various instruments of power together and, after a series of successful clashes with his principal rivals, became the unchallenged supreme ruler by the late 1920s.

By this time, another dictator, Benito Mussolini, had consolidated his preeminent position in Italy. Invited by King Victor Emmanuel III in 1922 to assume the premiership as a temporary solution to a political crisis, Mussolini manipulated the deputies in Parliament and gained emergency powers. Then, he systematically eliminated his opposition, beginning with the extreme left and moving to the right. Eventually, he and his Fascist Party ruled as a one-man, one-party dictatorship, much as Stalin and his Communist Party did in the Soviet Union.

While Stalin and Mussolini were establishing their leadership, in Japan military leaders and nationalistic politicians were in the process of undermining the unstable Japanese parliamentary regime. In 1931 they pushed the more liberal politicians aside and established a de facto military dictatorship. In the years that followed until Japan's defeat in World War II, the regime showed some similarity to those of Stalin and Mussolini, in that opposition found itself discredited and hemmed in by restrictions. But, as Edwin O. Reischauer has noted: "There was no dictator and the system was not the product of a well-defined, popular movement, but more a vague change of mood, a shift in the balance of power between the elite groups in Japanese society, and a consequent major shift in national policies, all occurring within the framework of the constitutional system established in 1889."[16] Totalitarianism came to Japan only with World War II itself, but the shift in leadership and policy focus in the 1930s started Japan along the road that led to war in the Pacific.

The extreme right in Germany, as elsewhere in industrially mature Western Europe, drew most heavily on those strata of society that had been the least dynamic during the stage of early industrialization and that had found themselves displaced during industrialization. Left behind by the dynamic sectors of organized capitalism, the petite bourgeoisie and small farmers were incapable of competing or coping with the industrial and commercial giants of the twentieth century. Right-wing attacks on trade unionism and communism probably focused more on the symptoms than on the causes of people's fears and frustrations, but the attacks appealed to the members of this class, especially where, as in Italy and Germany, they could be associated with frustrated national aspirations. Because a minority of Jews in certain countries such as Germany and France had achieved conspicuous success in business or politics, the Jews as a people became special targets for vitriolic attacks, again appealing to the frustrations of downwardly slipping social groups.

In Germany in the early 1920s anti-Semitism, combined with anti-communism, produced a number of right-wing threats to the new Weimar Republic during a time of postwar inflation and unemployment. In 1923 this unrest was further stimulated by the French occupation of the Ruhr and subsequent runaway inflation in Germany. In the fall of 1923, a rebellious segment of the army took control of the government of Bavaria and called on the central government in Berlin to yield power to the right wing. When Berlin refused, an obscure right-wing leader, Adolf Hitler, with the help of the former head of the General Staff, General Erich Ludendorff, staged an unsuccessful bid to gain power in Munich. Hitler was arrested and given a short jail sentence. Thereafter, the Weimar Republic found temporary solutions for its economic problems and began a five-year period of political stability. Nevertheless, Hitler had gained the public notoriety he needed to enable him to expand his organizational base, the National Socialist (Nazi) Party, to the national level.

By the early 1930s, the Great Depression, which had started earlier and hit with greater force in Germany than in most other advanced countries, had undermined the fragile stability of the Weimar Republic. Hitler's National Socialists as well as the Communists on the far left registered a series of spectacular gains in the Reichstag (parliament) elections of 1930 and 1932 and in the presidential election of 1932. By late 1932, the parties that were loyal to the Weimar Republic had virtually lost their majority in the Reichstag, and the country could be governed only by means of presidential emergency powers. Secret negotiations went on among conservative politicians and preeminent industrialists, leading to President Paul von Hindenburg's invitation to Hitler, in January 1933, to assume power as chancellor. This scenario resembled that of Mussolini's rise to power. Once again, a popular demagogue was invited to assume power because of his reputed ability to hold the left in check and, again, by a ruling elite who believed it could control his actions when in power. Even more rapidly than Mussolini, however, Hitler proceeded to eliminate all competing parties—those of the right, center, and left—and to construct a dictatorship in which the other power centers—the military, industrialists, and state bureaucracy—were subordinate to Hitler and his Nazi colleagues. The system of terror and domestic repression established by the Nazis was rivaled for its scope and ruthlessness only by that of Stalin at the height of the Great Purges in the late 1930s. By the eve of World War II, the Nazi and Soviet dictatorships stood as models of *totalitarianism*, a type of regime in which the individual is totally subordinate to the whims of the rulers of the state.

Totalitarianism is a system of rule that is fostered by political leaders seeking to engage an entire population in far-reaching projects for social, economic, and cultural change. Both Stalin and Hitler were preoccupied with strengthening their nations in preparation for the world war that each saw coming in the near future, the war that Hitler would, in fact, instigate. To accomplish this, each opted for a herculean program of mass mobilization. In Hitler's Third Reich, the individual was to be subordinated to the interests of the *Volk* ("nation"). Loyal German citizens would enthusiastically dedicate themselves to the tasks prescribed by the *Fuhrer* ("leader") and the Nazi Party, tasks designed to muster the maximum of human energy toward the goal of war preparedness. Even such previously private matters as the question of what career one might follow or whom one might marry were no longer left entirely up to individual choice but were required to fit within the regime's prescripts.

Totalitarianism attacks not only individual freedom of choice, but also (at least in theory) the individual psyche, aiming to mobilize the thoughts and feelings of individuals as well as their actions. Two means are employed toward this end: terror and propaganda. Terror is the instrument of a police state that creates diffuse uncertainty as to what is legal and what is illegal behavior. The individual must be constantly on guard lest a careless act or utterance lead to arrest, imprisonment, or death. The intense preoccupation that this uncertainty necessitates robs the individual of the freedom to express thoughts that do not fall within the bounds of what the regime officially permits. Simultaneously, the regime's propaganda bombards the citizen with its exclusive interpretation of situations and events inside and outside the country through a monopoly of the mass media and a forced screening out of contrary information emanating from whatever source.

The Nazi regime employed terror in essentially three domains: (1) as part of its racial purification program, designed to eradicate non-Aryan elements from the German population; (2) as part of Hitler's effort to eliminate political opposition, both inside and outside the Nazi movement; and (3) as a weapon against the German population at large, to enforce conformity to the regime's expectations and to weed out potential troublemakers. The instruments employed consisted of a confusing array of special police agencies, the most notorious of which were the Gestapo ("state police") and Hitler's elite corps of enforcers, the Schutzstaffel (SS; "Black Shirts"). It was the SS under Heinrich Himmler that maintained the concentration camps in Germany and eventually in German-ruled Eastern Europe. These were used systematically to snuff out the lives of millions of Jews.

Nazi propaganda was assisted by the perpetration of a myth, repeated and repeated until most Germans had internalized it—or so, at least, was the intention. The fundamental premise on which the myth rested was the superiority of the German people as the purest strain of the Aryan racial type. High points in the history of Germany were emphasized in the schools, whereas the lows were ignored or excused on the basis of the treachery of racial enemies. Especially stressed was the role allegedly played by Jewish business and political leaders in undermining the German war effort between 1914 and 1918. This, in turn, justified the Nazi demand for vengeance and the restoration of lost territory—if necessary, through military means. The myth of racial superiority was used to support Nazi claims to Eastern territory, the *Lebensraum* ("living space") rightfully owed to the German people although currently occupied by "inferior" Slavic and Jewish peoples. These peoples were marked for enslavement or, in the case of the Jews, extermination. The more extreme consequences of this doctrine may not have been spelled out to the German people, but the premises from which it might be inferred were systematically put forth in the schools, in the media, and in numerous speeches by Hitler and his propaganda chief, Joseph Goebbels. Pervading all of these messages was the glorification of Hitler as the infallible leader, with the implication that those anointed by Hitler as his principal collaborators—Himmler, Goebbels, Hermann Goering, and the *Gauleiters* (district party chiefs)—were to be obeyed without question as Hitler surrogates, chosen by the leader to implement his will and, in the event of his death, to carry on the work of "the 1,000-year Reich."

Although the word *Socialist* appeared in the party's title, in truth, the Nazi regime shored up German capitalism and enhanced the interests of employers, while doing away with independent trade unions and mobilizing the industrial workforce for war preparedness. This enhanced the profit-taking ability of German big business, although at a price—the reinstitution of central planning that even in the mid-1930s reached a scale rivaling that of World War I. In a sense, "organized capitalism" reached its pinnacle in Nazi Germany. Although it has also been argued that a social revolution took place in Hitler's Germany,[17] it took the form of the undermining of the aristocracy's superior social and political position inherited from pre–World War I Germany. The beneficiaries were those of the middle class who were to survive World War II. Any lowering of the social barriers between bourgeoisie and proletariat did not take place during the Nazi era.

## World War II

After the consolidation of Nazi rule in Germany, the world witnessed a series of daring expansionist thrusts by the dissatisfied powers. Italy invaded Ethiopia in 1935; Germany reoccupied the demilitarized Rhineland in 1936; Germany and Italy intervened successfully in the Spanish

Civil War (1936–39) to ensure victory for the forces led by General Francisco Franco; Japan moved out from its base in Manchuria, which she had occupied in 1931, to invade China proper in 1937; Germany forced Austria to join in a single German state ruled from Berlin in early 1938; German troops moved in the fall of 1938 into the Sudetenland (a part of Czechoslovakia inhabited by ethnic Germans) and into the rest of Czechoslovakia a few months later. Great Britain and France protested these various moves but did nothing to stop them.

By early 1939, it had become clear that what were to become known as the Axis Powers—the coalition of Germany, Italy, and Japan—had informally divided the world into spheres of influence; they felt strong enough to impose their will on the French and the British, who were timidly shrinking from confrontation, and on the Americans, who were deeply ensconced in isolation. In fact, Hitler enjoyed a fair amount of sympathy in these countries, especially from right-of-center politicians who saw him as a bulwark against communism. This perspective received a severe jolt when, in August 1939, Hitler concluded a mutual nonaggression pact with Stalin, thus neutralizing the other have-not power in any potential world conflict. Shortly thereafter, Germany and Russia invaded Poland from different directions, tearing apart the buffer state. This was too much for Britain and France, which had guaranteed Poland's security from just such an onslaught, and World War II began in September 1939. When Hitler turned his attention to the west, he quickly defeated and occupied France; Great Britain barely managed to escape a similar fate as the Royal Air Force (RAF) fought the Luftwaffe (German air force) to a standstill in the skies over the English Channel during the summer of 1940.

The alliance of the have-nots was relatively short-lived. When Hitler invaded the Soviet Union in May 1941, he gave Great Britain an instant ally. The Allied coalition was completed when the Japanese attacked Pearl Harbor in December 1941. Although Japan had little interest in what was happening in Europe or North Africa, her rulers saw the United States as the main obstacle to consolidation of a "Greater East Asian Co-Prosperity Sphere," a Japanese sphere of influence in the South Pacific and in Southeast Asia that would relieve Japan of her dependence on the rest of the world for raw materials. Her rulers hoped that the destruction of the U.S. Pacific fleet at Pearl Harbor would cripple American capacity to frustrate Japanese aims, and at first they succeeded.

Meanwhile, what was left of the French forces outside Occupied France had gradually come together under General Charles de Gaulle, and they participated alongside the British and Americans beginning with the North African campaign. Gradually, after the reversal of the tide in early 1943 at the battle of Stalingrad, the Soviet forces began pushing the Germans and their allies westward, while the British and Americans were winning battles in North Africa and then in southern Italy. After the establishment of the Western Front in France in June 1944, the ring soon closed on Germany, which surrendered in May 1945. Three months later the war in the Pacific came to an end with the Japanese surrender. Victory was total. The damage visited by the war on civilian populations in most of the belligerent countries had been catastrophic, and the prognosis for the future of mature industrial capitalism in most of these countries was not good.

## The Postwar Period (1945–60)

At the end of the war, Europe lay devastated. Germany was in ruins, her territory occupied by Allied troops. In all of the belligerent countries, economies needed rebuilding, with little or no capital available for the task. Great Britain and France still had commitments to their overseas empires, which promised to be more of a financial drain than an economic asset. The Soviet Union had extended its armed might far into Central Europe. Unless the United States was willing to retain its forces on the Continent, Western Europe would be vulnerable to any further Soviet expansionism. Germany was no longer a viable counterweight to Soviet power, and Soviet troops were occupying the smaller countries of Central and Eastern Europe, which had once been regarded as a buffer zone between Germany and Russia. At the end of the war, it was agreed that there would be four zones of occupation in Germany administered by the United States, Great Britain, France, and the Soviet Union. Berlin was also to be under four-power administration, although it was located well within the Soviet zone of occupation. The Soviet Union and Poland incorporated chunks of pre-Hitler Germany into their own territory (see map on page M-3).

By 1947, it had become clear to the Western powers that the world was once again dividing itself into hostile blocs. In a series of initiatives taken between 1947 and 1949, the United States, Great Britain, and France moved to consolidate Western Europe politically and militarily. A bizonal Economic Council was established in the British and American zones of occupation to begin the process of restoring Germany's economy. Massive American economic assistance began flowing into Europe under the auspices of the Marshall Plan. Although West Germany was not a sovereign unit when the Marshall Plan began in 1947, it received a large share of the assistance. By this time, Italy, the other defeated Axis Power in Western Europe, had been restored to full membership in the international community. Its government participated fully in the economic and political steps leading to Western Europe's recovery.

Japan, too, lay devastated after World War II and was subjected to Allied Occupation. In this case, however, one of the victors, the United States, was the sole occupying power. Under General Douglas MacArthur the American occupiers sought to instill in Japan a basic commitment to political and social democracy. The political side "took" in the acceptance of a sweeping "amendment" to the Constitution of 1889 by the emperor, who was permitted to continue his reign as even more of a figurehead than he had been before the war. The new constitutional arrangements were wisely patterned after the British parliamentary system, a model toward which Japan had been moving in the 1920s before the reimposition of oligarchical rule in the 1930s. The occupying authorities also attempted to break up the monopolistic hold on Japanese heavy industry by a few powerful family combines, the "*zaibatsu*," but this exercise in economic democracy, which would have gone farther than what antitrust policy in the United States had ever successfully accomplished, did not prove to be as long-lasting as the strictly political reforms incorporated in the constitution. Although it took about a decade for the Japanese economy to get back on its feet, assisted in the early years by American economic aid, the Korean War provided a substantial boost, launching Japan on the remarkable economic growth of the 1950s and 1960s. The Korean War, as well as the coming to power of the Communists in China, also created an atmosphere of anti-communism in Japan that helped solidify the rule of center-right politicians in the 1950s, just as the Cold War was doing in most Western countries during that decade.

By the late 1940s in Western Europe, the Western powers were moving to establish an effective military posture against the Soviet threat. In 1949, the North Atlantic Treaty Organization (NATO) was created. Then, in 1950, a beginning was made to unify Western Europe economically and politically through the announcement by the French Foreign Minister, Robert Schuman, of his plan to integrate French and West German coal and steel production. The first unit of today's European Community (EC)—the Coal and Steel Community (ECSC)—came into being in 1952. By this time, Western Europe had successfully completed its rebuilding program, thanks to American assistance and to the lessons learned by the failures of prewar economic policy. How these lessons were interpreted in postwar economic policy is part of the discussion in Chapter 2 of the transition from mature industrial to "postindustrial" society.

In domestic politics, the left emerged from World War II considerably strengthened in most Western European countries. Socialists and communists shared power in the early postwar governments of France and Italy as well as in several smaller countries.[18] But with the onset of the Cold War in 1947, the communists voluntarily left or were forced out of governments. Power, then, shifted to the right, with Socialist parties losing power or having to share it with center and center-right parties. Exceptions to these trends were the Scandinavian countries, which continued to be governed by coalitions dominated by the Socialists through the 1950s and 1960s, and Great Britain, where the Labour Party emerged the victor in the election of 1945 and remained in power until 1951. During these early postwar years, the Labour government under Clement Attlee was able to put into effect an extraordinary program of economic and social reform, most of which the Conservatives were to leave intact during their long tenure in power from 1951 until 1964.

In West Germany and Italy, the threat of communism immediately to the east helped propel voters in the direction of right-of-center parties after 1947. By the time the German Federal Republic (West Germany) came into being in 1949, the division of Occupied Germany into two hardened semisovereign entities was an established, if not yet accepted, fact. Because the eastern part of Germany (German Democratic Republic) was dominated by the Soviet-backed Communists, communism in West Germany was shunned by the voters. Torn between revulsion to communism and the suspicion that a too-Western-oriented foreign policy might postpone German reunification indefinitely, the Social Democrats were likewise disadvantaged at the polls, although not to nearly the same degree as the Communists. This opened the field for the new Christian Democratic Union (CDU), a union of former Catholic and Protestant parties led by former Cologne Mayor Konrad Adenauer. By the early 1950s, Adenauer's party had established its predominance over smaller center and right-wing parties.

In somewhat similar fashion, the strictly Catholic Italian Christian Democrats established its predominance over all rivals in the early postwar years. Left-oriented voters divided their support in the early years between the Communists and the Socialists. In the center and right regions of the political spectrum, however, the Christian Democrats easily outdistanced five smaller parties. With nearly a majority of seats in Parliament, the Christian Democrats could reward and punish potential partners, maintaining a stranglehold on the principal instruments of power. Somewhat similar, but even less encumbered by the necessity to accommodate smaller coalition partners, was the position of the center-right party in Japan, the Liberal Democratic Party. Both the Italian Christian Democrats and the Japanese Liberal Democrats had such a lock on power in their respective countries, in fact, that they could afford the luxury of open factional infighting. Neither party could boast a leader able to maintain himself in power for very long before having to cede leadership to one of his rivals in another faction of the party, a condition that contrasted with the fourteen-year reign of Konrad Adenauer as West German chancellor.

The withdrawal of the French Communist Party from government in 1947 had a significant impact on French politics. However, no party of the center-right was able to establish its supremacy in the ensuing years as happened in West Germany, Italy, and Japan. Instead, loose and shifting coalitions of fairly evenly matched parties, ranging from the Socialists on the left to the Independent and Peasant Party on the right, shared power between 1947 and 1958. In the meantime, war hero General Charles de Gaulle, after resigning as head of the provisional government in early 1946, waged a protracted battle to discredit the new Fourth Republic. He attracted a loyal movement of Gaullist followers who formed a political party in 1946. The combined pressure of strong opposition from Communists on the left and Gaullists on the right helped destabilize the Fourth Republic, which staggered from one crisis to another until it finally collapsed in May 1958 in the wake of a civilian/military revolt in Algiers, staged to protest the way the government in Paris was running the Algerian War. The result was the return of de Gaulle to power and a radical shift of voter support to parties of the right, enabling de Gaulle to solidify the position of his new republic, the Fifth. By 1960, parties of the center and right were in power in all five of our countries. The pendulum had shifted away from the reformism of the first postwar years to the conservatism of the consolidation years. Postwar politics in all of the countries, except, perhaps, France, were measurably more stable than the politics of the years between the wars.

In presenting the history of these contemporary polyarchies, we have shown the development of the elements of the political system on the one hand, and the elements of the economic, social, and international environment on the other. In the past 250 years these countries have been transformed from preindustrial to highly sophisticated industrial systems. Elements of the agrarian and semifeudal societies of the early eighteenth century have largely disappeared. Today power is much more widely distributed among various societal groups. In studying the background of contemporary political systems, we are not considering simply the ways in which political systems and their environments emerged in the past; we are also concerned with the received tradition of the present. When we are learning about countries with such richly received traditions as those of Western Europe and Japan, we must be alert to those developments of the past that help us understand (1) how these countries differ today from newer nations elsewhere and (2) how these countries differ from one another.

## *Suggestions for Further Reading*

**Bracher, Karl Dietrich.** *The German Dictatorship: The Origins, Structure and Effects of National Socialism*, trans. Jean Steinberg (New York: Praeger, 1970).

**Gerschenkron, Alexander.** *Economic Backwardness in Historical Perspective: A Book of Essays* (Cambridge, Mass.: Harvard University Press, 1966).

**Jansen, Marius B.** *Japan and Its World: Two Centuries of Change* (Princeton, N.J.: Princeton University Press, 1980).

**Kindleberger, Charles P.** *Economic Growth in France and Britain: 1851–1950* (Cambridge, Mass.: Harvard University Press, 1964).

**Kunio, Yoshihara.** *Japanese Economic Development: A Short Introduction* (Oxford: Oxford University Press, 1979).

**Landes, David.** *The Unbound Prometheus: Technological Change and Industrial Development in Western Europe from 1850 to the Present* (Cambridge: Cambridge University Press, 1969).

**Maier, Charles S.** *Recasting Bourgeois Europe: Stabilization in France, Germany, and Italy in the Decade after World War I* (Princeton, N.J.: Princeton University Press, 1979).

**Milward, Alan S.,** and **S. B. Saul.** *The Development of the Economies of Continental Europe, 1850–1914* (Cambridge, Mass.: Harvard University Press, 1977).

**Moore, Barrington, Jr.** *Social Origins of Dictatorship and Democracy: Lord and Peasant in the Making of the Modern World* (Boston: Beacon, 1967).

**Poggi, Gianfranco.** *The Development of the Modern State: A Sociological Introduction* (Stanford, Calif.: Stanford University Press, 1978).

**Rostow, W. W.** *Politics and the Stages of Growth* (Cambridge: Cambridge University Press, 1971).

**Stearns, Peter N.** *European Society in Upheaval: Social History since 1750*, 2nd ed. (New York: Macmillan, 1975).

**Thompson, E. P.** *The Making of the English Working Class* (New York: Random House, 1963).

**Tilly, Charles,** ed. *The Formation of National States in Western Europe* (Princeton, N.J.: Princeton University Press, 1975).

**Wallerstein, Immanuel.** *The Modern World System: Capitalist Agriculture and the Origins of the European World-Economy in the Sixteenth Century*, Vol. 1 (New York: Academic Press, 1974).

———. *The Modern World System: Mercantilism and the Consolidation of the European World Economy, 1600–1750*, Vol. 2 (New York: Academic Press, 1980).

**Wray, Harry,** and **Hilary Conroy,** eds. *Japan Examined: Perspectives on Modern Japanese History* (Honolulu: University of Hawaii Press, 1983).

## Notes

1. Arend Lijphart, *Democracies: Patterns of Majoritarian and Consensus Government in Twenty-One Countries* (New Haven, Conn., and London: Yale University Press, 1984).
2. Robert A. Dahl, *Polyarchy: Participation and Opposition* (New Haven, Conn.: Yale University Press, 1971).
3. Peter L. Berger, *The Capitalist Revolution: Fifty Propositions about Prosperity, Equality and Liberty* (New York: Basic Books, 1986), p. 220.
4. Gianfranco Poggi, *The Development of the Modern State: A Sociological Introduction* (Stanford, Calif.: Stanford University Press, 1978), Chs. 3 and 4.
5. For an illuminating discussion of industrialization, see David Landes, *The Unbound Prometheus: Technological Change and Industrial Development in Western Europe from 1850 to the Present* (Cambridge: Cambridge University Press, 1969).

6. Max Weber, *The Protestant Ethnic and the Spirit of Capitalism*, trans. Talcott Parsons (New York: Scribner's, 1958).
7. Fernand Braudel, *Civilisation materielle, economie et capitalisme, XVe–XVIIIe siecle*, Vol. 2 (Paris: Armand Colin, 1979), pp. 505–509.
8. Berger, *The Capitalist Revolution*, pp. 140–171.
9. David Landes, "The Creation of Knowledge and Technique: Today's Task and Yesterday's Experience," *Daedalus* 109 (Winter 1980), 111–120.
10. In 1707 the Act of Union brought England, Wales, and Scotland together under a United Kingdom. Thus, the term *British*, referring to the whole island of Great Britain, became a more appropriate term than *English* for reference to the political system.
11. Peter N. Stearns, *European Society in Upheaval: Social History since 1750*, 2nd ed. (New York: Macmillan, 1975), pp. 119–120.
12. Germany and Italy did not achieve unification until the second half of the nineteenth century. Italy was unified in 1860 and Germany in 1871, following Prussia's victory in the Franco–Prussian War. Unification meant the end of separate identities for the various parts of the two countries. Compare the map on page M-1 with that on page M-2.
13. Scott Lash and John Urry, *The End of Organized Capitalism* (Cambridge: Polity Press, 1987), Chs. 1–3.
14. Ibid., p. 4.
15. For the most authoritative 1950s formulations of this concept, see Carl J. Friedrich and Zbigniew K. Brzezinski, *Totalitarian Dictatorship and Autocracy* (Cambridge, Mass.: Harvard University Press, 1956); and Hannah Arendt, *The Origins of Totalitarianism*, 2nd ed. (New York: Meridian, 1958).
16. Edwin O. Reischauer, *The Japanese* (Cambridge, Mass., and London: Harvard University Press, 1977), pp. 100–101.
17. See David Schoenbaum, *Hitler's Social Revolution: Class and Status in Nazi Germany, 1933–1939* (Garden City, N.Y.: Doubleday, 1966).
18. The distinction between *socialist* and *communist* goes back to the Bolshevik Revolution in Russia and the establishment by Lenin of the Third International. Parties that remained part of the Second International, or pre-1917 world organization of socialist parties, are called "Socialist." Those following Lenin's lead are called "Communist." See Chapter 4 for contemporary differences and for a clarification of the terms *left*, *center*, and *right* used in this section.

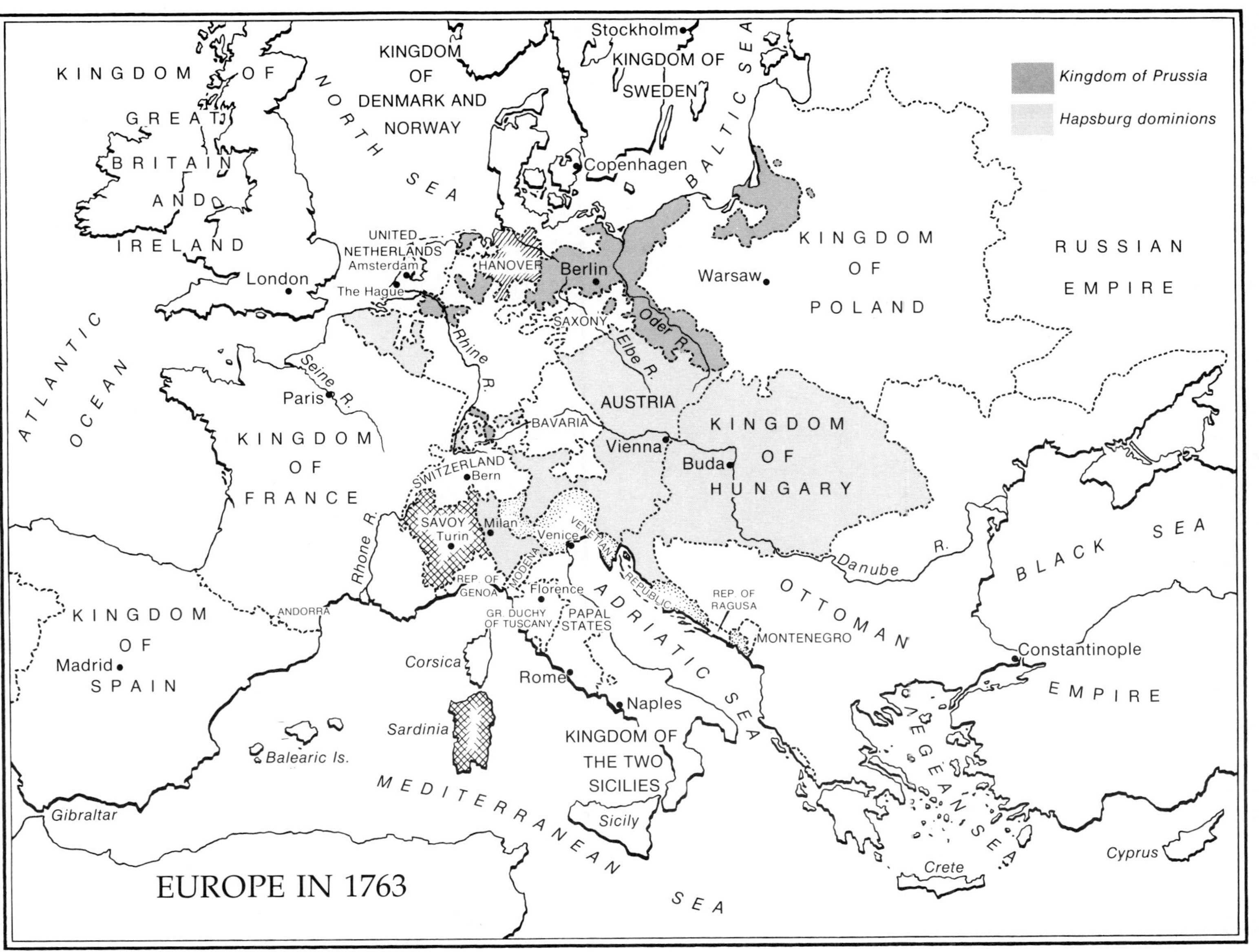
Kingdom of Prussia
Hapsburg dominions
KINGDOM OF GREAT BRITAIN AND IRELAND
London
KINGDOM OF DENMARK AND NORWAY
NORTH SEA
Stockholm
KINGDOM OF SWEDEN
Copenhagen
BALTIC SEA
UNITED NETHERLANDS
Amsterdam
The Hague
HANOVER
Berlin
SAXONY
Oder R.
Elbe R.
Warsaw
KINGDOM OF POLAND
RUSSIAN EMPIRE
ATLANTIC OCEAN
Seine R.
Paris
Rhine R.
KINGDOM OF FRANCE
AUSTRIA
BAVARIA
Vienna
Buda
KINGDOM OF HUNGARY
SWITZERLAND
Bern
SAVOY
Turin
Milan
Venice
VENETIAN REPUBLIC
MODENA
Rhone R.
REP. OF GENOA
Florence
GR. DUCHY OF TUSCANY
PAPAL STATES
ANDORRA
KINGDOM OF SPAIN
Madrid
Corsica
Sardinia
Balearic Is.
Rome
Naples
KINGDOM OF THE TWO SICILIES
Sicily
ADRIATIC SEA
REP. OF RAGUSA
MONTENEGRO
Danube R.
OTTOMAN EMPIRE
BLACK SEA
Constantinople
AEGEAN SEA
Crete
Cyprus
Gibraltar
MEDITERRANEAN SEA
EUROPE IN 1763

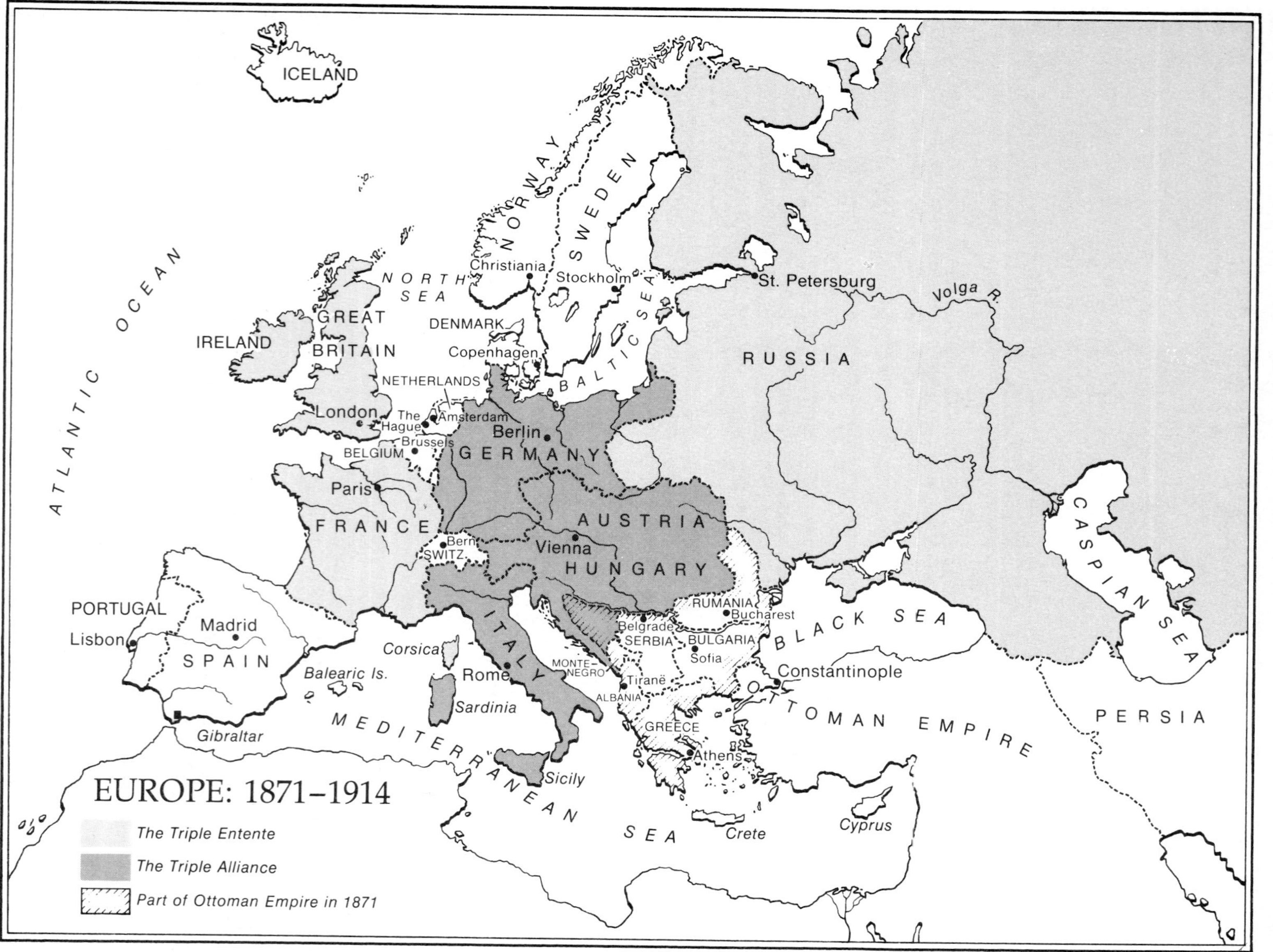
EUROPE: 1871–1914
The Triple Entente
The Triple Alliance
Part of Ottoman Empire in 1871
ICELAND
ATLANTIC OCEAN
IRELAND
GREAT BRITAIN
London
NORTH SEA
NORWAY
Christiania
SWEDEN
Stockholm
DENMARK
Copenhagen
BALTIC SEA
St. Petersburg
Volga R.
RUSSIA
CASPIAN SEA
NETHERLANDS
The Hague
Amsterdam
Brussels
BELGIUM
Berlin
GERMANY
Paris
FRANCE
Bern
SWITZ.
AUSTRIA
Vienna
HUNGARY
RUMANIA
Bucharest
Belgrade
SERBIA
BULGARIA
Sofia
BLACK SEA
Constantinople
MONTE-NEGRO
Tiranë
ALBANIA
GREECE
Athens
OTTOMAN EMPIRE
PERSIA
PORTUGAL
Lisbon
Madrid
SPAIN
Gibraltar
Corsica
Balearic Is.
Rome
ITALY
Sardinia
Sicily
MEDITERRANEAN SEA
Crete
Cyprus

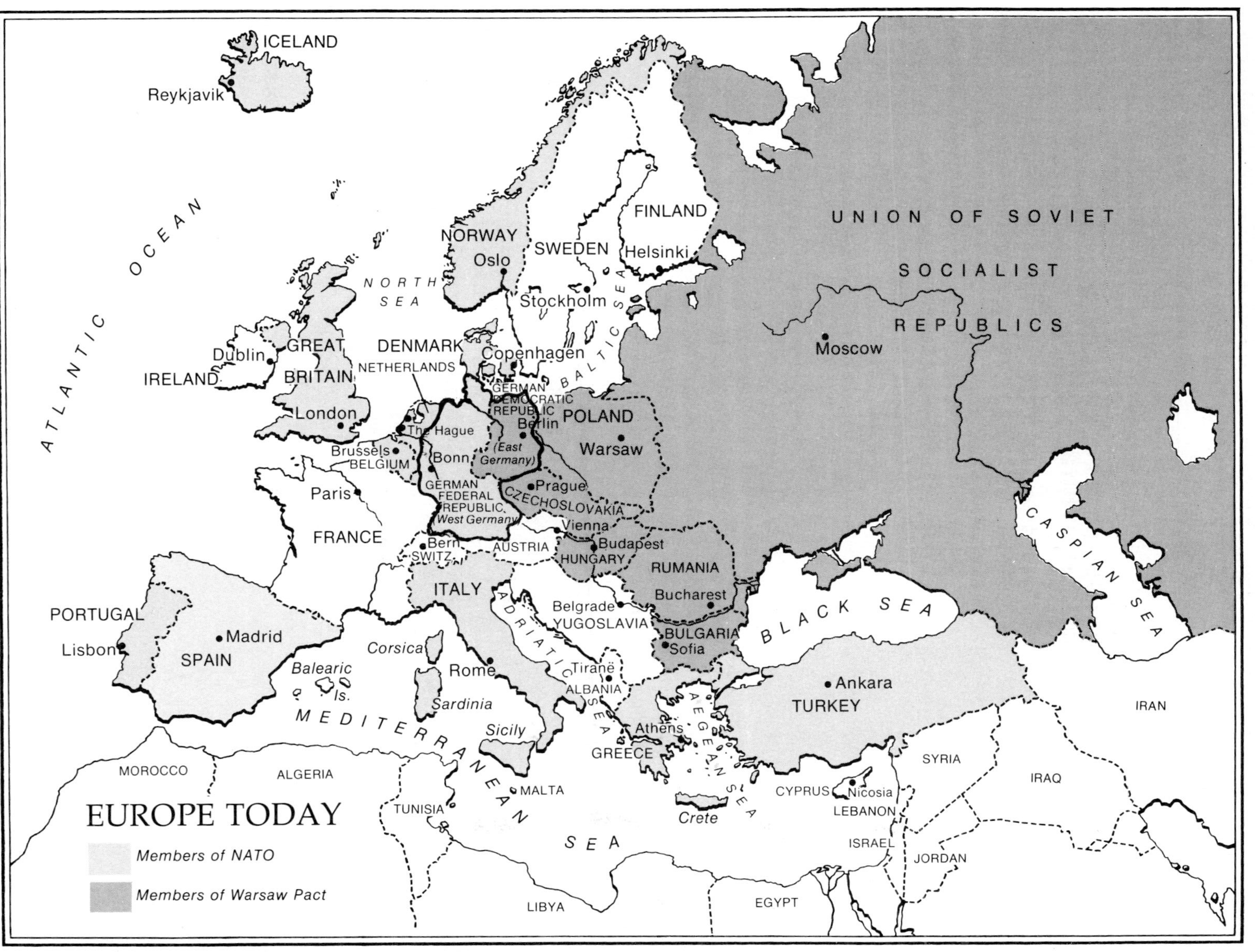

EUROPE TODAY
Members of NATO
Members of Warsaw Pact
ICELAND
Reykjavik
ATLANTIC OCEAN
NORTH SEA
IRELAND
Dublin
GREAT BRITAIN
London
NORWAY
Oslo
SWEDEN
Stockholm
FINLAND
Helsinki
BALTIC SEA
DENMARK
Copenhagen
NETHERLANDS
The Hague
Brussels
BELGIUM
Bonn
GERMAN FEDERAL REPUBLIC
(West Germany)
GERMAN DEMOCRATIC REPUBLIC
Berlin
(East Germany)
POLAND
Warsaw
Prague
CZECHOSLOVAKIA
Vienna
AUSTRIA
Budapest
HUNGARY
RUMANIA
Bucharest
UNION OF SOVIET SOCIALIST REPUBLICS
Moscow
CASPIAN SEA
BLACK SEA
Paris
FRANCE
Bern
SWITZ.
ITALY
Rome
ADRIATIC SEA
Belgrade
YUGOSLAVIA
BULGARIA
Sofia
Tiranë
ALBANIA
Athens
GREECE
AEGEAN SEA
Ankara
TURKEY
IRAN
SYRIA
IRAQ
CYPRUS
Nicosia
LEBANON
ISRAEL
JORDAN
PORTUGAL
Lisbon
Madrid
SPAIN
Corsica
Balearic Is.
Sardinia
Sicily
MEDITERRANEAN SEA
MALTA
Crete
MOROCCO
ALGERIA
TUNISIA
LIBYA
EGYPT

CHAPTER 2

# POSTINDUSTRIAL ECONOMY AND SOCIETY

The economic and social environments of the Western European political systems have experienced substantial changes since World War II. Some scholars have gone so far as to suggest that, by the 1960s, quantitative changes, such as dramatic increases in the gross national product (GNP) and a marked alteration in the proportions of the various occupational groups in the workforce, resulted in a qualitative leap, that a corner has been turned, and that we are now experiencing what they call *postindustrial society*.[1] If so, the first two postwar decades were the "late industrial" years during which postwar economic and social policy adjustments were laying the groundwork that enabled the corner to be turned.

## Late Industrial Social and Economic Policies

In all of our four Western European countries, the postwar period witnessed the expansion of the welfare state, featuring cradle-to-grave protection of those members of society unable, for whatever reasons, to cope with economic misfortunes. The upheavals of the 1920s and 1930s had left a lasting mark on Western Europe; leaders of both left and right in all countries converged on the Keynesian fiscal and monetary means of steering between the extremes of depression and runaway inflation. The result was a much improved level of personal security for individuals and families after World War II. Especially noteworthy were the provision of free medical care in Great Britain, through the National Health Service established in 1946, and the virtually equivalent result obtained in West Germany, through the extensive National Health Insurance Scheme. In Japan, as in the United States, more reliance was placed on private-sector provision of welfare, as in the worklife assurance of employment that Japanese corporations have provided their employees. However, there did not develop in the early postwar years in Japan a reliable pension or social security program caring for the needs of those beyond working age; nor was the security of employment enjoyed by workers in the large corporations an advantage enjoyed by the majority of the workforce, who were employed in smaller firms that were in a less secure position in the Japanese "dual economy."

But the more dynamic economic sectors in Japan and Western Europe pulled along the weaker sectors as all of our countries experienced a period of economic growth producing a remarkable transformation of their economies in the first two postwar decades. Although they were poor second cousins to the United States in the late 1940s, all of them experienced unprecedented economic growth in the 1950s and 1960s, to the extent that West Germany, France, and Japan, at least, became fully modern competitive equals by the 1970s. Even in Great Britain and Italy, countries whose economies suffered recurrent problems, the transformation in the lifestyles of ordinary citizens after World War II was dramatic.

One of the striking things about this record of economic success across five different countries is that there were considerable differences in approaches to economic policy, due to differences in past experiences and in the constellations of political forces and personalities in power. Participation by parties of the left in the earliest postwar governments resulted in important economic policy innovations in Great Britain, France, and Italy. Prominent among these were the extensive nationalizations of industrial sectors. In Great Britain and France, the postwar left-dominated parliaments converted the coal industry, railroads, major investment banks, and the electricity and gas supply utilities (among others) from private to public ownership. In Italy, nationalization was less of an innovation because the central government had already been buying into private industry during the Mussolini regime. Government financial participation through giant holding companies continued to spread in the postwar period, most notably in the energy sector.

In France, the governments of the latter 1940s began to make use of the leverage given them by government ownership to provide the leading wedge of a system of state economic planning, which was designed in the early years to modernize the war-damaged and seriously outdated French economy. Expansion of the public sector provided stimulus to the private sector by making energy, transportation, and raw materials more readily available at lower costs. The central planners assigned priorities to different industrial sectors and encouraged development of those with high priority through subsidies and tax incentives. As France emerged into the 1950s, this system of "indicative planning," which was to be given part of the credit for the subsequent economic boom, was developed further, providing French manufacturers and distributors greater certainty regarding the size of future markets and the availability of unfinished and semifinished goods needed in the productive process. France was one of two countries we are dealing with where the role of the state was probably decisive in fostering postwar economic growth. Japan was the other.

Once the Japanese government regained control over the pressure points that could influence the economic regeneration of the country, it followed a planning course that bore some resemblance to that of France, although the Japanese government was farther to the right and had closer links to industry than did the French government in the early postwar years. Because they were able to rely on an ample agricultural base, the French planners could hold the international economy relatively constant in their calculations and concentrate on building or rebuilding those industries that any relatively self-sufficient mature industrial economy would need. By contrast, Japan's dependence on the rest of the world for agricultural commodities and raw materials was, if anything, more acute than before the War, when she could rely on her colonial empire to supply a major portion of her needs. Therefore, her planners looked farther ahead than those in France, to the industries that would provide the greatest export mileage to earn Japan the U.S. dollars necessary to afford the commodities unavailable at home. Not only was massive government assistance, directed by the Ministry for International Trade and Industry (MITI), used to steer Japanese industry in the planned directions, as in France, but leading bankers and industrialists were at the very center of the priority assigning process, agreeing with their partners in MITI as to the appropriate uses to which both private- and public-sector investment would be put. Whereas mutual suspicions between the public and private sectors had to be broken down gradually in the evolution of French planning, a cooperative, information-sharing atmosphere prevailed from the outset in Japanese planning.

By contrast with the strong role played by the state in France and Japan, in West Germany the more conservative Christian Democrats, led by Chancellor Adenauer and Economics Minister Ludwig Erhard, evolved an economic system that relied much less on the state sector and placed its faith in the play of the free market. The market was expected to generate its own incentives, with the state intervening primarily in the interests of stabilizing the value of the deutsche mark and maintaining a steady money supply. Depending on the orientation of the economist, either Erhard's "social market economy," the French system of indicative planning, or the Japanese system of international trade-oriented industrial planning is cited as the model of effective economic policy for this period of late industrial recovery. The fact is that all three economies established remarkable records for economic growth coupled with relative stability, especially in the late 1950s and early 1960s. On the other hand, Great Britain and Italy, both of which opted for more mixed, eclectic, economic policy strategies, were to experience less impressive economic records during the same time span—Great Britain with relatively low growth rates and chronic balance-of-payments problems, and Italy with a record of economic instability and geographically uneven growth, despite an overall growth rate that was very high.

## Postindustrial Economy

*Postindustrial society* has been reached when a majority of a nation's workforce is employed in the *service sector* rather than, as in mature industrialism, in manufacturing. This is now true of all five of our countries. The term *post-industrial* has either positive or negative connotations depending on whether one is dependent on employment in the industry that is supposedly outdated (in which case the term may appear threatening) or whether one is optimistically looking forward to an economy in which computers and robots will perform the tasks that industrial workers once sweated over, and the "industry" remaining in the economy will be clean, safe, and healthy high-tech and service industry. In fact, all five of our countries, as has the United States, have moved a considerable distance from the era of smokestack industry and blue-collar labor. The changes that have taken place have accompanied the general process by which "organized capitalism" has become disorganized.[2]

### Disorganized Capitalism

Scott Lash and John Urry have provided a comprehensive list of the economic and social features of "disorganized capitalism," a list that encompasses both the positive and negative features of postindustrialism. The first feature is at the heart of the matter:

> (1) The growth of a world market combined with the increasing scale of industrial, banking and commercial enterprises means that national markets have become less regulated by nationally based corporations. From the point of view of national markets there has been an effective *de*concentration of capital.[3]

They are saying that capitalism has become disorganized at the national level, largely because it has become international in scope and organization. With the loss of national focus, the process of collective bargaining between management and labor becomes decentralized, and the economic policy that was previously made by national governments in close cooperation with private industry loses a good deal of its significance for industry. This is because the attention of private industry has become diverted beyond the national level. As for organized labor, because it is unable to come to grips with anonymous employers that may not even be headquartered in the same country, it finds it more rewarding to bargain with employers at the level of the individual manufacturing unit, whether these be branch plants of multinational corporations (MNCs) or local firms hiring local workers.

Three other features of economic change are central to disorganized capitalism, according to Lash and Urry:

> (2) Increased importance of service industry for the structuring of social relations (smaller plants, a more flexible labour process, increased feminization, a higher "mental" component . . .).
>
> (3) Decline in average plant size because of shifts in industrial structure, substantial labour-saving capital investment, the hiving off of various sub-contracted activities, the export of labour-intensive activities to "world market factories" in the Third World, and to "rural" sites in the First World. . . .
>
> (4) Industrial cities begin to decline in size and in their domination of regions. This is reflected in the industrial and population collapse of so-called "inner cities," the increase in population of smaller towns and more generally of semi-rural areas, the movement away from older industrial areas. . . .[4]

Accompanying these changes in demography and economic geography are changes in the occupational structure, and thus the class structure, of society. (5) The size of the manual workforce in manufacturing industry declines, first in relative terms, and then absolutely. In turn, (6) there is an expansion "of the number of white-collar workers and particularly of a distinctive service class (of managers, professionals, educators, scientists, etc.)."[5] This last feature is at the heart of the earlier writing about postindustrial society at the time these phenomena were first being recognized in the early 1970s. It is discussed in the next section, after which we turn to the phenomenon of "deindustrialization" and the high levels of unemployment that have characterized postindustrial societies since the 1970s.

## The Service Economy

Industrial society differed from preindustrial society because of the declining role of agriculture in the economy and the lower percentage of persons employed in the agricultural sector, especially when compared with the growing ranks of the industrial proletariat. By the same token, postindustrial society differs from industrial society because of the increasing importance of the service sector and the growing ranks of persons employed in the service sector as compared with both agriculture and industry. What is the service sector? According to Daniel Bell, it includes the following areas, where services rather than goods are produced: transportation, utilities, trade, finance, insurance, real estate, health, education, research, leisure, entertainment, and, finally—a catchall category—government. In the United States, the first country to achieve postindustrial status, employment in the goods-producing sectors of the economy increased from 25.6 million in 1940 to 29 million in 1968. In the service-producing sectors, employment increased from 24.3 million to 51.8 million during the same period.[6] Between 1968 and 1976, the number employed in the goods-producing sectors remained static, whereas the number in the service sector increased by another 7 million.[7] Among the service sectors, employment increased most rapidly in government, especially at the state and local levels.

Whether or not all First World countries have reached postindustrial status is a matter of definition. The most frequently used criteria are the percentage of employment of a country's workforce that is employed in service-sector occupations, and the country's gross domestic product (GDP) per capita. The combined rankings in the right-hand column of Table 2.1 give a very rough indication that the United States and Canada can be safely placed within the postindustrial society category, whereas Spain remains outside. The eight other countries are probably over the threshold into postindustrial society.

In Western Europe as in the United States, the service sector of the economy has become increasingly important in recent decades. This has meant that certain kinds of occupations

**Table 2.1 Rankings of Eleven First World Countries on Postindustrial Indicators (1987)**

| | *Percent of Employment in Service Sector* | *GDP per Capita* | *Combined Rankings* |
|---|---|---|---|
| United States | 1 | 3 | 2.0 |
| Canada | 2 | 5 | 3.5 |
| Sweden | 6 | 2 | 4.0 |
| *Japan* | 8 | 1 | 4.5 |
| Netherlands | 3 | 7 | 5.0 |
| *France* | 7 | 6 | 6.5 |
| *West Germany* | 10 | 4 | 7.0 |
| Australia | 5 | 9 | 7.0 |
| *United Kingdom* | 4 | 10 | 7.0 |
| *Italy* | 9 | 8 | 8.5 |
| Spain | 11 | 11 | 11.0 |

(*Source*) Organization for Economic Cooperation and Development, *OECD Economic Surveys 1988/1989: United Kingdom* (Paris: OECD, 1989), pp. 130–131.

have become more prominent than they were before. In general, nonmanual employment has increased more rapidly than manual employment. It was pointed out in Chapter 1 that, with the achievement of mature industrialization, a new social class—white-collar workers—appeared on the scene. This component of the workforce continues to grow in postindustrial society, but especially in the professional and technical category rather than in such white-collar occupations as secretaries and office clerks. Between 1958 and 1974, those in the professional and technical occupations increased by 77.5 percent in the United States, the largest increase in any single category.[8] This category includes those with the highest educational requirements, such as doctors, lawyers, engineers, teachers, scientists, and computer specialists.

As society becomes more complex, there is a growing demand for skills that involve the application of *knowledge* to large-scale problems. If Western Europe was slower than the United States to reach postindustrial society, it may not be simply because of inferior material resources and the disadvantages of working on a smaller national scale. European educational systems have been slow to change, whereas the American educational system has been decades ahead in the development of mass education and in the transition from the nineteenth-century classical curriculum to the more practical curricula of the twentieth century. The pool of talent available to meet the demanding standards of a postindustrial occupational structure is more restricted in Europe. On the other hand, if anything, the Japanese educational system has been freer than the American of traditional overhangs that impede the acquisition of the most up-to-date knowledge and skills. Indeed, Ezra N. Vogel attributes much of Japan's industrial surge of recent decades to the fact that, not only has she been able to borrow state-of-the-art technology from wherever in the world it can be found, but Japan can truly be called an "information society."[9] In Japan, according to Vogel, the quest for all relevant information bearing on a problem does not rely simply on its being retrievably stored in libraries or computer data banks, but on its being widely disseminated to all members of organizations, public or private, where it is needed to bear on decisions. Organizational members immerse themselves in available information and participate jointly in the decision to be made, rather than relying on the advice of a few experts, as would more likely be resorted to in the United States or Western Europe. Whether it would be correct to attribute Japan's economic success primarily to this characteristic, it is true that Japan was being labeled a "postindustrial society" not long after the term became fashionable, and sooner than it was applied to most Western European countries, precisely because of the high value placed on information, or what we are calling "enlightenment" in this text.[10]

Perhaps in part because of the higher earnings in real terms that workers in the skilled and professional categories realize today, there has been a growing demand for a wide variety of services, whose performances do not themselves require advanced education or refined skills. Thus, even in parts of northern England where unemployment among manual workers is high, there has been a striking growth of retailing and catering activities as those people who do have jobs have been spending significant portions of their incomes on consumption of goods and services that many could not afford ten years ago—for example, the sale of gourmet foods in grocery stores, of video recorders, of expensive suits, or of wine instead of beer in the pubs. The persons who sell these items are salesclerks and waiters or waitresses, normally classified as service-sector employees. Often they are employed on a part-time basis making earnings that are well below the average for manual workers, and for secretaries and other full-time white-collar workers. Such jobs have minimal educational or training requirements. In some ways the growth of the service economy has created a new postindustrial proletariat, one that is poorly organized in comparison with the factory workers of mature industrialism, and probably largely unorganizable, because of the high turnover in jobs of young people who perceive their location in this employment status to be temporary. In the meantime, the percentage of the workforce found in manual occupations is declining, and higher levels of unemployment have made it more difficult for trade unions to maintain the membership numbers of former days.

## Deindustrialization and Unemployment

The growth of the service sector has been much sharper in relative than in absolute terms. Whereas service employment has replaced manufacturing employment in percentage terms, it has been slow to make up for the number of manufacturing jobs that have been lost. Some service-sector categories are "labor-intensive," as in the case of catering, retailing, and tourism; others are less so. In the meantime, manufacturing has been experiencing technological transformation that has made virtually all branches of manufacturing more capital-intensive and less labor-intensive than they once were. Moreover, some branches of manufacturing are in decline in terms of their shares of gross domestic product as well as in numbers of jobs. First World countries are giving over the production of lower-cost steel, textiles, clothing, automobiles, and electronic products to Third World countries, whose wage structures are such that they can produce goods on a labor-intensive basis more cheaply. Some First World countries (Britain is the most startling example) have moved from the status of net exporters of manufactured products to net importers, compensating for the imports they buy with the proceeds of services or primary products (food, raw materials) that they have to sell to other countries. These are structural changes that are unlikely to be reversed. To the extent that other economic problems have been created by deindustrialization, especially unemployment and inflation, they are no longer likely to follow cyclical patterns as they did during industrial maturity. They are chronic problems that require long-term solutions rather than being susceptible to countercyclical manipulation. Yet the economic theories that we have used to cope with them have been developed at a time when economic problems were viewed as cyclical.

To the economist, unemployment is part of a larger phenomenon—underemployment of the nation's productive forces. As stocks of goods accumulate unsold in warehouses and retail outlets, factories shut down and employees lose their jobs. Some businesses weather the storm by cutting back production; others are swept away forever. Workers without jobs are forced to seek new employment. They often find that the only options are the unacceptable ones—moving to another part of the country (or to another country) to find work or going through the arduous process of retraining for a skill that is in greater demand. The impact of a recession on the individual and his or her family is often tragic, representing the loss of hope for a better future. To a country, recession means missed opportunity owing to unused productive capacity. Markets at home and abroad may be permanently lost to competition from companies in other countries because businesses have folded or have cut back production. Recession also means that national income falls short of its full potential; the standard of living of the nation fails to improve. Indeed, the standard of living for certain categories of the population actually declines as certain disadvantaged groups feel the brunt of unemployment.

The causes of recession and unemployment are varied. When economies of countries are compared with one another, it becomes clear that some countries suffer more severely than others during a worldwide recession. The relative losers lose to the relative winners because their producers cannot compete on an equal basis in the world market. If world demand is shrinking, it will be shrinking more rapidly for the less competitive and may not even be shrinking at all for those whose productivity and cost structures put them in a position to take over the markets of the losers. But why does a worldwide recession come about? The simple answer is that there is a worldwide shrinkage of consumer demand, a factor that itself may result from a variety of causes. Among these is government economic policy, especially the policies of the governments responsible for the largest economies, such as the governments in Washington, Tokyo, and Bonn. Government policies designed to curtail inflationary forces and trade deficits have an impact on the level of productive activity. If the measures (such as action to raise interest rates or fiscal policies designed to reduce consumer spending power) are too strong or are carried out for too long, the first consequence may be a downturn in economic activity, leading to a recession rather than to the desired result of bringing rates of inflation down to acceptable levels. Again, if we are talking about a major First World economy, declining demand in that country will mean a decline in world demand for the products of other countries. This may momentarily assist the balance of payments of the first country by improving its trade balances, but if the result is worldwide recession, it will mean that all countries will suffer from rising unemployment and a decline in living standards.

The more profound causes of unemployment, however, are structural rather than cyclical. They are the causes touched on in the opening paragraph of this section. The "second industrial revolution," symbolized by the advent of the microchip, has meant that many industries in postindustrial countries have turned to automated means of production that require fewer workers to turn out the same volume of products. If, for example, the textile industry in one country fails to join the new wave of technological modernization, it will be overcome by the competition of its rivals in other countries where automated production has been adopted. Firms in the country that stands still will fold or cut back production, with loss of jobs. Thus, the size of the workforce will decline, no matter whether the industry opts for automation or allows itself to be left behind by its overseas competitors.

Related to this is a third reason that unemployment has risen in postindustrial countries: competition from newly industrializing countries (NICs), which are able to produce the same goods at lower cost, not because of automation, but because wages for workers in these countries remain at a much lower level than those of First World industrial workers. Continuing with the example, employment in the First World textile and clothing industries further declines as manufacturers attempt to compensate for their relatively high labor costs by making production more capital-intensive.[11] Situations such as this have led some economists to despair of the possibility that First World unemployment percentages can ever again be reduced to their pre-1970s levels. Other economists point to the

West German children riding their bicycles alongside a Ruhr factory near Duisburg.

growing service-sector fields such as "fast food" and retailing as the eventual answer to the present scarcity of jobs for unskilled and semi-skilled workers.[12]

Left-of-center politicians, whether American Democrats or European Socialists and Communists, often appear to be saying that one must choose between protecting the value of money (avoiding inflation) and maintaining full employment (avoiding recession), and that the choice to be made is clear. They hold that, when the values that make up human dignity are considered, one must protect the underprivileged and disadvantaged. This means taking whatever action is necessary to maintain workers in their jobs, even if this runs the risk of adding to inflationary pressures. Those on the left are all the more inclined to approach the economic dilemma in this fashion because there are equally strong voices on the right who agree with the premise that one must choose between monetary stability and full employment, in the short run at least, and who argue that human dignity is best advanced if we protect the purchasing power of the dollar, the pound, or the yen.

The debate between left and right continues to be centered around versions of two theories that have been carried over into postindustrial economies. The first, *Keynesianism*, has its origins in the era of industrial maturity; the other, *neoclassical economics*, has roots that go back to the earliest years of industrialism.[13] One of the prime assumptions of Keynesianism is that there is a "trade-off" between unemployment and inflation, such that governments, in trying to contain one, will exacerbate the other. If left to itself, the economy will move through cycles, oscillating from one extreme of high unemployment with low inflation to the other of high inflation with low unemployment. Government fiscal policies can smooth out these cycles, keeping them within a much narrower range and allowing entrepreneurs greater certainty and employees greater job security. This is based on the belief that consumer demand is the primary driving force for economic activity, and that it can be at any time at too low or too high a level relative to the existing supply of goods and services. These levels are subject to manipulation in either direction by government taxing and spending policies, which either take money out of the hands of consumers to curtail inflation or put it into their hands to stimulate the economy, thus creating more jobs.

The neoclassical school of economics that is often labeled *monetarism* argues that Keynesian countercyclical policies over time are counterproductive and that they worsen the problem that they are trying to keep under control. When government has sought to stimulate an economy that is experiencing only modest levels of resource underemployment, it has produced the expectation among both buyers and sellers of commodities and labor that higher levels of inflation will result. This creates a sort of "self-fulfilling prophecy" in which wages and prices are pushed up in anticipation of that very thing happening. This will result in a decline in demand for commodities and labor, which will in turn result in an increase in unemployment. Thus, government efforts to raise economic energies produce the opposite effect. Instead of a trade-off between unemployment and inflation, the two rise simultaneously, a phenomenon that has been labeled "stagflation," that is, economic stagnation along with inflation.

There has been enough evidence to support the neoclassical claim since the early 1970s to raise the stock of neoclassical economics in the press, in public opinion, and in the eyes of government policymakers. The monetarist talks about money supply as the central variable to be controlled, rather than consumer demand. The monetarist seeks to smooth out business cycles, just as does the Keynesian, although the method recommended is to bring the increase in money supply down to modest levels, and to keep it there, because it is fluctuations in money supply caused by government policies that are responsible for business cycles. Neither monetarism nor Keynesianism places emphasis on the idea that longer-term structural changes in the productive forces of an economy may be reducing government's ability to control both unemployment and inflation simultaneously, while also rendering obsolete the phenomenon of business cycles encountered during industrial maturity.

Another sort of neoclassical economist puts emphasis on the "supply side" of the economy, arguing that orthodox economics, whether of the Keynesian or the monetarist variety, has been preoccupied with cyclical phenomena to the exclusion of structural problems that affect the quantity and quality of goods produced and services supplied. "Supply-siders" see the cause of both inflation and high unemployment to be insufficient investment in the modernization and equipment of home-based firms that produce goods, perform services, and supply jobs in the domestic economy. To supply-siders, the culprit is a tax structure that provides the wrong incentives to investors and feeds an overexpanded government that siphons off too many resources from the national economy in taxation without making compensating additions to the capital stock of the economy. Reduced taxation will provide the incentive for firms, individuals, and institutions to invest in increased productivity that will increase the supply of goods and services at lower cost, thus withstanding competition, creating jobs, and stimulating demand to meet the growing supply.

One problem with the supply-side prescriptions is that they assume that the extra capital available to investors as a result of tax cuts will be employed in the most productive directions. But Keynesians and socialists have argued that this gives no assurance that they will not be used for investment abroad, or in relatively unproductive exploits such as real estate. They argue that a genuine concern for the supply side would necessitate that government pay attention to the direction of investment, making sure that it is in sectors of the economy where future growth potential exists and where technological change and changing patterns of international competition have been taken into account. In part, investment could be influenced by the structure of tax incentives government offers to investors to judge investments in certain directions. Some supply-siders might go along with these suggestions. But the logical outcome of government guiding investment would be a "hands-on" government planning approach that goes well beyond Keynesian prescriptions and would be anathema to neoclassical economics of any stripe. Some *socialists* have argued that, with proper state control of economic resources, the problems of both unemployment and inflation could be better addressed. Government could make full use of the labor-saving potential of the electronics revolution to reduce working hours and to use the surplus produced to improve the quality of life of the mass of citizens who now have an abundance of leisure time on their hands. This would be a radical solution, but capitalism has made radical adjustments to crises in the past and has maintained itself as a system. Nevertheless, socialist solutions that stress central government planning are not popular at the end of the twentieth century, especially in the wake of the collapse of socialist economies in Eastern Europe.

## Postindustrial Social Structure

It was emphasized in Chapter 1 that a prominent feature of mature industrialism in Europe was intensified conflict between social classes. But in this chapter we have seen that the relatively simplified industrial class system has become complicated by the growth of the service sector, by the decline of manufacturing employment, and by the growth in importance of knowledge as a resource in economic affairs. A review of its more complex postindustrial class structure will enable us to assess the impact of social structure on the politics of postindustrial society. We focus on the hierarchy of social groupings that is based essentially on occupation and on the prestige assigned by society to each occupational category. In other words, we look at the varying shares that different social classes have of the four values of power, respect, well-being, and enlightenment. Do postindustrial societies distribute these values differently from those in earlier periods?

## The Complexities of Contemporary Social Structure

One factor that complicates the analysis of class structure for all Western European countries is that, even if one focuses on occupation for assigning individuals or families to positions on the scale, there is no single, unambiguous scale. Instead, one must deal with the concurrent existence of old and new occupations that require different criteria for placing them somewhere in a hierarchical order. Italian sociologist Luciano Gallino has suggested that the social structure in Italy today can be understood only if one realizes that there exist simultaneously a "traditional," a "modern," and a "contemporary" class structure.[14] The continuation of an agrarian economy in southern Italy, with its dominant land-owning class and numerically large peasantry, is a carryover of traditional society into the late twentieth century. In our terms, southern Italian society is still largely preindustrial or early industrial, although important changes are taking place. In different parts of northern and central Italy, what Gallino calls modern and contemporary social structures can be found. Gallino's modern class system corresponds roughly to what we describe as mature industrial society, whereas his contemporary class system would be what is found in postindustrial society. The industrial working class is numerically the largest in modern society, whereas those in the service sector predominate in contemporary society.

In some ways, southern Italy resembles the semi-industrial nations of parts of the Third World that exist economically in a symbiotic, but essentially dependent, relationship with the core nations of the First World. Investment capital comes from the north, but return on investment returns to the north. Migrant workers move from south to north, learning skills in northern industry and sending money to families back home. But many remain where the higher-paid jobs are found, and never return with their skills to their home region. Much of the technically sophisticated, highly paid supervisory personnel in the new industries of the south are northerners sent by their firms or agencies for tours of duty in the south; but their career objectives lie northward. As for the manual workforce in the newer plants that have been built in southern Italy, as in the less developed regions of other First World countries, automation has made it possible for large corporations to employ semiskilled workers in the branch plants in "peripheral" regions, confining the skilled work to maintenance and repair shops in the original "core" regions where these firms began their lives.[15] This means that the industrial workforce in the core regions is more highly skilled, is better paid, and enjoys higher rates of unionization and greater job security than that of the periphery.

Whether one is working for a large corporation in a more prosperous region or for the same firm in a poorer area with lower wage rates, one is still part of the relatively advanced and stable sector of what is called the "dual economy." By this we mean that large corporations move on a "faster track" than many, if not all, smaller businesses. Large corporations are more apt to employ the most advanced technology, meaning that their streamlined workforces are highly efficient. Large corporations are, on the average, able to provide better pay, working conditions, and employment security for each of their workers than are smaller firms for his or her equivalent. That is, a woman employed as a technician in a large engineering firm in a medium-sized city will have a better job by these measures than will her counterpart in a smaller engineering firm in the same city. This is because (1) the large corporation produces

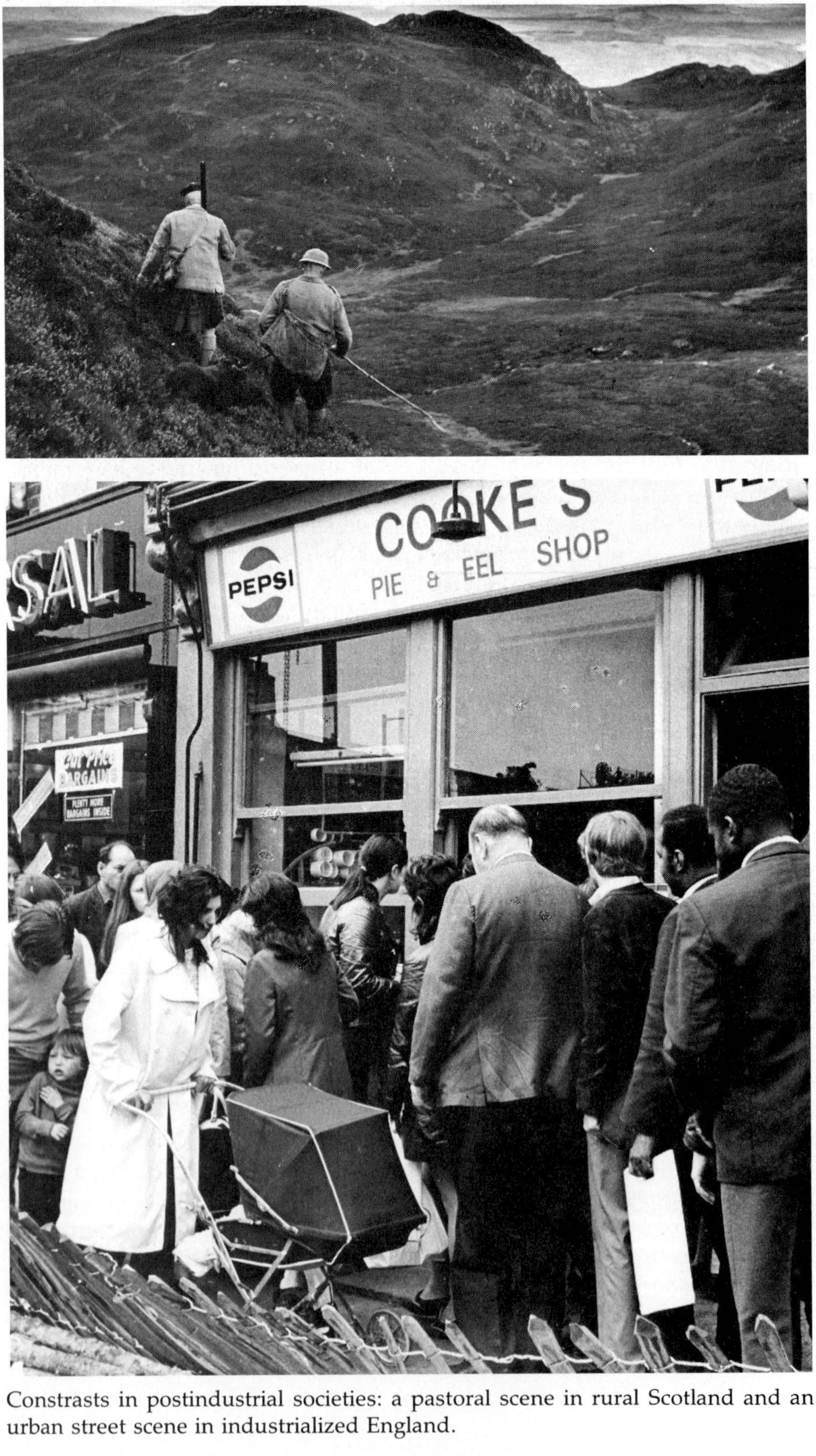

Constrasts in postindustrial societies: a pastoral scene in rural Scotland and an urban street scene in industrialized England.

more efficiently than the smaller one, and can afford to pay its workers more and provide better fringe benefits; (2) the large corporation is sufficiently diversified that it can carry unprofitable portions of its activities longer on the backs of its more profitable ones, or failing that, be able to transfer many of its employees to other parts of its operations—advantages the smaller firm that specializes in a single product line cannot offer its employees; and (3) there is a greater likelihood that the workforce in the larger firm is effectively unionized to promote better pay, better fringe benefits, and greater job security. These characteristics of the "dual economy" can be found in all First World countries to a greater or lesser degree, but it appears that the differences between advantaged and disadvantaged workers on either side of the divide are defined particularly sharply in Japan, where, in the absence of strong independent trade unions, the workers are dependent on the capacities of the firms they work for to define the positive and negative attributes of the jobs they hold. Larger firms organize their workforces themselves, guarantee their workers jobs for life, and solicit inputs into corporate decision making from the workers, who after all have a considerable stake in their companies' futures. Smaller firms in sectors where there is considerable competition and the struggle for survival is fierce are simply not in a position to accord such advantages to their workers, and the labor market in such a sector is more fluid that that in the more stable sectors.[16]

Nevertheless, the generalizations we make about the "dual economy" must be understood in light of certain postindustrial countertrends. As large corporations become multinational, they diversify and decentralize their operations so that the fact that parts of their operations are found in particular countries is of less significance to them than it once was. Security of employment has declined even in the more stable sectors of Japan's dual economy in recent years.[17] On the other hand, the advent of the microchip and the rise of the service sector have made it possible for smaller firms in some fields to operate more efficiently than larger ones, or to find market niches that are profitable for firms operating on a smaller scale, whereas they are not worth bothering with from the larger firm's standpoint. The recent buoyancy of the Italian economy, which in 1986 surpassed Great Britain on the scale of GNP per capita, moving into fourth place among our five countries, has been attributed in part to the proliferation of small manufacturing firms.[18] Found in traditional manufacturing areas of northern and central Italy, these firms typically have a few employees headed by one or two skilled workers. Often these are craftspeople who have lost their jobs or taken early retirement from large firms, and used lump severance payments to capitalize ideas they had dreamed up while watching increasingly standardized products being produced by increasingly automated processes requiring ever less skill and ingenuity. This is another example of ways in which the occupational structure of postindustrial society has become too complex to be understood in simplified dualistic terms.

## Postindustrial Social Classes

At the top of today's stratification system in Western Europe, the old aristocracy has been largely displaced by the executives of private corporations, as well as by professionals of various kinds (doctors, lawyers, government officials) who are in a favorable market position concerning the supply of, and demand for, their services. For example, a recent study of pay inequalities in Western European countries found that managers earn on the average 328.5

percent of the average earnings of full-time industrial workers in France, and 367.9 percent in Italy.[19]

In the middle range of the postindustrial stratification system, occupational categories are the most diverse. One finds both the declining ranks of small-business owners and independent farmers and the growing numbers of scientific and technical professionals, middle-management personnel, white-collar workers, and manual workers with marketable skills. The professional and managerial categories are the better paid, sharing with the upper-income earners a better education and a more favorable market position. Younger men and women in these categories may aspire to considerably higher incomes later in their careers as they move up the corporate ladder or shuttle back and forth between the public and private sectors. What distinguishes these various types of professionals from those below them in the middle-income ranks is their possession of knowledge that enables them to manipulate postindustrial technology and economic factors. They have invested time early in their careers to acquire this knowledge. The investment has more often than not been the result of early socialization in middle-class families, where acquisition of knowledge and investment for future gain are values on which high priority is placed. It is also likely to reflect a superior education at the primary and secondary levels, more readily available to middle-class than to working-class children in the relatively stratified Western European educational systems.

The distinction between manual and nonmanual workers has always been the basis of analysis of class structures under capitalism. Marxists believe that the class structure is based on exploitation of wage earners by their employers. Traditionally, Marxists either ignored classes that fell in between these two or else lumped them together with one or the other. Thus, nonmanual workers might be seen as part of the bourgeoisie or as part of the proletariat, with the former tendency being by far the more prevalent. Today one can question whether the earlier classifications of industrial Europe are still relevant—whether, for example, the social, economic, and political distance between skilled workers and unskilled workers has not become greater than that between white-collar workers and skilled workers. Indeed, it might be argued that by function and training, skilled workers belong more to the category of engineers and technicians than do the white-collar workers such as store clerks, secretaries, and key punch operators. The latter may be more akin to the unskilled-worker category, especially in levels of pay and in vulnerability to unemployment. Again, we see the importance of levels of education in leading to differences in life chances. Although most skilled workers have not gone to universities, in most European countries, as well as in Japan, there are public and private training programs based in part on the old apprenticeship systems that bring skilled workers into the full-time workforce only after considerable time has been invested in bringing them up to marketable standards.

Further contributing to the breaking down of the class system of industrial society is an easing of the traditional rigidities of the typical Western European educational system. Most European countries have until fairly recently made a relatively inflexible distinction at the secondary level between schools that prepare the student for university education and the professions and schools that prepare the student for various manual and nonmanual occupations which can be entered on finishing school at age sixteen or seventeen. The grammar school in

Great Britain, the *lycée* in France, and the *Gymnasium* in Germany are traditional means by which the "cream of the crop" are separated at around the age of twelve from the majority of their age group and are prepared for their roles in life that will mean higher income and status. Despite the fact that these schools were maintained by the state and were free and open to anyone qualified, children from middle-class families had a much better chance of meeting the entrance requirements than did children from working-class families. With the establishment of *comprehensive schools* in Western European countries, the distinctions between upper and lower "streams" remain, but they are administered more flexibly than before. This has reduced the disparity between the classes in the likelihood of one's advancement to higher education. In the 1960s and 1970s there was a massive expansion of the state-supported university system, but the net result was to improve the chances of middle-class children for higher education much more than to improve those of working-class children. In Japan, as we will see in Chapter 7, the chances of working-class children for higher education are appreciably better than those in Western Europe. Nevertheless, the point to be emphasized in the present context is that the expansion of higher education in Western Europe has broadened the pool of talent from both strata that is entering the expanding middle ranks of the occupational structure. Therefore, changes in educational opportunities appear at one and the same time to be reducing the proportion of the population left to compete for the less remunerative and less secure jobs of both a manual and a nonmanual nature in postindustrial society, while reinforcing the gulf between the more and the less advantaged occupational positions, a gulf that runs through many families, dividing not only working-class parents from their better-educated offspring, but also dividing the better educated from their disadvantaged siblings and childhood friends.

## Women and Immigrants in the Workforce

The above generalizations leave aside a crucial factor of increasing significance in Western Europe as well as in the United States and Japan: the fact that large percentages of white-collar workers are women and that overwhelmingly the largest percentages of women are found in the lowest-paid white-collar jobs. In Western Europe, as in the United States, efforts are being made by governments and by private employers to place more women in higher-paid positions of greater responsibility. Yet, the chief beneficiaries thus far have been women with advantageous social and educational backgrounds. Young women from middle-class families are entering universities in greater numbers and are coming out with qualifications that enable them to compete with men on a more equal basis in the liberal professions and for junior management positions. But young women from working-class families are even less likely than their male counterparts to go on to higher education; nor are they anywhere nearly as likely to go on to technical schools or the apprenticeships that will lead to their becoming skilled workers. Accordingly, on leaving school at around age sixteen, perhaps having learned to type and take shorthand, they seek jobs as store clerks, secretarial assistants, or members of typing pools.

Prospects for advancement are limited for women in the lowest-paid white-collar jobs. The expectation of their employers is that they will soon get married and raise families, thus becoming dependent on their husbands for their future economic and social positions. After the child-raising years, they may return to similar jobs at about the same rank as before, but with even less chance for future promotion to higher-paying jobs because they have less future ahead of them. What this adds up to is the fact that, when one says that the white-collar worker has better long-term job prospects than the manual worker, it is clearly the *male* white-collar worker that one has in mind. In terms of both the tangible and intangible rewards of their work, women in the lower-paid clerical jobs should probably be classified with the semiskilled and perhaps even the unskilled workers at the bottom of the occupational scale.

An industrial proletariat still exists in Western Europe. It consists of manual workers who now perform the tasks that technological advances have not yet rendered unnecessary—and perhaps never will. These include a wide variety of jobs, from watching over and occasionally adjusting the automated machines to serving as waiters in restaurants, from collecting trash to sweeping public buildings. If women occupy the lowest-paid levels of the nonmanual occupational categories, migrant workers, both men and women, are their counterparts in the manual categories. Like women white-collar workers, migrant workers occupy the jobs that are the worst paid and the least likely to enjoy union protection. As individuals, they are marginal to the employment structures of the countries where they work. As a class of workers, however, they are indispensable. They perform tasks that must be performed by someone if the factories are to be kept running and the streets are not to become blocked by mountains of garbage. Workers (especially men) indigenous to the more highly industrialized regions and countries of Western Europe will no longer engage in such work. If necessary, they prefer unemployment compensation while waiting for more desirable jobs to reopen. To meet the need for unskilled labor at a time of near full employment, governments and employers in northern Europe (and recently in Italy as well) encouraged the immigration of hundreds of thousands of unskilled workers from countries along the shores of the Mediterranean and, in the case of Great Britain, Commonwealth citizens from West Indian, Asian, and African countries that were formerly part of the British Empire.

During the 1960s, large numbers of young men from Portugal, southern Italy, and Spain; from Greece, Turkey, and Yugoslavia; and from Algeria, Morocco, and Tunisia arrived in northern Europe and became important percentages of the working populations of Belgium, France, Great Britain, Switzerland, and West Germany, among others. In France, by 1968 their numbers had reached 6.3 percent of the labor force, including 8.7 percent of skilled workers, 10.6 percent of semiskilled workers, and 21.6 percent of unskilled workers. Moreover, they concentrated in the larger cities. Immigrants in the West German cities of Frankfurt, Munich, and Stuttgart constituted 17 percent of the population of those cities by the early 1970s. Approximately one-third of the immigrants in Great Britain and France lived in the London and Paris areas. This meant approximately 500,000 residents in each city. Paid the poorest wages and discriminated against by landlords, they occupied the lowest standard of housing, often crowded several to a room.[20]

When economic conditions took a turn for the worse in the 1970s, the governments of the host countries sought to restrict the flow of immigrants, and, indeed, the numbers of workers entering these countries declined. But, because indigenous workers could not be found to take over jobs that were still available in the recession, many of the immigrants who originally had entered on a temporary basis stayed. Much of the influx of the 1970s came in the persons of wives and children who had earlier been left behind. Second-generation southerners were now entering the schools and the job market in increasing numbers. What had been regarded as a temporary expedient, to assist the economy in a boom period, now was becoming a chronic social condition. Homogeneous societies like those of West Germany and France were becoming multiethnic, and neither governments nor private corporations nor trade unions were geared to deal with the resulting problems. There has been increasing militancy on the part of migrant workers. They have formed their own organizations and have engaged in wildcat strikes, sit-ins, and demonstrations, sometimes touching off backlash violence by native workers who feel economically and socially threatened. In France, a right-wing political party has capitalized on this unrest. Called the *Front National*, its candidate received 14 percent of the popular vote in the presidential election of April 1988. By 1989 a right-wing party in West Germany, the *Republikaner* (Republicans) was pursuing a similar anti-immigrant line. But its "anti-foreigner" message became confused with the influx into West Germany of several 100,000s of ethnic Germans from East Germany and elsewhere in Eastern Europe. Postindustrial society may have lessened the social distance among the relatively highly paid and skilled indigenous men workers (manual and nonmanual), but it seems to have created the roots of a new class struggle, which may be all the harder to resolve because occupational and economic bases of distinction are overlaid by racial, linguistic, and gender distinctions.

## Postindustrial Inequality

Despite growing affluence, the shares of the expanding pie have been inequitably distributed in postindustrial society, and those with the smallest shares—in many cases the elderly, the handicapped and disabled, single mothers, orphans, and the unemployed—might be right to perceive the social order as unjust. A study sponsored by the Organization for Economic Cooperation and Development (OECD), published in 1976, lent some support to this possibility. The author of the study, Malcolm Sawyer, measured income distributions in twelve selected First World countries. He measured both pretax and post-tax income, employing a variety of standard measures that gave somewhat different, but not radically different, results. In measures of pretax income, France and the United States consistently showed the greatest inequality, and France consistently showed the most unequal distribution of income after taxes in Western Europe. Figure 2.1 shows the shares of post-tax income of the two lowest deciles of the population in each of the twelve countries. It can be seen that the poorest 20 percent in France had 4.3 percent of the post-tax income, whereas the comparable group in West Germany had 6.5 percent, in Italy 5.1 percent, and in Great Britain 6.3 percent. On the other hand, the richest 20 percent in France had 46.9 percent of the post-tax income. The comparable percentages were 46.1, 46.5, and 38.7 for West Germany, Italy, and Great Britain respectively.[21]

These intercountry differences probably mask differences in the trends of postindustrial societies toward or away from greater social

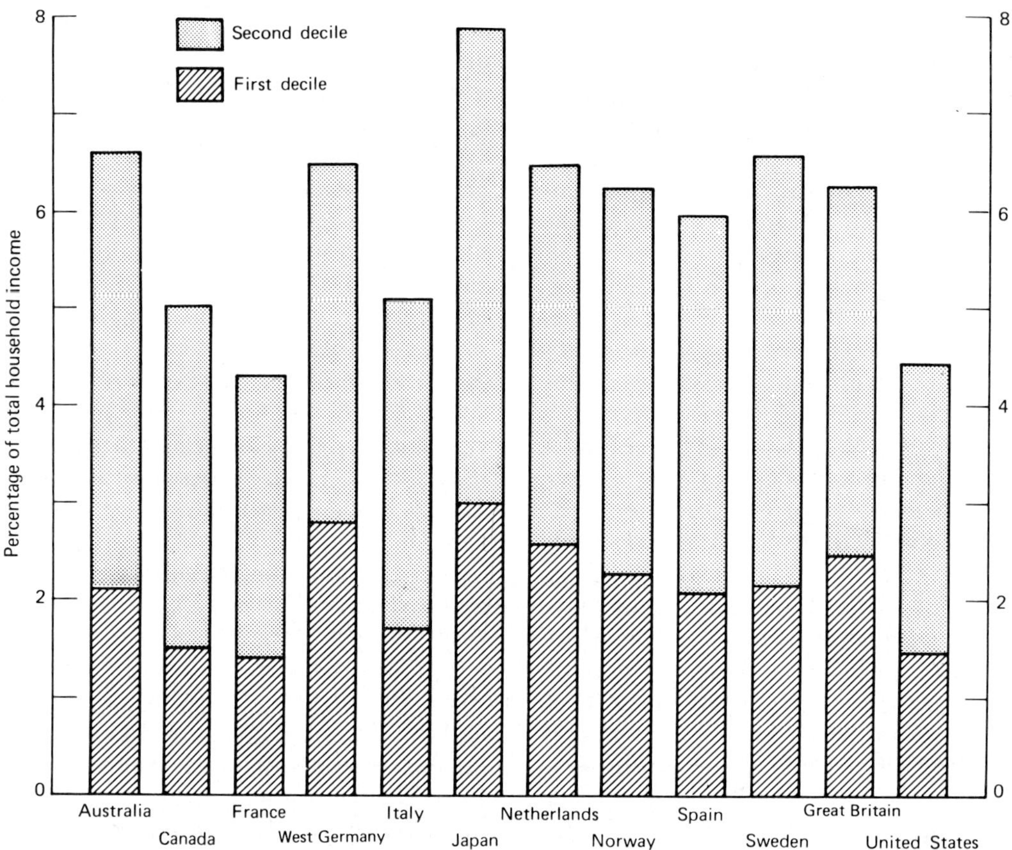


*Figure 2.1* Shares of lowest two deciles in post-tax household income distribution. [Malcolm Sawyer, "Income Distribution in OECD Countries," in Organization for Economic Cooperation and Development, *Occasional Studies* (Paris: OECD, 1976), p. 15.]

equality. In 1979 the British Royal Commission on the Distribution of Income and Wealth reported its findings from a comparison of studies undertaken in several First World countries from the early 1950s to the mid-1970s. Very tentatively the Commission concluded that, insofar as the distribution of total personal income among households (family and single-person units) is concerned:

There was a trend toward greater inequality in the USA after 1967. A similar but more uneven trend was evident for the UK from the same date, having been preceded between 1959 and 1967 by a decline in the level of inequality. The Japanese estimates indicate a long run trend toward greater inequality, though this was not confirmed by . . . less complete . . . data. . . . In West Germany there has been little change since 1955 whereas in France an increase in inequality between 1956 and 1962 was reversed between 1962 and 1971. If the trend has persisted since 1971 then more up-to-date French data might show a level of inequality of roughly equal magnitude to other European countries in our study.[22]

It may be the case that France, less urbanized and industrialized in 1960 than the other countries in the study, assumed a social profile closer to that of the other First World countries during the next decade. But the finding that inequality appeared to be growing among some of the most advanced industrial countries during the same period of time, and at a time of relatively high economic growth—relative to the most recent decade at any rate—leads one to suggest that, despite the "trickle-down" gains for all classes, those at the top of the scale were gaining the most. It should be stressed, however, that these are estimates of pretax inequality. Post-tax figures for Britain and West Germany show little change in either direction over the late 1960s and early 1970s.[23] The same may likewise be true of France, whose tax structure was regressive by Western European standards.

According to economist Lester C. Thurow, the high levels of inflation and unemployment of the 1970s probably resulted in greater inequality in First World countries than was ac-

"Instant slums" outside Paris. These are called Bidonvilles (shanty-towns, or literally "tin-can towns"). Such slums in France and in other Western European countries house North African and other immigrant workers who perform low-paid service labor.

tually found in the mid-1970s.[24] Inflation produced an unwillingness on the part of middle-income earners to continue "to pay the transfer payments necessary to keep the income of the bottom quintile rising in pace with the rest of the nation."[25] Furthermore, inflation motivated middle-class wives, who have the education and skills to enable them to enter the postindustrial workforce at relatively high levels of remuneration, thus expanding the share of the pie held by upper-middle- and middle-income households, advantages that lower-income families usually do not possess. Thurow also sees rising unemployment as directly contributing to growing inequality, because market trends are distinctly unfavorable to the employment hopes of unskilled and semiskilled workers at the lower end of the income scale. Although his findings apply to the United States, the same phenomena have occurred in Western Europe, and thus the same reasoning applies. It seems reasonable to conclude that postindustrial society does not, of itself, generate forces that will lead to greater equality. If this is true, there will have to be some political impetus if First World societies are to become more equal or even to remain at approximately their present state.

## Preindustrial Social Divisions and Politics[26]

During mature industrialism, political parties in Western Europe could be distinguished from one another as parties of the left or the right partly in terms of the social classes to which they directed their appeals. Parties of the left, particularly those calling themselves Socialists and Communists and seeing their intellectual inheritance in the writings of Karl Marx, primarily sought the voting support of the industrial working class, whereas parties of the right aimed their messages at the various portions of the middle class. This was never a perfect correlation, particularly because of the tendency of a sizable minority of the working class to vote for the party or parties of the right. By the early post–World War II years, it was generally assumed that social class, or the division between manual and nonmanual workers, was the most important factor in determining whether voters voted for parties of the left or parties of the right.[27] Early in the century this assumption helped account for the long-range optimism of socialist parties in Western Europe, for they set the assumption of stable working-class support alongside the assumption that, with growing industrial maturity, the size of the working class would continue growing until socialist parties could be assured of majority voting support from the electorate as a whole.[28] Postindustrial society has confounded these expectations. Indeed, no party in any of our Western European multiparty systems has been able to gain a majority of the popular vote for any but fleeting moments during the entire post–World War II era.

There are two principal reasons for this failure on the part of socialist parties to reach majority status among Western European electorates. First, as previously noted in this chapter, social class structures have become more complex, with the portion of the working population properly labeled "manual worker" receding in size. Second, social class has declined in importance as a determinant of party voting.[29] In one First World country after another, the evidence mounts against the assumption that social class is any longer the primary basis of party politics. As social class has declined in electoral importance, other identifying features of electorates—some of which are older characteristics, some newer—have gained in significance. In the remainder of this chapter we concentrate on two of the longer standing social distinctions in Western Europe—religion and ethnicity. In

Chapter 3 we look at some post-industrial dividing lines of growing political significance.

## Religion

Historically, religion has played a very important role in the politics of all Western European countries. The Protestant Reformation had an immense impact on the countries of northern Europe, as did the reaction to it of the Roman Catholic Church in southern Europe. Religious political parties have, at different times and in different places, been central to the politics of almost all continental Western European countries. Our four Western European countries can readily be characterized as follows: Great Britain is a Protestant country, France and Italy are Catholic countries, and West Germany is approximately half Protestant and half Catholic. But the situation is actually much more complex than that.

In the first place, in the late twentieth century, despite signs of a renascence here and there, organized religion has not been such an important factor in the average European's life as it was earlier in the century. Many people, especially in urban areas, are atheists, agnostics, or nominal church members who never attend services. Church membership figures in Western European countries usually far exceed that portion of the membership that could be regarded as "religious." This is particularly true in Great Britain, where 61 percent of the population identify themselves with the established Church of England, but where actual Church of England attendance is only a small fraction of the potential.[30] Generally, the same holds true for the Scottish Presbyterians (the established Church of Scotland). Although British Catholics and non-Anglican Protestants show higher attendance rates, those Britons who take religion seriously are decidedly a minority of the overall population.[31]

Religion is more important to more people in the three other countries, and it has greater political significance elsewhere than it has in Great Britain. The Anglicans tend to vote Conservative and the other religions lean to Labour, but social class is much more important in Great Britain in accounting for the two-party vote than is religion. Although class as a factor in British party voting has been declining since the early 1970s, it has not been replaced by religion or any other social factor as the principal determinant.[32] In West Germany, 50 percent of the population is Protestant and 46 percent Catholic. A majority of Catholics support the CDU, the successor to the old Catholic Center Party of the Weimar Republic. But the Christian Democrats have renounced a strictly confessional orientation. They have sought Protestant support and have obtained about one-third of the Protestant vote. Indeed, they have captured about 50 percent of the vote of self-employed, middle-class Protestants, which helps account for the inability of their rival, the Social Democrats, to gain much more than 50 percent of the Protestant vote.[33]

Although France and Italy are both Catholic countries, Roman Catholicism is much more solidly entrenched in the latter. In France, there has always been a very strong strain of anticlericalism. This is not the same as a personal philosophical position about the existence of God. The anticlerical French need not be atheists or agnostics, although many are. What distinguishes the anticlerics is their opposition to any church influence in political matters. What is sought is a complete separation of church and state, which means, for example, the abolition of state subsidies to religious schools.

Although anticlerics are difficult to distinguish from other French men and women, at least for purposes of census taking, voting studies show that there is a strong relationship between anticlericalism and left-wing voting. This can be seen from electoral maps of France that show what regions of the country have the strongest left-wing voting. Anticlericalism flourishes in the south and southwest, the regions that have consistently provided the greatest support for the left for more than a century. It has also been found that strong adherents to the Catholic faith in France tend to vote right of center. For example, in a 1981 survey, the Socialist Party was chosen by only 28 percent of weekly churchgoing Catholics, whereas it was chosen by 47 percent of the nonreligious and nonchurchgoing Catholics. By contrast, the Gaullists, the leading party of the right, were supported by 26 percent of the former group and only 9 percent of the latter.[34]

This distinction between church attendance and nonchurch attendance is also important in Italy and West Germany. Parallel studies in the two countries showed that, in both cases, church attendance was the most important variable explaining left-wing versus right-wing voting; it was more important than social class, trade union membership, or, in the case of West Germany, Catholicism versus Protestantism.[35] Thus, religion in its usual sense—that is, one religion versus another or religion versus nonreligion—as an environmental factor affecting politics in postindustrial societies, may no longer be so important as it once was. But, in some Western European countries, the intensity of religious participation still plays an important role in politics. This is particularly true in countries with substantial Catholic populations; other examples include Austria, Belgium, the Netherlands, Spain, and Portugal.

## Ethnicity

In two of the smaller Western European countries, Belgium and Switzerland, there is another important factor—the concentration of people who speak different languages in separate regions of the country. In Belgium, the division is between French-speaking Belgians (Walloons) in the south and Dutch-speaking Belgians (Flemish) in the north. In Switzerland, there are four separate regionally based linguistic groups, of which the most important are the French-speaking Swiss in the west and the German-speaking Swiss in the north and east. Political party support in both countries has been profoundly affected by these linguistic divisions, but in Switzerland they have not disrupted the overall political harmony in this century. The opposite has been true in Belgium. There, the numerically superior Flemish have claimed that the Walloons enjoy a privileged political and economic status, and the Walloons resent the economic decline of their region relative to prosperous Flanders. Disruptions of the Belgian political system have sometimes approached the scale of those in Canada, where a similar division can be found between French-speaking and English-speaking Canadians.

In each of our four Western European countries, the principal language group far exceeds the minorities in terms of its share of the population. West Germany has no significant geographically based minority. In Italy and France, linguistic minorities are found in border areas that adjoin other countries: the Alsatians on the French side of the Franco–German border speak a dialect that is similar to German; the Basques and Catalans in southern parts of France that adjoin the corresponding regions of Spain have their own languages; the French-speaking Italians are found in the Alpine region adjacent to France; and the people of the South Tyrolean Alps speak German but live on the Italian side of the Austro–Italian border. In all these areas, except Alsace, there are movements seeking attachment to the appropriate ethnographic entity. The most serious conflict has been in the French Basque region. Basques on the French side of the Franco–Spanish border have harbored fugitive Basque separatists from the Spanish side. This has been a source of strain in relations between Paris and Madrid, although both governments have taken steps in recent years to seal off the border to the refugees.

There is a different kind of problem for certain minorities in regions of France and Great Britain where there are no international boundary lines dividing linguistic groups who speak the same language. In these cases, a combined cultural and economic deprivation is felt by the minorities in relation to the dominant populations. In France, this is the case of the Bretons in Brittany, the westernmost region of the country, and of the Corsicans on the Mediterranean island of Corsica, which is legally and administratively an integral part of France. In Great Britain, it is true of the Welsh and the Scots. In all of these cases, the political system has been affected—by outbursts of violence in Brittany and Corsica and by the electoral success of Welsh and Scottish nationalist parties. The responses in these cases have been halting attempts by the central government to provide greater material resources to the aggrieved regions and to experiment with means of giving more power to regional levels of government to stave off the demand for full-scale independence. Regionally based ethnicity bears watching as an old source of a new strain in postindustrial societies, especially if social class and religious divisions become less important politically than they once were and if economic disparities between regions within a country continue.

## The Anomaly of Northern Ireland

In a class by itself is the division between peoples in Northern Ireland, an area that is physically part of the island of Ireland but is politically a part of the "United Kingdom of Great Britain and Northern Ireland," which we have been referring to as "Britain" or "Great Britain" (i.e., the larger of the two main islands of the British Isles). At the time Catholic Ireland gained its independence from the United Kingdom after World War I, heavily Protestant Ulster (the northern six counties of Ireland) remained part of the United Kingdom and remains so today. Its population is divided along what are both religious and ethnic lines. Between 35 and 40 percent of the population are historically indigenous Irish Catholics; the remaining 60 to 65 percent are Protestants, mainly Presbyterians whose ancestors migrated to Ulster from lowland Scotland two or three centuries ago. Religion is a more salient dividing line than ethnicity today, as church attendance is much higher for both Catholics and Protestants in Northern Ireland than it is for either religion in Great Britain. But sociologists argue that the dividing line is as much a social class division as a religious one. All of the indicators of well-being, employment indicators, levels of pay, and standard of living favor the Protestants, who, until 1969, dominated the government of Northern Ireland, which was allowed a great deal of autonomy from control by the British Parliament.[36]

In 1969 the Catholics staged civil rights demonstrations that produced intergroup violence and eventuated, in 1971, in the British government's dismissing the local parliament and establishing direct rule from London. The arrival of the British army stimulated resistance from more militant Catholics organized in the Irish Republican Army (IRA). Militant Protestants are also organized in paramilitary fashion, and their political parties have defended the social, economic, and political advantages of Protestants with single-minded determination. Most Catholics today support the independence of

Northern Ireland from Great Britain and its unification with the Irish Republic in the south. But militant Protestants have made it clear they will turn to violent means themselves if the governments in London and Dublin were to move overtly in that direction. Talks have gone on between the two governments, both of which believe some form of joint Protestant–Catholic rule must form the basis of an ultimate solution for Northern Ireland itself, but there is not a clear-cut agreement on the question of who should have ultimate sovereignty, the United Kingdom or the Republic of Ireland. In Northern Ireland itself, too much of the present political leadership of both communities appears too far removed from willingness to seek a compromise solution for it to be a realistic hope before the arrival of the twenty-first century. However we view the social basis of the conflict in Northern Ireland, the violence it has produced far exceeds that in any other part of the First World. In Great Britain itself, religious conflict has not produced such violence since the early 1700s.[37]

In summary, it would seem clear that socioeconomic environmental factors are important in influencing politics. The level of a country's economic development and the degree of equality in the distribution of well-being among its social groups will help determine the shape of its political system. But these economic factors will undoubtably be affected by the country's predominant social cleavages, some of which have existed since before the Industrial Revolution.

## *Suggestions for Further Reading*

**Acquaviva, S. S., and M. Santuccio.** *Social Structure in Italy: Crisis of a System*, trans. Colin Hamer (London: Robertson, 1976).

**Atkinson, A. B.,** ed. *Wealth, Income and Inequality* (Oxford: Oxford University Press, 1980).

**Bell, Daniel.** *The Coming of Post-Industrial Society* (New York: Basic Books, 1973).

**Coates, David.** *The Context of British Politics* (London: Hutchinson, 1984).

**Gallie, Duncan.** *Social Inequality and Class Radicalism in France and Britain* (Cambridge: Cambridge University Press, 1983).

**Goldthorpe, John H.** *Social Mobility and Class Structure in Modern Britain* (Oxford: Clarendon Press, 1980).

**Hirsch, Fred, and John H. Goldthorpe,** eds. *The Political Economy of Inflation* (Cambridge, Mass.: Harvard University Press, 1978).

**Jacobs, Jane.** *Cities and the Wealth of Nations: Principles of Economic Life* (New York: Random House, 1984).

**Krejci, Jaroslav.** *Social Structure in Divided Germany* (New York: St. Martin's, 1976).

**Lash, Scott, and John Urry.** *The End of Organized Capitalism* (Cambridge: Polity Press, 1987).

**Marceau, Jane.** *Class and Status in France: Economic Change and Social Immobility, 1945–1975* (Oxford: Clarendon Press, 1977).

**Offe, Claus.** *Disorganized Capitalism: Contemporary Transformations of Work and Politics* (Cambridge, Mass.: MIT Press, 1985).

**Okimoto, Daniel L., and Thomas P. Rohlen,** eds. *Inside the Japanese System: Readings on Contemporary Society and Political Economy*

(Stanford, Calif.: Stanford University Press, 1988).

**Parkin, Frank.** *Class Inequality and Political Order: Social Stratification in Capitalist and Communist Societies* (New York: Praeger, 1971).

**Sabel, Charles F.** *Work and Politics: The Division of Labor in Industry* (Cambridge: Cambridge University Press, 1982).

**Taylor, Robert.** *Workers and the New Depression* (London: Macmillan, 1982).

**Vogel, Ezra N.** *Japan as Number One: Lessons for America* (Cambridge, Mass., and London: Harvard University Press, 1979).

## Notes

1. Among many works that discuss postindustrial society, see Daniel Bell, *The Coming of Post-Industrial Society* (New York: Basic Books, 1973); Leon N. Lindberg, ed., *Politics and the Future of Industrial Society* (New York: McKay, 1976); and Alain Touraine, *The Post-Industrial Society*, trans. Leonard F. X. Mayhew (New York: Random House, 1971).
2. Among the earlier uses of this term is that by the German Socialist Claus Offe. See his *Disorganized Capitalism: Contemporary Transformations of Work and Politics* (Cambridge, Mass.: MIT Press, 1985).
3. Scott Lash and John Urry, *The End of Organized Capitalism* (Cambridge: Polity Press, 1987), p. 5.
4. Ibid., p. 6.
5. Ibid., p. 5.
6. Bell, *The Coming of Post-Industrial Society*, pp. 129–142.
7. Statistical Office of the European Communities, *Basic Statistics of the Community*, 16th ed. (Luxembourg: The European Communities, 1978), p. 18.
8. Bell, *The Coming of Post-Industrial Society*, p. 135.
9. Ezra N. Vogel, *Japan as Number One: Lessons for America* (Cambridge, Mass., and London: Harvard University Press, 1979), Ch. 3
10. Taketsugu Tsurutani, *Political Change in Japan: Response to Postindustrial Challenge* (New York: McKay, 1977); Ardath W. Burks, *Japan: A Postindustrial Power* (Boulder, Colo., and London: Westview, 1981).
11. Donald B. Keesing and Martin Wolf, *Textile Quotas against Developing Countries*, Thames Essay no. 23 (London: Trade Policy Research Centre, 1980).
12. Angus Maddison, "Economic Growth and Structural Change: Issues and Prospects," in Irving Leveson and Jimmy W. Wheeler, eds., *Western Economies in Transition: Structural Change and Adjustment Policies in Industrial Countries* (Boulder, Colo.: Westview Press, 1980), pp. 41–60.
13. Jane Jacobs, *Cities and the Wealth of Nations: Principles of Economic Life* (New York: Random House, 1984), Ch. 1.
14. Luciano Gallino, "Italy," in Margaret Scotford Archer and Salvador Giner, eds., *Contemporary Europe: Class, Status and Power* (London: Weidenfeld and Nicolson, 1973), pp. 110–115.
15. Charles F. Sabel, *Work and Politics: The Division of Labor in Industry* (Cambridge: Cambridge University Press, 1982), pp. 71–77.
16. Tadashi Hanami, *Labor Relations in Japan Today*, 1st paperback ed. (Tokyo: Kodansha Interna-

tional, 1981), pp. 89–90.

17. Edward J. Lincoln, *Japan: Facing Economic Maturity* (Washington, D.C.: Brookings, 1988), p. 4.
18. Sabel, *Work and Politics*, pp. 220–231; "The Flawed Renaissance: A Survey of the Italian Economy," *The Economist* (February 27, 1988), special section, pp. 4–9.
19. Duncan Gallie, *Social Inequality and Class Radicalism in France and Britain* (Cambridge: Cambridge University Press, 1983), Ch. 1, fn. 33.
20. Thierry Baudouin et al., "Women and Immigrants: Marginal Workers?" in Colin Crouch and Alessandro Pizzorno, eds., *The Resurgence of Class Conflict in Western Europe since 1968*, Vol. 2 (New York: Holmes & Meier, 1978), p. 74.
21. Malcolm Sawyer, "Income Distribution in OECD Countries," in Organization for Economic Cooperation and Development, *Occasional Studies* (Paris: OECD, 1976), pp. 3–36. Estimates in the study are carefully made from a variety of sources, including government statistics and surveys of households. Narrow differences among countries should be interpreted cautiously; wider differences should be quite reliable.
22. Report no. 7 of the Royal Commission on the Distribution of Income and Wealth, reprinted in part in A. B. Atkinson, ed., *Wealth, Income and Inequality* (Oxford: Oxford University Press, 1980), pp. 93–95.
23. Ibid., p. 94.
24. Lester C. Thurow, "Equity, Efficiency, Social Justice and Redistribution," in Organization for Economic Cooperation and Development, *The Welfare State in Crisis* (Paris: OECD, 1981), pp. 140–145.
25. Ibid., p. 142.
26. Because of the absence of politically relevant *pre*industrial cleavages in Japan, we confine our discussion in this section to our four Western European countries. *Post*industrial cleavages in Japan are considered, along with those in Western Europe, in the next chapter.
27. Robert R. Alford, "Class Voting in the Anglo-American Political Systems," in Seymour M. Lipset and Stein Rokkan, eds., *Party Systems and Voter Alignments: Cross-National Perspectives* (New York: The Free Press, 1967), p. 68.
28. Adam Przeworksi, *Capitalism and Social Democracy* (Cambridge: Cambridge University Press, 1985), pp. 16–19.
29. Russell J. Dalton, *Citizen Politics in Western Democracies: Public Opinion and Political Parties in the United States, Great Britain, West Germany and France* (Chatham, N.J.: Chatham House, 1988), Ch. 8.
30. Richard Rose, "Britain: Simple Abstractions and Complex Realities," in Rose, ed., *Electoral Behavior: A Comparative Handbook* (New York: The Free Press, 1974), p. 517.
31. Ibid., pp. 517–518; Dalton, *Citizen Politics*, p. 162.
32. Regional differences in Great Britain, where unemployment levels and other economic indicators show substantial differences between the more prosperous south of England and the poorer northern English regions and Scotland and Wales, are becoming of greater political importance. In 1987 the Conservative Party won 51.8 percent of the vote in the south, against 36.6 percent of that in northern England, 29.5 percent of the Welsh, and 24 percent of the Scottish vote. For Labour, the percentage of the southern vote was only 20.9, against 42.1 percent in northern England, 45.1 percent in Wales, and 42.4 percent in Scotland. David Butler and Dennis Kavanagh, *The British General Election of 1987* (London: Macmillan, 1988), p. 284.
33. Derek W. Urwin, "Germany: Continuity and Change in Electoral Politics," in Rose, ed., *Electoral Behavior*, pp. 133, 148; Dalton, *Citizen Politics*, p. 164.

34. Dalton, ibid.

35. Urwin, "Germany," and Samuel H. Barnes, "Italy: Religion and Class in Electoral Behavior," in Rose, ed., *Electoral Behavior*, pp. 109–170, and 171–225, respectively.

36. Although he accepts this statistical evidence, Richard Rose contends that it is still religion, rather than social class, that is the predominant politically relevant social cleavage in Northern Ireland. *Governing without Consensus: An Irish Perspective* (Boston: Beacon Press, 1971), pp. 286–387.

37. David Coates, *The Context of British Politics* (London: Hutchinson, 1984), p. 184.

CHAPTER 3

# POLITICAL CULTURE

It should be clear from the preceding chapter that First World economies have been struggling in the past two decades and that the accompanying social strains have been growing in severity. In subsequent chapters, we will see how the political systems of these countries have adjusted to these strains. In some cases, as in Great Britain and France, important changes have taken place in voting patterns, partisan alignments, and public policy goals. The West German and Japanese political systems, which earlier underwent the greatest transformations from pre–World War II patterns, had been the most resistant to the winds of change, probably because, as we have seen, the economy and social order in the two countries have been the least subject to strain during the past decade. But, even in West Germany, if not in Japan, the 1980s brought some political surprises. Thus, we can see a relationship between the stability of the socioeconomic order and political stability. Disequilibrium in one realm is likely to produce discontinuity in the other.

Social and economic strains do not simply translate into political events without first having some impact on the people who make the political events. In First World polyarchies, the political stage is a relatively crowded one. Political actors include not only the elites who make the principal policy decisions that affect society, but also ordinary citizens—citizens acting as voters and in other ways participating in the political process. The importance of voters for political outcomes should be obvious to anyone who has witnessed the changes at the top that have occurred as a result of elections in Great Britain, the United States, France, West Germany, and Italy since 1979. But political participation of other kinds—participation in strikes, public meetings, and demonstrations and even acts of violence—have an impact on the political system, although often a less calculable impact than that of dramatic changes in voting behavior.

How do ordinary citizens respond politically to the traumas of daily life? The answer depends on how citizens view politics. Do they see it as a very distant realm inhabited by a few knowledgeable persons, or as an arena affording opportunities for personal involvement and potential relief from social, economic, and even psychological ailments? In other words, what are the political beliefs of ordinary citizens? How do they perceive the values of power, well-being, enlightenment, and respect to be distributed within their society, and what responsibility do they assign to government for these distributions? What role do they see for themselves in reinforcing or bringing about changes in these distributions? Do the citizens of different countries have different political beliefs? In what ways do different segments of the population of the same country differ in their political beliefs? The study of political culture is the study of such belief systems. It enables us better to explain and make predictions about the ways traumatic events affect the political behavior of citizens in different societies.

## *Definitions*

The term *political culture* was coined in the 1950s by the political scientist Gabriel A. Almond.[1] Its meaning has changed somewhat since then as perspectives borrowed from social psychology have come to have greater influence in the fashioning of the concept. According to Almond and G. Bingham Powell:

> Political culture is the pattern of individual attitudes and orientations toward politics among the members of a political system. It is the subjective realm which underlies and gives meaning to political actions. Such individual orientations involve several components, including: (a) cognitive orientations, knowledge, accurate or otherwise, of political objects and beliefs; (b) affective orientations, feelings of attachment, involvement, rejections, and the like, about political objects; and (c) evaluative orientations, judgments, and opinions about political objects, which usually involve applying value standards to political objects and events.[2]

Essentially, Almond and Powell are saying that political culture is a pattern of individual attitudes and orientations toward political objects. The key words are (1) *pattern,* (2) *individual attitudes and orientations,* and (3) *political objects*.

Let us begin with the second of these elements. "Attitudes and orientations" should lead us into the realm of individual psychology. How do people think and feel about themselves and about the world around them? How they think or feel, of course, is not necessarily an indication of how they will act. At best, it simply gives us some insight into their *potential* for action. One must also take into account the situational opportunities and constraints that surround any such potential action. I might have a very strong feeling that the mayor of my city is corrupt and has been robbing the city blind for years. Yet I might hesitate to take action unless I know others feel the same way and unless I believe something could be done to get the mayor out of office. Still, if many people feel the same way I do (impotent), that is one significant reason why the mayor has been able to get away with it for so long. If such people could know who shared their view and realize that the discontent was widespread, perhaps the mayor could be ousted from office. The potential is there; the problem is to convert the potential into action.

This brings us back to the first element—the pattern of attitudes and orientations. Suppose that only a tiny minority of relatively well-educated citizens opposed the mayor, whereas the vast majority of people were either apathetic or believed he was doing a good job. The mayor would have less to be concerned about in this situation than if the city were polarized, that is, fairly evenly divided between strong supporters and strong opponents. Here we see the difference between two attitudinal patterns: a consensual and a polarized pattern; these patterns can be depicted graphically as distribution curves. (See Figure 3.1.) The J-shaped and normal curves represent consensual patterns, whereas the U-shaped curve indicates polarization. In the case of the J-shaped pattern, there is what one might call a one-sided consensus because there is a minority that is far removed from the majority in this case. The normal curve reflects something of a middle-of-the-road consensus. Here, it would be easier to work out a compromise between the competing opinions than in the first situation.

The final element of our definition is the political object toward which the attitudes and orientations are directed. In the case at hand, the incumbent mayor is the political object. But political culture encompasses a much wider array of political objects; these may include a number of questions of public policy, how government should allocate scarce resources among competing needs. Also included are attitudes and orientations toward the structures of politics and government and how power is distributed between citizens and their government and between government offices. In other words, the political culture of a country is the pattern of attitudes and orientations of its citizens toward power, well-being, respect, and enlightenment, and how they are distributed.

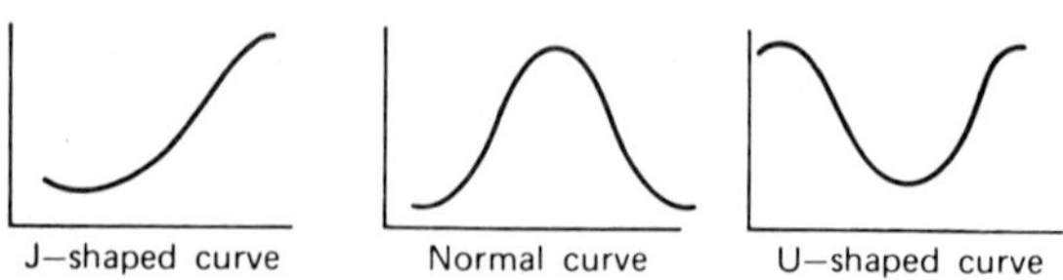


*Figure 3.1* Three types of attitudinal distribution.

In studying political culture, we may want to know whether certain political attitudes and orientations are distributed among the entire population of a country or only among a portion of its citizenry. We have already used the political culture of a single city as an example. Any national political culture can be subdivided into a variety of political *subcultures* if certain groups that can clearly be differentiated on the basis of certain attributes also have distinct political orientations. For example, the youth of a country, who are distinguishable on the basis of age, may also share distinct political beliefs and feelings. Perhaps women or the elderly or Catholics share sufficiently distinctive political orientations to warrant being treated as subcultures in certain countries. In Chapter 4, we consider the political elites of our five countries—those public officials and influential private citizens with the greatest share of political power—and ask whether there are distinct subcultures among political elites, that is, the different ideologies that divide political parties, such as Socialists and Conservatives, from one another. In some countries, such as the United States, the ideological differences between political parties are probably not fundamental enough to warrant the judgment that all but their most active members belong to different subcultures. In other countries, however, the ideological walls are steeper and thicker, and such subcultures can be found.

We should not be surprised to learn that French communist ideology constitutes a separate political subculture. But the active Communists, after all, constitute only a small minority of the population, almost professionally separate from the rest—like doctors, lawyers, or engineers. What about the masses of people? In postindustrial society, do typical French people differ enough from typical Britons or Germans to make it worthwhile to examine differences in political culture? If you have ever traveled in these countries, perhaps you can answer this question. People *do* differ in how they feel about things, and their reactions may seem unpredictable to anyone who is unfamiliar with their culture. By and large, Britons were able to empathize with the trauma that Watergate represented to Americans, but they could also better sympathize with the plight of a disgraced president, whose stature as a world leader they respected, than could most Americans. Germans, on the other hand, could understand neither. They could not relate to the agony most Americans were experiencing. Obviously, Richard M. Nixon had done wrong; obviously, he should be removed from office. What was all the fuss about? The French displayed a third reaction—cynicism. To them, all politicians are corrupt and what Nixon did was no better or worse than what most politicians do. But if Americans wanted to clean up their political system, they should have started much earlier; in any event, it probably would not have done much good.[3]

How can people living in such close proximity to one another have such different responses? Part of the answer lies in the fact that people are brought up differently in these countries. Here we come to the subject of *political socialization.* Each country has typical ways in which children are brought up and typical ways in which adults are politically influenced that continue to reshape the orientations they learned in childhood and adolescence. In these social learning experiences, one acquires a set of "correct" attitudes that enables one to get along with one's fellow human beings with a minimum of friction. This training and conditioning process is only partly at the conscious level. Parents have certain ideas about how to bring up their children, but most of them are not trained child psychologists. Children growing up in France during the presidency of Charles de Gaulle may have gotten a clear impression from their parents that the general was greatly admired and respected, even though their parents may never have said anything explicitly to this effect. Later on, this same respect and admiration may have transferred to the office of the president itself, with de Gaulle's successors benefiting from the "halo effect." Whatever orientations children gain from parents will not easily be changed later in life.

Certain kinds of political orientations are also learned in school. In Western European polyarchies, children are not as likely to learn partisan affiliations as they are to learn of their position in the larger world. No longer screened from this world by the warmth of the family circle, children begin to experience the various authority patterns with which they will have to live later on, and they begin to get an idea of their position in the hierarchy of respect within the general society. The relatively elitist educational systems of Western Europe help transmit a stronger sense of class difference than is true of the schools in the United States and Japan. European children going through the privileged upper stream are likely to have greater confidence in their ability to influence political events than are children in the lower stream, who are learning that they will have lesser shares of well-being, respect, and enlightenment. But as larger numbers of young persons in Western Europe have gone on to higher levels of education, so the level of confidence of the younger generation as potential wielders of political influence exceeds that of older people.

Political socialization takes place elsewhere as well. Peer influences can be quite important in shaping attitudes both in school and later on in various occupations and organizations. Such influences may reinforce or conflict with those learned in the family and the school. In postindustrial society, many individuals are exposed to influences that lead them to become quite different from their fathers and mothers. The acceleration of change has been so great in recent decades that could a time machine transport average Italian adults from the 1940s to the 1990s, their efforts to adjust to the new Italy might bring about a severe trauma requiring confinement in a mental institution. Older Italians have gone through precisely this process, but at a slower pace, which has enabled them to build up their psychological defenses. But how well can an Italian of twenty communicate with an Italian of seventy? Change the word *Italian* to *American* and see what your answer is.

Television and the other media have also helped break down the attitudes acquired early in life. The process of challenge probably begins in late childhood, accelerates in adolescence, and comes to full bloom in adulthood. The degree to which the media are deliberately purveying certain messages varies from country to country. The matter of government control over French broadcasting is one of the most important issues in France, and has been ever since the Gaullist leadership began shaping media messages more than thirty years ago. Opponents of the Gaullists argued that they used radio and television to condition attitudes in ways that helped them remain in power. Today the Gaullists are making similar complaints about their Socialist successors. But the potential influence of the media goes far beyond partisan advantage and disadvantage. The crises of inner cities, the tragic struggle of Northern Ireland, terrorist attacks, the killing of fish by chemical pollution of the Rhine River, the grim economic statistics of the last decade—all reach the livingrooms of people in Western polyarchies. So does emotionally charged good news, such as the steps taken toward democratic regimes nearby in Eastern Europe. No matter how objectively these traumatic events are portrayed by media news staffs, they are bound to affect people's confidence in the efficacy of political systems and in the dependability of their own future.

## *Political Allegiance*

### Allegiant and Alienated Political Cultures

When political scientists compare the political cultures of different countries, much of their attention is focused on what we have called the value of *power*. Political scientists have asked two very general sorts of questions about attitudes toward the distribution of power. The first relates to the way people view the structure of political elite roles within the political system; the second concerns people's view of themselves and of people like themselves as nonelite political actors. The political elite is a body larger than that set of individuals who hold important public offices at any given time. In Western Europe and Japan (as we will see in Chapters 4 and 5) the political elite includes the leaders of the opposition party or parties who hold seats in the legislative body (parliament) and who stand ready to replace the leaders of the majority party or parties who presently hold power.

The first aspect of political culture is the study of how nonelites perceive the political elites of their country. When we ask how people view political elites, we are not asking simply how well they like the incumbents. Such questions are frequently found in public opinion polls: People are asked how well they think President George Bush or Prime Minister Margaret Thatcher is doing, for example. In studying political culture, we ask a more fundamental question: how well people believe the country is being run by *whoever* is in power. This question has a longer-term quality to it. It is a question about what political scientists call the *regime*. We are interested in how well the ordinary citizen feels his or her country has been run in recent experience, including periods of time during which more than one president or prime minister or, for that matter, political party has been in power. In essence, we are asking both (1) how well the system of political institutions is structured to ensure that the most appropriate team of political elites will be in a position to make public policy and (2) how reliable the *entire pool* of political elites is.

Individual citizens who have positive attitudes toward their political institutions and political elites can be termed *allegiant*. They are so in more than the sense that they have a strong national identification, meaning a sense of patriotism. They also believe that their system of government is one that works, at least most of the time, and that the people who specialize in the work of government are capable of making it work. *Alienated* citizens, on the other hand, are those who lack confidence in their governmental system and in their political elites. They may not trust those in power, they may be disenchanted with all politicians, and they may very well be searching for substantial changes in the structures of the system that will make it work better. It is possible to go from the level of the individual to the citizenry as an aggregate and say that the political culture of a country is allegiant or alienated if a strong majority of the citizenry shares attitudes of one type or the other. These two types of political culture are depicted in Figure 3.2.

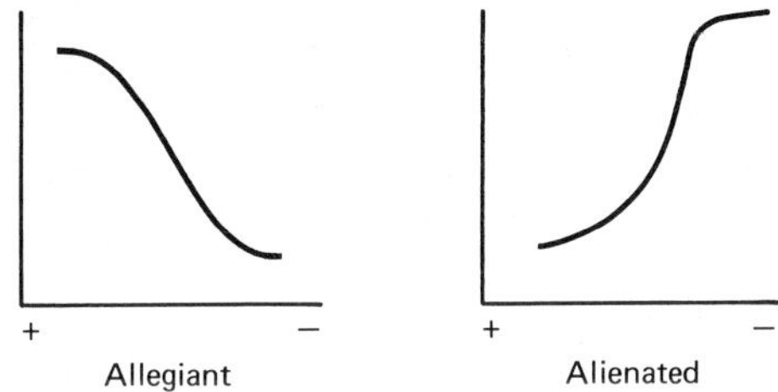

*Figure 3.2* Two types of political culture.

It is easier to define aspects of political culture, such as political allegiance, than it is to measure them. Ideally, one would like to be able to determine how every citizen of a particular country felt at a given time about the political elites. Although this is impossible, the next best thing—the public opinion poll or attitude survey—is in principle available and reliable. Prohibitive costs, however, have limited its use on a cross-national basis so that, although we have many good surveys of the political attitudes of people in individual countries, they can seldom be combined with similar studies of other countries to enable comparative analyses. One of the pioneering cross-national studies in this field—a five-nation survey conducted by Gabriel A. Almond and Sidney Verba in 1959–60[4]—is still a landmark, but its findings are now quite out of date. Therefore, we supplement some of those findings with more recent studies made either cross-nationally or within single countries.

Almond and Verba asked their respondents in the United States, Great Britain, West Germany, Italy, and Mexico the following question: "Speaking generally, what are the things about this country you are most proud of?"[5] The respondents came up with their own answers rather than being compelled to answer in categories supplied by the interviewer. The responses were then coded into a discrete number of categories. (See Table 3.1.)

The Americans and British most often cited aspects of their governmental or political institutions, including social legislation. Nearly twice as many Americans as British said they felt most proud about aspects of their political

**Table 3.1 Aspects of a Nation in Which Respondents Report Pride (by Nation)**

| *Percentage Who Said They Were Proud of:* | *U.S.* | *U.K.** | *West Germany* | *Italy* |
|---|---|---|---|---|
| Governmental, political institutions | 85% | 46% | 7% | 3% |
| Social legislation | 13 | 18 | 6 | 1 |
| Position in international affairs | 5 | 11 | 5 | 2 |
| Economic system | 23 | 10 | 33 | 3 |
| Characteristics of people | 7 | 18 | 36 | 11 |
| Spiritual virtues and religion | 3 | 1 | 3 | 6 |
| Contributions to the arts | 1 | 6 | 11 | 16 |
| Contributions to science | 3 | 7 | 12 | 3 |
| Physical attributes of country | 5 | 10 | 17 | 25 |
| Nothing or don't know | 4 | 10 | 15 | 27 |
| Other | 9 | 11 | 3 | 21 |
| Total percent of responses† | 158 | 148 | 148 | 118 |
| Total percent of respondents | 100 | 100 | 100 | 100 |
| Total number of cases | 970 | 963 | 955 | 995 |

(*Source*) Gabriel A. Almond and Sidney Verba, *The Civic Culture: Political Attitudes and Democracy in Five Nations* (Princeton, N.J.: Princeton University Press, 1963), p. 102. Reprinted with permission of Princeton University Press.
* Great Britain.
† Percentages exceed 100 because of multiple responses.

system, but more British cited this category than any other aspect of their country or its people. Only negligible percentages of the Germans and Italians mentioned this category at all. The largest percentage of German respondents mentioned characteristics of the people, such as industriousness and efficiency, and the success of the West German economy. As for the Italians, the largest single category was "nothing, or don't know." The physical attributes of the country came ahead of any category dealing with the qualities or achievements of the Italian people. Clearly, allegiance to the political system was higher at that time in the United States and Great Britain than in West Germany or Italy.

## Recent Developments

In the past twenty years, changes have taken place in mass attitudes in the countries Almond and Verba studied.[6] In a recent study of attitudes toward democracy in our four Western European countries and the United States, Ulrich Widmaier found that there had been a general tendency for support for democracy to decline during the troubled economic times of the late 1970s and early 1980s.[7] This expressed itself differently in the five countries. In the United States, support for democracy declined gradually from a very high level before the economic decline began, and even by the early 1980s it rested at a higher level than was true in the four other countries.

The next highest level was found in Widmaier's own country, West Germany, where, he noted, support for democracy had risen dramatically in the 1960s and early 1970s but had declined somewhat since then. France and Britain showed fluctuations during the period studied, but they seemed to be related to different factors that might explain them. In the case of France, Widmaier noted that support for democracy rose around the times elections were held and declined thereafter. He interpreted this to mean that the French voters' hopes for democracy were raised each time the evenly balanced parties went into combat against each other, but typical French cynicism set in again once the outcome had been declared and the new incumbents had settled into office. As for Britain, support for democracy closely followed support for the incumbents. Thus, for example, when public opinion polls were registering an upsurge in support for Prime Minister Margaret Thatcher at the time of the Falklands (Malvinas) War, the attitude surveys on which Widmaier relied were showing a similar improvement in British views of democracy. In Italy, support for democracy was lower than in the other countries and showed less movement over time. However, in all five countries, levels of support for democracy were lowest in the mid-1970s and the early 1980s, when economic fortunes were likewise at a low ebb. They rose again in the mid–1980s with the return of good economic times.[8]

The substantial differences in patterns of support for democracy among these five countries suggests more caution in interpreting the findings than Widmaier displays. For one thing, the term *democracy* itself may have different meanings in different political cultures. It has always enjoyed a sort of "halo effect" in the United States, whose people see themselves as the pathbreakers who have led the rest of the world in making the abstract concept of democracy work in reality. The American view of democracy probably had a substantial impact on the generations of West Germans who have grown up since World War II, experiencing an educational system that features civics courses that are, if anything, more sophisticated than those found in American schools. Such explicit socialization in democratic norms and values is not found in British, French, or Italian schools, where greater continuity prevailed between prewar and postwar educational patterns. The tendency of the British to subordinate their view of democracy to their view of the way the government is performing at the moment suggests that democracy is not a concept that is grasped early and retains strong emotional attachment in Britain, as it does in the United States and seems to do in West Germany. It also suggests that questions about attitudes toward democracy do not really reach the deepest levels of political allegiance in European countries. Older symbols, relating to the nation-state, may reach further.

There have been other recent studies of political allegiance that have gone deeper into the subject for each of these countries. The increased allegiance among citizens of West Germany has been a consistent finding. In 1978, a sample of West Germans was asked to specify what things about their country made them proudest, and the results were noticeably different from what Almond and Verba found in 1959–60. The percentages who volunteered some aspect of governmental or political institutions had risen from 7 percent to 31 percent, the second highest category after the economic system, which had risen to the 40 percent level.[9] Although West Germans were still proud—indeed, even prouder—of their economic record in 1978, they were now registering allegiance to the political system in much higher frequencies than twenty years before. It can be imagined that the sustained superiority in economic performance of West Germany had built up a stock of *specific support* among its citizenry. This is allegiance to the existing regime that is based on a positive evaluation of its performance but that is not necessarily indicative of a deeper sense of allegiance to the political institutions. The latter has been termed *diffuse support* by political scientists.[10] It may be developing in West Germany, but one wonders whether the high levels of allegiance shown in recent surveys would be sustained in the face of a sustained reversal in the performance of the West German economy. However, it seems safer today than twenty years ago to predict that democracy as a general system of government will continue to receive support. This has been shown in survey after survey taken over the past two decades in which West Germans in overwhelming percentages consistently expressed positive feelings toward democracy and rejected authoritarian forms of government.

The positive movement of West Germans along the allegiance/alienation dimension is all the more striking because, if anything, the movement of American and British citizens has been in the opposite direction in the past twenty years. The evidence for Americans is quite clear. Periodically, Americans have been asked about their levels of confidence in various political and social institutions. Comparisons of results for 1966 and 1972 show a remarkable decline in confidence for all institutions, including the medical profession, major companies, organized labor, and the various branches of national government. Among the latter, the Supreme Court declined from a 51 percent expression of public confidence to 28 percent in the six-year period. The Senate and House of Representatives were supported by only half as many respondents in 1972: 21 percent for both houses of Congress versus 42 percent in 1966. Support for the executive branch declined from 41 percent to 27 percent. This declining confidence appears to have been accompanied by a growing cynicism among Americans. The percentage of those who agreed with the statement that government is "run by a few big interests" increased from 29 percent in 1964 to 65 percent in 1974.[11] The latter figure can be compared with that of only 27 percent in West Germany who agreed with the statement the same year. Also in 1974, 47 percent of British respondents agreed with the same cynical proposition, a figure approximately midway between those for West Germany and the United States.[12]

Although West Germans are gaining in allegiance and Americans seem to be moving in the direction of disaffection, if not alienation, the evidence for Great Britain is less clear. Cynicism appears to have reached only a moderate level in the evidence just cited, but it is noteworthy that the strong support for the British two-party system, registered in election after election in the 1950s and 1960s, dropped off significantly in the 1970s, both in terms of the votes for the two major parties in elections and in terms of the levels of party identification. As in the United States, increasing numbers of voters, especially young voters, are showing a lack of attachment to the two political parties that have dominated British politics since World War II. However, it should be pointed out that the identification of Britons with the social classes of the industrial era has also declined in postindustrial Great Britain. Loss of party identification can be partially explained by the fact that the two political parties, Labour and Conservative, are strongly associated in the public mind with the manual and nonmanual classes of the industrial social order.[13]

It is possible that the British have recently withdrawn specific support from their political elites, at least to an extent; it is not so certain that the same can be said of the diffuse support that had accumulated in Great Britain over centuries of gradual political development.[14] Surveys have shown that the British still support the institution of the monarchy in overwhelming numbers, something that cannot be said of any of the American political institutions, including the presidency and the Supreme Court. However, British respondents also acknowledge that the monarch has little power, so that the appropriate American analogue might be a purely symbolic feature of the American political system, such as the flag or the Washington Monument.

More to the point, perhaps, is the continued support in Great Britain for the system of law and for the obligation of the citizen to obey the law. Higher percentages of British respondents, in a 1979 survey, were willing to give approval to police using force against illegal demonstrations than was true of American or West German respondents.[15] One comparative study of teenagers in London and Boston found satisfaction with the political system to be higher among British young people, but expectations of democratic performance to be lower. Perhaps Britons are less alienated because they have not demanded as much responsiveness from their political system as have Americans.[16] To repeat, it appears that specific support has declined in recent years but that the stock of diffuse support, built up over a long period of time, has scarcely been depleted, despite the waning of British power in the world and the country's dismal economic record of recent decades.

Almond and Verba found a substantial degree of alienation and cynicism among their Italian respondents in 1959. This fit the stereotypes that most observers shared in viewing the Italian political culture of the time. During the 1960s, with the Italian economy booming, attitude surveys revealed more positive assessments, especially in policy-related areas, such as jobs, housing, and income. The political system seemed to be gaining its share of popular credit for improving well-being in Italy. But the 1970s brought a reversal in this trend. In 1971, only 17.5 percent of an Italian national sample agreed with the statement that "there is something basically wrong with the social and political system." By 1974, the percentage had risen to 34.6. In 1975, more than 77 percent of respondents assigned to government great responsibility for solving problems in the fields of jobs, crime prevention, and inflation. Less than 18 percent evaluated government performance positively in any of these areas. It is unlikely that evaluations have improved in the years since 1975. Still, as Joseph LaPalombara has emphasized, political cynicism is worn as a sort of badge of honor by Italians. One wonders how seriously it should be taken.[17]

In light of the evidence from the United States, Great Britain, and Italy, the West German case seems all the more striking. It is difficult to escape the impression that economic success can engender and help sustain political support, whereas poor or mediocre economic performance can have the opposite effect. Especially when one considers the disastrous earlier German experiment with democracy, the Weimar Republic, does the West German case seem significant. Generalizations about the German national character have long stressed the tendency of the German people to accept authority unquestioningly as a civic obligation. The early attitude surveys taken after the establishment of the Federal Republic of Germany indicated that the acceptance of the authority of the state, its laws, and the actions of its official state agents—bureaucrats and the police—did not necessarily mean a strong attachment to the existing political leadership found in the governing and opposition parties. More recent studies have found that not only are the governmental institutions of the Federal Republic accepted today, but the phenomenon of competing political parties, always viewed with ambiguity at best, has now become an accepted feature of the institutional framework.[18]

## France: Allegiance or Alienation?

In the case of France, the fact that Almond and Verba did not include that country in their study deprives us of a similar baseline for comparing today's political culture with that of thirty years ago. Nor have French scholars been preoccupied with asking the same kinds of questions about political culture as have students of American, British, and West German political cultures. There is some evidence regarding attitudes toward the two most recent political regimes that have prevailed in France—the Fourth and Fifth Republics. As in West Germany and, briefly during the 1960s, in Italy, evaluations of the new French regime improved swiftly during the economic boom years of the 1960s.[19] French citizens assess the Fifth Republic instituted by General Charles de Gaulle more positively than they do its predecessor, but the disparity is in no way as striking as that between West German evaluations of the Weimar and Bonn republics.[20]

Students of French political culture have focused a great deal of their attention on French attitudes toward authority, viewed in the abstract and studied in a variety of settings, such as offices of large bureaucratic organizations and classrooms at various educational levels.[21] The prevailing view is that most of the French are ambivalent toward authority, whether it be found in their more immediate small-group experiences or as they view the authority of their political leaders and the state. There is a strong distaste for manifestations of authority that are experienced at too close range. The French reputedly have an abhorrence of face-to-face contact with those who hold authority over them. They prefer that authority remain impersonal and distant and that they be expected to adhere to formal rules that apply equally to all in the same situation as well as that allow them a maximum of freedom to assert their own individuality within the framework established by these rules. If authority becomes too immediate and oppressive, the French may well rebel against rules that they consider arbitrary or unjust. The rebellion may be covert, taking the form of surreptitious noncompliance with the rules—as in the case of tax fraud or of students ridiculing teachers behind their backs—or it may take a more overt and collective form—as in 1968, when tens of thousands of French men and women discovered, almost spontaneously, a common resentment against the authority of the French state and went on a collective strike that eventually evaporated as suddenly as it had formed, once the pent-up resentment had been sufficiently vented.

The other side of this ambivalence is a need for order and a fear of chaos that will be reasserted when rebellion against authority threatens to get out of hand. General de Gaulle is said to have fit the French expectation of authority especially well, in that he was an aloof, aristocratic figure, preferring Delphic generalities to specific commands. It was reassuring that de Gaulle was *there*, as living proof that the capacity of the state to maintain law and order was intact; and it was especially comforting in that de Gaulle did not appear to be making excessive demands on his people to achieve goals of *his* choosing, goals that they as individuals had not chosen for themselves. His grand designs tended to be directed outward toward the leaders of other countries, especially the superpowers and his European neighbors. His people could watch his maneuvers, as they would watch a spectator sport or the performance of a great actor, without feeling any obligation being thrust on them, other than the obligation to admire. Contrast this style of leadership with that of John F. Kennedy, which was better attuned to the

American culture. Kennedy said, "Ask not what your country can do for you; ask what you can do for your country." At the same time in history, de Gaulle was saying, in effect: Ask not what you can do for France; observe and be proud of what de Gaulle does for France.

French ambivalence toward authority is also related to a tendency, as in Germany, to disassociate the state from the current political regime.[22] In the French case, the concepts of state and nation are intermingled. Throughout the many successive political regimes that France has experienced since the French Revolution of 1789, the state has remained relatively intact, meaning that the bureaucracy, the courts, the army, and the diplomatic corps have not experienced great upheaval, whatever has happened at the political level. The state, with its permanent bureaucratized institutions housed in their elegant old buildings, is the living proof of the nation's permanence. By contrast, state and nation for West Germans cannot be so readily equated. Whatever its historic meaning as a geographic and cultural expression, Germany did not exist until 1871; its boundaries were subject to radical fluctuation between 1918 and 1945. Thereafter, what was left of its former territory was divided into two separate states fashioned on rival political and social philosophies. With the removal of physical barriers between the two Germanies in November 1989, we again see the territorial question attaining a predominant place on the political agenda on both sides of Germany. Although the West Germans continue to feel a strong sense of civic obligation to obey the commands of the state and do not feel the same sense of ambivalence toward the state's authority as do the French, there is not the same confidence in the state's permanence. Had support been withdrawn from the Bonn Republic (the political regime), one could not have predicted with confidence that there would not be a convulsion affecting the structure and authority of the West German state and threatening the viability of West Germany as a political entity. Should support for the French Fifth Republic be withdrawn, on the other hand, the institutions of the state would likely survive without difficulty even if a Sixth Republic came into being.

In fact, the question of regime support is at the heart of the issue of how German reunification should take place. Those who, like West German chancellor Helmut Kohl, believe that East Germany should simply "join" the existing Federal Republic (FRG), are asserting that the FRG is an established, legitimate regime, whereas the East German regime (the German Democratic Republic) is not. Those who, like West German opposition leader Oskar Lafontaine, would prefer the creation of a new all-German regime with a new constitution, agree that the East German regime lacks popular support; but they believe that, for a reunited Germany to be established on a secure basis, the existing FRG must be replaced with a constitutionally based regime that will be designed from the outset to be permanent, which the FRG was not. Only then can the new regime begin to accumulate the support of both East and West Germans that will eventually evolve into support of the diffuse kind. (See the Postscript at the end of Chapter 7 for a more extended discussion of German reunification).

## *Attitudes toward Political Participation*

### Earlier Findings

The second aspect of political culture that concerns us is the question: How do people feel about themselves—ordinary citizens—as political actors? Much of the Almond and Verba study was directed toward answering the question: Do people believe that they—as ordinary citizens—can influence the decisions made by those in power? This question taps people's perceptions of the way political power is, in fact, distributed. Such perceptions may not actually be correct. People may naively feel that they have a greater share of power than they in fact have, or they may be overly cynical, believing that power is concentrated in fewer hands than it really is. But whether their perceptions are correct or not, they are of interest because they can help predict the way people will act. It is likely that citizens who believe they have access to the political system would be more apt to try to do something about a political situation they regard as unfavorable. On the other hand, citizens who cynically detach themselves from a political system they believe is rigged against them would be more likely to ignore opportunities that may actually be available to them.

To answer this, Almond and Verba asked their respondents questions designed to discover levels of what they called *civic competence*. The citizen who feels competent is one who believes he or she actually has the capacity to influence government decisions. Almond and Verba asked whether the individual, if confronted with an unjust national regulation, felt he or she could do something about it.[23] Table 3.2 presents the percentages who responded affirmatively to this question about both a nationally and a locally imposed regulation. Intercountry differences are not particularly great on the question of local decisions, but the differences are striking at the national level. Clearly, more Americans and Britons felt they were competent to influence national decisions than did West Germans or Italians.

Almond and Verba made certain judgments on the basis of the response patterns to their whole array of questions.[24] They found that the Italians were highly distrustful of one another, were preoccupied with self-protection, and were dubious that the government can be enlisted to help them.[25] They believe that government is run by the few in the interest of the few; democracy is an illusion. Therefore, why not accept the fact and live with it? Italians find they can get along most comfortably in life if they let the politicans worry about politics while they worry about the welfare of their family. In this way, Italians avoid disappointment; therefore, their cynicism may be of positive value for them psychologically.

Almond and Verba made a more complex judgment of West German political culture. They observed what they called political detachment

**Table 3.2 Percentage of Respondents Who Said They Could Do Something about an Unjust Local or National Regulation (by Nation)**

| *Country* | *Can Do Something about Local Regulation* | *Can Do Something about National Regulation* |
|---|---|---|
| United States | 77% | 75% |
| *Great Britain* | 78 | 62 |
| *West Germany* | 62 | 38 |
| *Italy* | 51 | 28 |
| Mexico | 52 | 38 |

(*Source*) Gabriel A. Almond and Sidney Verba, *The Civic Culture: Political Attitudes and Democracy in Five Nations* (Princeton, N.J.: Princeton University Press, 1963), p. 185. Reprinted with permission of Princeton University Press.

and subject competence among the West Germans.[26] Voter turnout is high in West Germany, and Almond and Verba found that the West Germans were more knowledgeable about politics than were their respondents in the other countries. But they also found that the Germans were more preoccupied with economic than with political matters. Voting is seen as a civic obligation, and keeping informed about political matters is only prudent for people in a country that has undergone such drastic political upheavals in this century. But Almond and Verba's study shows that a majority of West Germans in 1960 did not feel particularly competent to influence political events, and there was no majority who even felt one ought to try. The conclusion is that, although the West Germans were not necessarily antidemocratic, they had not yet internalized truly democratic norms and values. On the other hand, it appeared that they felt themselves competent as *subjects*, that is, as consumers of the goods and services provided by government. Relatively large percentages of West Germans trusted government administrators and the police to treat them fairly. Apparently, the professional traditions of these officials could be relied on as a protective device against arbitrary official behavior, despite the inclination of the German people not to exercise effective popular control.

To characterize Great Britain and the United States, Almond and Verba coined the term *civic culture*.[27] A civic culture is a political culture in which citizens value popular participation in political affairs and an equal distribution of political power, but where they are sufficiently content with the political system that they have no motivation to participate very actively in politics. Most of the time they prefer to leave politics to their leaders, the specialists. Almond and Verba found that the British were more passive than the Americans, but the differences were not great; therefore, they labeled the former a *deferential* civic culture and the latter a *participant* civic culture. In both cases, the commitment to democracy was strong enough to ensure that the political system would operate essentially as a democracy; but the commitment was not so strong that large numbers of people would be constantly intervening in the decision-making process, overloading the normal channels and threatening to destabilize the system. Almond and Verba felt that the civic culture is a solid underpinning for stable democracy. The future of democracy seemed more certain in Great Britain and the United States than it did in West Germany and Italy.

What about France, which was not included in the five-nation study? Students of French political culture are generally agreed that the French tend to be cynical (like the Italians) about the extent to which France is indeed a democracy.[28] In 1969, a survey was taken in France that asked a number of questions similar to those in the Almond–Verba study. Among these, the respondents were asked if they agreed with the following statement: "The people decide how the country shall be run through the vote." The percentage of the French who responded positively (58 percent) was lower than that for any of the five Almond–Verba countries, in which the percentages ranged from 83 percent (Great Britain) to 62 percent (Italy).[29]

## More Recent Findings

Once again, we must ask whether attitudes in the various countries have changed in the years since the Almond–Verba study. If we take the idea that these countries have since entered or are now entering the postindustrial era, we might expect certain changes to have occurred. Russell J. Dalton has called attention to certain socioeconomic changes associated with postindustrialism that might suggest a growth of participant orientations: (1) The growth of government involvement in society since the middle of the twentieth century has increased citizens' awareness of the importance of government's decisions for their lives. (2) The growth of the service sector and the expansion of educational opportunities has meant that more persons rely on their intellectual skills in their occupational lives, which may mean that more have developed the capacity to analyze public affairs and make their own judgments. (3) The last point has been reinforced by improvements in the flow of information between citizens, through the growth of voluntary associations and the availability of electronic means of storing, retrieving, and communicating information. (4) New issues have arisen involving ordinary citizens more directly, a point that is developed later in this chapter. Dalton has reviewed the findings of various recent studies of political participation and has concluded that the amount of change that has occurred since 1959–60 depends on the country examined and the type of political participation one has in mind.[30]

Three of the countries Almond and Verba examined—the United States, Great Britain, and West Germany—were included in a more recent five-nation study in which the focus of attention was on popular attitudes toward political participation. The international team of researchers who conducted the study in the mid-1970s was headed by an American, Samuel Barnes, and a West German, Max Kaase.[31] The Barnes–Kaase team conducted surveys in the Netherlands and Austria as well as the United States, Great Britain, and West Germany. An important feature of this study was to answer those critics of Almond and Verba who stated that they had paid insufficient attention to modes of political participation often considered *unconventional*. Activities such as demonstrations, unofficial strikes, boycotts, and sit-ins had not been prevalent in the late 1950s, and, in neglecting to inquire into popular attitudes toward these less common modes of behavior, Almond and Verba's study rapidly became outdated as the instances of unconventional participation multiplied during the 1960s and 1970s.

Many of the questions Barnes and Kaase asked differed from those that Almond and Verba had posed, but, in some cases, comparison of the two time periods is possible. Regarding conventional modes of participation, Barnes and Kaase asked what types of activities respondents actually had engaged in, such as attending public meetings, contacting public officials, or trying to convince friends to vote in particular ways. Leaving aside those respondents who had done no more than read about politics in newspapers or discuss politics with friends in a neutral fashion, we find the percentages for the more active respondents listed in Table 3.3.

In 1974, when the Barnes–Kaase survey was administered, Americans still rated at the top of the scale in political participation, at least of the conventional type. But the British no longer ranked higher than the West Germans—quite the contrary. As in the case of the allegiance/alienation dimension, democratically relevant attitudes have increased in West Germany. Table 3.3 also suggests that today the West Germans rank high among Western Europeans in their propensity to employ conventional modes of

**Table 3.3 Conventional Political Participants**

| *Country* | *Percent* |
|---|---|
| United States | 42% |
| *West Germany* | 28 |
| Austria | 21 |
| Netherlands | 20 |
| *Great Britain* | 16 |

(*Source*) Samuel H. Barnes et al., *Political Action: Mass Participation in Five Western Democracies* (Beverly Hills: Sage, 1979), p. 85. Copyright © 1979 by Sage Publications, Inc.

participation. At least in northwestern Europe, the British political culture now appears to rank among the least participant.

A similar impression is gained if we look at the Barnes–Kaase findings on civic competence. The Almond–Verba study found the United States, Great Britain, and West Germany to rank first, second, and third, respectively, in both local and national civic competence. Table 3.4 displays percentages for both 1959–60 and 1974 for these three countries as well as percentages for 1974 for the Netherlands and Austria. The rankings for local competence have changed, with West Germany replacing Great Britain in second place. The rankings for national competence remain the same. But it is noteworthy that the gap between West Germany and the Anglo-Saxon countries has narrowed markedly. Civic competence has increased among West Germans at the local level, whereas it has declined among the British at both levels and among Americans at the local level, but not at the national level.[32]

When Barnes and Kaase asked their respondents about unconventional modes of political participation, they shifted the focus from activities in which respondents *had* engaged to those in which they *would* engage given proper stimulus. The principal dividing line was between legal activities considered unconventional, such as legal demonstrations and boycotts, and activities that were illegal as well as unorthodox, such as rent strikes. In terms of the percentages of those who said they would engage in the illegal type of activity, the ranking of the United States, West Germany, and Great Britain remained the same (in that order); the only change was the rise of the Netherlands from fourth to first place (tied with the United States), with 46 percent of the respondents willing to engage in at least one of the illegal activities (compared with 31 percent in West Germany and 30 percent in Britain.[33]

Reviewing these and similar findings, Russell Dalton poses two competing explanations for the rise of unconventional participation in these industrialized polyarchies. The first is that there has been a rise of dissatisfaction with the performance of these political systems on the part of disadvantaged and alienated persons, that is, a decline in allegiance and a rise in alienation. As we have seen, the evidence for this on a cross-national basis is mixed, appearing stronger, or at least more consistent, in the United States than in Western Europe up to the beginning of the 1980s. But, when the corre-

**Table 3.4 Percentage of Respondents Who Said They Could Do Something about an Unjust or Harmful Local Regulation or National Law, 1959–60 and 1974**

| | *Local Regulation* | | *National Law* | |
|---|---|---|---|---|
| *Country* | *1959–60* | *1974* | *1959–60* | *1974* |
| Netherlands | —% | 62% | —% | 43% |
| *Great Britain* | 78 | 64 | 62 | 57 |
| United States | 77 | 71 | 75 | 78 |
| *West Germany* | 62 | 67 | 38 | 56 |
| Austria | — | 43 | — | 33 |

(*Source*) Samuel H. Barnes et al., *Political Action: Mass Participation in Five Western Democracies* (Beverly Hills: Sage, 1979), p. 141. 

lates of unconventional participation are examined on an individual level, it is seen that unconventional participants tend to be more highly educated and younger than conventional participants. This suggests the validity of a second thesis, according to Dalton. It may be that the boundary lines between conventional and unconventional participation are shifting, and at least some of what was considered unconventional for an older (and less well educated) generation is considered conventional by those who have reached adulthood since the Almond–Verba study, given their own experiences.[34] We examine further evidence to support this interpretation at the end of this chapter.

## Italy and France

In the past (as noted earlier), the Italian and French political cultures have not seemed to have as heavy an incidence of participant orientation as has been the case with the other countries we are examining. Earlier studies focused primarily on conventional modes of participation. It is clear that France and Italy have been among those European countries in which the rise of unconventional, including illegal and even violent, political activity has been most striking since the late 1960s. However, speculation that the Italians rate high in propensity for unconventional activity is belied by a survey taken in 1975 in which Italians were asked whether they would engage in various forms of activity. Violent forms were overwhelmingly repudiated, and, at most, only about 20 to 25 percent of respondents indicated a willingness, in theory, to engage in any illegal activities.[35] This can be compared with the figure of 30 percent that Barnes and Kaase found for Great Britain and West Germany. It must be remembered that Italy is a Catholic country. Despite strong support for the Italian Communist Party (PCI), a great many Italians are taught by the church and at home to respect the authority of the established government and the police who enforce its laws. This is especially true because the established government is primarily in the hands of the Christian Democratic Party and, therefore, enjoys the church's blessing. It is even likely that many communist voters would disdain illegal activity. The PCI has become an established part of the structure of political institutions in Italy, and communist leaders have little desire to see those institutions rocked by widespread acts of defiance of the state's authority, as they have demonstrated in condemning terrorist acts and in seeking to discourage unauthorized strikes in industrial disputes.

What we might call the theory of French political culture suggests that the typical Frenchman or -woman, ambivalent about established authority, will avoid conventional modes of participation approved by those in authority and potentially involving face-to-face contact. They will avoid such contact with the authorities themselves and with other like-minded citizens in any organized context in which the legitimacy of the authorities is mutually acknowledged.

Although France is officially a Catholic country, nonbelievers and lukewarm Catholics are found with greater frequency there than in Italy. Thus, the restraining hand of the church and Catholic family are less likely to inhibit attitudes toward unconventional participation in France. The other side of the coin is that the French would not be expected to engage in sustained, organized protest. Their ambivalence toward authority would mean oscillation between periods of intense antagonism and periods in which the desire for order and predictability would return. The tendency of French leftist groups toward endless internal bickering and splintering into innumerable offshoots would be an expression of the reputed French disdain for long-term stability in relations with peers as well as with those in authority. However, the success of the French Socialist Party (PS) in channeling youthful energies into the successful campaigns of the 1981 presidential and legislative elections challenges these speculations. More of the French may today be gaining respect for, and confidence in, conventional modes of political action.

## Japanese Political Culture

Until now we have deliberately left the Japanese political culture out of consideration. This is because the Japanese have a system of social values and norms that differs markedly from that typically found in Western countries. Whereas Western value systems are predominantly individualistic in nature, that of Japan, like other Asian countries, is essentially collectivistic. This means that the very question of whether the Japanese are allegiant or alienated toward their political system lacks cognitive meaning, if, as we have done so far, it is thought of in an individualistic sense (i.e., in the sense of the relationship between the individual and the state). To the Japanese, individuals are a part of a social order that is hierarchical and all-encompassing. Given centuries of isolation from the rest of the world, this society is viewed by its members much as is an extended family in agrarian societies[36]—and, remember, Japan was an agrarian society until early in this century. Holders of authority in the state are seen as the natural leaders of this extended family, and challenges to their authority are unthinkable, not because authority holders are considered to be always right, but because the individual is not an autonomous actor who can counterpose his or her judgment against them.

In smaller social settings, as in the immediate family, the neighborhood, or the workplace, conflicts do occur, but they tend to be resolved in favor of the views held by those in positions of power and authority within the group. Appeals to the seniority or higher social status of the stronger person will suffice to remove the substance of the weaker person's disagreement.[37] Yet traditionally, or during the centuries of isolation and feudalism, conflict among different groups within Japan were frequent and often cataclysmic. As Japan became more vulnerable to the rest of the world from the sixteenth century onward, her leaders made great efforts to draw society together into a tightly knit defensive posture. Individuals, families, towns, and other groups within society were expected to defer to the common interest as defined by society's rulers. But the potential for explosive group conflict existed just below the surface, making it imperative for individuals, when dealing with other persons from other parts of society, to subordinate individual needs to social needs and thus to stifle potential conflict voluntarily.[38] In our terms, the Japanese concept of respect involves the desire for respect for one's group rather than for one's self as an individual. Or, perhaps better put, Japanese self-respect is dependent on how well one believes one has conformed to group expectations—that is, how well one has earned the respect of the group.

The Japanese, therefore, are group-oriented rather than self-oriented[39] to such an extent that questions about their own sense of political efficacy can have little meaning to them unless there is a group reference. The company for which they work might be such a reference, and the individual may rely on the company-as-group, and of course the executives of that company, to promote his or her interests as an employee in the political arena. Individual Japanese with strong objections about aspects of Japanese life, such as conservationists concerned about the threat of population pressure on the natural habitats of migratory birds, will feel politically efficacious only as members of organizations committed to their goals. But if the organization takes on the character of a community of persons with strong dedication to the cause, its members may be capable of employing unconventional means of participation at great potential risk to themselves as individuals, subordinating what we might consider to be their own personal interests to the needs of the group as defined by the group's leaders. If asked an abstract survey question such as "Could you do something about an unjust law?" the individual Japanese would be less likely than the Westerner to give a positive answer yet be more willing than the Westerner to engage in self-sacrifice on behalf of a collective objective. Had Japan been included in the original Almond–Verba study or, for that matter, the more recent study by Barnes and Kaase, it is difficult to say what the results would have been, because the questions asked and the categories employed grow out of Western political science preoccupations.

Nevertheless, Japan has experienced the same social and economic trends that were discussed as postindustrial phenomena in the preceding chapter and that Dalton argues are bringing about changes in Western political cultures. We consider certain accompanying features of postindustrial political culture that have been hypothesized by political scientists such as Dalton and Ronald Inglehart in the final section of this chapter and return to the question of whether Japanese political culture has any traits that liken it to the political cultures of other advanced industrial countries.

## *Factors Underlying Political Participation*

The differences among our Western European countries with respect to the dimensions of conventional and unconventional participation do not stand out as clearly as do those on the allegiance/alienation dimension. A possible explanation may be that there are underlying factors that account for attitudes toward participation essentially in the same ways in all of our countries. For example, Almond and Verba found that civic competence increased in all countries with level of education. Citizens with university-level educations, for example, would be more likely than those who had not completed secondary education to display civic competence, regardless of whether they were American, German, or Italian.

### Demographic Factors

In point of fact, the relationship between level of education and political participation is one of the most consistent findings in the research on political culture.[40] Studies have also found that it is a stronger predictor of political participation than are indicators of social class, such as occupation and family income. The consistent finding that level of education is the strongest predictor of political participation can be explained in terms of the heightened awareness and understanding of politics that the student gains at the higher levels of education. Alternatively, it may reflect a higher personal investment and stake in a system that can be influenced by political participation.

Other possible predictors of political participation are gender, age, and religion. Of the three, Barnes and Kaase found that gender was the most strongly related to conventional political participation. Age and religion bore little or no relationship to conventional participation, although there was a tendency for participation to increase with age, only to level off in the oldest age brackets. In all five countries, men were more likely to participate through normal channels than were women, but the difference was greatest in West Germany, least in the United States. This suggests that one aspect of the greater liberation of women in the United States is their greater involvement in politics, whereas the gap between West German men and women remains relatively wide.

With respect to unconventional participation, age assumes an importance at least equal to that of education. In fact, in the United States, Great Britain, and West Germany, age was a somewhat better predictor of attitudes toward unconventional participation than was education. The relationship is a negative one in the case of age; that is, the older the individual, the less likely he or she is to favor unconventional participation. The relationship between education and unconventional participation is a positive one; that is, the higher the educational level, the greater the inclination toward unconventional participation. Gender and religion showed some relationship to unconventional participation, but the correlations are weaker than in the cases of age and education. Men are slightly more likely than women to favor protest activity. Those who have no religious belief or little intensity of belief (whatever their religion) are somewhat more likely than the more intensely religious to favor unconventional participation.

## Political Socialization

The strong relationship between level of education and conventional political participation is a standard finding that we should expect on the basis of common sense. But that the social category most likely to engage in unconventional activities is that of younger people with higher levels of education would not have been so self-evident before the era of the campus protests of the 1960s and 1970s. Those with higher levels of education would have been expected to display a greater appreciation for the beneficial qualities of the democratic political system because they were the very people who had benefited most from the educational opportunities provided by that system and could also command the other values that education can bring. Because young people were typically less likely than their elders to participate in conventional ways, it might also have been expected that they would not show a penchant for unconventional participation. Nor did many students in either the United States or Western Europe spend much time protesting perceived political injustices before the mid-1960s.

When the student rebellions began, the older generation was hard pressed to understand the new phenomenon. These young people certainly were not behaving in ways taught them by their parents. Young people participating in demonstrations and university sit-ins, on the other hand, could not comprehend the lack of comprehension on the part of their parents. Observers of this new dimension of political conflict in the First World—parents versus children—began to speak of a generation gap.

Concern about a generation gap came at about the same time that political scientists were exploring an area of research that was new to them and that they conceived to be closely related to the study of political culture. The study of *political socialization* is the study of the ways in which political orientations are transmitted from generation to generation through the mediation of institutions in which older people communicate with younger people. Especially noteworthy among these institutions are the family, the school, and the media of communication. Something seemed to be happening in Western society that was interfering with traditional lines of communication between the generations. The same sort of break in continuity was being observed in studies of political socialization in Third World countries, but it was to be expected there, given the fact that such countries were undergoing rapid modernization. What students of political socialization in the First World in the 1950s and early 1960s failed to recognize was that rapid change was occurring in the First World as well, and that it was affecting the perceptions the younger generation held of their elders and of the institutions in which the authority of the older generation had always prevailed. The family, the school, and the political system were becoming arenas of conflict that centered around the question of the right of the older generation to command the obedience of the younger generation. It was a conflict between the power asserted by the older people as their right and the respect demanded by younger people as their right. What has been happening to the process of political socialization in Western Europe during this era of institutional change?

If we begin with the traditional role played by the primary socializer—the family—we are struck immediately with the more authoritarian nature of the family in our three continental European countries than in Great Britain or the United States. Almond and Verba found a higher percentage of Britons and Americans than of West Germans or Italians who (1) remembered having had an influence in family decisions as children, (2) remembered being free to protest family decisions, and (3) remembered that they had actually protested family decisions on occasion.[41] In the past, the typical European (non-British) family was dominated by the father, whereas the father and mother played (and continue to play) more equal roles in family decision making in the United States. The latter is also true among British middle-class families. However, in the British working class, the father was an authoritarian figure, although he was traditionally absent when it came to bringing up the children. Thus, the mother played a greater role by default. The resulting authority pattern was probably more ambiguous than that found in a working-class family on the Continent.

Traditionally, authority patterns learned in the family served as models as the child grew up. If he or she had experienced the father having the final decision-making responsibility and had been used to obeying these decisions without question, the child would assume this pattern to be normal and, thus, expect to find it in later-life situations. In this connection, European (including British) school systems were more authoritarian than the American, as the Almond–Verba study documented.[42] The authority of the teacher was absolute. In French schools, the child learned certain principles by rote and was then expected to reproduce them to the teacher's satisfaction. If the child failed, the teacher might call on the ridicule of the other children as a means of reinforcing the expectation.[43] In Italy and in parts of France and West Germany, religious instruction in the public schools or instruction in church schools added the absolute authority structure of the Catholic Church to an already authoritarian pedagogical system.

Once again, it should be pointed out that the Almond–Verba surveys were conducted thirty years ago. In the meantime, important changes have taken place in Western Europe, some of which were discussed in Chapter 2. A decrease in family size has made it more likely that the wife will work at least part of the time to supplement the family income. This increases her status within the family and gives her a stronger voice in the family decision-making process. With a more pluralistic family power structure, the children are not so overwhelmed that they cannot exert influence, especially as they grow older. The schools have been doing a certain amount of experimentation in curriculum development and teaching methods, often along American lines. West Germany has gone especially far in this direction. Ever since the Allied

Occupation, a concerted effort has been made to democratize the educational system with respect to both the authority patterns within the schools and the explicit content of the teaching.[44] German children are given a much more extensive civics education than are British, French, or Italian children, and the content is often of a superior quality to what can typically be found in American schools. A recent study has shown a marked increase in the past two decades in the tendency of West Germans to discuss politics with one another. It is true of all generations, but the tendency of West Germans born after World War II to discuss politics is substantially greater than is that of their elders. The advent of television as well as quantitative and qualitative educational improvements have helped bring about this change.[45]

As in the case of West Germany, the American occupiers of Japan after World War II paid considerable attention to the structure and content of the educational system, with the explicit objective of changing what had been an authoritarian structure and a traditional content. From the time of the Meiji Restoration, Japanese educational authorities had wrestled with the problem of how to control the process of psychological modernization of the Japanese so that modern technology could be learned while traditional Japanese values would not be swept aside in favor of subversive Western value systems. What steps were taken in the late nineteenth and early twentieth centuries to liberalize education were reversed during the decade preceding World War II, as nationalism and emperor worship were reinforced in the school curricula. Any teacher who believed that children should gain the capacity to think through public issues on their own and participate in the political process was stifled.[46]

The American occupation of Japan from 1945 to 1951 failed in several of its objectives to democratize Japanese education. Control over the West German educational system became decentralized in the hands of the state (*Länder*) governments, thus permitting a certain amount of educational pluralism to develop. Despite the wishes of the Occupation authorities to decentralize Japanese education, it reemerged with control over curriculum concentrated in the hands of the central Ministry of Education. This has meant that the conservative politicians who have ruled at the center have made sure that the traditional values retained their place. Although General MacArthur had hoped, probably unrealistically, that the school system would adhere to the Western liberal principle of separation of church and state, traditional religious values still form part of what the students learn today. Perhaps most important, the Japanese teenager lives under what could almost be called a totalitarian regime of preparation for state examinations that will determine his or her future, with much more time spent on studies both inside and outside school than is true of students in Western countries. Much of the time spent involves rote learning; it does not involve much consideration and discussion of controversial ideas.[47] These conditions have persisted in postindustrial Japan, such that one wonders whether the impact of education on participant orientations in Western countries is reproduced there.

There is evidence in political socialization studies to suggest that postindustrial society, with its higher levels of education and increased media exposure of young people, is witnessing the declining political influence of traditional political socializing agencies, especially the family and the political party.[48] As was noted in Chapter 2, the industrial maturity link between family, social class, and party identification has been breaking down in the past decade or so in Western Europe. It is possible that these long-standing agents of political attitude shaping have become weaker as well. British political scientist Dennis Kavanagh argues that people in Western societies have become more adept at "determining their own political attitudes" based on the wide array of conflicting messages about politics that reach them from many directions, and that attitudes are less likely than once was the case to fit neatly into predictable patterns along class and party lines. Thus, the likelihood that two individuals, one of whom is allegiant and the other alienated politically, will be from predictable social backgrounds—the one from a middle-class family and pursuing a professional career, the other growing up in a working-class family and holding down a blue-collar job—is less today than it was a generation ago, just as it is less likely that the one will vote to the right and the other to the left.[49]

Kavanagh sides with the "recency" side of the "primacy versus recency" argument among students of political socialization. That is to say, he feels that political attitudes are more likely to be shaped by influences experienced in one's adult life than by those in childhood and adolescence. Earlier influences may still show up in today's attitudes, but the individual is not foreordained as a political thinker by the beliefs that prevailed in the family and neighborhood where he or she was raised. More people are exposed to information and ideas about politics today in a way that does not reinforce attitudes learned early in life. Or perhaps the attitudes learned earlier in life are not as clear and consistent as they tended to be before the arrival of the mass media, such that the recent adult is freer than were his or her parents to choose among a variety of ways of thinking about and reacting to political stimuli.[50]

## The Value Gap

What has brought about the generation gap? Why has it manifested itself in an expanded repertory of political participation modes? An answer to these questions was implied in the preceding section. In making it more explicit, we draw on the work of American political scientist Ronald Inglehart, who has examined the changing structure of values in First World countries.[51]

Inglehart has been interested in whether the affluence and relative security of postindustrial society has shifted people's value preferences from a preoccupation with getting on in daily life to more abstract, less mundane values. In our terms, this would mean a shift from the values of well-being and power to those of enlightenment and respect. He hypothesized that older citizens, having experienced the Great Depression and World War II, would be more concerned with maintaining a healthy economy, as well as domestic and international order. Younger citizens would see less value in such things because they had experienced them all their lives. Instead, they would be concerned with expanding the scope of individual expression, both politically and in their personal lives. Table 3.5 indicates that Inglehart's expections were essentially borne out by the findings. In all five of the countries included in the table, the percentage of respondents exhibiting what he called *materialistic* values increases as one moves to successively older age categories (cohorts), whereas the percentage of his respondents exhibiting *postmaterialist* values declines.[52] The same was true of the five smaller countries included in his study—Belgium, the Netherlands, Luxembourg, Denmark, and Ireland.

Table 3.5 also reveals several differences among the larger countries. For one thing, the range of percentages from younger to older respondents is greater for three of the countries—West Germany, France, and Italy—than it is for the other two—the United States and Great Britain. Inglehart explained this by citing events that caused a greater generation

**Table 3.5 Value Type by Age Cohort in Five Countries, 1972–73 (Percentage of Each Country's Respondents in Each Age Cohort)**

| | *West Germany* | | *France* | | *Italy* | | *U.S.* | | *Great Britain* | |
|---|---|---|---|---|---|---|---|---|---|---|
| *Ages* | *Mat.** | *P-M*† | *Mat.* | *P-M* | *Mat.* | *P-M* | *Mat.* | *P-M* | *Mat.* | *P-M* |
| 19–28 | 24%‡ | 19% | 22% | 20% | 26% | 16% | 24% | 17% | 27% | 11% |
| 29–38 | 39 | 8 | 28 | 17 | 41 | 8 | 27 | 13 | 33 | 7 |
| 39–48 | 46 | 5 | 39 | 9 | 42 | 7 | 34 | 13 | 29 | 6 |
| 49–58 | 50 | 5 | 39 | 8 | 48 | 6 | 32 | 10 | 30 | 7 |
| 59–68 | 52 | 7 | 50 | 3 | 49 | 4 | 37 | 6 | 36 | 5 |
| 69+ | 62 | 1 | 55 | 2 | 57 | 5 | 40 | 7 | 37 | 4 |
| Total point spread across cohorts | 38 + 18 = 56 | | 33 + 18 = 51 | | 31 + 11 = 42 | | 16 + 10 = 26 | | 10 + 7 = 17 | |

(*Source*) Ronald Inglehart, "The Nature of Value Change in Postindustrial Society," in Leon N. Lindberg, ed., *Politics and the Future of Industrial Society* (New York: McKay, 1976), pp. 70–71. Reprinted with permission of Longman Inc.
* Mat. = Materialistic value system.
† P-M = Postmaterialistic value system.
‡ Percentages do not total 100 for each country because of respondents in intermediate categories.

gap in continental Europe than in the Anglo-Saxon countries. World War II was experienced more directly and probably left a greater and more lasting impression on the generations who experienced it in Germany, France, and Italy than on generations in the United States and Great Britain; in addition, postwar economic growth has been more rapid in the former countries than in the latter, suggesting that younger people in the former countries have become as accustomed as younger people in the latter countries to expecting progressive improvement of material conditions.

In addition to his independent research, Inglehart participated in the Barnes–Kaase five-nation study and measured the relationship between his materialism/postmaterialism dimension and the Barnes–Kaase measures of conventional and unconventional political participation. He found a strong association between materialism/postmaterialism and conventional/unconventional participation, postmaterialists being more favorably disposed than materialists to protest activity.[53] Extending Inglehart's theory, therefore, we can suggest that the reason younger people are more inclined to protest what they perceive to be wrong in their societies is not that they have a greater sense of material deprivation than do their elders; rather, they are likely to have a different ordering of value priorities. Among those values that they are likely to rank in high position are (1) the value of power, which they believe should be distributed more widely in their societies instead of being concentrated in the hands of the few, especially when the few are apt to be older persons; and (2) the value of respect, which they feel is denied to them to the extent that there are limits placed on their ability to communicate their political beliefs. Material values (well-being) are of lesser concern to them, but this does not mean that they are, for that reason, politically quiescent; quite the contrary. In the case of their parents, the experience of enhanced material well-being had occurred in their formative years. The solidification of these gains remained a principal preoccupation for them as they grew older, and has not completely left them even today. Moreover, in Western Europe, at least, few of them were afforded the opportunity for higher education, something their sons and daughters have had available in much greater numbers. These young persons do not experience material deprivation, but it is possible that the value deprivation they *do* feel is of a greater magnitude than that of their parents.

Although Japan was not included in the earlier Inglehart studies of value change in industrialized countries, there have been surveys undertaken over the years in which similar values were tested with different age groups in the Japanese population, and some of the same questions have been asked in periodically repeated surveys over a number of years. If these have turned up findings similar to those of Inglehart, then we may have reason to wonder whether the group-oriented emphasis that the Japanese political culture puts on the values of power and respect (see the treatment of Japanese political participation, discussed earlier) still holds among the younger generation, which, like the younger generation in Western Europe, is better educated than its elders. Japanese political scientist Nobutaka Ike[54] summarized one series of surveys of Japanese values in which respondents were asked to choose which among several alternatives were their "goals in life." It was found that over a fifteen-year period from 1953 to 1968, the percentage who answered that "work hard and get rich" was one of their major goals had held fairly constant, but that the goal "just lead a life that suits your tastes" had risen in frequency of choice from 21 percent of the respondents in 1953 to 32 percent in 1968. The latter was particularly true of the youngest cohort of respondents, ages twenty to twenty-four, 34 percent of whom chose this highly "individualistic" value in 1953, while 51 percent did so in 1968.

On the other hand, a very traditional goal—"resist all evils in the world, and live a pure and just life"—had lost favor over time, supported by only 17 percent in 1968, against 29 percent fifteen years earlier. There was some evidence that materialism was receding as in Western Europe. The percentage of respondents who agreed with the proposition that schoolchildren should be taught "that money is the most important thing" had fallen from 65 percent in 1953 to 57 percent in 1968.[55] But what was replacing both traditional values and materialistic values among the youngest generation was individualistic pursuit of self-determined goals, something even the older generation of Western Europeans had taken for granted when they were young. According to Ike, "in Western culture, which has long stressed individualism, youth may seek a sense of belonging, whereas in Japanese culture, which has emphasized the group, youth may yearn for individuation and privatization."[56] Unlike Ike, Scott C. Flanagan believes that what Western youth seek is more complex than this. There is a commitment both to ideal goals and to fulfillment of self.[57] For some Western youth these would be in contradiction with one another; for others the two would be compatible, as in the case of young people who find *self*-fulfillment in the pursuit of "*other*-directed" causes such as the ecology movement espouses.

Among the elements that Inglehart expected to find within a postmaterial value system was an ecological concern, the value of preserving our natural environment for future generations.[58] This might be considered a long-term perspective on the value of well-being, that is, well-being not for the here and now but for the future. Or it might be seen as the assertion of the right of future generations to the same respect generations currently alive are given. For a growing number of First World citizens, ecology is of the utmost importance. The Green Party of West Germany (see Chapter 4) has attained considerable political prominence in the 1980s with a program that features four "pillars": ecology, social responsibility, grassroots democracy, and nonviolence.[59] Of the four, ecology has the widest support among Green Party members, who came together behind this program in 1979–80 from a wide variety of earlier political and ideological loyalties.

The ecological perspective is holistic, in the sense that all things related to life are seen as interconnected and interdependent. This accords with a desire to see the power concentrations of modern states broken down into smaller entities that are closer to the problems of human beings living within their everyday environments. The Greens raise the value of environmental well-being to a higher priority than the values of economic well-being and national security, which, materialists would argue, can only be adequately promoted by the nation-state with power instruments concentrated in the hands of its government. The Greens see a radical divergence between their agenda—which includes nuclear disarmament, governmental decentralization, the ending of sexist exploitation, the controlling of automobile emissions, and elimination of acid rain, nuclear waste, and other forms of pollution—and the agendas of the other political parties that accord such items low priority. Inglehart's terminology has not been part of the Green lexicon, but their arrival on the scene in the 1980s accords generally with his predictions of a decade earlier.

Inglehart's principal study was undertaken in the early 1970s, before the economic difficulties associated with the 1970s had been perceived as a chronic condition of postindustrial society. It has often been observed in more recent years that young people have turned their backs on the idealism of the previous two decades and are showing greater tendencies toward conformity with their elders' expectations because they are concerned with their futures in terms of economic security. In fact, follow-up studies that Inglehart undertook later contained some evidence that postmaterialism had receded among the very youngest age cohort, making them more materialistic than their immediate elders, the Sixties generation.[60] But the differences are slight, and, at any rate, the youngest cohort is less materialistic than are the cohorts of the parents and grandparents of today's teenagers. As we have seen, younger people appear to be less allegiant and more inclined (in all countries) toward protest activity than are their elders.[61]

As we move to the study of political parties and party systems in the next chapter, it is worth noting that Inglehart's theory of value change points to the growth of parties of what are called sometimes "the New Left" or "the New Politics," parties that burst on the scene in the later 1960s and have undergone a series of subgenerational shifts every half-dozen years or so, including the Green phenomenon. Inglehart appears to relegate to his materialist category another new, or perhaps resurgent, political phenomenon—the New Right—which is particularly strong in France, but which has come close to or actually succeeded in capturing control of conservative parties in other countries, notably the United States and Great Britain since the mid-1970s. Yet, as Flanagan has argued, the New Right is not necessarily materialist in the strictly economic sense of the word. Its economic philosophy stresses national self-restraint from material overindulgence in order to achieve longer-term material benefits, in a sense similar, though not identical, to the longer-term view of the Greens.[62] Its stress on moral issues, such as "the right to life" and "law and order" are materialist only in the concept-stretching sense in which Inglehart defines the term. To Flanagan, both the New Left and the New Right are "nonmaterialist" (and, we could add, equally postindustrial) manifestations of the breakdown of early socialization patterns just discussed. This still raises the question of whether different groups in society support the New Left and the New Right or whether adherence to one or the other is essentially a random matter. And it leaves open the further question of why the New Left has taken different forms and achieved different measures of success in different countries, and likewise the New Right. The converse of these questions is: What has been happening to the "Old Left," the "Old Right," and, for that matter, the "Old Center"?

As for Japan, the survey findings that Ike and Flanagan have reviewed leave considerable room for doubt as to whether "New Right" and "New Left" have the same meaning that they do in the West, and even whether such terms have any relevance to Japanese politics. As we shall see, there are still "Old Right" and "Old Left" political parties in Japan, but if younger people are seeking meaning in themselves instead of in large causes—turning away, as Ike suggests, from the traditional loyalty to larger bodies of persons, including especially the family and the nation—then they are becoming apolitical and less available for mobilization on behalf of causes that can be related to these primordial loyalties.

## *Suggestions for Further Reading*

**Almond, Gabriel A., and Sidney Verba.** *The Civic Culture: Political Attitudes and Democracy in Five Nations* (Princeton, N.J.: Princeton University Press, 1963).

———, eds. *The Civil Culture Revisited* (Boston: Little, Brown, 1980).

**Baker, Kendall,** et al. *Germany Transformed: Political Culture and the New Politics* (Cambridge, Mass.: Harvard University Press, 1981).

**Barnes, Samuel H.,** et al. *Political Action: Mass Participation in Five Western Democracies* (Beverly Hills: Sage, 1979).

**Barzini, Luigi.** *The Italians* (New York: Bantam, 1965).

**Christopher, Robert C.** *The Japanese Mind: The Goliath Explained* (London and Sydney: Pan Books, 1984).

**Dalton, Russell J.** *Citizen Politics in Western Democracies: Public Opinion and Political Parties in the United States, Great Britain, West Germany, and France* (Chatham, N.J.: Chatham House, 1988).

**Dogan, Mattei,** ed. *Comparing Pluralist Democracies: Strains on Legitimacy* (Boulder, Colo., and London: Westview, 1988).

**Hart, Vivien.** *Distrust and Democracy: Political Distrust in Britain and America* (Cambridge: Cambridge University Press, 1978).

**Inglehart, Ronald.** *The Silent Revolution: Changing Values and Political Styles among Western Publics* (Princeton, N.J.: Princeton University Press, 1977).

**Kavanagh, Dennis.** *Political Science and Political Behaviour* (London: George Allen & Unwin, 1983).

**LaPalombara, Joseph.** *Democracy, Italian Style* (New Haven, Conn., and London: Yale University Press, 1987).

**Nakane, Chie.** *Japanese Society* (Berkeley and Los Angeles: University of California Press, 1972).

**Schonfeld, William R.** *Obedience and Revolt: French Behavior toward Authority* (Beverly Hills: Sage, 1976).

**Wylie, Laurence.** *Village in the Vaucluse*, 3rd ed. (Cambridge, Mass.: Harvard University Press, 1974).

**Zeldin, Theodore.** *The French* (London: Fontana, 1984).

# Notes

1. Gabriel A. Almond, "Comparative Political Systems," *Journal of Politics* 18 (1956), 391–409.
2. Gabriel A. Almond and G. Bingham Powell, *Comparative Politics: A Developmental Approach* (Boston: Little, Brown, 1966), p. 50.
3. These generalizations are based on direct observations by the author in Western Europe during 1974.
4. Gabriel A. Almond and Sidney Verba, *The Civic Culture: Political Attitudes and Democracy in Five Nations* (Princeton, N.J.: Princeton University Press, 1963).
5. Ibid., p. 102.
6. See the collection of essays in Gabriel A. Almond and Sidney Verba, eds., *The Civic Culture Revisited* (Boston: Little, Brown, 1980). These essays evaluate the Almond–Verba study in light of findings of more recent studies.
7. Ulrich Widmaier, "Tendencies toward an Erosion of Legitimacy," in Mattei Dogan, ed., *Comparing Pluralist Democracies: Strains on Legitimacy* (Boulder, Colo., and London: Westview, 1988), pp. 143–167.
8. Ronald Inglehart shows differences between Western European countries in life satisfaction, relative levels of which remain fairly constant between countries, but political satisfaction levels fluctuate more unpredictably. Ronald Inglehart, *Culture Shift in Advanced Industrial Societies* (Princeton, N.J.: Princeton University Press, 1990), p. 33.
9. David P. Conradt, "Changing German Political Culture," in Almond and Verba, eds., *The Civic Culture Revisited*, p. 230.
10. David Easton, *A Framework for Political Analysis* (Englewood Cliffs, N.J.: Prentice-Hall, 1965), pp. 124–126.
11. Alan I. Abramowitz, "The United States: Political Culture under Stress," in Almond and Verba, eds., *The Civic Culture Revisited*, pp. 189–190.
12. Conradt, "Changing German Political Culture," p. 235.
13. Samuel H. Beer, *Britain against Itself: The Political Contradictions of Collectivism* (New York and London: Norton, 1982), pp. 110–120.
14. Philip Norton, *The British Polity* (New York and London: Longman, 1984), pp. 32–34.
15. Samuel H. Barnes et al., *Political Action: Mass Participation in Five Western Democracies* (Beverly Hills: Sage, 1979), p. 88.
16. Vivien Hart, *Distrust and Democracy: Political Distrust in Britain and America* (Cambridge: Cambridge University Press, 1978), p. 42.
17. Findings reviewed by Giacomo Sani, "The Political Culture of Italy: Continuity and Change," in Almond and Verba, eds., *The Civic Culture Revisited*, pp. 308–310. But see the argument

by Joseph LaPalombara that Italians are critical of their politicians in the same way they are of their football stars and opera singers. They demand perfection in performance and when, rarely in the case of politicians, it is attained, they applaud wildly. This may not be true political alienation. LaPalombara, *Democracy, Italian Style* (New Haven, Conn., and London: Yale University Press, 1987), pp. 88–91.

18. David P. Conradt, *The German Polity*, 3rd ed. (New York and London: Longman, 1986), pp. 55–58.
19. Henry W. Ehrmann, *Politics in France*, 3rd ed. (Boston: Little, Brown, 1976), p. 131.
20. Support for the Fifth Republic no longer is confined to voters on the right, as power passed to the left in the 1980s, and the regime rather easily survived the experience of "cohabitation," or the sharing of power by left and right in the 1986–88 period.
21. See the discussions in Ehrmann, *Politics in France*, Ch. 3; and John S. Ambler, *The Government and Politics of France* (Boston: Houghton Mifflin, 1971), Ch. 3.
22. That is, the political regime may change but the state, as a set of permanent bureaucratic institutions, is seen to carry on unchanged. Americans and Britons do not tend mentally to separate the concepts of state and regime, in part because the two have not been disjoined historically.
23. Almond and Verba, *The Civic Culture*, p. 184.
24. Ibid., pp. 402–414.
25. Ibid., pp. 135–136, 267. See also Edward C. Banfield, *The Moral Basis of a Backward Society* (New York: The Free Press, 1958).
26. Almond and Verba, *The Civic Culture*, pp. 428–439.
27. Ibid., pp. 440–469.
28. A classic analysis is Laurence Wylie, *Village in the Vaucluse*, 3rd ed. (Cambridge, Mass.: Harvard University Press, 1974), pp. 206–239.
29. Ambler, *The Government and Politics of France*, p. 54.
30. Russell J. Dalton, *Citizen Politics in Western Democracies: Public Opinion and Political Parties in the United States, Great Britain, West Germany, and France* (Chatham, N.J.: Chatham House, 1988), Ch. 8.
31. Barnes et al., *Political Action*, pp. 57–94.
32. Some British scholars are highly critical of the concept of civic competence. They argue that negative responses to questions such as those the cross-national studies have posed may reflect negative evaluations about the political system (especially its economic performance), not a weak sense of personal efficacy. This would make the findings of declining allegiance and lower civic competence in Britain consistent with one another. Evidence to support such a contention is at best mixed. See Alan Marsh, *Protest and Political Consciousness* (Beverly Hills: Sage, 1977), Ch. 6; and Hart, op. cit.
33. Barnes et al., *Political Action*, p. 81.
34. Dalton, *Citizen Politics*, pp. 66–70.
35. Sani, "The Political Culture of Italy, p. 306.
36. Robert C. Christopher, *The Japanese Mind: The Goliath Explained* (London and Sydney: Pan Books, 1984), Ch. 2.
37. Mitsuyuki Masatsugu, *The Modern Samurai Society: Duty and Dependency in Contemporary Japan* (New York: American Management Associations, 1982), pp. 77–92.
38. Ibid., pp. 1–9.
39. Chie Nakane, *Japanese Society* (Berkeley and Los Angeles: University of California Press, 1972), Ch. 1.
40. The discussion in this section is drawn from material in Barnes et al., *Political Action*, pp. 97–135.
41. Almond and Verba, *The Civic Culture*, p. 331.
42. Ibid., pp. 332–333.
43. Wylie, *Village in the Vaucluse*, pp. 84–87.

44. See Sidney Verba, "Germany: The Remarking of Political Culture," in Lucien W. Pye and Sidney Verba, eds., *Political Culture and Political Development* (Princeton, N.J.: Princeton University Press, 1981), pp. 130–170.
45. Kendall L. Baker et al., *Germany Transformed: Political Culture and the New Politics* (Cambridge, Mass.: Harvard University Press, 1981), Chs. 2 and 3.
46. J. E. Thomas, *Learning Democracy in Japan: The Social Education of Japanese Adults* (London: Sage, 1985), Ch. 3.
47. Ibid., pp. 53–54.
48. Dalton, *Citizen Politics*, Ch. 8.
49. Dennis Kavanagh, *Political Science and Political Behaviour* (London: George Allen & Unwin, 1983), Ch. 3.
50. Ibid., pp. 44–46.
51. Ronald Inglehart, "The Nature of Value Change in Postindustrial Society," in Leon N. Lindberg, ed., *Politics and the Future of Industrial Society* (New York: McKay, 1976), pp. 57–99.
52. Materialists, in our terms, express a preference for stability of economic well-being and political power. Postmaterialists seek a redistribution of all values to those in society who are relatively deprived of them; but they are most concerned with the values of power and respect.
53. Ronald Inglehart, "Political Action: The Impact of Values, Cognitive Level, and Social Background," in Barnes et al., pp. 343–380.
54. Nobutaka Ike, "Economic Growth and Intergenerational Change in Japan," *American Political Science Review* 67 (December 1973), 1194–1203.
55. Ibid., p. 1198.
56. Ibid., p. 1203.
57. Scott C. Flanagan, "Value Change and Partisan Change in Japan: The Silent Revolution Revisited," *Comparative Politics* 11 (April 1979), 260–261.
58. Ronald Inglehart, *The Silent Revolution: Changing Values and Political Styles among Western Publics* (Princeton, N.J.: Princeton University Press, 1977), p. 45. Inglehart's findings did not support the expectation that ecological goals fit within his postmaterial value cluster. However, this only means that ecology has a broad appeal to people in many walks of life in Western Europe, as in the United States.
59. Fritzof Capra and Charlene Soretnak, *Green Politics* (New York: Dutton, 1984), Ch. 2.
60. Ronald Inglehart, "Political Dissatisfaction and Mass Support for Social Change in Advanced Industrial Society," *Comparative Political Studies* 10 (1977), 452–472; and "Postmaterialism in an Environment of Insecurity," *American Political Science Review* 75 (December 1981), 880–900.
61. This is not to suggest that a majority of young people are clearly postmaterialistic. Inglehart has consistently found that those from lower-income families exhibit the materialism of their elders. This may be especially true of those who are upwardly mobile, for whom the term *Yuppies* has traveled across the North Atlantic from the United States.
62. Ronald Inglehart and Scott C. Flanagan, "Value Change in Industrial Societies," *American Political Science Review* 81 (December 1987), 1303–1318.

# CHAPTER 4

# POLITICAL PARTIES

## *Parties, Participation, and Pluralism*

In First World political systems, political parties serve as a medium through which ordinary citizens are able to express their political preferences in a way that reaches the attention of the makers of public policy. This is because, as voters, citizens may choose to support one of the parties presently in power with their votes or to shift their support to an opposition party. If enough voters do likewise, the party or parties in power could find themselves outside government looking in after the election. So those who make policy must be alert to voter preferences, both directly in terms of their policy preferences and indirectly in terms of their preferences between competing political parties and candidates.

Parties serve as a medium for political participation both as mobilizers of popular support at election time and as organizations in which ordinary citizens participate as more or less active members. In Western Europe and Japan, parties play a more distinct role in structuring political participation than is true of parties in the United States. This is partly due to the nature of political party organization in these countries. In the United States, those who vote regularly for the Republican Party's candidates are likely to think of themselves as members of that party. In Western Europe and Japan, the larger parties have an official definition of what a party member is; there is usually a dues-paying requirement and perhaps a certain minimal expectation of participation in party activities. The membership will therefore be easily identifiable and stable; it will not fluctuate wildly from year to year, and the party itself will function on a continuous basis. Party meetings will be held—locally as well as nationally—with regularity, whether it is an election year or not. Party activity will naturally increase at election time, just as it does in the United States; but the point is that the ground troops are already in place, ready for action. They do not have to be recruited on the eve of the campaign.

What this suggests is that the political party in the countries we are studying offers opportunities as a channel for popular participation, but one must first establish his or her credentials as a party regular before having any hope of playing a weighty role either in the electoral or in the public policymaking process. The rules of the game of popular participation are thus more firmly established in Western Europe and Japan. Because the two major parties are looser and more fluid in the United States, the participant may be in a position to help redefine the rules as well as to influence the outcome. Nevertheless, the existence of a larger number of political parties in most First World countries means that the individual has a variety of choices. This may be a reason why voter turnout rates are higher in most other First World countries than in the United States.

On both sides of the Atlantic (and of the Pacific), the electoral process is the principal means by which most people participate in politics. The political parties are the instruments through which the electorate expresses its preferences at election time as follows: (1) Those citizens who are active in the political parties may have a role in selecting candidates for elective office, and (2) the choices that are offered on the ballot are usually distinguishable to the average voter according to the differences between the parties they represent. The first point is more true of the United States than of other First World countries, which do not have primary elections for choosing the parties' candidates. The second point is more true of Western Europe and Japan, where the voters may not be clearly aware of who the candidates for legislative office are, but they feel competent to choose anyway because of the candidates' party (or factional) affiliations.

In each of the political systems we are studying, two or more political parties interact with one another in what we call a *party system*. The central focus of this interaction is the contest among political parties for the power to govern the country—a contest that takes place at two levels: (1) in elections, where the voters determine the respective share each party will have of the seats in parliament, and (2) within parliament, where the distribution of seats among the parties and the coalitions worked out among them will ultimately determine what party or parties will constitute the government. These are *pluralistic* party systems, because there are two or more parties among which competition is meaningful. It makes a difference how people choose among these parties. If the choice goes in one direction, one party or coalition of parties will govern the country, with one set of policy consequences; if it goes in another direction, there will be a different set of governors and policy consequences.

Italian political scientist Giovanni Sartori has made two important observations concerning pluralistic party systems: First, they operate very differently with quite different consequences for human dignity than do political systems in which there is only one political party of consequence. Second, there is, however, the danger that pluralistic party systems may become *too* pluralistic, with adverse consequences for the capacity of those governing the country to make headway in the pursuit of human dignity. In other words, *viable* pluralistic party systems are found in a range that is terminated by the one-party system at one end and what Sartori calls "extreme pluralism" at the other.[1] Although there may be more than one party, it may be the case that a single party so dominates the other parties that the party system is pluralistic in form only. Critics of the Japanese party system have sometimes characterized it in this fashion.[2] Or it may be the case that there are many parties of roughly equal strength and of sufficiently divergent policy views, so that it becomes impossible for coalitions of parties to solidify around common programs that will enable effective government to persist. Sartori sees the Italian party system as belonging to the extreme pluralism category.[3]

In Sartori's view, there are three important variables that differentiate party systems which should be taken into account in deciding whether a given party system is close to the one-party or the extreme pluralistic end of the continuum, or somewhere safely in between them. These are (1) the nature of the *ideological spectrum* the parties occupy, (2) the number of parties of significance in the system, and (3) their relative strengths.[4] Let us begin with the fascinating and complicated subject of party ideologies.

## The Ideological Spectrum

In Chapter 3 our focus was on the political beliefs of ordinary citizens. Political culture is a diffuse set of attitudes that are generally shared by large numbers of citizens. The individual citizen may or may not be able to relate his or her political attitudes to an integrated set of political beliefs that we would dignify with the label *ideology*. Only a minority of citizens have this capability. Usually, they are those who are more highly educated, who follow politics regularly, and who at least discuss politics on a regular basis with friends and associates. Political ideologies are more highly developed than is political culture. They can usually be traced to the writings of influential political philosophers who fit into established philosophical traditions, and they can be assigned recognizable labels, such as *liberalism*, *conservatism*, or *socialism*. This chapter considers the political parties in Western Europe and Japan that are readily identifiable in terms of political ideologies and that compete with one another for power—contesting elections and seeking government office on the basis of their stated, ideologically based programs.

Ideology plays a more important role for European political parties than for their American counterparts. Americans, who are used to thinking of themselves as Democrats or Republicans as long as they more or less consistently vote for the candidates of one or the other party, have difficulty understanding that political parties in Western Europe have corporate identities that separate them clearly and distinctly from the body of voters to whom they appeal for votes. The parties, in effect, are groups of men and women who fill party offices and actively participate in party functions. They constitute a small minority of the population. Thus, if French political parties are sharply at odds with one another on ideological grounds, that does not necessarily mean that the average French man or woman cares much about these battles between activists.[5] If French voters divide their votes among a relatively large number of parties, it could be because the French political elites give them a relatively large number of choices. The separate ideological families in France are subsets of political activists—the minority of the French who devote their time and energy to such matters. Thus, to speak of ideologies that divide political parties from one another in Europe is to speak of several different political subcultures—essentially elite subcultures.

Let us briefly survey the range of these subcultures as they are typically found in Western Europe. We use the traditional left–right spectrum because most subcultures can be fairly easily placed along it. (See Figure 4.1.). Two of the eight subcultures, *liberalism* and *conservatism*, have their origins in the nineteenth century; one, *democratic socialism*, was a turn-of-the-century creation; the remainder are distinctly twentieth-century phenomena.

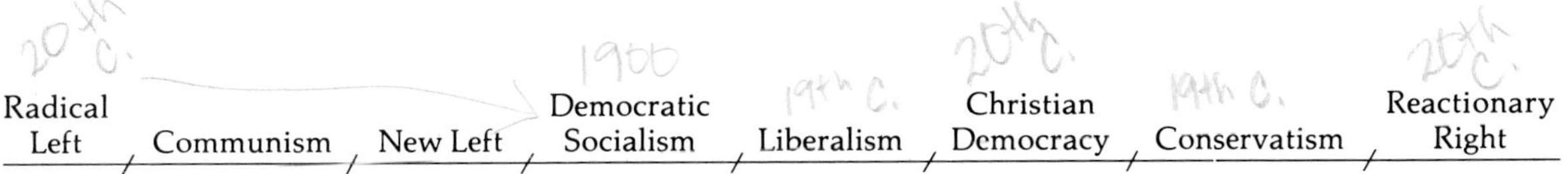


*Figure 4.1* The left–right ideological spectrum.

Nineteenth-century liberalism and conservatism differed from one another primarily in terms of the struggle to democratize European political systems. Liberals favored a measured, steady reform that would expand the electorate and reduce the power of the entrenched aristocracy, whose privileges and prerogatives conservatives sought to protect. In Europe today, there is little to distinguish liberalism from conservatism; both accept political, economic, and social institutions essentially as they are. Although conservatives resist efforts to redistribute well-being, respect, and enlightenment through government action, liberals are amenable to moderate reform but are not likely to be in the vanguard advocating it. Liberalism and conservatism have both adapted to modern capitalism. Indeed, it is not clear to what extent they can any longer be regarded as separate subcultures, although most Western European countries have separate liberal and conservative political parties.

Socialism as an ideology and as a subculture goes back nearly as far as liberalism and conservatism. In the nineteenth century, there were both utopian and scientific versions of socialism existing side by side; the former was more prevalent in France, whereas the latter was more prevalent in Germany, the home of Karl Marx. By the end of the century, Marxist socialism was the predominant variety, but there was emerging within Marxism a doctrinal conflict over the appropriate means for achieving the agreed-on ends. The revisionist wing of the movement became stronger after the turn of the century as its prescription to work within the parliamentary democratic system began to pay dividends. What we now call *democratic socialism* is the product of early twentieth-century revisionism. The democratic socialists advocate a substantial redistribution of the values of well-being, respect, and enlightenment in favor of those social classes that have relatively small shares of them. However, they do not believe a major redistribution of power is also necessary because parliamentary democracy enables classes that are weak in other resources to use their superior numbers to gain the necessary power to make redistributive decisions.

Western European *communism*, on the other hand, is a direct descendant of that branch of socialism that remained faithful to the Marxist revolutionary blueprint. Until recently, at least, these Communists denied that a fundamental redistribution of well-being, respect, and enlightenment could take place unless the political system were radically changed. Thus, if the Communists had come to power in Western European parliamentary democracies, they would have used their newly acquired political resources to destroy the power base of the capitalist class, thus removing resistance to socialist redistribution and achieving "dictatorship of the proletariat." Recently, however, communism has become more ambivalent about how to achieve socialist goals. Leading Communists in Italy, the country in Western Europe where communism is strongest, have argued (much as the democratic socialists have argued all along) that it would not be necessary to change the rules of parliamentary democracy. Although this would mean living with capitalism longer than the Communists in the Soviet Union, Poland, or East Germany were willing to do, contemporary Western European communism seems content to let the existing distribution of power remain intact while working on the redistribution of other values. Thus, differences between communism and democratic socialism have been considerably lessened.

In the mid-1970s, the term *Eurocommunist* was applied to most of the Western European Communist parties, implying that they had evolved in a direction different from that of the Soviet Communist Party (CPSU) and its fraternal parties in Eastern Europe. The term was first assumed by the Spanish Communist Party (PCE), which even went so far as to deny that it was any longer a Marxist–Leninist party, preferring to be regarded as simply a Marxist party, thus implicitly denying any necessity to follow the guidance of the CPSU, the party of Lenin. Both the Italian and the French parties permitted themselves to be labeled Eurocommunist, but there have been important differences between the two parties, including differences of an ideological nature. The Italian Communist Party (PCI) went a considerable distance in pragmatically adapting its program to the expectations of the ruling Christian Democrats with whom it sought a partnership. This search for a *historic compromise* led the PCI into close working relationships with private capitalists in those cities where the PCI held power, as well as with the Christian Democrats in the Parliament, where the PCI has frequently played a cooperative role in the fashioning of legislative compromises. More recently, the PCI has sought the establishment of a "popular front" coalition with the Socialist Party (PSI). PCI leader Achille Ochetto intends to bring about a change in the party name, removing the word "Communist." The French Communist Party (PCF) persisted in a determined opposition to the parties in power until the victory of the Socialist Party in the 1981 legislative election. Their participation in the Socialist-led government formed in that year ended only three years later. Many observers who take at face value the claim of the PCI that they have abandoned the objective of a dictatorship of the proletariat are more skeptical of the same claim when it is made by the PCF. One indicator of the difference between the two parties is the fact that the Soviet invasion of Afghanistan was denounced by the PCI, whereas the PCF defended it. However, the upheavals in 1989–90 affecting Communist parties in Eastern Europe may have removed some of the causes of disagreement among Western European Communists, as the Leninist model of one-party rule appears to be on its way to becoming a museum piece of modern history, at least in the nearest Eastern European neighbors.

Younger Socialists have moved into the vacuum left by the communist drift away from the extreme left since the mid-1960s. Calling themselves Marxists, Leninists, Trotskyites, Maoists, or anarchists, they have rejected Moscow-oriented communism as defensive of the status quo. But their position on the distribution of basic values in Western capitalist systems is essentially the same as that of the revolutionary Socialists at the turn of the century or of the Communists of the 1950s. They feel that only a thorough destruction of the capitalist base of power will make it possible to achieve a radical redistribution of other values. This *radical left* differs from the earlier brand of communism by dividing its criticism equally between Western capitalism and the socialist regimes of Eastern Europe. Because inequalities persist in the latter regimes, the radical left in Western Europe argues that this is a form of state capitalism that does not differ in principle from the private capitalism of the West. But their wholesale rejection of the Western institutional structure places them on the far left of the ideological spectrum. Political parties of the radical left, such as the Democratic Proletarians in Italy, have seldom received more than 1 or 2 percent of the popular vote in recent national elections.

Another primarily twentieth-century development in some Western European countries was the emergence of Christian democracy, which came about as an effort to reconcile Europe's Catholics with parliamentary democracy and with economic and social reform. Before World War II, there had been strong Catholic elements who rejected democracy and sought to preserve the existing distribution of values in society. These groups were especially strong in the Mediterranean Catholic countries—Italy, Portugal, and Spain—but they constituted at least a minority among the politically active Catholics in France and Germany. In all of these countries, some leading Catholics embraced fascism. Yet, Catholics also played an important role in resisting Mussolini's fascist rule in Italy and the German occupation of France during World War II. In France and Italy, Christian democracy, which stemmed from smaller parties of earlier decades, earned its democratic credentials during the resistance and emerged from the war with a large mass following. In Germany, Christian democracy was made up of the leaders of the old Catholic Center Party of the Weimar Republic, who had gone into deep retirement during the Nazi years and emerged after the war untainted. But Christian democracy in West Germany has taken a somewhat different turn from that in Italy and France because half of the West German population is Protestant. In West Germany, Christian democracy has been able to appeal to liberal and conservative middle-class Protestants as well as to Catholics of all social classes.

What is Christian democracy today? It remains the ideological basis of two strong political parties—in Italy and West Germany—whereas its political expression in France became weaker and weaker, until today there is no longer a Christian Democratic Party, properly speaking. The party's survival in Italy and West Germany has depended on the capacity of Christian democratic leaders to broaden their appeal, adopting in their party platforms elements of conservatism, liberalism, and even democratic socialism. In the early years after World War II, Christian democracy in all three countries had a strong reformist strain, a commitment to a truly democratic political system and to moderate redistribution of well-being, respect, and enlightenment. After the onset of the Cold War in the late 1940s, these reformist aspects became increasingly muted in favor of a strong anticommunism. In the 1950s, it was customary to classify Christian democracy with conservatism. But since the early 1960s, the willingness of Christian democratic political leaders to cooperate with the Democratic Socialists in programs of moderate reform has made it much harder to place them very far to the right on the ideological spectrum. Christian democracy today is a mixture of many ideological elements with considerable pragmatism and even opportunism. It is probably safest to locate Christian democracy in the center-right of our ideological spectrum.

As for the *far right*, it is not as easy to find bona fide right-wing extremists in Western Europe as it was a few decades ago. With respect to political movements, there is nothing even faintly resembling the virulent Nazis in Germany or Mussolini's Fascists in Italy. Short-lived right-wing movements have appeared from time to time, such as the Poujadists in France in the mid-1950s, which was a movement of small-business owners who were protesting the dislocations that affected them as France moved toward a postindustrial society. Today's longest-lived right-wing party, the Neo-Fascists in Italy, is a somewhat similar phenomenon, likewise appealing to threatened social groups and gaining its principal strength in the less advanced southern portion of Italy, just as the Poujadists were strongest in the rural areas of central and southwestern France. It is not easy to characterize what today's reactionary right represents ideologically. In some ways, it resembles the radical left in its aversion to big capitalism and big government. But prewar Nazism and fascism showed that bringing the reactionary right to power will only lead to bigger capitalism and bigger government without effecting any real redistribution of well-being, respect, and enlightenment, whatever the upheavals in the structure of power. The racism of the Nazis finds some faint echoes today, as in campaigns against immigrant workers carried on in France by the National Front, a party that rose very rapidly in electoral strength through the 1980s, peaking at 14% for its leader, Jean-Marie Le Pen in the 1988 presidential election. A similar phenomenon in West Germany, the *Republikaner*, rapidly captured attention in West Germany in 1989. However, the strong nationalism of the Republikaner was made redundant by the rising voices from left, center, and right calling for German reunification.

Jean-Marie Le Pen, leader of the French right-wing party, National Front.

As Western European countries have entered postindustrial society, *new left* parties have emerged of late, attracting the support especially of the educated "postmaterial" youth, whose preoccupation is with the expansion of political rights, including the right to engage in forms of political action labeled in Chapter 3 as "unconventional." One such party has been the Radical Party in Italy, which came from almost nowhere in the 1979 national election to capture 3.4 percent of the popular vote and eighteen seats in the Chamber of Deputies. Sometimes encompassed within new left parties and sometimes constituting separate parties on their own are the Environmentalists (or Greens). The Green Party in West Germany was strong enough in the 1983 parliamentary election to take crucial segments of votes away from the larger parties. It captured 5.6 percent of the popular vote and twenty-seven seats, becoming the fourth party in the Bundestag, or lower house of Parliament. In 1987 it increased its share of the popular vote to 8.3 percent, and of seats to forty-two.

Another type of fringe party found in many Western European countries is the regional or ethnic separatist party—exemplified by the Scottish Nationalist Party in Great Britain and the South Tyrolean People's Party in Italy—

which, at a minimum, seeks greater autonomy for the region in which its ethnic minority is concentrated. In some cases, as for some Scottish Nationalists, actual independence from the larger nation is sought. It is difficult to fit many of these new or resurgent parties into the traditional left–right spectrum that reflects the "materialist" agenda of issues of advanced industrialism. As we saw in Chapter 3, postindustrial society is bringing forth a new agenda to which the older parties are trying to adjust.

Table 4.1 matches ideologies with the more important political parties in our five countries. Some parties defy classification, such as the Union for French Democracy (UDF), which is a mixture of Liberals, Christian Democrats, and Conservatives. For want of a better solution we categorize them as liberals, in order to distinguish them from the French Gaullists (RPR), whom we have placed in the conservative category. However, both the UDF and the RPR are broad coalitions of elements much like the Christian Democrats in Italy and West Germany. Some Gaullists are liberals, others are clearly conservatives, and still others, in their strong nationalism at least, resemble adherents of the reactionary right. Indeed, it was customary to classify the forerunner of the contemporary

**Table 4.1 Location of Political Parties on the Ideological Spectrum**

| *Country* | *Radical and New Left* | *Communism* | *Democratic Socialism* | *Liberalism* | *Christian Democracy* | *Conservatism* | *Reactionary Right* |
|---|---|---|---|---|---|---|---|
| *Great Britain* | | | Labour Party | Democrats (SLD)<br>Social Democrats (SDP) | | Conservative Party | |
| *France* | Ecologists | French Communist Party (PCF) | Socialist Party (PS) | Union for French Democracy (UDF) | | Gaullists (RPR) | National Front (FN) |
| *West Germany* | Greens | German Communist Party (DKP) | Social Democratic Party (SPD) | Free Democratic Party (FDP) | Christian Democratic Union (CDU) | Christian Social Union (CSU) | Republikaner |
| *Italy* | Proletarian Democracy (DP)<br>Radicals (PR)<br>Greens | Italian Communist Party (PCI) | Italian Socialist Party (PSI) | Republican Party (PRI)<br>Social Democratic Party (PSDI) | Christian Democratic Party (DC) | Liberal Party (PLI) | Italian Social Movement (MSI) |
| *Japan* | | Japan Communist Party (JCP) | Japan Socialist Party (JSP) | Democratic Socialist Party (DSP)<br>Komeito | | Liberal Democratic Party (LDP) | |

Gaullist Party, the Rally of the French People (RPF) of the late 1940s and early 1950s, as a party of the far right. Still, in terms of the behavior of the Gaullist leadership since the party came to power in 1958, it seems appropriate to classify the party as conservative, but it is a very practical, flexible kind of conservatism—like that of the British Conservative Party.

A similar judgment can be made about the ruling party in Japan, the Liberal Democratic Party. Two parties in the center of the Japanese party spectrum, the Democratic Socialist Party (DSP) and the Komeito, or "Clean Government Party," are very difficult to classify in Western terms. They are placed in the liberal category here, mainly because of their center position between Japanese socialism and conservatism. Both call themselves "socialist," but the DSP gets substantial financial support from private business, and the Komeito, a Buddhist party dedicated to peace and a clean environment, combines elements of liberal reformism with what in the West would be associated with Christian democracy on the one hand, and the new left on the other.

## Ideology and Organization

Traditionally, the parties of the left and right in Western Europe were distinguished from one another not only in terms of their beliefs and programs, but also in terms of the ways in which they were organized. Socialist parties, being parties of the working class, sought large mass memberships, particularly of industrial workers, who could be readily organized in advanced industrial society because of their concentrations in large factories and in homogeneous residential areas. Liberal and conservative parties of the center and right sought to mobilize the financial contributions of wealthy supporters, while confining party membership to a relatively small circle of middle-class activists. Thus, according to French political scientist Maurice Duverger, democratic socialist parties were *mass parties*, while liberal and conservative parties were *cadre*, or "framework," parties.[6]

In postindustrial societies, parties of the left, center, and right are not as easily characterized in organizational terms as they were nearly four decades ago when Duverger made the mass/cadre distinction. On the left, parties that previously relied heavily on working-class support have had to come to grips with the fact that the industrial working class is diminishing in size and is losing what cohesion it once had. Democratic socialist and even communist parties have had to redouble their efforts to capture middle-class support if they wish to hold the shares of the popular vote they once enjoyed. This has meant a dilution of the working-class bases of socialist parties and a decline in membership, as middle-class supporters have been harder to recruit to dues-paying membership status and the pool of available working-class members has been evaporating. On the other hand, those parties of the center and right that have broadened their party programs in order to appeal to working-class as well as to middle-class voters (e.g., the British Conservative Party and the French Gaullists) or to Protestants as well as to Catholics (the Christian Democrats of West Germany) have found their memberships growing as they reach into new social categories that are amenable to organizational efforts. Thus, as parties of the advanced industrial era have become "catch-all" parties,[7] trying to reach as many voters as possible with the broadest possible appeals, the old organizational differences have disappeared. At least the larger parties of Western Europe are no longer strictly mass parties or strictly cadre parties, although some smaller parties are found in the latter category. They are parties with respectable dues-paying memberships, but their focus is electoral. They rely on the financial support of both the dues paid by their formal membership and the substantial contributions made by wealthier adherents; and they make use of both the army of doorbell-ringing ordinary members and the media skills of paid professionals. Although there are slight differences in organizational form as one moves from one party to another, such differences assume less importance in light of the trends discussed in Chapter 2 under the heading "Disorganized Capitalism." It is not that political parties have become less organized than they once were; it is that party organization has become a standardized, professionalized feature of all parties that are successful in attracting significant shares of the popular vote. It would be relatively easy to substitute the organizational characteristics of one party for those of its most serious rival with relatively little adjustment trauma for the personnel involved.

A more telling question to ask about the ways in which today's political parties in First World countries are structured is to ask abut the nature of intraparty conflict. Some political parties have easily identifiable ideological left and right *wings*. Within-party conflict in such parties is nearly as serious as the ideological warfare that goes on between parties. Political scientist Richard Rose has distinguished between the British Labour and Conservative parties in these terms. The Labour Party, he says, is a party of *factions*, whereas the Conservative Party is a party of *tendencies*.[8] In the Labour Party there are readily identifiable left and right wings that take different positions on a wide variety of issues and that have stable memberships, almost as if there were two separate political parties within one Labour Party. The Conservatives, on the other hand, divide in different ways on different issues. Thus, there are certain party members who are opposed to capital punishment and others who favor it, but some of those who are at odds with one another on this issue will join forces against still other members on the issue of whether Britain should be a member of the European Common Market. Each of these pro and con positions is a tendency, but a set of tendencies will not add up to stable factions that could be disruptive of Conservative Party unity, as the constant battle between left and right has done in the Labour Party.

There is another meaning of the word *faction* that has been applied in particular to two of the parties we are considering here: the Italian Christian Democratic Party (DC) and the Japanese Liberal Democratic Party (LDP). Both parties are the largest vote getters in their countries, and both have monopolized or held the lion's share of power since normal politics resumed after World War II. Both have publicly identifiable factions, but they are factions defined more in terms of the *persons* who belong to them than of the ideological beliefs their members share. It is possible to give rough "left" or "right" labels to some of the factions that vie for leadership of the DC and the LDP, but many others occupy shifting ground somewhere between the center-left and center-right of the within-party spectrum. More appropriately, the factions are named for their present or past leaders. Their inner cores are sets of parliamentary members of the respective parties, led by one or more nationally prominent figures, who ordinarily will be found occupying ministerial positions in government, or party organizational posts, or both. Younger members of a given faction count on the support of their seniors for promotion up the political ladders so that they will in turn become faction, party, and governmental leaders later in their careers.

Most observers feel that the Italian and Japanese type of factionalism just described is less damaging to internal political unity than is the ideologically defined factionalism often found in parties of the left in Western Europe. However, the other side of the coin is that a great deal of energy is expended in the DC and LDP in interfactional maneuvering and bargaining. On the face of it, both parties have been strong enough to have provided effective policy leadership during the many years they have dominated their political systems; yet, especially in Italy, the infighting that has gone on between factions has assumed greater significance for the contestants than just the policy issues that an outsider would think are at stake. Still, it could be argued that both countries have been governed more effectively than the critics would lead us to expect, especially when we look at indicators of economic growth and international trade balances.[9] The ideological factionalism found in the British Labour Party has been one of the prime targets for criticism of the poor economic record of Britain during the years of Labour government in the 1960s and 1970s.[10] At any rate, the amount of pluralistic competition within party systems is a function not only of the number of parties in the system, but also in the degree to which the parties are factionalized in either of the senses discussed here.

## Party System Pluralism

In the two preceding chapters we have examined the structure of social cleavages and the pattern of psychological orientations (political culture) as they relate to politics in Western Europe and Japan. It has typically been the function of political parties in these parts of the world to translate social cleavages and mass political orientations into political action, through the medium of the contests between parties for power. These contests take place within the framework of what we call *party systems*. They involve competition between political parties for the support of members and electors and a system of cooperation and conflict between parties in the process of forming governing coalitions and making public policy. The party system will reflect the principal lines of cleavage within a society (Chapter 2) and the principal political subcultures (Chapter 3) by appealing to different sets of voters with competing party leaders, competing slogans, and competing ideologies. Those parties that succeed in gaining power or a share of it in governing coalitions will put their leaders in office and see that the leaders adhere more or less closely to the promises the parties have made to their adherents in the electorate.

However, we must not suppose that there are one-to-one translations of voter wishes into party intentions and of party intentions into the actions of their leaders when in government office. Intervening factors can distort the one translation or the other. Some of these factors are indigenous to the party system itself; others are external to it, operating elsewhere in the political system or in its environment. Factors internal to the party system, such as fragmentation, polarization, and coalition formation, are discussed in this chapter, as is an influential external factor, the way the system of elections is organized. Additional external factors are discussed in other chapters: The changes occurring in the economy were discussed in Chapter 2, the rules of parliamentary practice are discussed in Chapter 5, and the ways in which conflicts of interest between major interest groups in society, such as trade unions and employers groups, are resolved are discussed in Chapter 6. Such constant or uncontrollable factors can influence the electoral fortunes of political parties as well as their capacity to make good on their promises once in office.

There are many ways of characterizing political party systems, depending on the purpose of the analysis. Since we are concerned with the problem of where party systems fall in the range between too little pluralism and too much pluralism,[11] we focus on three criteria for differentiating party systems that are related to this problem. These are (1) the degree of fragmentation, (2) the distribution of strength across the ideological spectrum, and (3) coalition patterns. The first of these, *fragmentation*, combines two measurable characteristics, the number of parties in a system and the strengths of those parties. The fewer the number, the less the fragmentation; and the more even the strengths of the parties, the greater the fragmentation. A four-party system ordinarily would be more fragmented than a three-party system. But if the strength of the three parties in the latter system is evenly distributed, each party having one-third of the voters' support, it would be more fragmented than would a four-party system in which two parties each had 45 percent of the voters' support and the remaining two parties each had 5 percent. That is, voter support is more concentrated in the four-party system than in the three-party system. Presumably, it would be easier to draw together a majority coalition when you start with a 45 percent party as one of the building blocks than it would be when you have to find ways of reconciling two proud 30–35 percent parties in the same coalition government. Fragmentation, then, makes the cohesion of government more tenuous, thus adversely affecting the productivity and ultimately the stability of government. This, at least, is what theorists of party systems have argued for a long time.[12]

There are a number of indexes that political scientists have devised for party fragmentation, some of the best known of which are rather complex. One of the simplest, the *index of aggregation,* measures the converse of fragmentation.[13] It divides the percentage of the largest party by the number of parties in the system. We follow the practice of regarding a party as being "in the system" if it obtains at least 2 percent of the popular vote in legislative elections. By this measure, aggregation has been greater in the United Kingdom in the last four elections (aggregation index = 14) than in France (aggregation index = 7). Party system aggregation has an average index of 14 in West Germany, substantially higher than that of Italy, which is 8. Japan, with an average index of 9, is closer to the more fragmented systems.

The *distribution of strength across the ideological spectrum* refers to the left–right spectrum outlined in the previous section and the distribution of party strengths across that spectrum. Even if all of the ideological types are represented in a particular party system, if the strongest parties are concentrated near one point on the spectrum, the system could be labeled left-leaning, centrist, or right-leaning, depending on the location of that point. Another party system might have more of a bimodal distribution with twin peaks on the left and right, such that it could be labeled *polarized*, although the degree of polarization would depend on whether the large parties of left and right are of the extremes or of the more moderate left and right. The party systems could be differently characterized depending on whether we are talking about the distribution of electoral strength or the distribution of strength in Parliament. Thus, the British party system appears to have a rather centrist appearance if electoral strengths of the parties are considered, as the center Liberal and Social Democratic Alliance captured more than 20 percent of the popular vote in 1987, but, because the number of seats it obtained in the House of Commons constituted only about 3 percent, it nearly disappears from a diagram of parliamentary party strength, and the British system appears moderately polarized between the Labour Party on the near left and the Conservative Party on the near right. At this stage we concentrate on the distribution of party strength as reflected in the popular vote, and then later we look at the parliamentary distribution when we consider the effects of electoral systems on party systems.

Figure 4.2 shows how our five party systems appear when the distribution of party electoral strengths across the ideological spectrum[14] is diagrammed. From the figure we can see that the mild polarization of the British party system finds echoes in the West German and Japanese party systems, in each of which a Democratic Socialist Party and a party of the moderate right are the two strongest. In France and Italy, there are Communist parties with sufficient strength to extend the left bloc in Parliament farther to the left, creating greater polarization, especially

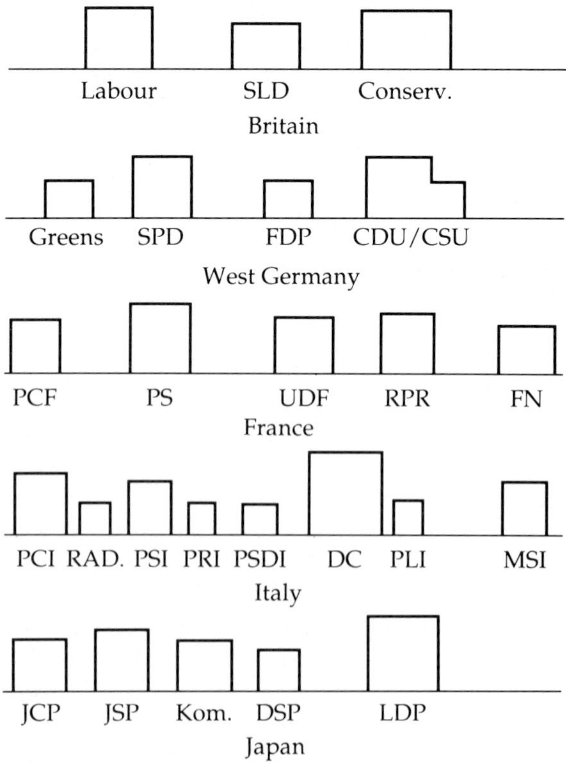

*Figure 4.2* Party left–right spectrums for five countries.

as there is some strength on the far right in each country as well. Both the French and the Italian party systems exhibit both polarization and the highest levels of fragmentation among the five countries.

*Coalition formation* occurs in party systems in cases where no party is strong enough to command a majority in the legislative body, called the House, the Assembly, the Chamber, or the Diet, depending on the country in question. (See Chapter 5.) In three of our five countries—France, West Germany, and Italy—coalitions are usually necessary because of the fact that seldom, if ever, can one party gain a majority in its own right. In Britain and Japan, on the other hand, coalitions have not been found in recent decades, because one party has, with rare exceptions, always had a majority of seats in parliament. Whether coalitions are found or not, the same question can be asked: Does power remain anchored at one point on the left–right spectrum, or does it alternate between left and right over the course of, say, a twenty-five-year generation? In Britain, alternation is fairly frequent, with power having changed hands between left and right four times in the past twenty-five years. In France, changes have occurred three times during that span and in West Germany, twice. But power has remained anchored on the right in Japan and in a broad area of the Italian spectrum stretching from center-left to center-right. In the Italian case, the width of the coalition has expanded and contracted from time to time, but it has remained anchored around the center of the spectrum. Italy is the only one of the five countries to exhibit coalitions of the center, a characteristic Sartori associates with extreme pluralism, because the parties on the extreme left and right of the spectrum are not seen as suitable partners by those closer to the center. So the center parties remain one another's coalition partners by de-

British Labour party supporters demonstrating their opposition to Conservative Prime Minister Margaret Thatcher during the June 1987 general election campaign.

fault. In the four other countries, the coalitions have been clearly either to the left or to the right of center, although France edged slightly toward a center coalition in mid-1988. The coalition patterns and locations of government and opposition in the five party systems as of mid-1988 is depicted in Figure 4.3.

## Electoral Systems

It is a long-accepted generalization among political scientists that the number of political parties a country has is, in part at least, dependent on the type of electoral system it has. Two-party systems tend to be found in countries with *single-member district plurality* electoral systems, and party systems with more than two parties, especially party systems with five or more parties, are associated with *proportional representation*. The United States and Great Britain are said to have two-party systems, and Italy, always with more than five parties, is said to have a multiparty system that features extreme pluralism.

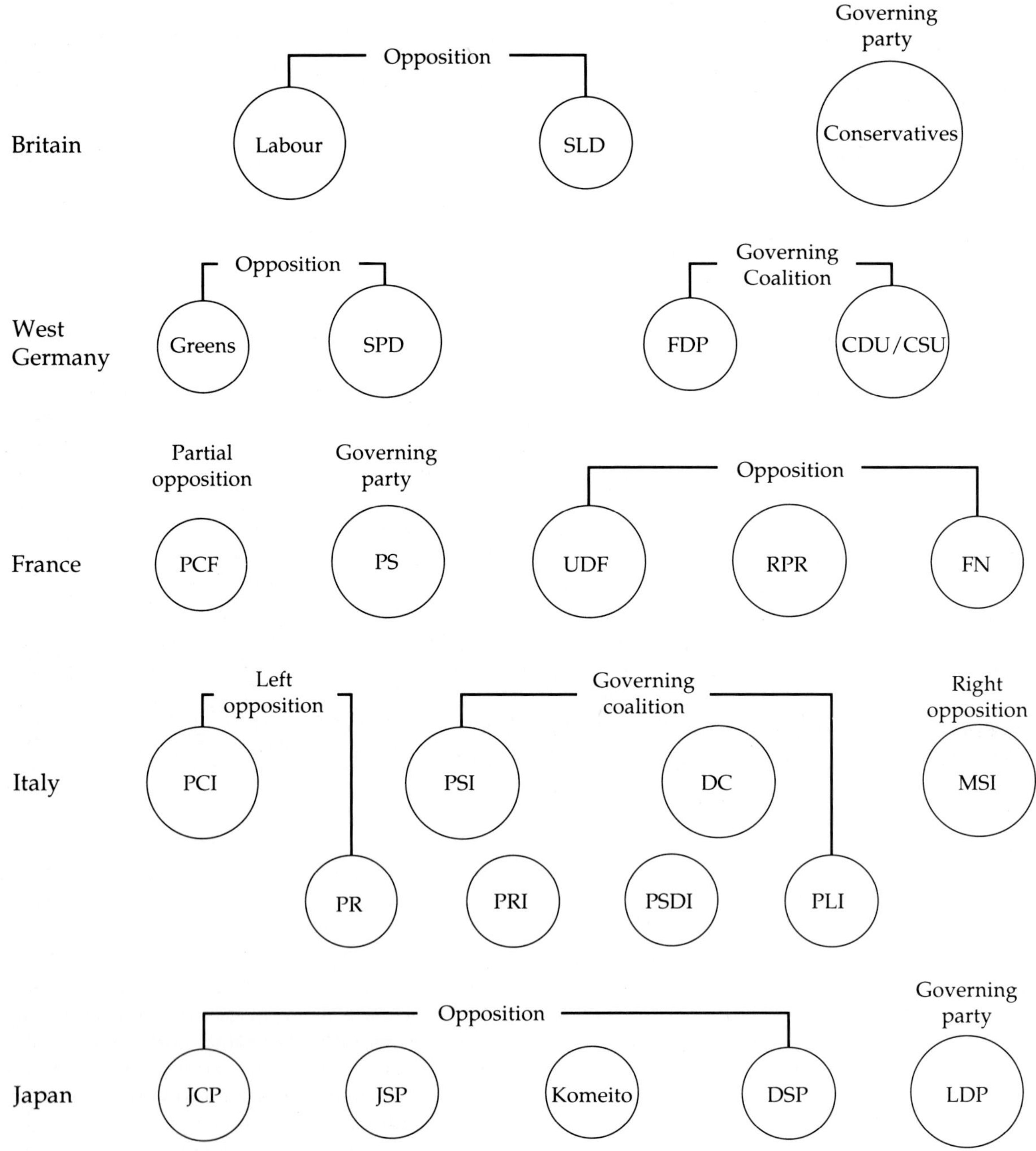


*Figure 4.3* Governing parties or coalition, and opposition parties.

But do the United States and Great Britain really have two-party systems? And does it matter whether they do or they do not? Are there not important differences between three-party systems and, say, eight-party systems? In other words, the dividing line between two and three parties is a rather arbitrary one and may not capture a significant distinction. Look at the British party system today. In the general election held in June 1987, the two leading parties, Labour and the Conservatives, together gained 73 percent of the popular vote. The third largest contending unit, the Alliance of Liberals and Social Democrats, captured 23 percent, whereas other parties, including Scottish Nationalists, Welsh Nationalists, Ulster Unionists, Communists, the right-wing National Front, and various independents, totaled nearly 5 percent. Clearly the two largest parties far outdistanced the others, but can we really omit the Liberals and Social Democrats from consideration? Is the British party system not really at least a four-party system?

One reason political scientists have clung to the two-party label for Great Britain is that, at least until very recently, the British electoral system has seriously discriminated against all but the two largest parties. As in the case of the U.S. House of Representatives, Great Britain is divided into geographical units, each returning 1 member to the 650-member House of Commons. When a general election is held, all 650 seats are contested. Some of these are safe Labour seats, returning the Labour candidate in election after election; some are safe Conservative seats. Few can be taken for granted by the Alliance. In fact, Liberal and Social Democratic strength is quite evenly distributed around the country, unlike that of the Scottish, Welsh, and Ulster parties, which, of course, is concentrated in their respective geographic regions. Because only one candidate can win the seat in a given constituency and because the winner is whoever gains a plurality—not necessarily a majority (more than 50 percent) of the votes—the Alliance often runs a strong second to one or the other of the two major parties, but seldom takes the first spot. Thus, in June 1987, although the Alliance won 23 percent of the popular vote, it captured only 22 of the 650 seats. With 73 percent of the popular vote, the two largest parties obtained 93 percent of the seats. So, is the British party system a two-party system or a four-party system, or even an eight-party system?

Now let us look at the situation in West Germany, whose party system bore some resemblance to that of the British until recently. There, too, the three leading parties have been a large party on the left, the Social Democrats (SPD); a large party on the right, the Christian Democrats (CDU/CSU); and a smaller party in the center, the Free Democrats (FDP). In January 1987, the two larger parties (the Christian Democrats are federated with the Bavarian CSU) gained 81 percent of the popular vote, and the FDP obtained 9.1 percent. If this result has occurred in Great Britain in June 1987, the Alliance would have been fortunate to have gotten its twenty-two seats. Yet, the FDP captured 46 seats out of 497. This enabled them to hold the balance of power between the two major parties, neither of which had secured a majority of seats in the Bundestag.

It is the electoral system that accounts for the more advantageous position of the FDP. West Germany has a complex combination of proportional representation and the single-member plurality system; however, the proportional representation principle predominates. This means that seats are distributed among parties in proportion to their percentages of the popular vote. Half of the 497 Bundestag seats are based on single-member constituencies, as in Great

Britain. The other half are distributed on a proportional basis among party lists drawn up at the state (*Land*) level. The distribution among Land lists corrects for any disproportion that arises in the single-member district results so that the total distribution of seats among the parties will be proportional to their percentages of the national popular vote.

Proponents of the proportional representation system argue that it is only simple justice to allow a party the parliamentary representation it has earned. Otherwise, the votes of those who support a party such as the British Liberals are often discounted. The counterargument stresses the fact that proportional representation tends to encourage the proliferation of parties. The horrible example often cited is the Weimar Republic of Germany (1919–33), where a pure system of proportional representation encouraged literally dozens of parties to vie for Reichstag seats and actually rewarded many of them. Building and maintaining governing coalitions under such circumstances is extremely difficult. The framers of the Bonn electoral law had the Weimar experience in mind when they sought to modify the extreme proliferating effect of proportional representation. They accomplished this by denying representation in the Bundestag to any party that could not gain at least 5 percent of the national list vote. This rule has kept the Communist Party out of the Bundestag since the earliest years of the Federal Republic, and it has worked to the disadvantage of right-wing parties and various regional splinter parties. Among the smaller parties, only the FDP was able to remain above this minimum level before March 1983. The advantage that the FDP gains by means of proportional representation is somewhat offset by its uncertain future. In March 1983, the FDP fell to 6.9 percent of the popular vote, thus coming close to elimination from the Bundestag. In the meantime, the Green Party, which had gained only 1.5 percent of the vote in 1980, climbed to 5.6 percent in 1983, thus increasing to four the number of parties with seats in the Bundestag. In 1987 the two parties both increased their shares of both votes and seats. (See Table 4.2.)

Italy, on the other hand, retains a multiplicity of parties. There are nine listed in Table 4.2, which excludes parties of a strictly ethnic-regional character. This is because Italy is the only one of our five countries to have essentially unrestricted proportional representation. However, five of the Italian parties are of a distinctly minor nature, typically polling 5 percent or less of the popular vote. It seems likely that only the proportional representation system is keeping them alive at the national level.

The capacity of proportional representation to encourage the proliferation of political parties has also been seen in the case of France since World War II. During the Fourth Republic, France had a proportional representation system that discriminated in favor of parties of the center that were able to form electoral alliances with one another, but which nevertheless permitted six or seven parties to play important roles in the National Assembly at any given time. When the Fifth Republic came into being in 1958, the electoral system was changed to a single-member district basis, the system that is found there today. But is is not a plurality system like that in Britain. Rather, a majority of votes in a district are required for a candidate to be elected on the first ballot. Failing that, a second ballot is held a week later, at which time a plurality of votes, or more than any other candidate obtains, is all that is required to win the seat. This system encourages alliances of parties of the left to form against alliances of parties of the right. The candidates of the left who do not receive the largest number of votes for left candidates on the first ballot will step aside and urge their

**Table 4.2 Distributions of Seats and Votes in Three Recent Legislative Elections**

*United Kingdom*

| | *1979* | | *1983* | | *1987* | |
|---|---|---|---|---|---|---|
| *Party* | *Votes* | *Seats* | *Votes* | *Seats* | *Votes* | *Seats* |
| Labour | 36.9% | 268 | 27.6% | 209 | 30.8% | 229 |
| Liberal (Alliance) | 13.8 | 11 | 25.4 | 23 | 22.6 | 22 |
| Conservative | 43.9 | 339 | 42.4 | 397 | 42.3 | 376 |
| Others | 5.4 | 16 | 4.6 | 21 | 4.3 | 23 |

*France*

| | *1981* | | *1986* | | *1988* | |
|---|---|---|---|---|---|---|
| *Party* | *Votes* | *Seats* | *Votes* | *Seats* | *Votes* | *Seats* |
| Communists | 16.2% | 44 | 9.8% | 35 | 11.3% | 27 |
| Socialists and Left Radicals | 37.5 | 285 | 32.7 | 214 | 37.5 | 276 |
| Giscardists (UDF) | | 64 | | 131 | | 130 |
| Gaullists (RPR) | 40.0 | 85 | 44.7 | 158 | 40.5 | 128 |
| National Front | 0.4 | — | 9.7 | 33 | 9.6 | 1 |
| Others | 5.9 | 13 | 3.1 | — | 1.1 | 13 |

*West Germany*

| | *1980* | | *1983* | | *1987* | |
|---|---|---|---|---|---|---|
| *Party* | *Votes* | *Seats* | *Votes* | *Seats* | *Votes* | *Seats* |
| Greens | 1.5% | — | 5.6% | 27 | 8.3% | 42 |
| SPD | 42.9 | 218 | 38.2 | 193 | 37.0 | 186 |
| FDP | 10.6 | 53 | 6.9 | 34 | 9.1 | 46 |
| CDU/CSU | 44.5 | 226 | 48.8 | 244 | 44.3 | 223 |
| Others | 0.5 | — | 0.5 | — | 1.3 | — |

*Italy*

| | *1979* | | *1983* | | *1987* | |
|---|---|---|---|---|---|---|
| *Party* | *Votes* | *Seats* | *Votes* | *Seats* | *Votes* | *Seats* |
| Communists | 30.4% | 201 | 29.9% | 198 | 26.6% | 177 |
| Greens | — | — | — | — | 2.5 | 13 |
| Radicals | 3.4 | 18 | 2.2 | 11 | 2.6 | 13 |
| Socialists | 9.8 | 62 | 11.4 | 73 | 14.3 | 94 |

(*Table continues on p. 114.*)

**Table 4.2** (*Continued*)

| | *Italy* | | | | | |
|---|---|---|---|---|---|---|
| | *1979* | | *1983* | | *1987* | |
| *Party* | *Votes* | *Seats* | *Votes* | *Seats* | *Votes* | *Seats* |
| Social Democrats | 3.8 | 20 | 4.1 | 23 | 3.0 | 17 |
| Republicans | 3.0 | 16 | 5.1 | 29 | 3.7 | 21 |
| Christian Democrats | 38.3 | 262 | 32.9 | 225 | 34.3 | 234 |
| Liberals | 1.9 | 9 | 2.9 | 16 | 2.1 | 11 |
| Italian Social Movement | 5.3 | 30 | 6.8 | 42 | 5.9 | 35 |
| Others | 5.9 | 12 | 4.7 | 1.3 | 5.0 | 15 |

| | *Japan* | | | | | |
|---|---|---|---|---|---|---|
| | *1980* | | *1983* | | *1986* | |
| *Party* | *Votes* | *Seats* | *Votes* | *Seats* | *Votes* | *Seats* |
| Communists | 9.8% | 29 | 9.3% | 26 | 8.6% | 27 |
| Socialists | 19.3 | 107 | 19.5 | 112 | 17.2 | 86 |
| Komeito | 9.0 | 33 | 10.1 | 58 | 9.4 | 57 |
| Democratic Socialists | 6.6 | 32 | 7.2 | 38 | 6.4 | 26 |
| Liberal Democrats | 47.9 | 284 | 45.7 | 250 | 49.5 | 304 |
| Others | 7.4 | 26 | 7.8 | 27 | 8.4 | 12 |

(*Source*). Great Britain: David Butler and Dennis Kavanagh, *The British General Election of 1987* (New York: St. Martin's, 1988), p. 283. France: J. E. S. Hayward, *Governing France: The One and Indivisible Republic,* 2nd ed. (London: Weidenfeld and Nicolson, 1983), p. 76; *The Economist,* June 11, 1988, p. 49, and June 18, 1988, p. 48. West Germany: Stephen Padgett and Tony Burkett, *Political Parties and Elections in West Germany: The Search for a New Stability* (New York: St. Martin's, 1986), p. 200; Christian Soe, ed., *Comparative Politics 88/89* (Guilford, Conn.: Annual Editions, 1988), p. 40. Italy: Frederic Spotts and Theodor Wieser, *Italy: A Difficult Democracy* (Cambridge: Cambridge University Press, 1986), p. 295; Mark Donovan, "The 1987 Election in Italy: Prelude to Reform," *West European Politics* 10 (1987), 127; Japan: Ronald J. Hrebenar, *The Japanese Party System: From One-Party Rule to Coalition Government* (Boulder, Colo., and London: Westview, 1986); *Keesing's Contemporary Archives* 32 (August 1986), 34555; *The Economist,* July 12, 1986, p. 29.

supporters to vote for the leading candidate of the left. Something similar will happen on the right, so that ordinarily on the second ballot the two strongest candidates are left facing one another. The first ballot has been likened to the primary elections in the United States, by which party candidates are nominated to appear on the ballot in the general election, which corresponds to the French second ballot. The system encourages weaker parties to remain in existence in the hope they will be able to win a few seats with the support of their partners on the same side of the political spectrum. It does not ruthlessly weed out the weaker parties, as does the single-member plurality system.

In the Fifth Republic, the two-ballot system for legislative elections has had the effect of reducing the number of effective contending parties to four, two on the left (the Communists and Socialists) and two on the right (the RPR and UDF). However, before the 1986 legislative elections, the then Socialist majority in Parliament succeeded in enacting a new electoral law that returned France briefly to proportional representation. The Socialists wished to distance themselves from the Communists, who had been losing electoral support and no longer appeared to be a very useful electoral alliance partner, while at the same time neutralizing the more effective alliance on the right. The strategy failed to produce a majority that would enable the Socialists to retain control of the government, but it did have the predicted effect of increasing the number of parties in the National Assembly from four to five, with the success of the right-wing National Front in attaining 10 percent of the popular vote, thus entitling them to the same percentage of seats in the Assembly under the proportional rule. Upon regaining a majority in the assembly despite the socialist maneuver, the RPR and UDF gave their support to a reversal of the electoral law change, restoring the single-member district, two-ballot system. The result of the subsequent 1988 legislative election was the virtual elimination of the National Front from the Assembly and therefore a return to the four-party system at the legislative level.

The different effects of the single-member district and proportional representation systems can be seen if we compare indexes of aggregation for our party systems in terms of the extent to which the index changes when we move from measuring the aggregation of electoral support among parties to an index of the aggregation of seats in parliament. Table 4.3 presents indexes of aggregation for both votes and seats for our four Western European countries and Japan in the early 1980s.

The table shows, first of all, that, in terms of the distribution of the popular vote among parties, Britain and West Germany have relatively aggregated party systems, whereas France and Italy have relatively fragmented ones, and the Japanese system falls in between. But, in terms of the seat distribution, the British and French systems appear the most aggregated, the Italian and Japanese the least, and the West German in between. The index of aggregation increases markedly for the British and the French systems, but only very modestly for the Italian and the Japanese, and not at all for the West German. Proportional representation clearly lives up to expectations in accurately translating votes into seats in West Germany, whereas the single-member district plurality system has the expected distortive effect in Britain. Distortion

**Table 4.3 Indexes of Party Aggregation in Elections and in Parliament**

| *Country* | *Year* | *Index (Votes)* | *Index (Seats)* |
|---|---|---|---|
| United Kingdom | 1983 | 14.1 | 30.5 |
| France | 1981 | 8.4 | 14.5 |
| West Germany | 1983 | 12.2 | 12.2 |
| Italy | 1983 | 6.6 | 8.9 |
| Japan | 1983 | 9.1 | 9.8 |

in France occurs in the aggregative direction as well, in this case because the Socialist Party in the 1981 legislative elections was able to outdistance not only its opposition on the right, but also its communist allies on the left. This put it in the position to win more seats than it would be entitled to on the grounds of strict proportionality. The French electoral system, unlike the British, allows more than two parties realistically to contend for voter support, but, like the British—indeed even more so—it piles up seats in the column of any party that is able to put appreciable daylight between it and its nearest rival. Some distortion also occurs in the Italian case, despite the fact Italy has a proportional representation system, because many of the electoral districts are small and do not have enough seats to distribute to the fourth, fifth, or sixth largest parties. This favors the two or three largest parties, especially the Christian Democrats, which obtained 34.3 percent of the popular vote in 1983, but 37.1 percent of the Chamber of Deputies seats.

In the case of Japan, the electoral system combines features of the plurality system and the proportional representation system in ways that favor the largest party, the Liberal Democrats, but that do not tend greatly to distort the translation of its share of the votes into its share of seats. Districts for the House of Representatives are of medium size—three to five seats. The seats are not distributed proportionately among party lists as in West Germany and Italy, but among individual candidates. In a constituency with three seats, the three candidates receiving the highest number of votes are elected, so that candidates of one party are competing against other candidates of the same party, as well as against candidates of other parties. Parties must calculate what share of the vote they can reasonably hope to attain and then put the optimum number of candidates up for election. Too few candidates in a district would mean some other party would gain a seat that might otherwise go to one's own party; but too many candidates would risk losing the extra seat as well, because the vote might be too evenly divided between them, and another party with the optimum number of candidates would win the seat instead. This feature of the Japanese electoral system has tended to freeze the relative proportions of party strength that existed in earlier postwar years, making it very difficult for smaller parties to make up ground on the dominant LDP. Although it does mean a fairly accurate translation of the vote distribution into the seat distribution, the lack of surprises such as are possible in Britain and France is of dubious value, because it is purchased at the cost of interparty competitiveness.

## Coalition Patterns

It should be clear by now that none of the five political party systems can be labeled two-party without serious qualification. On the other hand, two of them—the British and the West German—have at least the potential of behaving very much like two-party systems because each system has two strong parties that can serve as poles of attraction for the coalescence of the smaller parties. In fact, this is clearly what does happen in West Germany, and it potentially could happen in Britain. If one of the characteristics of a viable two-party system is that the two major parties alternate with one another in power, such has been the case in both of countries. In the 13 elections for the House of Commons since World War II, power has changed hands between the Conservatives and Labour six times, most recently in May 1979. Since the Bundestag was first established in 1949, there have been eleven elections in West Germany. Power really has changed hands there only twice. This occurred in 1969, when the Social Democrats came to power in a coalition with the Free Democrats; and in October 1982, when the FDP switched coalition partners a second time, abandoning the center-left coalition headed by Chancellor Helmut Schmidt and joining a new coalition government under CDU leader Helmut Kohl. If the West German electoral system was as sensitive to shifts in support for the two major parties as is the British, the most recent change in power holders probably would have occurred six years earlier, in October 1976, when the Christian Democrats recaptured the lead in popular votes but were outdistanced by the coalition of the Social Democrats and Free Democrats, a result that was reproduced four years later.

Because of its strategic position, the FDP is the key to whether or not power will change hands frequently in West Germany. Most of the time from 1949 to 1966, the FDP was in coalition with the CDU; then, in 1969, it joined a coalition government with the SPD. Between 1980 and 1982, some CDU leaders sought to woo the FDP away from the left-center alliance and into a right-center alliance; and some FDP leaders became increasingly attracted by the prospect. After the formation of the CDU/CSU–FDP government in October 1982, the issue was put to the voters, who approved the change in the March 1983 Bundestag election. Thus, in West Germany there is a two-*tendency* rather than a two-*party* system. Clearly, the strategic moves of the FDP have been taken cautiously at times when FDP leaders calculated the electorate would approve. There are two alternative coalitions; this means that the potential exists for a fairly frequent alternation in power, but that the process is complicated by rigidities in the coalition pattern. But the fact that the FDP has the potential at any time to switch partners means that its current partner must be attentive to its policy preferences. Although the relatively small size of the FDP means that it is always the junior partner, it is a partner with considerable influence. Because of its central position on the left–right ideological spectrum, this influence is usually exercised in the direction of moderation. The FDP is often at odds with the Bavarian CSU, which occupies the far-right position in the governing coalition. Before it switched sides, the FDP was frequently in conflict with the left wing of the SPD, for similar reasons. Chancellors Schmidt and Kohl frequently have had to mediate these disputes.

The arrival of the Green Party on the national scene in West Germany complicates the coalition pattern. Although the percentage of the popular vote gained by the Greens in the 1983 and 1987 elections only barely enabled them to gain seats in the Bundestag (Table 4.2), it had been thought each time that they might take enough votes away from the FDP to close the doors of the lower house to the latter party. If this had occurred, assuming that the CDU/CSU had remained short of a majority of seats, it would have made the discovery of a majority coalition extremely difficult. The Greens have been publicly disdainful of the "parliamentary game" as it is normally played in West Germany as well as in other Western European polyarchies. They presumably would have resisted a coalition with the Social Democrats, something that the right wing of the latter party would not have wanted anyway. A return to the Grand Coalition government of the SPD and the CDU/CSU (1966–69) might then have become necessary, although it would not have been to the taste of many in both parties. As it happened in both elections, the FDP surmounted the 5 percent barrier, and the center-right government was maintained in office. But the Greens have served notice that the future of three-cornered coalition politics in the Federal Republic is very much in doubt.

This uncertainty has increased with the rise of the right-wing Republikaner, foreshadowing a possible five-party system.

Recent developments in Britain have likewise raised doubts as to the continued alternating pattern of the near two-party system there. After the May 1979 election victory of the Conservative Party led by Margaret Thatcher, internal strife in the Labour Party led to a schism in 1981, with four prominent ex-Cabinet ministers on the right of the party resigning their party membership and calling for the formation of a new Social Democratic Party. Later in the year, the new SDP joined the centrist Liberal Party in an electoral arrangement called the Alliance, designed to strengthen both against the two major parties in election contests. The Alliance succeeded in winning several by-election battles to fill vacant seats in Parliament during the next year and appeared to be poised to take enough parliamentary seats in the next general election to deprive the Conservatives of their majority. However, the success of the Thatcher government in bringing down inflation and the British victory in the Falklands (Malvinas) War of the spring of 1982 elevated Mrs. Thatcher's popularity just when the Alliance appeared on the verge of a breakthrough. Perceiving the occasion to be advantageous, the prime minister called an early election in June 1983 and the Conservatives scored an easy victory, raising the number of their seats in the House of Commons from 339 to 397 (Table 4.2).

The Conservatives were actually helped along to their victory by the success of the Alliance in taking votes away from the Labour Party, whose percentage of the popular vote dropped from 36.9 in 1979 to 27.6 in 1983. The Alliance took nearly the same percentage (25.4) as Labour and increased the share the Liberals alone had held in 1979 by 11.6 percent. Had the Alliance been able to gain an appreciably larger share of the vote (30–35 percent), it undoubtedly would have been at the expense of the Conservatives; so, although the Conservatives were helped by the Alliance to a smashing victory in 1983, the government was served notice that further gains by the Alliance could deprive the Conservatives of their majority in the next election, given the effect of the electoral system in exaggerating swings in popular support. Meanwhile, the Labour Party under the youthful leadership of Neil Kinnock, elected leader in October 1983, attempted to repair the damage of the internal party divisions that were so devastating to the party in the period up to June 1983.

But the 1987 general election and its aftermath revealed that the long-term viability of a third force between Labour and Conservatives could not be taken for granted. As the election approached, differences between the Liberals and Social Democrats over policy issues began to surface. The Social Democratic leader, Dr. David Owen, showed considerably greater sympathy for the domestic and foreign policies of the Thatcher government than did the Liberal Party and its leader, David Steel, who were closer to the Labour Party on a number of issues, especially the question of nuclear disarmament. During the election campaign Owen even hinted that, in the absence of a single party majority, the Alliance should consider offering itself to the Conservatives as a coalition partner, whereas Steel insisted that the Alliance parties should keep their options open. Aware of the divisions in the Alliance ranks, many voters who might have voted Alliance a few months earlier turned to the Labour and Conservative parties or stayed away from the polls. As a result, although the Labour Party made modest gains, the Conservatives did not lose electoral ground, and they retained a considerable majority in Parliament (Table 4.2).

Neil Kinnock, leader of the British Labour Party, shown at the October 1983 Labour Conference, where he was elected to the leadership at the age of 41.

Following the 1987 election, the conflict between the Alliance leaders expanded into a conflict over the future of the Alliance itself. The Liberals remained fairly cohesive, but the Social Democrats split into two factions—the supporters and the opponents of David Owen and the positions he had taken during the election. Owen's opponents called for a fusion of the two parties into one, thus ending the confusion that had reduced voter support in the recent election. In this they had the support of most Liberals. Owen and his supporters preferred to hold onto a separate Social Democratic party. As a result, the SDP split, with the anti-Owenites joining the Liberals in a new party called the Social and Liberal Democrats (SLD), or "Democrats" for short. Owen remains the leader of what is left of the Social Democrats, which was reduced by the election and by defections to only three members of Parliament. If we drop this minority of a minority from consideration, Britain still appears to have a three-party system, but the "third party" in the center is considerably weaker than it was not too long ago.

In Italy and Japan, it is not clear whether there is even the potential for alternation between the two leading parties. The Christian Democrats in Italy have governed either alone or in coalition since 1946. The Communists have not had a share of power since 1947 and, until the mid-1970s, there was little likelihood that they would regain it. Until 1962, the Christian Democrats relied on the support of smaller parties in the center and on the right to maintain their majority. Then, the coalition pattern shifted to the left, with the Socialists replacing the Liberals as the principal coalition partner. Unable to gain a majority in their own right and unwilling to turn either to the Communists on the far left or to the neo-fascist MSI on the far right, the Christian Democrats and Socialists became virtual prisoners of one another, although the former were clearly the senior partner. Both parties were divided internally over whether to keep the coalition alive.

Finally, in 1974, the Socialists abandoned their partners and joined the Communists in opposition. This left the Christian Democrats without a majority. They continued on for several months as a minority government but were finally forced to call new elections for June 1976. Both of the major parties gained or maintained strength, whereas some of the smaller parties lost ground. But the parliamentary situation remained basically unchanged. A new Christian Democratic government was formed with the tacit willingness of the Communists to allow it some breathing space in exchange for a more progressive program. Following the June 1979 election in which the PCI lost twenty-seven Chamber of Deputies seats, a Christian Democratic–Socialist coalition again became possible. This is what was governing Italy in the 1980s, the Communists having returned to the role of constructive opposition. The principal innovation in the 1980s was the selection of non-DC leaders as prime minister. Before the 1983 election, the office was held briefly by Republican Giovanni Spadolini. From that election (in which the Socialists gained nine seats) until 1987, PSI leader Bettino Craxi was prime minister. In these cases the Christian Democrats supported the government in Parliament and held the largest number of ministerial posts. Since June 1987, the DC has again held the prime ministership, while governments have succeeded one another as coalitions of the same so-called pentarchy of five centrist parties—the Socialists, the Republicans, the Social Democrats, and the Liberals, as well as the DC. Although the present system works, the Italian party system remains fraught with uncertainty for the future. It is not really a two-tendency system of the type found in Great Britain and West Germany. There may be two political parties that are numerically superior, but no mechanism has yet been worked out by which there can be an orderly transfer of power as there was in West Germany in the late 1960s and early 1980s. Nevertheless, the Socialists have been gaining ground on the Communists over recent elections, and one might foresee the time, perhaps in the 1990s, when they will replace the PCI as the second largest party. As they have a greater potential for forming coalitions with smaller parties other than the Communists and the Christian Democrats, an alternative coalition headed by the Socialists may someday come to power, finally relegating the DC to unaccustomed opposition status.

There are a number of similarities between the Japanese and the Italian party systems, not the least of which is the predominant role of one party of the center-right. Like the Christian Democrats in Italy, the Liberal Democratic Party (LDP) in Japan has not been out of power for more than three decades. In Italy, in fact, the DC has been in power for more than four decades, but the Liberal Democrats in Japan did not merge into their present identity until 1955. However, since doing so, they have been able to govern most of the time by themselves, without the need for coalition partners. In the early years, as in Italy, the two strongest Japanese opposition parties were the Communists (JCP) and the Socialists (JSP). Unlike the Italian left, the Socialists have been stronger electorally than the Communists and are the second largest party in Japan in terms of both voting support and seats in Parliament. But partly because of the rigidities imposed by the electoral system discussed in the last section, the JSP has remained frozen at a level of support far below that of the LDP. For this reason, writers in the 1950s and 1960s referred to the Japanese system as a "one-and-one-half-party system."

There are two reasons why the term "one-and-one-half parties" is misleading. It is especially so today, but has always been so in a sense, because of the factionalized nature of the leading Japanese parties, and especially the LDP. As noted earlier in the chapter, another way in which the Japanese party system resembles the Italian is in the personalized factionalism of the parties. The LDP is said to consist of some four or five factions, each identified with one of the principal leaders of the party.[15] These leaders vie with one another for positions in the government, especially for the top prize of prime minister. In turn, their supporters among the LDP members of Parliament (Dietmembers) and supporters among regional and local-level politicians compete with one another on an interfactional basis for lower-level elected offices. The system for electing Dietmembers, described in the preceding section, contributes to the interfactional competition, because, as noted, voters choose not only between parties, but between competing candidates of the same party. Given the relatively fixed ratio of seats between the parties from one Diet to the next, it can be seen that, for Japanese who follow politics closely, the contest among LDP factions for Diet seats is more fascinating than the interparty contest. It is only a mild exaggeration to say that, far from having a highly aggregated party system with one dominating party, Japan really has an extremely pluralistic multiparty system, if we imagine each of the within-party factions as a party in itself. Nevertheless, when it comes to governing the country, the factions of the LDP are sufficiently cohesive that the party's monopoly of power is not threatened by such intraparty pluralism.

Also militating against the "one-and-one-half-party" label is the fact that the number of political parties with significant shares of votes and seats has grown over the years since the label seemed most applicable. After the merger of the Liberal Party and the Democratic Party into the LDP in 1955, Japan had only three national parties of significance—the LDP, the JSP, and the JCP—and of these, the Communists held only two Diet seats. In the 1960 election a fourth party emerged with seventeen seats, the Democratic Socialist Party, a right-wing offshoot of the JSP. This four-party system persisted in the Diet until the arrival with the 1967 election of the Clean Government Party, or Komeito. All five of these parties remain in the Diet today, all of them capable of capturing at least 10 percent of the popular vote and at least twenty-five seats in Parliament. In addition, a breakaway party from the LDP, the New Liberal Club (NLC), obtained representation in the Diet beginning in 1976. With that breakaway, enough seats were taken away from the LDP to threaten its ability to retain a majority in Parliament. In the latter 1970s and in the early 1980s, for the first time the LDP was forced to govern as a minority government and, for a time, even as a coalition government, with at least the token incorporation of a few NLC ministers. Although the LDP majority was regained in 1986, the loss of the long-standing certainty that there will always be a majority makes the "one-and-one-half-party" label a dubious one when applied to Japan today.

Curiously, although France does not have two dominant parties (as West Germany and Great Britain do), something like a two-tendency system has emerged, with a fairly stable alliance on the right facing a fairly stable alliance on the left. Part of the reason for the two-tendency system lies in the two-ballot-type election for both president and legislative representatives that encourages electoral alliances. As is discussed at some length in Chapter 5, France's system of government differs from the parliamentary regimes of the four other countries. There are both an elected president and an elected legislative body. Because they share power, both elections are important. The balance of power established at the last legislative election can be upset by the next presidential election, and vice versa. To reiterate, France is divided into single-member constituencies, as is Great Britain. But a candidate must win a majority of the vote on the first ballot to be elected. Otherwise, there will be a second ballot the following week, during which any candidate who obtained at least 12.5 percent of the registered voters on the first ballot can remain in the race or withdraw. The second ballot operates the same way the single ballot does in Great Britain: Whoever receives a plurality of the vote will be elected for that constituency. The arrangement for the presidential election is similar, except that (1) France is one entire constituency, and (2) the second ballot is automatically a runoff between the two candidates who receive the most votes on the first ballot.

Because no French party is strong enough to win a majority in its own right in the majority of constituencies in legislative elections, the parties need to have allies who will agree with them in advance that there will be only one candidate mutually representing the parties against a common enemy on the second ballot. Traditionally, the left has been better able than the right to work out such arrangements. During the Third Republic (1870–1940), the Socialists and Radicals were quite successful in maintaining discipline between the two ballots. The expectation was that, in any given constituency, whichever candidate, Socialist or Radical, did better on the first ballot, the other would step aside and urge his supporters to vote for the first candidate on the second ballot. In the Fifth Republic, the Socialists and Communists have had a similar agreement. In response, the right has had to work out its own arrangement. From 1967 to 1988, with only one exception (1978) there has been only one candidate of the majority coalition (primarily the Gaullists and the Giscardist liberals) in each constituency on the first ballot.

For the presidential election, such prior agreements are not necessary because all except the two top candidates are automatically eliminated after the first ballot. But there is a special need for unity on both the left and the right. If the parties on one side cannot agree on a common candidate before the first ballot but those on the other side can, the common candidate will far outdistance his rivals on the first ballot so that the parties on the divided side will really have to scramble to try to secure support for the surviving candidate during the two weeks between the first and second ballots. An excellent example is the 1969 presidential election. Georges Pompidou, the only candidate of the right, was facing three rivals of the left and center. Pompidou won nearly twice as many votes as his nearest rival on the first ballot and then went on to win the runoff easily, partly because one of the losing parties on the first ballot, the Communists, refused to support his second-ballot opponent. In 1981, neither the left nor the right presented a single candidate on the first ballot. The failure to do so was more costly to the surviving right-of-center candidate on the second ballot, incumbent President Valery Giscard d'Estaing. His defeated rival, Jacques Chirac, refused to give him a clear endorsement whereas the Communists endorsed François Mitterrand, the eventual victor. Thus, the presidential election as well as the legislative puts a premium on solidarity between the parties on either side.

One must not put too much stress on the importance of the electoral systems in France. The country has had electoral alliances of a fairly stable nature in the past. However, what was truly remarkable in the first twenty-three years of the French Fifth Republic was a stable governing coalition, consisting of Gaullists, Giscardists, and minor partners on the center right. At least three factors were responsible for this: (1) the strong leadership exercised by General de Gaulle in the early years of the Fifth Republic; (2) the superior electoral position of the Gaullists, which enabled them to play the role of senior partner, rewarding their allies for loyalty; and (3) the fact that the office of president of the Republic is the preeminent prize to be won and that, because important decision-making powers are concentrated in the president's hands, the coalition partners must mute their dissent.

With the capture in 1981 of the presidency and a majority in the National Assembly, the Socialists under François Mitterrand found themselves in a position similar to that enjoyed by the Gaullists between 1968 and 1974. Strictly speaking, it would not have been necessary for the Socialists to offer their Communist electoral allies a share of power, because the Socialists claimed a parliamentary majority in their own right. However, concern for maintaining Communist cooperation in the trade union movement was a potent reason for Mitterrand to offer the Communists four seats in his first cabinet (headed by his fellow Socialist Pierre Mauroy as prime minister). The positions were filled by relatively junior members of the PCF leadership, and they were not the most prominent or strategically significant ministerial offices. However, inclusion in the Socialist-dominated government meant that the Communists had to support that government's domestic and foreign policy initiatives. This they did with little public dissent for the first year of the Mitterrand presidency. But as his domestic policy began to move away from an initial reflationary and redistributive strategy and his pro-Western, anti-Soviet inclinations came into sharper focus, criticism from PCF leaders outside the government and communist trade union leaders began to mount. By mid-1984, the Communists were leading an outcry against the industrial restructuring carried on by the government (see Chapter 6) that was acknowledged to be increasing the already high level of unemployment. When, in July 1984, Mitterrand dismissed Mauroy as prime minister and appointed in his place Laurent Fabius, a young technocrat who had been the minister in charge of the disputed industrial policy, the Communists read the signal correctly and declined to be included in the new government. Thus, the one-sided coalition of the left was dissolved.

By the time the next legislative election was held, in March 1986, both parties of the left had shown losses in electoral strength in the various local elections held in between national elections, as well as in the election to the European Parliament of June 1984. But the decline in Communist Party strength had more than doubled the Socialist decline. On the right, the gains of the mainstream RPR and UDF were less impressive than that of the extreme right party, the National Front. These changes were solidified in the 1986 legislative election, which gave the RPR and UDF a majority in the National Assembly and necessitated a change in government.

Although there was speculation that President Mitterrand would resign with the loss of a Socialist majority in the Assembly, his seven-year term had two years to run, and he preferred *cohabitation* with Gaullist leader Chirac as prime minister rather than to return to the wilderness of opposition. For the next two years Mitterrand and Chirac shared power in an uneasy division of responsibilities in which, like Charles de Gaulle before him, the president shouldered primary responsibility for foreign affairs and the prime minister was mainly responsible for domestic policy. In some ways, this was like the Grand Coalition of the CDU/CSU and the SPD in West Germany in the 1960s. Only the parties of the extreme left and the extreme right were left outside. Although the Communists only managed to slow down their decline in support as registered in the public opinion polls, the National Front continued its gain, and its leader, Jean-Marie Le Pen, looked like he might be in a position to affect the outcome of the next presidential election. He did not fail to highlight the fact that the parties of the center-left and center-right were, in effect, governing together, applying the term "Gang of Four" to all four of the other parties: not only to Mitterrand's Socialists and to the RPR and UDF, in the coalition government under Chirac, but also to the Communists, which, many of its working-class voters believed, had sold out while its members had been ministers in a government that pursued an economic policy course seen as contributing to the rise in unemployment.

History came close to repeating itself in May 1988, when François Mitterrand won a second term as president, with an enhanced majority over his 1981 margin. Once again, he relied on Communist votes, although they were less numerous than they had been seven years earlier. The RPR and UDF showed greater solidarity behind Chirac as their second-ballot candidate than they had behind Giscard, who was not a candidate in this election. But Le Pen succeeded in capturing 14 percent of the first-ballot vote, and many of his supporters may have abstained on the second ballot or even shifted their votes to Mitterrand. Mitterrand appointed moderate socialist Michel Rocard as his prime minister, and it became his role to form a government that contained enough politically neutral or centrist ministers to ensure that the additional votes could be found either to the left (PCF) or to the right in order to get legislative measures through Parliament. Once again, Mitterrand dissolved the National Assembly and legislative elections were held in the month following the presidential elections. However, this time his Socialists failed to obtain an absolute majority in the National Assembly, falling thirteen seats short. Thus, the Rocard government is technically a minority government, rather than a coalition government, because only one party as such—the PS—is included within it.

## Conclusion

Despite the various dissimilarities among our five political party systems, they do appear to fall into three separate categories, based on the distinctions by Giovanni Sartori discussed earlier in this chapter. In three of the cases, there is sharp, clear-cut competition between left and right, whether it is a case of a party on the left facing a party on the right or of a coalition of parties facing one party or another coalition. Sartori would call the West German and British cases "moderate pluralism," because they enable one party to control all or most government offices at a given time, but do not prevent the occasional changing of the guard, as there are two parties with this sort of governing potential. It will be recalled that these are the two-party systems with the consistently highest indexes of aggregation. One might ask how Sartori would judge the French system, where, since 1986 at least, there have been three parties of fairly even strength, preventing any single one of them from gaining exclusive control of government. Here there would not seem to be sufficient aggregation, or in Sartori's terms, too much pluralism, especially considering that there are also parties of the far left and far right that limit the options of the larger parties still further. Nevertheless, once formed, coalitions have held together reasonably well in France, including the "coalition" of cohabitation between President Mitterrand and Prime Minister Chirac. And, on the other hand, there have been three changes in power between left and right in the 1980s, which has not occurred in Britain and has happened only once in West Germany during the decade. Therefore, Sartori's term *moderate pluralism* seems applicable.

Actually, the existence of such left–right competition is remarkable when we consider the history of two of these three-party systems—the French and the German. If we go back to the 1920s in Germany, and as recently as the 1950s in France, we see a different sort of party system, one in which power is anchored in the center of the spectrum and opposition comes from the left and right extremes. In the Weimar Republic of Germany, the center parties were committed to the existing democratic regime. But during much of the Republic's life, these parties were scarcely able to maintain majorities in the Reichstag because of the anti-democratic parties on the left and right. A similar situation prevailed in France in the 1950s. For this reason, one has to view the present prospects for a return to center coalitions in France with some misgivings.

Anchoring power in the center of the political spectrum in a coalition of beleaguered parties that are committed to the preservation of the existing regime means there is no possibility of alternating power from left to right. Power remains where it is, or the regime falls. From the voters' standpoint, either they support the coalition in power or they face unknown upheavals. This is really not a choice for many voters who may feel disenchanted with the performance of the governing coalition. Some will abstain; others will vote for one of the parties opposing the governing regime under the assumption that it could not come to power anyway; still others will resign themselves to the continuation of the present regime and will vote accordingly, although not out of any great conviction. Under the circumstances, the disgruntled voter will feel disenfranchised.

This description is not far from the case today in Italy, whose party system comes closest to what Sartori called *extreme pluralism*. The characteristics of this system that keep it out of the moderate pluralism category have not changed appreciably since the early 1960s, when the Socialists were invited into what had theretofore been government anchored on the center-right. Since then it has been government anchored more symmetrically at the center. However, it does not exemplify extreme pluralism to quite the degree the Weimar Republic and the French Fourth Republic did so, because the Christian Democrats have remained easily the strongest party in the system, both in electoral terms and in terms of the position of indispensability they occupy for coalition formation. No party occupied such a position with any consistency in Germany of the 1920s or France of the 1950s. The Italian Christian Democrats have done so for more than forty years.

But the Italian Christian Democrats do not enjoy the same sort of hegemony as that of the Liberal Democratic Party in Japan. In the mid-1970s Sartori employed the term *dominant party system* to characterize Japan. Clearly it falls into a third category. There is pluralism, but not of the kind that allows power to be shared with other parties of any size and strength, let alone to be transferred to another party or coalition of parties entirely. Although our measure of aggregation does not quite capture the fact, because there are five parties that are able to surmount our rather arbitrary 2 percent barrier in Japan, it seems appropriate to consider the Japanese party system to be one of "minimum pluralism." But the loss of the earlier assurance on the part of the LDP that they will always have a working majority in the Diet suggests that the potential for Japan to move to moderate or even extreme pluralism is greater than it was before the late 1970s.

Finally, if the politics of postindustrial society is becoming the politics of "disorganized capitalism," as was broached in Chapters 2 and 3, is it possible that political party systems in postindustrial capitalist societies are becoming "disaggregated" party systems? One way in which this has been happening has been in the tendency of larger parties of the left and right to shed their close ties to segments of society that are themselves no longer as cohesive as they were during the height of industrial maturity. The nexus between working-class voters and democratic socialist parties has been weakened because of (1) the numerical decline of the working class, (2) the decline of working-class support for parties of the left, and (3) the resulting effort of democratic socialist parties to reach out to other classes in society for electoral support. On the right, the most reliable supportive groups for conservative and Christian democratic parties—farmers and the self-employed middle class—have also experienced numerical decline. Although the middle class as a whole has grown, it has been largely a new urbanized middle class, which has shown great volatility in shifting support among parties of the left, center, and right. With minor modifications, these trends are discernible in all five of our countries. Added to this volatility is the appearance of new issues in First World politics, of particular interest to young, well-educated voters. (See Chapter 3.) The cultivation of these trends has had two effects on party systems: It has reduced the percentage of support for the largest political parties in each system, an effect that has been particularly noteworthy in Britain, Italy and Japan; and it has increased the number of viable competitors, as in the case of the rise of the Greens in West Germany and the National Front in France.

## *Suggestions for Further Reading*

**Baerwald, Hans H.** *Party Politics in Japan* (Winchester, Mass.: Allen & Unwin, 1986).

**Bell, D. S., and Byron Criddle.** *The French Socialist Party: Resurgence and Victory* (Oxford: Clarendon Press, 1984).

**Butler, David, and Dennis Kavanagh.** *The British General Election of 1987* (New York: St. Martin's, 1988).

**Daalder, Hans, and Peter Mair,** eds. *Western European Party Systems: Continuity and Change* (London: Sage, 1983).

**Doring, Herbert, and Gordon Smith,** eds. *Party Government and Political Culture in Western Germany* (New York: St. Martin's, 1982).

**Duverger, Maurice.** *Political Parties: Their Organization and Activity in the Modern State*, 2nd English ed., trans. Barbara and Robert North (New York: Wiley, 1959).

**Hrebenar, Ronald J.** *The Japanese Party System: From One-Party Rule to Coalition Government* (Boulder, Colo., and London: Westview, 1986).

**Kavanagh, Dennis.** *Thatcherism and British Politics: The End of Consensus?* (Oxford: Oxford University Press, 1987).

**Lane, Jan-Erik, and Svante O. Ersson.** *Politics and Society in Western Europe* (London: Sage, 1987).

**Merkl, Peter H.,** ed. *Western European Party Systems: Trends and Prospects* (New York: The Free Press, 1980).

**Padgett, Stephen, and Tony Burkett.** *Political Parties and Elections in West Germany: The Search for a New Stability* (New York: St. Martin's, 1986).

**Penniman, Howard H.,** ed. *Italy at the Polls, 1983: A Study of the National Elections* (Washington, D.C.: American Enterprise Institute, 1987).

**Rose, Richard.** *Do Parties Make a Difference?* 2nd ed. (Chatham, N.J.: Chatham House, 1984).

———, ed. *Electoral Behavior: A Comparative Handbook* (New York: The Free Press, 1974).

**Ross, George.** *Workers and Communists in France: From Popular Front to Eurocommunism* (Berkeley: University of California Press, 1982).

**Sartori, Giovanni.** *Parties and Party Systems: A Framework for Analysis* (Cambridge: Cambridge University Press, 1976).

**Wilson, Frank L.** *French Political Parties under the Fifth Republic* (New York: Praeger, 1982).

## *Notes*

1. Giovanni Sartori, *Parties and Party Systems: A Framework for Analysis* (Cambridge: Cambridge University Press, 1976), Ch. 5.
2. Ibid., p. 299.
3. Ibid., p. 128.
4. Ibid., pp. 121–128.
5. For supporting evidence, see Philip E. Converse and Georges Dupeux, "Politicization of the Electorate in France and the United States," in Angus Campbell et al., eds., *Elections and the Political Order* (New York: Wiley, 1966), pp. 269–291.
6. Maurice Duverger, *Political Parties: Their Organization and Activity in the Modern State*, trans. Barbara and Robert North, 2nd English ed. (London: Methuen, 1959), pp. 63–71.
7. Otto Kirchheimer, "The Transformation of the Western European Party Systems," in Joseph LaPalombara and Myron Weiner, eds., *Political Parties and Political Development* (Princeton, N.J.: Princeton University Press, 1966), pp. 177–200.
8. Richard Rose, "Parties, Factions and Tendencies in Britain," in Rose, ed., *Studies in British Politics: A Reader in Political Sociology* (New York: St. Martin's Press, 1966), pp. 314–329.
9. Regarding Italy, see the argument by Joseph LaPalombara in *Democracy, Italian Style* (New Haven, Conn., and London: Yale University Press, 1987).
10. S. A. Walkland, "Economic Planning and Dysfunctional Politics in Britain 1945–1983," in A. M. Gamble and S. A. Walkland, *The British Party System and Economic Policy 1945–1983* (Oxford: Clarendon, 1984), pp. 92–151.
11. Sartori, *Parties and Party Systems*, Ch. 6.
12. Ibid., pp. 131–145.
13. Lawrence Mayer, "A Note on the Aggregation of Party Systems," in Peter H. Merkl, ed., *Western European Party Systems: Trends and Prospects* (New York: The Free Press, 1980), p. 517.
14. The height of each party's column in Figure 4.2 is based on its share of the vote in the three most recent legislative elections.
15. Ronald J. Hrebenar, *The Japanese Party System: From One-Party Rule to Coalition Government* (Boulder, Colo., and London: Westview, 1986), p. 248.

CHAPTER 5

# THE DISTRIBUTION OF GOVERNMENT POWER

In this chapter we consider most directly the question of how power is distributed in First World polyarchies. Chapter 6 discusses how power is used to affect the distribution of well-being; Chapter 7 assesses the outcomes of these uses of power. In this chapter, for the most part, we examine the formal power relationships among units of government. Wherever informal forces, especially the system of political parties, come into play and affect the working of the formal mechanisms, this is taken into account. Our focus is on those institutions and roles that, legally speaking, are *supposed* to have the power to make decisions for society as a whole. In First World polyarchies, the distinction between formal and informal power structures is somewhat easier to make than in the case of political systems in the Second and Third Worlds. Western polyarchies are characterized by an adherence to the form of their constitution and organic laws to a greater extent than is true elsewhere. A description of the forms does provide some understanding of the way a political system works in the First World, although it is certainly not the entire story.

In analyzing both the formal and the informal distributions of power in a country, it is convenient to make a distinction between what might be called the *vertical* and the *horizontal* distributions. Vertically, power is distributed among the various levels of government—national, regional, and local. We are concerned with the vertical distribution of power in the United States whenever we talk about the system of federalism—the distribution of power between the federal government and the states—or when we discuss the problem of the cities attempting to gain financial assistance from the federal or the state governments. The horizontal distribution of power, on the other hand, exists among units of government that are all located at the same level. Power, as we know, is distributed at the federal level in the United States among the three branches of government—legislative, executive, and judicial. Further, each of these branches has subunits so that power of the branch itself is further distributed. For example, the federal executive is divided into a multitude of agencies that vary widely in the amount of power they exercise and in their relationship to the White House. Let us begin our discussion of the formal distribution of power by seeing how our four European political systems and Japan divide power horizontally at the national level of government.

## *Horizontal Power Distribution*

### Parliamentary Systems

**Britain, Italy, and Japan.** In the first place, it is important to understand that most Western European political systems differ from the American political system in that power is distributed horizontally according to the principle of *parliamentarism*. Parliamentarism exists in a relatively uncomplicated form in Great Britain, Italy, and Japan. It is qualified in certain respects in West Germany, and it has been partially displaced in favor of the alternative system of presidentialism in France. Figure 5.1 depicts basic formal differences among British parliamentarism, American presidentialism, and the mixed French system.

In a parliamentary system of government, unlike the presidential type of system, the voters do not directly elect the executive head of government. They elect only the members of the legislative body, called Parliament. The head of government, usually called the prime minister (chancellor in West Germany), is then chosen on the basis of the distribution of political party strength in the newly elected Parliament. The prime minister must be someone who is able to hold together a majority of members of the Parliament. He or she will be the leader of the party with the most seats in Parliament, or perhaps the leader of a smaller party capable of forming a coalition with other parties large enough to ensure majority support for the prime minister. The prime minister will then form a cabinet, consisting of heads of government departments (ministries) and drawn usually from among leading members of the party or the coalition of parties that the prime minister leads in Parliament. The prime minister and the cabinet may continue in office as long as they retain the voting support (confidence) of a majority of the Parliament. If they do not lose majority support, they may stay in office until the end of the Parliament's term (four or five years). Should the majority be lost on a vote of confidence or a vote of nonconfidence, the prime minister will resign or ask the head of state to dissolve Parliament, meaning that new elections will be held before the end of the Parliament's term.[1] Resignation may also come as a result of shifts in parliamentary support that are not formally registered in votes of confidence or nonconfidence.

The characteristics of parliamentarism as seen in Great Britain, Italy, and Japan are such that, in a formal sense, these three systems operate in an essentially similar fashion, but there are certain informal differences that make their actual functioning different in important respects. In all three, there is an organic relationship between the composition of the legislative body and the composition of the leading executive body, the cabinet. In each country, if a single political party wins a majority of the seats in Parliament at the general election, it has the right to form a cabinet on its own without seeking coalition partners. In fact, this happens regularly in Great Britain and Japan. It has happened only once since World War II in Italy—in 1948—when the Christian Democratic Party won a slim majority in both houses of Parliament, the Chamber of Deputies (the lower house) and the Senate (the upper house). Since that high point, the Christian Democrats have declined in strength. Although still the largest party in Parliament, they must find coalition partners to have the

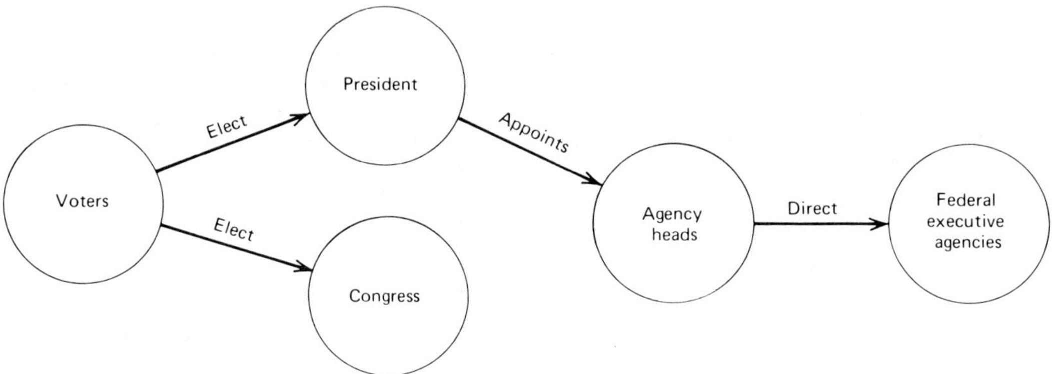


The American presidential system

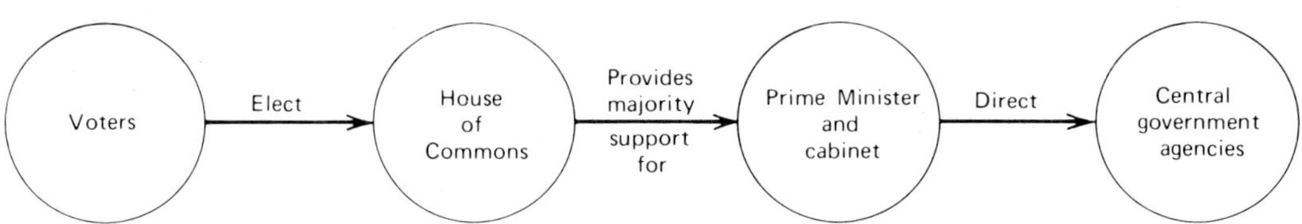


The British parliamentary system

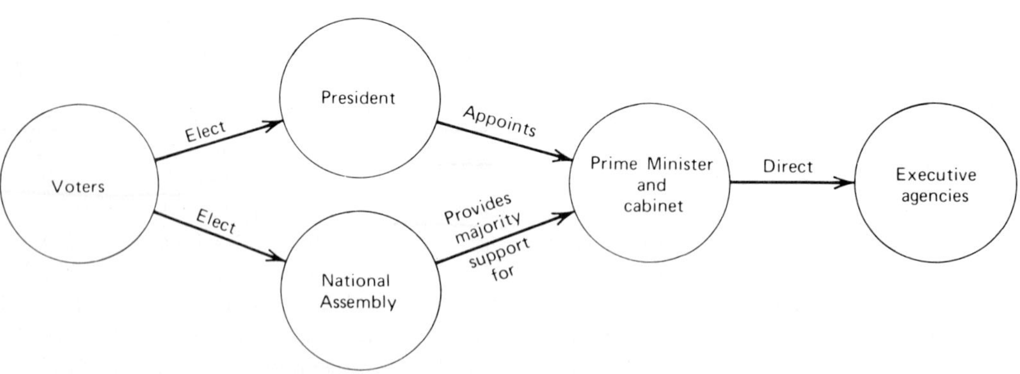


The mixed French system

*Figure 5.1* Essential elements of three systems of government.

majority necessary to form and sustain a government.

In parliamentary countries generally, if a single party has won a majority, there will probably be a single-party cabinet. If a coalition of parties wins the majority, either the cabinet will be a coalition cabinet, made up of leaders of the parties in the coalition, or it will be a minority cabinet, like the Labour government in Great Britain from 1976 to 1979. The Labour Party held office by itself but required the support of other parties to remain in power. A similar situation has existed in both Japan and Italy at various times in recent years.

In comparison with the American presidential system of government, leadership of government in parliamentary systems is exercised by cabinets as bodies that *collectively* make decisions and are *collectively* responsible to Parliament. The prime minister may be, and often is, the strongest figure in the cabinet. In Great Britain (but usually not in Italy or Japan) some prime ministers have even been dominant figures. But political preeminence is not inherent in the office to the degree it is in the American presidency. Such generalizations, of course, are subject to considerable modification when specific personalities are compared. Compared with Helmut Kohl, Konrad Adenauer was a dominant chancellor. Compared with Margaret Thatcher, her predecessor James Callaghan was simply "one among equals," in his cabinet. But an indicator of the greater importance of the American chief executive is that there is an entire subfield of American political science that makes such comparative judgments about, say, Lyndon B. Johnson versus Jimmy Carter. A similar preoccupation is not found among West German or British political scientists, let alone Japanese or Italian.

The British and Italian lower houses of parliaments have five-year terms, at the end of which elections must be held. In Japan, the Diet has a maximum four-year term. If, however, a cabinet loses its majority in Parliament, it has the option of calling new elections, as Harold Wilson, then Great Britain's prime minister, did in September 1974; or it may resign and allow a new cabinet to be formed, as has happened frequently in Italy.[2] Thus, elections may be held before the end of the term, depending on the political situation and the judgment of the leaders of the existing cabinet.

Westminster Palace, London, which houses the mother of parliaments, the famous Big Ben clock and tower.

Suppose that the result of an election is not a clear-cut one. Neither the February 1974 British election, the 1980 Japanese election, nor the 1987 Italian election produced an automatic majority. What then? Who decides what cabinet should be chosen? The place to look is the internal deliberating processes of the leading political parties: the Labour and Conservative parties in Great Britain; the Christian Democrats, the Socialists, and several smaller parties in Italy; and the Liberal Democratic Party in Japan. Formally, there is a sort of referee, although it would be misleading to emphasize the importance of this role. In all three countries, there is a head of state who performs essentially ceremonial and nondiscretionary functions. In Great Britain and Japan, it is the hereditary head of state, the queen in the United Kingdom and the emperor in Japan. In Italy, the head of state role is played by the president of the Republic. Parliamentary heads of state are to be distinguished from the political leader of the country—the head of government, called the prime minister in all three countries. Two of these rulers, of course, gained their positions through the accident of birth. Because the monarchical principle is so far removed from late twentieth-century democratic norms, it is unthinkable for the sovereign to exercise real political discretion. The Conservative and Labor parties in Britain elect their leaders, as does the Liberal Democratic Party in Japan. Thus, there is no scope for the hereditary sovereign to exercise a personal choice in naming the prime minister.

The president of the Italian Republic, on the other hand, is usually a politician of some prominence who has been elected to that office by members of the two houses of Parliament voting jointly. It is expected that the president will defer judgment to the leaders of the party (or parties) in power. During the life of the Italian Republic this principle has been followed, although with some notable exceptions. However, the extreme polarization of the Italian party system, as outlined in the previous chapter, means that the president can play a useful role in bringing the parties together behind a choice of one of their leaders for prime minister. One can even imagine a potential role for the president as a safety valve, a national asset held in reserve in case of total stalemate. Should the party leaders be incapable of steering Italy out of one of her recurrent political crises, it might become necessary for the president of the Republic to take a more active part. The precedent, however, is ominous. It was the head of state in an earlier era, King Victor Emmanuel III, who handed power to Mussolini. This memory undoubtedly has played a part in convincing the leaders of the coalition parties to keep the reins of power in their hands.

One additional formal difference between the systems should be noted. Although the British, the Italian, and the Japanese parliaments are bicameral—that is, divided into two houses—the upper houses differ considerably in power. The House of Lords in Great Britain is a body of residual importance whose principal function may be to enable leading politicians, government servants, businesspersons, and trade union leaders to be honored for service to their country. Such an honor is likely to be given rather late in life, at a time when the individual is handing over responsibilities to younger colleagues. Elevation from the House of Commons to the House of Lords is actually a sort of political demotion when viewed in these terms. The Lords debate and amend bills coming from Commons, but they seldom refuse them passage, and the amendments stay in effect only if Commons (which usually means the cabinet) accepts them graciously. The Lords usually avoid direct confrontations with the majority in Commons. The upper chamber suffered two reductions in its power in this century (1911 and 1949) because the cabinet of the left felt it was necessary to overcome the real or potential opposition by the Conservative-dominated Lords to its legislative program. The clue to the weakness of the Lords is that, because of the hereditary principle, it has a permanent Conservative majority.[3] This has been tempered somewhat since the 1950s by the creation of life peers, new members of the House of Lords whose titles will not pass on to their heirs. Although many of these are Labour and Alliance peers or political independents, the Conservative majority remains. Thus, the composition of the House of Lords does not reflect changes in popular support for the parties. Its wishes are not taken into account when a new cabinet is being formed or when it is being decided whether the present one should stay in power.

By contrast, the Italian Senate is nearly a coequal of the lower chamber, the Chamber of Deputies. Legislation must pass both houses; the Senate can just as easily be a stumbling block as the Chamber. The cabinet must retain the support of the Senate as well as the Chamber to stay in power. Nevertheless, having two chambers in Italy is actually rather arbitrary and of limited significance for two reasons. First, the electoral systems for the two chambers are similar; they are both based essentially on proportional representation. (See Chapter 4.) Whenever one house is dissolved, the other is as well; therefore, elections are held at the same time, and the results are usually quite close. Thus, it is possible to form a cabinet on the basis of the distribution in either chamber without doing injustice to the distribution in the other. Second, major decisions about the disposition of legislative matters are made at party headquarters among leaders representing factions of the party in both chambers. A decision made for the party, whether Christian Democrats, Communists, or Socialists, will generally be binding on members of the party in both chambers, and the voting on legislation cannot be expected to differ significantly in either house.[4] This is not to suggest that there is never disagreement between the two; it is still important to recognize the formal coequal status of the Italian Senate in comparing its power with that of the House of Lords.

As for the Japanese upper house, the House of Councillors, it is an elective body, like the House of Representatives, the lower Diet chamber. But its composition differs from that of the House of Representatives, as there is a different type of electoral system—one that favors the ruling LDP even more than does the electoral system for the lower house. Like the House of Lords, the House of Councillors has only a delaying power, which is used sparingly, because the government is able to ensure through LDP party discipline that both houses will comply with its wishes.

When one turns fully to the informal aspects of the horizontal distribution of power, especially when one asks about the role of party systems, there is a sharp contrast between Great Britain's near two-party system and the Italian multiparty system, with Japanese legislative behavior resembling the British more than the Italian. The similarity between Britain and Japan is especially apparent in the high level of party discipline in Parliament. Members of parliamentary parties in both countries vote as blocs most of the time. If the control exercised by party leaders over these legislators shocks American students, they should remember that party discipline in legislative bodies is generally greater in Western Europe than it is in the United States. Great Britain is certainly no exception. As in Japan, the many in the major parties are directed by the few who are party leaders, although the proper term for Japan is *faction leaders*. The chief difference lies in the greater role the British members of Parliament (MPs) actually play in choosing their leaders and in their capacity to withhold their approval, forcing the leaders to bend to their will. But this rank-and-file control is not exercised very often. On a day-to-day basis, the leadership formulates policy, communicates it to the rank and file, and expects to see them filing into the appropriate division lobbies when a vote is called.

Mention should be made of the method of voting on important questions in the House of

Commons. Figure 5.2 shows the physical layout of the House. In contrast to the houses of Congress in the United States as well in most other parliamentary bodies, MPs do not sit in rows facing a common podium. Instead, they sit in rows of benches facing each other. On one side are the governing party's benches; on the other are the opposition's. Third- and fourth-party MPs sit on the opposition's side. Debate flows back and forth between the two sides. Much of it is informal and impromptu, a characteristic that is facilitated by the small size of the chamber because there are fewer seats than there are MPs.

On either side of the chamber are rooms known as division lobbies. MPs vote by filing into the appropriate lobbies whenever the division bell rings. The bell can be heard throughout Westminster Palace, in nearby MPs' offices, and out on the street as well, so that any MP in the vicinity is alerted. Actually, the party whips will have informed MPs when to expect the division. It is their job to see that the troops are marshaled whenever a vote is important. If the balance between the two parties is very close, MPs on both sides remain away only at the risk of their leaders' severe dipleasure. But even if there is a comfortable majority, both sides will want to make a good showing. Too many absentees will indicate weakness in the current leadership's support on the back benches. The convenient aspect of the division lobbies from the leadership's point of view is that the whips can station themselves at the heads of the lobbies and make sure that their back-benchers are whipped in. To file into the opposite lobby takes an act of overt defiance, which most MPs would rather avoid most of the time.

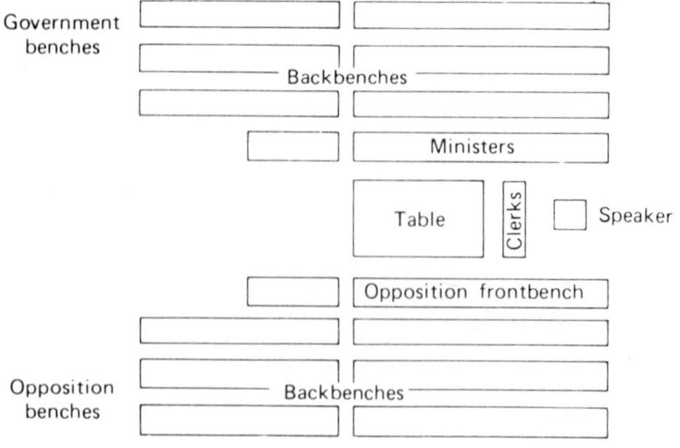


*Figure 5.2* Floor plan of the House of Commons.

However, too much should not be made of these physical aspects. Most observers find two other explanations for party cohesion in the House of Commons more persuasive.[5] In the first place, Labour and Conservative MPs are team players. The results of the divisions are like cricket scores. It looks better for the party in power to win a division by, say, 330 to 261, than by 305 to 286. The latter score would be at least a moral victory for the other side if the normal spread between the two parties is wider. Of course, if the party balance in Commons is very close, a poor result could actually mean the government's defeat. (This happened to the James Callaghan government in the spring of 1979.) Such a result on a motion of confidence would force the government either to resign or to call a new election. Although the latter is the more likely choice in Great Britain, it could still mean the loss of power if the electorate so decides (as also happened in 1979). Taking all these factors into consideration, the team player usually goes along with his or her mates.

A second consideration is the practical consequence for the MP of violating party discipline. If an MP should lose the backing of his or her political party, he or she would be in the political wilderness. Candidates without the backing of one of the major parties stand little chance in a general election in Great Britain. Although it does not happen very often that a party in Parliament expels an MP from its ranks, it is possible that an MP who votes with the opposition on a crucial division will be dropped by the local party constituency association in favor of another candidate.[6] Moreover, within the parliamentary party, potential dissidents who are ambitious for higher office may find their path blocked by the leadership whom they have defied and who controls access to government office. However, despite all of that, party cohesion in the House of Commons declined in the 1970s. Back-bench dissent, or voting in the opposite lobby, occurred within the majority party on a number of important issues, causing difficulties for both Labour and Conservative governments. Party cohesion has generally held on motions of confidence and nonconfidence, but the dissent registered on important policy questions probably reflects a greater spirit of independence among back-bench MPs and, in the case of the Labour Party, serious within-party conflict over domestic and foreign policy.[7]

Japanese Dietmembers are likewise known for the high level of party cohesion they display in Parliament. However, in both the Japanese and Italian legislative bodies, votes are taken only after elaborate negotiations among factional leaders have been undertaken and common party positions worked out.[8] The result is a much more cumbersome process of *intra*party deliberations that must go on before a majority can be built behind a single position. The individual Italian or Japanese legislator may be able to influence this process, as can the MP in Great Britain with respect to particular policy areas where the interests he or she represents are at stake. But, for the most part, the legislator is dependent on his or her factional and party leaders to get results. Whether or not the leaders can get results depends on the stands of other leaders and on the overall distribution of party strength in Parliament. However, once the decisions are made, in Japan cohesion will hold, whereas this has not been a certainty in Italy. This is because, until the practice was abolished in 1988, important votes in the Italian Parliament were taken by secret ballot, giving individual members of parties the opportunity to vote in unexpected ways. So-called sharpshooters were free to vote against a government in which their party participated—indeed, voting counter to the way the party leaders had pledged that the party would vote.[9] This is a principal reason that cabinets in the Italian Republic have had an average life of only ten months.[10]

When a British or Japanese party leadership comes to power after gaining a solid electoral victory, it can proceed to put its program into effect. However, this certainty is not possible in a party system like Italy's where no single party can hope to gain a majority. Even in a country like the Netherlands, where the differences between the parties on substantive issues are not as great as in Italy, it usually takes several weeks or even months of negotiation before a governing coalition can be formed with an agreed-on program. But in Italy, the members of a new coalition cabinet have come to power with only the vaguest idea of a common program. Policy tends to emerge on an ad hoc basis in response to urgent necessities when decisions can no longer be postponed. Under similar circumstances in France in the 1950s, the political system was characterized as *immobile*; and this term accurately describes the situation in Italy today.

**West German Parliamentarism.** Immobility of the above type had plagued the earlier German attempt to construct a polyarchy—the Weimar Republic (1919–1933). Just as in the Italian Republic today, a multiplicity of political parties had hampered policymaking. As was shown in Chapter 4, the West German party system has come a long way from the extreme multipartism of the Weimar period. As of 1949, however, when the Basic Law (constitution) of the new Federal Republic was being formulated, it was not at all clear whether or not there would be the same multiplicity of parties as in the past. Accordingly, the framers of the Basic Law added certain complications to the model of a parliamentary system to prevent the potential destabilizing effects of a multiparty system. Because of the subsequent consolidation in the party system, these complications have not been as significant in the Bonn Republic as they might otherwise have been.

The two most important additions to the normal rules of a parliamentary system are the so-called constructive vote of nonconfidence and the important role played by the upper chamber of Parliament, the *Bundesrat* (Federal Council). In most parliamentary systems, when the cabinet decides that a vote in Parliament will be a motion of confidence, it must resign or call for new elections if defeated. Under the West German Basic Law, resignation is forced on the federal chancellor (the West German counterpart of a prime minister) only if the vote of no confidence has been on an opposition motion that names a new chancellor and passes by a majority vote. If this does not occur, the chancellor may remain in office even if his or her majority has been lost on the vote of confidence, or he or she may call for new elections. This was the situation facing Chancellor Willy Brandt in 1972. He had lost his majority in the lower house, the *Bundestag* (the Federal Diet), but no alternative chancellor could secure a majority. Therefore, Brandt called for new elections, which his coalition (SPD-FDP) won comfortably; this changed the balance in the Bundestag in his favor and gave him a reliable majority. In October 1982, a constructive vote of no confidence was adopted by the Bundestag for the first time in the history of the Bonn Republic. SPD Chancellor Helmut Schmidt was defeated and a new chancellor, Helmut Kohl, leader of the CDU, was elected in his place.[11]

Helmut Kohl, the West German chancellor, addressing the lower house of the Parliament, the Bundestag. Former Chancellor Helmut Schmidt is in the background.

Both the 1972 and 1982 cases show the importance of having few political parties in West Germany. The calculations necessary to avoid a loss of confidence in the first place or, once it is lost, to find a new majority are much easier to make when there are only four political parties operating at the national level. The number of potential defectors from a governing coalition are far fewer than in the Weimar Republic, and there are fewer alternatives to any given coalition. As noted in Chapter 4, the appearance of the Greens as a fourth party in the Bundestag complicates matters. However, had the extreme multiparty system prevailed after 1949, it is conceivable that the provisions of the Basic Law on motions of confidence would have been used more often. This might have increased the importance of the president of the Republic, who plays a neutral role in the political process, as does the Italian president, unless a stalemate arises between the chancellor and the Bundestag.

The role of the upper chamber, the Bundesrat, is a unique feature of the Basic Law. Its composition is based neither on the hereditary principle that prevails in the House of Lords nor on direct popular election found in the Italian Senate and the Japanese House of Councillors. It reflects the fact, as is outlined later, that West Germany is a federal republic and, therefore, gives an important place in its system to its regional units of government, the *Länder*. Members of the Bundesrat are actually members of the Land cabinets who are sent to Bonn to represent the interests of their governments in the upper house of Parliament. The Bundesrat enjoys an absolute veto over the acts of the Bundestag whenever they directly affect Land interests. This is true for more than half the bills adopted by the lower house because much federal legislative policy is actually administered by the Länder. On other legislative measures, the Bundesrat has a suspensory veto, meaning that bills must be repassed by the Bundestag by a majority (in certain cases by a two-thirds majority) if they are to become law without the Bundesrat's consent.

These powers actually put the Bundesrat in a strong position, not only with respect to the Bundestag itself, but also with respect to the federal chancellor and the cabinet, who reflect the wishes of a majority in the Bundestag. When the party balance in the Bundesrat differs from that in the Bundestag, as it did before 1982, the opposition party or coalition is in a position to stymie the actions desired by the party or coalition in power. Until 1982, the situation was one in which the SPD-FDP coalition with a majority in the lower house faced a majority of CDU/CSU votes in the upper house. This is all the more likely to occur because, unlike the case of Italy, members of the upper house are not chosen at the same time as those of the lower house. Land elections, which determine the composition of Land governments, are staggered at different times during the period between federal elections. This partial veto power held by the upper chamber in West Germany (potentially, at least) interferes with the responsibility of a cabinet to its majority in the lower one. A cabinet could bend to the wishes of the majority in the upper house and find itself losing the confidence of the majority in the lower house. When this danger exists, the party or coalition in power has no choice but to give the opposition a role in its policymaking deliberations.

Thus, the Basic Law has some built-in features that could, under certain circumstances, produce instability or immobility. On the other hand, a cabinet can keep going despite the loss of its Bundestag majority as long as it has the support of the federal president and the Bundesrat. But what the framers of the Basic Law may have gained in flexibility, they seem to have lost in terms of the parliamentary theory of democracy. Neither the president nor the Bundesrat is directly elected by the people. Still, because the party system has permitted stable government, power has been concentrated in the chancellor and the cabinet at least as much as in the case of the British prime minister and cabinet.[12] Once again, a high degree of party discipline works to the advantage of party leaders. Because they have the support of a majority in the popular house of Parliament and because this majority has been chosen from essentially only two alternatives by the voters, the democratic link is there.

## The Mixed French System

From the establishment of the Third Republic in the 1870s until the fall of the Fourth Republic in 1958 (except for the brief interlude of German occupation, 1940–1944), France, too, had a parliamentary system of government. However, because of the fragmented party system, cabinet coalitions were unstable and government was weak throughout the Third and Fourth Republics. The Fifth Republic, instituted under the leadership of Charles de Gaulle in 1958, represents a departure from French parliamentary traditions in a number of important respects. As the Fifth Republic has matured, it has developed features that are more typical of a presidential system—as in the United States. The result has been a combination of constitutional elements.

As Figure 5.1 indicates, French voters elect both the lower house of Parliament (the National Assembly) and the head of state (the president of the Republic). This feature of the Fifth Republic constitution resembles the American presidential system, as does the fact that the terms of the president and the National Assembly do not coincide, the former being elected for a seven-year term and the latter for five years. On the other hand, like the monarch in the British parliamentary system, the French president appoints a prime minister, whose role is to preside over the cabinet. In the French case this is not a mere formality: The French president exercises discretion in this choice. However, the choice must be one that can be supported by the National Assembly, because the prime minister can be forced to resign if a motion of censure is adopted by the Assembly. This could potentially neutralize the president's control over the prime minister, although the president has the power in such cases to dissolve the National Assembly, forcing a new legislative election that might return a majority favorable to a prime minister of the president's choosing. Circumstances such as these have occurred three times in the history of the Fifth Republic—in 1962, when Prime Minister Georges Pompidou, appointed by President de Gaulle, was defeated on a motion of censure; and in 1981 and 1988, when the election of François Mitterrand as president on both occasions produced the situation in which a president of the left faced a National Assembly majority of the right. In all three cases the assembly was dissolved and the subsequent elections produced an assembly that was more compatible with the president's wishes. However, in 1986, new legislative elections produced a National Assembly with a majority of the right facing a president of the left—Mitterrand. For two years the president had to "cohabit" power with a prime minister—Gaullist leader Jacques Chirac—he would have preferred not to appoint.

French President François Mitterrand. With his Socialist Party, he won the presidential and legislative elections of May–June 1981, and was reelected seven years later.

Several features of the constitution of the Fifth Republic were designed to reduce the hold of Parliament over the process of policymaking and turn power decisively over to the executive. In the Third and Fourth Republics, Parliament's ability to withdraw majority support from cabinets on short notice deprived the latter of the capacity to make strong, coherent policy—at least in areas where Parliament was sharply divided (for example, on colonial policy during the Fourth Republic). Among the new procedural means, several enable the prime minister and the cabinet virtually to ignore or circumvent the legislative process. For example, the National Assembly has been deprived of the power to lay down more than the basic principles of legislation in many areas; in other areas that are relegated to the administrative sphere, it cannot legislate at all. Furthermore, in those areas where the Assembly can still legislate, the prime minister is authorized to deny it an actual vote! Whenever the prime minister declares that a bill is a matter of confidence, the bill will pass without a vote, unless the opposition puts down a motion of censure. In that case, the motion must pass by an *absolute majority* (that is, 50 percent plus one of all members of the Assembly—not just a majority of those voting). During the life of the Fifth Republic, some prime ministers have been more heavy handed than others in using these and other provisions in short-circuiting Parliament. But the stability of governing majorities has consistently made sure that the power of Parliament in the Fifth Republic to assert its will against the prime minister and cabinet has not been as great as that of its predecessors.

Although it was not necessarily the intention of its framers, the Constitution of 1958 departed further from the parliamentary principle by creating a potentially powerful president of the Republic without incorporating a system of checks and balances, such as that found in the American Constitution. Since 1965 the president has been elected for a seven-year term. The more important powers of the office include (1) the power to decide when to dissolve the Assembly, something the president could do before only on the advice of the prime minister; (2) the power to put a question to the voters in the form of a popular referendum (on the advice of the prime minister); (3) the power to choose the prime minister without having to secure approval for this choice by a parliamentary vote; (4) the power to conduct the nation's foreign policy; and (5) the power to declare a state of emergency, thus suspending Parliament's power to legislate. The last of these was a cause of grave concern to many French observers, but it was deemed a necessary evil because of the Algerian War, which was raging at the time the constitution came into effect and because of the near-military coup that had brought down the Fourth Republic.

Charles de Gaulle was elected the first president of the Fifth Republic in December 1958 and served until his resignation in 1969. Of the various powers available to him, the emergency power—potentially the most extensive—was exercised with moderation and essentially within constitutional limits. He declared a state of emergency only once, in April 1961, in the face of an imminent coup d'état by army generals in Algeria. The powers he assumed at that time were phased out gradually with what experts regarded as only minor breaches of legality. There was no doubt in anyone's mind that a real emergency existed and that strong measures were needed to save the Republic. By contrast, in another civil crisis seven years later, the May–June revolt of 1968, de Gaulle refrained from invoking the emergency clause, Article 16. Nor has it been used by any of his successors.

In other areas, de Gaulle seemed to be fashioning the role of the president into something beyond that of a mere referee among competing political forces. He appointed his own prime minister, Michel Debré, who had been a loyal follower of the general from the beginning; he also decided who the members of Debré's cabinet should be—a practice he continued with subsequent cabinets. Furthermore, he intervened on a daily basis in policy decisions, essentially devising his own national security strategy and often interjecting his views among those of his ministers in the area of domestic policy.

In short, de Gaulle acted much more like the very partisan and powerful president of the United States than like the neutral and largely powerless heads of state of Great Britain, Italy, Japan, and West Germany. His prime minister was not expected to be a political leader in his own right, but rather a policy coordinator and manager of the majority in the National Assembly; however, the long tenure of Georges Pompidou as prime minister (1962–1968) enabled him to transcend the limits of the role and ultimately to rival de Gaulle himself. Yet Pompidou as president (1969–1974) and his successor, Valery Giscard d'Estaing (1974–1981), largely continued to exercise the function of the presidential office along the lines established by de Gaulle. The president of the republic is by far the most powerful figure in the French political system.

That having been said, it must be acknowledged that the unique circumstance of *cohabitation* between a president of the left (Mitterrand) and a prime minister (Jacques Chirac) and parliamentary majority of the right, which was the case between 1986 and 1988, restricted the normal presidential powers. In order to have a relatively free rein in the sphere of foreign affairs, Mitterrand found it necessary during this time to allow Chirac wide scope to formulate and implement domestic policy. In fact, this worked to the president's advantage, because it was a period of improving relations with the Soviet Union and other Eastern block nations, whereas the domestic ventures of the prime minister lurched from one disappointment to another. Accordingly, Mitterrand won reelection to the presidency in 1988, rather easily outdistancing Chirac on the second ballot. In the following legislative elections, however, his Socialists failed to gain an absolute majority in the National Assembly. This means that his prime minister, moderate Socialist Michel Rocard, has had the spotlight focused on his efforts to sustain coalitions behind his domestic policy. Mitterrand plays a more passive role similar to the one he played during cohabitation. It appears that France has moved beyond the period of recurrent crises that marked the de Gaulle presidency and that forced him to play a more active role than perhaps he himself had regarded as ideal, even though necessary in the circumstances. Indeed, whenever possible, de Gaulle preferred to remain publicly aloof from domestic political infighting, exposing his prime minister and other members of his government to the risk of public opprobrium when things went wrong. Mitterrand has by both choice and necessity played a similar role.[13] But, again, at no time in the Fifth Republic has the presidency reverted to the figurehead status of the Third and Fourth Republic presidents or of the heads of state of our four other countries.

Probably the most controversial use President de Gaulle made of the presidency was his attempt on two occasions to use the popular referendum to amend the constitution. Although Article 89 of the Constitution of 1958 provides several methods of constitutional amendment, all of them require the participation of both parliamentary chambers—the National Assembly and the Senate. Yet in October 1962 and April 1969, de Gaulle submitted constitutional amendments to the voters without first consulting the two chambers. The first, which changed the method for selecting the president to direct popular vote, was adopted by the voters with a wide margin.[14] The second, designed to change the composition and powers of the Senate and to give certain powers of the central government to new regional units of government, was rejected—which brought about de Gaulle's retirement from politics. Both referendums were heavily criticized by non-Gaullists. Part of the criticism was directed at the unconstitutional method of amendment, a criticism that probably carried more weight with political elites than with the general public.

In fact, the referendum of October 1962 profoundly changed the spirit of the Constitution of 1958. It introduced something foreign to French political traditions. The idea of a popularly elected president had been anathema to dyed-in-the-wool republicans ever since the middle of the nineteenth century, when the only previous popular presidential election had resulted in the victory of Napoleon Bonaparte's nephew and the consequent transformation of the Second Republic into the Second Empire. By making the president of the republic a popularly elected official, the 1962 amendment went a long way toward changing the French system of government from a modified parliamentary system to a near-presidential system. Because the longest standing and most copied presidential model is the American one, it may be worthwhile to compare the present Fifth Republic with the American political system (Figure 5.1). In both systems, whatever the original intentions, the president is the central figure in the structure of power. Both presidents name whomever they choose to their cabinets. Both are in charge of foreign and defense policies. Both are popularly elected, with major attention in the election being given to the personalities of the competing candidates. Both carry a great deal of authority with the public, the press, the legislature, and their subordinates in the executive branch of government.

Nevertheless, the president of the French Fifth Republic has a greater share of horizontal power than does the president of the United States. The French president is elected for a seven-year, rather than a four-year, term and unlike the case of the American president, there are no constitutional limits on the number of times a French president can be reelected. The American president cannot do three things that are permitted to the French president under the Constitution of 1958:

1. The U.S. president cannot dissolve Congress and call new elections. The terms of members of Congress are fixed, and the dates of the elections are determined by the U.S. Constitution. However, the French president cannot dissolve the National Assembly twice during a one-year period.
2. The American president cannot submit a proposition to the voters in the form of a referendum. De Gaulle made effective use of this device in mobilizing support for his objectives in the Algerian War. Presidents Lyndon B. Johnson and Richard M. Nixon might have found a similar device useful in handling the war in Vietnam.
3. The American president cannot declare a state of emergency, thus suspending the legislative powers of Congress. American presidents sometimes assume extraordinary powers during a crisis, but their actions can be revoked by Congress or declared invalid by the Supreme Court. The French Parliament is powerless to act if Article 16 is invoked, and no judicial body in France is as powerful as the U.S. Supreme Court.

On the other hand, there is a counterweight in the French system that is not found in the American system—the capacity of the National Assembly to censure the president's hand-picked prime minister, forcing either the prime minister to resign or the president to dissolve the Assembly. It is this provision that made it inadvisable for Mitterrand to choose a Socialist colleague as his prime minister after his party had lost the legislative education of 1986. If the U.S. Congress had this power, it could remove members of the president's cabinet from office by a majority vote. But this is not a means for removing the French president. There is a procedure in the French Constitution that resembles impeachment and removal from office of the American president. The French president can be indicted by an absolute majority of both chambers in an open ballot and then be tried by a High Court of Justice made up of members of Parliament elected by their colleagues in the two chambers. However, according to Article 68, "The President of the Republic shall not be held accountable for action performed in the exercise of his office except in the case of high treason." This would seem to constitute a greater limitation on the capacity of the French Parliament to remove a president from office than is true in the case of Congress, which has twice instituted impeachment proceedings against a president thought to be guilty of "high crimes and misdemeanors." Thus, rather paradoxically, the French president seems to be more immune from removal by the legislature than is the American president, but the latter's cabinet cannot be brought down on a motion of censure.

In fact, what the French Constitution seems to guarantee is that, in normal times, the president will have enough power to fashion policy, to gain its acceptance by Parliament, and to coordinate its implementation, relatively free of the kind of roadblocks and detours that often confront American presidents. The French president enjoys the position normally held by British and West German cabinets that are assured of stable majorities in their respective parliaments. Even an American president whose party has majorities in both houses of Congress faces cross-party coalitions that can block passage of certain bills. The threat of dissolution might make quite a difference here, but it would also disrupt the balance in the American system that has developed during two centuries of trial and error. On the other hand, the French president enjoys at least as much immunity against removal from office as does the American president, in a position superior to that of the British prime minister and the West German chancellor, who serve only as long as they can retain the support of majorities in Parliament. What this means is that the French president has the best of both the parliamentary and the presidential worlds. If we are speaking of the normal situation (i.e., leaving cohabitation aside), it seems that this is the single most powerful government office in the countries we have been examining.

But the "normal" situation is not always the case. The constitution, because it mixes together elements of the presidential and the parliamentary systems of government, has the potential for deadlock between executive and the legislature even more severe than what often beset the Third and Fourth Republics. Thus far, either the French voters or their elected officials have managed to avoid absolute deadlock, although the period of cohabitation is unlikely to be remembered as one of inspired, dynamic government. There are some very delicate balances in the French system. Perhaps it is not possible to combine the two constitutional principles into one system without running the risk of deadlock. The flexibility may be there to enable the political elites to work out their difficulties, but the heat of partisan battle may dictate otherwise. Still, we have seen problems in the other countries. In Great Britain and West Germany in the early 1980s, the former certainty that stable majorities could be found in Parliament was lessened by the appearance of new actors on the scene, the Alliance in Great Britain and the Green Party in West Germany. In Italy, there is the great difficulty of finding a stable majority as long as the Communists are not invited to share power. Even in Japan, there has been uncertainty about the ability of the LDP to maintain a clear-cut majority in the Diet. In all five countries, the least workable situation seems most likely to materialize whenever the balance between left and right is closest, because the ability of executive leaders to command the support of legislative majorities is most uncertain at such times. Under such conditions, the usual executive initiative-taking role and more passive role of the Parliament can be undermined by the potential veto capacity held by the latter.

## Administrative Elites

On the right-hand side of Figure 5.1 are the administrative agencies that implement the policies formulated by presidents, prime ministers, and cabinets and enacted into law by legislative bodies. In Western Europe and Japan, administrative authority is largely in the hands of permanent civil servants, especially those in the higher ranks—the *administrative elites*.

For our purposes, the term *administrative elite* is reserved for higher echelon civilian administrative officials. In Western Europe, the line between the political heads of government agencies and neutral civil servants who are their subordinates is drawn at a higher level of the administrative hierarchy than it is in the United States. At the top levels of executive branch agencies in the United States, the patronage system remains, to the extent that at least the top two or three layers are staffed with fellow partisans of the president who have been rewarded for their service to the party and to the president. In most Western European countries, on the other hand, only the top-line position in each department is held by a leader of the party or parties in power. Below that level are high-ranking civil servants, who are chosen, in large part, for their demonstrated merit according to criteria established for the civil service of that country. These civil servants are highly educated experts in the art of governing. They are expected to maintain neutrality between the contending political parties, and, unlike American higher officials, they are insulated from the political infighting of the legislative body. When compared with the United States, the principle of political neutrality of high-ranking government officers in at least three of our countries holds up, but, when compared with each other, it appears that the British higher civil service maintains a higher level of political neutrality than do the others, although the reasons this is so differ from country to country.

The leading study of administrative elites in First World countries is *Bureaucrats and Politicians in Western Democracies*, by Joel D. Aberbach, Robert D. Putnam, and Bert A. Rockman.[15] During the early 1970s the authors interviewed more than 1,400 politicians and civil servants in seven countries, including the four Western European countries covered in this text. A similar study was undertaken in Japan in the middle 1970s by Michio Muramatsu and Ellis S. Krauss.[16] Both studies examined the different role perceptions of administrators and politicians in the countries studied. Aberbach et al. set forth four models of role relationships between political leaders and administrative elites and classified their respondents according to which of the models they carried in their heads while they performed the duties of their respective offices.

The first model (Type I) is close to the one set forth at the outset of this section. It is a very formal relationship in which politicians make policy decisions, which administrators implement faithfully. Although this may be a sort of constitutional ideal of Western democracies, as the politicians are elected by the voters and the administrators are appointed by the politicians, in fact this image did not recommend itself to many politicians or bureaucrats in any of the countries as an approximation either of the way things should operate or of the way they do in fact operate.

Both politicians and bureaucrats recognize that the civil servant is invaluable to the policymaker as a supplier of information the policymaker needs to make competent decisions. The civil servant is the real expert on the substance of the issue at hand, but the politician recognizes the *value* implications behind the issues. The way the decision goes will have important consequences for the values of power, well-being, enlightenment, and respect. The second model of political and administrative roles (Type II) draws a dichotomy between *fact* and *value*. It is the political leader's job to decide between values and the administrator's job to supply the politician with the relevant facts, including the facts bearing on what the value consequences of each decision will be. The administrator in this model plays a crucial role in policymaking. It is not a passive role, simply waiting for a decision to be made so that it can be implemented; rather, it is an active role of providing the information the policymaker needs to make an informed decision. In the studies in question, administrators were much more inclined than policymakers in each country to define their roles vis-à-vis policymaking in something like these terms. This was particularly true of civil servants in West Germany and Italy. For example, more than 80 percent of the civil servants in these countries saw the role of the administrator as that of technician, whereas the percentages fall to 66 percent and 59 percent in the cases of British and French administrators.[17] On the other hand, Italian administrators were much less likely than those in any of the other Western European countries studied to express a tolerance for political interference in what they considered to be their sphere of activity.[18] In Japan, it was found that administrators had an aversion to politics similar to that of the Italians, and that the Japanese were as likely to say that "technical considerations should outweigh politics" (49 percent of the Japanese administrators) as were the West Germans (50 percent), although not as much as the Italians (77 percent). On this question, only 21 percent of the British administrators agreed.[19] In general, it appears that the Type II model is popular with the West German, Japanese, and especially the Italian higher civil servants, but less so with the British and the French.

The third model suggested by Aberbach et al. (Type III) is one in which the politician supplies the energy and will to accomplish policy objectives, whereas the administrators react to the politician's initiatives, trying to be helpful when possible, but seeking to strike an equilibrium between the wishes of their political "masters" and the network of interest groups and other bureaucratic agencies with which they work on a continuing basis. The politicians are there for brief periods; the civil servants stay on in their jobs. The latter must make certain that the former do not so upset things that the environment in which they work will become a hostile one. This means that they will often attempt to dissuade the politicians from courses of action that appear too rash and will attempt to steer them into safer waters. Viewers of the television series "Yes, Minister" and "Yes, Prime Minister" will recognize this tendency in the relationship between the British political leader and the top-ranking permanent civil servant. Much of the recent literature critical of the British civil service has suggested that this third model is, indeed, eminently applicable to Britain.[20] In fact, Aberbach et al. conclude their study by arguing that their findings identify Type III as uppermost in the minds of higher civil servants in all of the countries they studied. Although the second model is one those interviewed frequently cited as a formal statement of the role relationship, when pressed for a more realistic picture, they brought in elements of the third model. We might say that in Italy, Japan, and West Germany, the formal model serves as a stronger inhibition against subtle bureaucratic undermining of political will than it does in Britain. There are reasons for this, as we can see in the next section.

Finally, the fourth model tested in these studies (Type IV) removes any distinctions between politicians and administrators at the top levels, blending them together into a hybrid type. This may take the form of the political leader with administrative experience or of the politician taking over the functions of the bureaucrat. In either event, gone are any inhibitions against bureaucratic involvement in politics, including interest brokering, the making of choices between competing values, and the exercise of political will. In essence, the administrative elite becomes part of the political elite. Aberbach et al. find this to be most true of the United States, where persons playing roles similar to those of higher civil servants in Western Europe and Japan are, in fact, political appointees. Significantly, they found that the role image most prevalent among American civil servants is that of *trustee* (74 percent), which they define as a "focus on one's role as representative of the state."[21] This suggests that the permanent civil servants in the United States see themselves as providing the continuity that is otherwise lacking in a system where so many of the leading personnel change when new leadership comes to the executive branch. France is another case in which the trustee role is chosen by many administrators (77 percent). An even larger number in France (82 percent) saw elements of the *policymaker* in their role, which suggests that French administrators find little to inhibit them from playing a strong administrative role, while at the same time they regard this as necessary from the standpoint of protecting the interests of the French state. Of our five countries, France seems to be the one whose higher civil servants, even those who are not political appointees, most closely approximate the Type IV hybrid image.

**The Socialization of the Administrative Elite.**[22] Part of the explanation for these differences can be found in the administrative traditions of the five countries, traditions that have been handed down from generation to generation through the process of socialization. In part, this process takes place in the family. A fair percentage of recruits to the administrative elite in all five countries come from families headed by civil servants. But, in general in these countries, a very high percentage of the administrative elite is recruited from the upper strata of society, is educated in the most prestigious schools and universities, and enters the ranks of the civil service at a level commensurate with its education and high enough to guarantee that these individuals will end their service careers in positions of considerable responsibility.[23] Family and school socialization patterns for Europe's and Japan's upper classes do not vary greatly from country to country. What is different is the type of professional training recruits to the upper administrative ranks have received, both in their formal education and in the years of their apprenticeship as higher civil servants. Three essential patterns may be distinguished for our five countries: the classical *generalist* (Great Britain), the *legalist* (West Germany, Italy, and Japan), and the *technocrat* (France).

In Great Britain, the administrative elite is a well-defined minority within the civil service, known until recently as the administrative class. It consists of only a few hundred officials in the top nonpolitical ranks of agencies headed by ministers. Below this elite is a much larger body of subordinate officials who follow the orders of their administrative class superiors. However, they may in turn be responsible for supervising the activities of large numbers of employees. Elite civil servants have university degrees, whereas those below them may or may not, and if they do, they will probably not be as distinguished as the degrees held by those in the elite category. The examination for the elite-level civil servants is partly an academic-style written examination and partly a test of the candidate's capacity to respond to situations designed to simulate actual administrative experiences. Because the curriculum in the elite university–preparatory secondary schools is classical in its orientation—emphasizing history, literature, languages, and philosophy—and because the civil service examination allows university graduates with a humanistic education to specialize in their subjects, well-rounded generalists are not at a disadvantage and may even have an advantage over their more technically specialized peers.

The British education system produces liberally educated generalists at the baccalaureate level. Therefore, the administrative class of the British civil service is filled with generalists, whose forte is the ability to master the general terms of a particular problem and to offer a solution that takes a maximum number of considerations into account. The solution may not, however, be a clean, economical way of optimizing any given objective. To achieve that end, the technical specialist—the economist, the natural scientist, the accountant, the engineer—may be better equipped. But the British way has been to keep the expert "on tap, not on top." Administrative agencies consign the highly trained specialists to staff positions, which are subordinate in the hierarchy to generalists, who occupy the principal decision-making posts. This practice has been heavily criticized since the 1960s by academic specialists in public administration and, most significantly, by the Fulton Commission, which made a number of sweeping recommendations for changing the civil service. Although the Fulton Report appeared in the late 1960s, its most important recommendations—to phase out the administrative class and to place specialists on an equal footing with generalists—have been implemented very slowly, if at all. Although the administrative class has now ceased to exist as such, its spirit is likely to continue to pervade the British administrative elite.[24]

The counterpart of the British generalist in the West German, Japanese, and Italian administrative services is the higher civil servant with a generalized legal education. In these countries, officials trained in law are more likely than those with other academic specialties to be found at the topmost levels of the administrative hierarchy, although, in West Germany, economics has been gaining in favor in recent years as a preferred academic background second only to law. Civil servants in these countries are expected to pay strict attention to the procedural and substantive legalities of their work. This helps to ensure a relatively impartial bureaucracy, in West Germany at least, but it may also lead to overly cautious and even obstructive implementation of the state's business—a characteristic that numerous critics of the Italian bureaucracy have noticed. In both Italy and Japan, impartiality between political parties may not appear particularly important to civil servants, as power has not shifted to the Opposition since the present regimes came into being following the post–World War II occupations.

The route for legally trained candidates to administrative elite positions in West Germany leads from the Gymnasium (upper-stream secondary school) through the university to a first state examination in law. The requisite qualifications are determined by the state, and the universities are expected to gear their curriculum in law to fit these expectations. This is unlike the situation in Great Britain, where university standards have been used since the late nineteenth century to determine the content of the examinations. Success in the first state examination will enable the German aspirant to begin a training period of about two-and-one-half years in one of the administrative agencies at the federal, Land, or local level or in the administrative service of a court at one of these levels. Here, the prospective civil servant will build on this background in the study of law and prepare to take a second state examination, which will determine whether he or she is qualified to become a higher level civil servant (*Beamter*). The criteria for admission to this elite are precise and objective, unlike those in Great Britain where a fair amount of emphasis continues to be given to the intangibles of style.

If anything, training in the law is even more exclusively the academic mode of entry into the Italian and Japanese administrative elites than it is in West Germany. However, the recruitment process is not as carefully regulated in Italy as it is in West Germany. In the Federal Republic of Germany, one seeks to enter the civil service of the federal government or of one of the Länder just as, in Great Britain, one is recruited into the civil service of the central government. In both countries, generalized criteria apply, regardless of the government agency or level in which the recruit ultimately will be employed. In Italy, on the other hand, one seeks employment in a given ministry, not (in general) in the service of the Italian central government. And, to be assured of employment in that ministry, one ought to have family or political connections in addition to a law degree. Without such connections, the waiting period may last several years, no matter how well the recruit does in the entrance examination. Here, the power of the Christian Democratic Party (DC) can be clearly perceived. Certain ministries have been headed by leaders of the DC for years. Different factions of the party regard particular ministries as their exclusive fiefdoms. This is especially true of those factions whose power base is located in the area south of Rome. Ambitious young people from southern Italy are more likely to be attracted to a relatively secure position in the central government than to a riskier, if potentially more rewarding, job in the private sector.

As in other aspects we have examined, the fact that one party is dominant and that that party is factionalized means there are similarities between the recruitment of Italian and Japanese civil servants. Besides the fact that legal training is paramount for both, it is also the case that connections with one or another of the ruling party's factions is a means in both countries of attaining a post in the appropriate ministry. But the academic standards are higher for admission to the higher civil service in Japan than they are in Italy. Typically, those recruits who attain the most attractive initial posts and who are most likely to be "high flyers," rising rapidly in their early years, have received their degrees from either the University of Tokyo or the University of Kyoto, the two most prestigious Japanese universities. In this respect they resemble their British counterparts from "Oxbridge."[25]

In the four countries thus far considered in this section, civil servants who have been trained in such academic disciplines as economics, mathematics, engineering, and the natural sciences—disciplines that are most apt to put them in touch with the most decisive changes taking place in postindustrial society—are more likely to have positions that are subordinate and advisory to the more traditionally educated civil servants, who hold the real decision-making power in the administrative elite. This is not the case in France, which has a long-standing tradition of relying on the state to take a dynamic part in driving and shaping the economy. The elite corps of highway and mining engineers were already playing a major role in laying the basis for French industrialization early in the nineteenth century. After World War II, France established a model for training an administrative elite by creating the École Nationale d'Administration (ENA), where recruits to the higher civil service undergo a three-year training program containing a heavy dose of economics—not the classical laissez-faire economics that prevailed in France and elsewhere in Western Europe before the War, but rather the Keynesian, growth-oriented economics that rapidly caught on in government circles in France after World War II. Graduates of ENA have come to occupy top-ranking positions in the central agencies that direct and regulate the French economy, including the Ministry of Finance and the important Planning Commissariat. Aside from ENA, there is the École Polytechnique, which provides the finishing academic touches for future state engineers, some of whom will spend their entire careers in the Ministry of Industrial Production or the Ministry of Transport. These various kinds of technocrats can anticipate careers in which they will eventually reach high-level positions with important decision-making responsibilities. The expert, whether economist, legal specialist, or engineer, can eventually hope to get to the top rather than to remain on tap in the French bureaucracy.

**The Role of the Administrative Elite in Policymaking.** What are the consequences of these differing socialization patterns for the positions that administrative elites occupy in the horizontal power structures of our four countries? As noted earlier, these elites differ with respect to the self-perceptions they carry with them in fulfilling their role specifications; these self-perceptions, in turn, affect their actual performances. Generally speaking, it can be said that the British administrative elites are relatively self-restrained in their approach to the exercise of administrative discretion, whereas the French are relatively free of self-restraint. The West German, Italian, and Japanese administrative elites fall somewhere in between these two other types.

Administrative neutrality is a well-established tradition in both Great Britain and Germany. However, it has been severely strained in the latter country at certain times in the past and recently has been challenged by the appearance of politically oriented administrators occupying positions that are held by neutral civil servants in Britain. In Great Britain, the role of the neutral civil servant prepared to serve whichever party comes to power goes back to the middle of the past century. If it were ever in doubt, it met the supreme test after World War II, when the Labour Party came to power and put into effect its sweeping program of economic and social reform. Although the program contained many items that must have been fundamentally at odds with the personal views of many senior civil servants, the Labour ministers later said that the administrative elite carried out the directives of the Labour government as loyally as they had those of earlier Conservative governments. The higher civil servant is a career officer whose professional standards require a high degree of intelligence employed in the mastery of detail and in the assessment of the implications of alternative courses of action. It is the duty of civil servants to advise their political superiors about these implications; however, even if civil servants privately disagree with the latter's judgment, they will implement the chosen action with skill and dispatch. That, at least, is the formal role image of the British administrative elite.

There is, however, the other side of the coin. Although the senior civil servant has been trained as a generalist, he or she has spent a career in government service. If successful, the civil servant has gained the reputation of being a quick study, which means that one can master the essential details of whatever problem might arise. The civil servant is very likely, therefore, to be more of an expert and less of a generalist than his or her political superior, the minister. As a result, it would be foolish to suggest that such civil servants do not have a great deal of influence on the policymaking process, especially where complicated adjustments to the needs of particular interest groups are concerned. They have information, something their minister, who may be new to the job, desperately needs. In this respect, British civil servants may even have an edge over their counterparts in Italy, where turnover in particular ministerial positions occurs less often than it does in Great Britain. Of the civil servants examined here, the British seem to come closest to the Aberbach et al. Type III of politician–bureaucrat relations. They try to see that their ministry maintains an *equilibrium* in its relationship with powerful groups in its environment. If this means translating the intentions of the occasional headstrong minister into less threatening policy implementation, so be it.

The lawyers who occupy important positions in the West German administrative structure are probably not as deferential to their political superiors as are their British counterparts. After all, they regard themselves as experts. They view the politicians as generalists against whose intervention they (the specialists) must safeguard their professional standards. In the past, this insistence has escaped the boundaries of administrative neutrality. For example, the Socialist ministers in the early Weimar Republic (about 1920) did not benefit from the civil servants' willingness to carry out their wishes as did the Labour Party ministers in Great Britain during the late 1940s. When Adolph Hitler came to power, he made certain that he would not encounter the same obstructiveness, so he abolished the security of tenure that the German administrative elite traditionally had enjoyed. This was restored after World War II for the reconstituted West German administrative elite; and, since that time, the civil service has rediscovered the principle of political neutrality. This time, when the Social Democrats replaced the Christian Democrats in power, they could count on the loyal implementation of their programs.

Nevertheless, the advent in 1969 of the Social Democratic–Free Democratic coalition was accompanied by the implantation of persons loyal to the coalition parties in some top positions and important auxiliary positions normally occupied by career civil servants. Besides the desire to be able to rely on the loyalty of the top administrators, this was done to ensure a greater sensitivity to political considerations on the part of higher civil servants than could be expected from the traditional, legally minded German administrator. This is perhaps the major reason that West German respondents to the Aberbach et al. study could not so readily be classed in the Type II category, which confines the role of the civil servant to that of supplying information while ministers make the decisions. The more politically oriented administrative elites of the post-1969 West German government see themselves in Type III or even Type IV roles, with any meaningful distinction between politics and administration removed.

This suggests that the higher West German and French civil servants are coming to resemble each other. High-ranking French civil servants expect to have an important voice in the policymaking process, and they do. Their demanding, relatively highly specialized academic training, capped with a final period of socialization at one of the grands écoles, gives them a sense of their own self-importance. The self-assurance exhibited by the French diplomatic corps in international negotiations, often to France's advantage, can be observed among the higher civil servants who are responsible for administering domestic policy as well.

The high degree of formal concentration of power in the hands of the executive of the French central government enhances the position of the administrative elite in the horizontal power structure. Deputies in the National Assembly cannot hope to influence the course of policymaking through their own legislation. Often, what they want to accomplish can be achieved only through administrative action or, if legislation is necessary, only if the government will draft it and present it to Parliament. Either way, it will be necessary to work with civil servants who will be sure to incorporate their own views into whatever decision is made by the appropriate ministry. The political heads of these executive units frequently are former civil servants who have moved to the political level either directly or indirectly from the permanent civil service.[26] Even when ministers have not had administrative experience, they will include in their inner cabinets rising young members of the Conseil d'État or the Finance Inspectorate—men and women on loan from their respective agencies. Their role will be frankly a political one, to aid the minister in making decisions that will enhance his or her career. Such rising young stars are likely to move back and forth between administrative and political positions in their careers. The newer breed of French administrators who have come out of ENA since World War II are pragmatic men and women of action.

Whatever advantages there may be when the state is expected to play a dynamic, innovating role—stimulating other social institutions to change in keeping with the changing times—this aggressive type of role presents a problem from the standpoint of political theory. Administrative self-restraint is a guarantee that the ultimate rulers will be representatives of the people. Professional civil servants who have the security of tenure are responsible, first and foremost, to their own professional standards. If those standards permit a forceful, imaginative policymaking role, then considerations of what the public really wants are likely to take second place to the civil servants' beliefs as to what is best for the public.

An additional reason there may be cause for concern in the French case is the tendency of higher civil servants to leave their government jobs in mid-career and take executive positions in industry, or else to enter politics in the hope of being elected to Parliament and then assuming ministerial positions when and if their parties come to power. These prospects can hardly be conducive to the most public-spirited application of their responsibilities as public servants. A very similar situation is found in Japan, where civil servants, particularly in the ministries concerned with economic policy, can look forward to occupying high-ranking positions in industrial or banking firms whose interests have been in their hands while they have occupied important government positions. In both France and Japan, observers of this phenomenon have noted a certain arrogance in public posturing of the administrative elites. This is suggested also by the high number of French administrators who saw their roles as *trustees*, removed from effective public control.[27] This description of the Japanese administrator by Muramatsu and Krauss is similar:

> Almost all of the Japanese civil servants believe that political parties often needlessly intensify political conflicts, and a large majority of them also believe that the clash of interest groups seriously endangers the national welfare. Further, they believe that it is they, not the parties or legislature, who ensure reasonable public policy and that technical factors should have precedence over political ones.[28]

Muramatsu and Krauss claim that Japanese civil servants are "more like the classical bureaucrats of Italy"[29] than like the civil servants of the other countries we are studying. By this they mean that the formal legal training of civil servants in both Japan and Italy make them particularly defensive against the intrusion of politics into their domain. This may well be true of the Japanese, as it was of the traditional German, civil servant. But it is not an element of Italian culture to hold fast to legalities to the exclusion of all other considerations, and we have seen that the Japanese political culture stresses that such modern concerns are in constant conflict with more traditional values and loyalties, to family, village, and friends. (See Chapter 3.) But one wonders if "modern concerns" of administrative neutrality and adherence to legal norms have the meaning in Italy they do for the elegantly educated Japanese administrative elite. In Italy, if it is a question of adhering to a legal principle as opposed to the interests of one's political friends, there may not be much conflict for the administrator. If these friends have been responsible for one's getting a job in the bureaucracy in the first place, for example, as a favor to a member of one's family, the civil servant will find an excuse to ignore the legal principle. In the eyes of an Italian, this is not necessarily corruption. It may even be regarded as highly moral behavior—loyalty to one's family and friends, displaying reliability (in their eyes), and even demonstrating a sense of one's responsibilities. Such personal responsibilities come before the abstract responsibilities associated with the role of public servant. A jealous guarding of one's status also leads to a conservative stance regarding ideas for reform. Italian civil servants are not the dynamic force for innovation their French counterparts are reputed to be.[30] They also lack the firm commitment to political neutrality found in Great Britain. Accordingly, the Italian civil service is a force to be contended with in the policymaking process. But it is not likely to be a force for change.

## *The Vertical Distribution of Government Power*

When we speak of the vertical distribution of power in a political system, we mean the relationship among various levels of government rather than among different units at the same level. In any system of government, there will be at least a national (or central) level of government and a local unit that corresponds to the city, town, or village in which people reside and interact with one another. Usually, there are also one or more intermediate levels between the center and the localities. There may be some sort of district that is larger than the locality, which includes several nearby localities and the adjoining countryside—a district that resembles the county in the United States. In some countries, there will be a larger intermediate level, which can be called a regional level—an area that comprises more than one city and a significant proportion of the country's population or territory. The states in the United States would fit this definition, as would various kinds of regional units in the countries we are studying. Western polyarchies differ substantially from one another with respect to their intermediate and local units and the distribution of power among national, intermediate, and local units.

The first, and most basic, distinguishing question is: What, if any, regional level of government is there? There are two types of answer to this question among Western polyarchies. Either there is a regional level with powers that are clearly defined by a constitution and protected from encroachment by the central government, or there is not. If there is such a regional level, then the system can be called *federalism;* if there is no regional level or it is weak and dependent on the center, the system should be termed a *unitary* one. The United States is generally regarded as having a federal system of government because the regional units—the states—have powers reserved to them by a constitution, and these powers are protected by a court system that is pledged to uphold the constitutional balance. Great Britain, on the other hand, has a unitary system in that the regional level of government is very weak, to the extent that it exists at all, and the local level of government is dependent on Parliament for whatever powers it has. The courts in Great Britain defer to acts of Parliament. There is no constitutional distribution of powers to which Parliament must defer when it defines what local government units may and may not do. Of our five political systems, only West Germany can properly be called a federal system; the four others are unitary systems.

## Unitary Systems

In our four unitary systems, cities, towns, and villages generally constitute what is often called the first tier of local government. In France and Italy, this first tier is made up of *communes,* irrespective of their size; in Great Britain and Japan, the terms for the units vary depending on their size. In all four countries, there is a second tier comparable to the American county: It is called the *county* in Great Britain, the *département* in France, the *province* in Italy, and the *prefecture* in Japan. Both tiers of government in all four countries exercise powers that have been granted to them by laws enacted through the normal lawmaking processes of the central government. They are not, however, simply administrative arms of the central government any more than, say, the city of Detroit is just an administrative arm of the state of Michigan. They have their own elected councils, which make policy for the local area subject to certain restrictions imposed from above.

As in the United States, local units of government do not monopolize the administration of government policies within their boundaries. In Detroit, there are offices of both the federal and the Michigan governments, with administrative responsibilities and jurisdiction within the city of Detroit. Similarly, there are central government field offices in Newcastle, England; Nancy, France; Naples, Italy; and Nagoya, Japan—the post offices in these cities, for example. But, to varying degrees, the city governments are responsible for such things as maintaining law and order, fighting fires, and collecting refuse.

Among unitary systems there is a wide variety of ways in which the relationship between central and local levels of government is organized. This variation is between countries and between different functional areas of government as well. In general, the legislative body of the central government is free in a unitary system to change the boundaries and powers of local governments at will; but powerful political forces may make such change impossible or may make only certain kinds of change possible. For example, a political party that holds power nationally may be restrained by local leaders of that party from making certain changes in the powers of local governments they control, even though to do so might make fulfillment of the national party's program easier. Within a given country, implementation of policy may vary in the enthusiasm with which local governments carry it out, and even in the direction that it takes from one area of the country to another, because different political parties or coalitions of interest groups are powerful in different localities.

In Italy today—and until recently in France and until the "MacArthur constitution" in Japan—there is a single official of the central government, called the *prefect*, with power to bring local governments into line within the intermediate level of government under his or her control. The prefect has the powers to veto acts of local councils and to withhold funds otherwise provided by the central government. In Japan today, executive power at both the local and the intermediate levels is held by locally elected, rather than centrally appointed, officers. The same has been true of France since the office of prefect was eliminated by legislation during the period of the Socialist government in the early 1980s. It was replaced by the office of councillor of the republic, who is weaker than the prefect was, but still retains the power to nullify acts of the local governments after the fact, rather than to stop them from being taken in the first place, as was in the prefect's power. Some observers are skeptical as to how much difference the reform has actually made, especially in less populous areas that are heavily dependent on government financial support. The reform seems to have strengthened the hand of elected officers in larger cities and in some départements, but elected officials had been gaining on the prefects in an informal process of decentralization before the socialist reform. The exact significance of the decentralization continues to be debated by students of French sub-national government.[31]

In these unitary systems, central government agents have always acted in a very crowded political–administrative environment in which their authority frequently is challenged not only by local units of government, but by other agents of other divisions of the central government. Each of these actors views policy from a different perspective, and conflicts are inevitable.[32] Centralization has never been as monolithic as stereotypes of these systems suggest; but the very complexity of the process defeats efforts to make it less technocratic and more democratic.

In First World polyarchies generally, power is sufficiently divided on the vertical dimension as well as on the horizontal, that whoever holds the upper hand at the central level faces an extremely difficult task trying to get local authorities, even if they are of the same political persuasion, to conform to central policy objectives. And in the case of local authorities with markedly different policy objectives, the frustration of central power holders can be acute. This has been the case especially of governments that have been trying since the high-inflation years of the 1970s to bring the spending of local government under control. During the 1960s and 1970s, in most First World countries local governments took on added responsibilities for providing social services such as public housing, transportation, higher education, and welfare. Many of these functions were added at the behest of central governments trying to keep their own administrative burden from becoming unmanageable; others were assumed at the initiative of the local governments themselves. Whatever the case, by the late 1970s local government spending had increased to the point of becoming the largest component of public spending in many Western countries. By the late 1970s, central governments were seeking to contain government spending generally as part of macroeconomic policies strongly influenced by monetarist economic thinking. (See Chapter 2.) However, they were not always able to convince local governments to rein in their spending and often lacked the political strength to force them to do so. Some governments were able to reduce the amount of central grants used to fund local programs, but this could be countered by local governments' raising the taxes imposed on their residents.

In 1979 the new Conservative government led by Margaret Thatcher came to power in Britain and pledged to bring the high levels of local-authority spending under control. During the early and middle 1980s, it was able to steer legislation through Parliament designed to set upper limits not only on local-authority spending, but also on the rates, or property taxes, that can be levied on local businesses and private residences. In 1988 legislation was enacted to replace residential property taxes with a poll tax, or a tax on each local resident that would be the same regardless of income or wealth. This is designed to make the less affluent voters more aware of the costs as well as the benefits of local-government spending programs, but it has been heavily criticized as regressive (i.e., as extracting a higher percentage of the assets of lower-income than of higher-income persons). Businesses will no longer be taxed by the local governments, but will be taxed at rates determined by the central government, the proceeds to be remitted to the local governments by the central government. This very substantial withdrawal of traditional local revenue-gathering power has been matched by withdrawal of other powers in the areas of law enforcement, education, housing, and economic regeneration of depressed local economies.[33]

In some ways, this recentralization of government in Britain runs counter to the trend toward disaggregation of social, economic, and political institutions discussed in earlier chapters. The trends in Italy and France appear to be toward greater decentralization, with the creation of elected regional bodies in Italy in the 1970s and in France in the 1980s. A 1974 movement in that direction in Britain, with the creation of elected county councils in large metropolitan areas, was canceled in 1986, with some of the functions of these bodies, instead of being devolved back to the smaller governmental units, being concentrated in nonelected bodies under central government control. It remains to be seen whether the centralization going on in Britain at present can be sustained in the face of strong centrifugal forces represented by local business, labor, and community groups organized both locally and regionally, especially if the resurgence of the economy registered in the period from 1985 to 1989 can be sustained. Local resistance to central control can take a variety of forms. The fact that the central state acts in the various parts of its territory through a multiplicity of agencies, and that the various localities have representation in the legislative body on which government is dependent, makes it likely that the current centralizing thrust of the Conservative government will lose its momentum. It does not have close parallels in other First World countries.[34]

## West German Federalism

Federalism in the United States is of a type that political scientist Gordon Smith calls a *dual* system of vertical power distribution.[35] The federal government and the states each have their own spheres of power. Under the U.S. Constitution, the federal executive implements policy that has been enacted in the form of legislation by Congress. Spheres of power that have not been explicitly granted to the federal government in the constitution are, according to the Tenth Amendment, reserved to the states. We know, of course, that the meaning of the constitution has been stretched considerably as the powers of the federal government have expanded. But the states continue to exercise primary responsibility in many areas that are of direct importance to people's lives—providing for public education, maintaining public order, and caring for the indigent, the elderly, and the mentally infirm. The federal government plays an important auxiliary role in these areas, but the discrepancies in the quality of the service and in the amount of money per capita spent by individual states attests to the fact that state prerogatives are jealously guarded against extensive federal encroachment.

In West Germany, there are fewer obvious regional disparities in the quality of public services than in the case of the United States. Part of the reason for this is that the Basic Law of the Federal Republic encourages greater per capita revenue and expenditure standardization among the Länder, as part of what Smith calls a *fused* system of vertical power distribution.[36] It must also be acknowledged, however, that West Germany is a much smaller country than the United States and one would, therefore, expect less diversity. Moreover, except for Bavaria and the two city-states of Hamburg and Bremen, the Länder are new entities emerging from boundary rearrangements by the Allied Occupation after World War II and, thus, do not maintain such local particularisms as do, say, a Mississippi or a New Hampshire. Still, regional differences have always been important in German life, and it must be remembered that Germany as a national political unit has existed for only about 120 years. Parts of what is now West Germany, such as Bavaria, Baden, and Wurttemberg, were sovereign states before 1871.

Under the Basic Law, both the federal government and the Länder possess explicitly delineated spheres of power. The most important powers held exclusively by the federal government are, as for any sovereign state, those pertaining to national security. For the Länder, education, religion, and cultural affairs are among the more important areas that are exclusively within their jurisdiction. There is a further area of concurrent powers—for example, transport, nuclear energy, and criminal law—where both may legislate but with the stipulation that federal law supercedes Land law. In still other areas, the federal government may enact broad framework laws, but implementation is left up to the governments of the Länder. The federal government plays more of a supervisory role than a direct administrative one. This means that, in relation to the other countries with which we are dealing, the Federal Republic of Germany maintains a relatively small central bureaucracy. Public employment is, relatively speaking, dispersed in West Germany.

On the other hand, the federal government holds the upper hand with respect to taxation. The taxes with the highest total yield, including the income tax, go into the federal treasury. These are then distributed to the Länder so that they can implement federal policy. This has much more of a redistributive effect than have revenue distributing systems tried in the United States. Taxes collected in the richer Länder, like Hamburg and Baden–Wurttemberg, are used to help bring public services in the poorer Länder, such as Lower Saxony or the Saarland, up to a common national standard. This financial power gives the federal government considerable leverage to make sure the states are carrying out federal policy as intended by those in power in Bonn, but the primary purpose of the arrangement is to equalize resources to implement policies determined at both central and regional levels.

Divided Germany before the 1990s. West German states (Länder) are separated by broken lines.

Two counterweights protect the Länder against excessive federal control. The Federal Constitutional Court plays a role resembling that of the U.S. Supreme Court in refereeing the system. Even by American standards, this is an activist court that seeks to accommodate the Basic Law to existing social realities. Important constitutional decisions have sometimes gone against the Länder and sometimes against the federal government. The second counterweight is an organ discussed earlier—the Bundesrat. Through this body, the state governments are able to play a direct role in the federal legislative process. Although the federal government has powerful means for guiding and controlling the management of Land affairs, the Länder can help shape the ways in which this guidance and control will be exercised.

As for the local level of government in the Federal Republic, there has been an increasing tendency of the federal government, as in the United States, to bypass the states and deal directly with local units of government—the counties (*Kreise*) and the municipalities. Both federal government and Länder have shown a tendency, with the intensification of economic problems in the late 1970s and early 1980s, to increase their shares of revenue at the expense of the localities, while at the same time shifting responsibility for implementing policies downward to the local level. This has helped stimulate a citizens' movement in defense of local autonomy, which has stressed the problems of urban decline and ecological peril. Part of the same "citizens' initiative" phenomenon that has given rise to the Green Party, this movement has been particularly threatening to entrenched Social Democratic city governments and has had the local support of Christian Democrats and Free Democrats reflecting middle-class urban concerns—yet another example of political disaggregation in postindustrial society.[37]

Although central–local relations do not seem to be at the forefront of the Japanese policy agenda in the same way they are in the Western European countries considered here, the problems of the cities have been a focus of the citizens' action movement there as in West Germany. They also have arisen within the British Labour Party to challenge its traditional centralist focus and suggest that the vertical dimension of power is becoming a battleground in the face of the centralizing tendencies of the Thatcher government. The "politics of disaggregation" can be expected increasingly to feature such conflicts between "center" and "periphery" in the years to come.

## *Conclusion*

In summary, it seems clear that the greatest concentration of power in the countries we have examined is found in France. This is true on both the horizontal and vertical dimensions. If we take as the standard for horizontal concentration the amount of executive predominance over Parliament, the French president has more power than the cabinets of the strictly parliamentary countries. This power is reinforced by the strong role played by French civil servants. On the vertical scale, France has had a high concentration of power in the central government, and long-standing habits at both the central and local levels will not readily be erased by recent efforts to decentralize the system. Closely following France in these respects is Japan, with the long reign of the Liberal Democratic Party having meant an accumulation of power in the executive, facing a relatively docile legislature. Japan's elite civil servants do not escape the control of the LDP politicians as readily as their French counterparts have habitually been able to do in what has, except for the 1960s and early 1970s, always been a more evenly balanced system politically, which no set of politicians is quite able to dominate. On the vertical plane, the recent French reforms may have brought the French and Japanese systems closer together. Formally, they are unitary systems; informally, networks of local politicians are able to steer courses that escape tight central control.

In the West German and British parliamentary systems, there is a more collective form of leadership than is found in France, although perhaps with more scope for the head of government to lead than is the case in Japan and certainly more than is found in Italy. As in Japan, power is held securely in West Germany and Britain by the cabinet as a collective body, with little scope for Parliament to play more than a marginal role collectively in policymaking. In Italy, on the other hand, the existence of a minority or weak coalition government and the inefficiency of the bureaucracy makes it difficult for the cabinet to assert its will over Parliament. Secret voting and instantaneous coalitions of opposition parties with "sharpshooters" in the majority parties have made it necessary for governments to spend much of their time minding their legislative fences, a problem that is hardly unknown to U.S. presidents. Thus, power is more dispersed in the horizontal sense in Italy than in any of the other countries. West Germany, on the other hand, with its federal system, goes farthest toward decentralization on the vertical scale, although the country has a higher degree of actual centralization than is found in the United States. Like the cities and states in West Germany, the local units of government in Britain and Italy have a longer tradition of autonomy and of corporate identity than do those in France and Japan, so when the various reorganizations of the unitary systems are sorted out, it is still safe to say that Britain and Italy fall somewhere in the middle of our scale of vertical power distribution.

## *Suggestion for Further Reading*

**Aberbach, Joel D.,** et al. *Bureaucrats and Politicians in Western Democracies* (Cambridge, Mass., and London: Harvard University Press, 1981).

**Armstrong, John A.** *The European Administrative Elite* (Princeton, N.J.: Princeton University Press, 1973).

**Ashford, Douglass E.** *British Dogmatism and French Pragmatism* (London: George Allen & Unwin, 1982).

**Conradt, David P.** *The German Polity*, 4th ed. (New York and London: Longman, 1986).

**Drucker, Henry,** et al., eds. *Developments in British Politics 2* (rev.) (New York: St. Martin's, 1988).

**Gurr, Ted Robert, and Desmond King.** *The State and the City* (Basingstoke and London: Macmillan, 1987).

**Hayward, Jack.** *The State and the Market Economy: Industrial Patriotism and Economic Intervention in France* (New York: New York University Press, 1986).

**Loewenberg, Gerhard, and Samuel C. Patterson.** *Comparing Legislatures* (Boston: Little, Brown, 1979).

**Nordlinger, Eric A.** *On the Autonomy of the Dem-*

*ocratic State* (Cambridge, Mass., and London: Harvard University Press, 1981).

**Norton, Phillip.** *The British Polity* (New York and London: Longman, 1984).

———. *The Commons in Perspective* (New York: Longman, 1981).

**Reischauer, Edwin O.** *The Japanese* (Cambridge, Mass., and London: Harvard University Press, 1977).

**Richards, Peter G.** *The Local Government System* (London: George Allen & Unwin, 1983).

**Rose, Richard, and Ezra Suleiman,** eds. *Presidents and Prime Ministers* (Washington, D.C.: American Enterprise Institute, 1980).

**Smith, Gordon.** *Politics in Western Europe: A Comparative Analysis*, 4th ed. (London: Heinemann, 1983).

**Spotts, Frederic, and Theodor Wieser.** *Italy: A Difficult Democracy* (Cambridge: Cambridge University Press, 1986).

**Suleiman, Ezra N.** *Elites in French Society: The Politics of Survival* (Princeton, N.J.: Princeton University Press, 1978).

## Notes

1. A vote of confidence is a vote in Parliament on a motion introduced by supporters of the prime minister; a vote of nonconfidence is a vote on a motion introduced by the opposition. Dissolution of Parliament is an act that prematurely terminates the life of the present Parliament and means that new parliamentary elections will be held.
2. This presents the alternatives a bit too sharply. It is possible for a government to soldier on for a few months without a majority if a negative majority cannot (or will not) vote it out of power on a confidence or nonconfidence motion.
3. Paradoxically, the House of Lords has been quite active in amending legislation passed by the Conservative-dominated House of Commons elected in 1983 and in 1987. This appears to be partly because dissent within the ranks of Conservative MPs is lost in the large majority the Thatcher government holds in Commons. Conservative peers have thus joined non-Conservative peers in forcing the government to take a second look at the more controversial provisions of its bills, a function that the House of Commons is not performing as adequately as it might with a slimmer majority.
4. This was less than a certainty as long as important votes in the Chamber were taken by secret ballot. Individuals or factions within parties could break ranks and defeat, even bring down, the government on such votes. The practice of secret voting was abolished in 1988.
5. Robert J. Jackson, *Rebels and Whips* (London: Macmillan, 1968).
6. As a result of recent changes in party rules, the "deselection" of sitting MPs has occurred more frequently than in the past in the Labour Party, but it is an extremely rare occurrence in the Conservative Party.
7. Philip Norton, *Dissension in the House of Commons 1974–1979* (Oxford: Oxford University Press, 1980).
8. It should be noted, however, that the enactment of many bills in the Italian Parliament is done by smaller committees where party control may not be as strong as it is in the entire Chamber

or Senate, thus providing the individual legislator somewhat wider scope.

9. Joseph LaPalombara, *Democracy, Italian Style* (New Haven, Conn., and London: Yale University Press, 1987), p. 114.

10. Frederic Spotts and Theodor Wieser, *Italy: A Difficult Democracy* (Cambridge: Cambridge University Press, 1986), p. 115.

11. Stephen Padgett and Tony Burkett, *Political Parties and Elections in West Germany: The Search for a New Stability* (New York: St. Martin's, 1986), pp. 236–248.

12. Until recently it was customary to remark on the greater role played by the West German chancellor vis-à-vis his cabinet than of the British prime minister. This undoubtedly reflected the strong personal authority of long-standing chancellors Konrad Adenauer and Helmut Schmidt. However, recent commentary suggests that Margaret Thatcher has come to enjoy a similar preeminence, especially since the Falklands (Malvinas) War. Gillian Peele, "Government at the Center," in Henry Drucker et al., eds., *Developments in British Politics* (London: Macmillan, 1983), pp. 100–105; Dennis Kavanagh, *Thatcherism and British Politics: The End of Consensus*? (Oxford: Oxford University Press, 1987), p. 264.

13. President Mitterrand has at least wanted to be *seen* to be detached from day-to-day policymaking. It is likely that his real role is stronger than what outward appearances would suggest. Olivier Duhamel, "The Fifth Republic under François Mitterrand: Evolution and Perspectives," in George Ross et al., eds., *The Mitterrand Experiment: Continuity and Change in Modern France* (Cambridge: Polity Press, 1987), pp. 153–154.

14. Under the Constitution of 1958, the president was to be elected by a sort of electoral college that was made up of more than 80,000 members, consisting mainly of small-town mayors and councillors. This was the mode by which de Gaulle was first elected in December 1958.

15. Joel D. Aberbach, Robert D. Putnam, and Bert A. Rockman, *Bureaucrats and Politicians in Western Democracies* (Cambridge, Mass., and London: Harvard University Press, 1981).

16. Michio Muramatsu and Ellis S. Krauss, "Bureaucrats and Politicians in Policymaking: The Case of Japan," *American Political Science Review* 78 (March 1984), 126–146.

17. Aberbach et al., *Bureaucrats and Politicians*, p. 97.

18. Ibid., p. 220.

19. Muramatsu and Krauss, "Bureaucrats and Politicians," p. 134.

20. Peter Kellner and Lord Crowther-Hunt, *The Civil Servants: An Inquiry into Britain's Ruling Class* (London: Macdonald, 1980). More balanced is James B. Christoph, "High Civil Servants and the Politics of Consensualism in Great Britain," in Mattei Dogan, ed., *The Mandarins of Western Europe: The Political Role of Top Civil Servants* (New York: Wiley, 1975), pp. 25–62.

21. Aberbach et al., *Bureaucrats and Politicians*, pp. 87, 97.

22. In the preparation of this section, John A. Armstrong's *The European Administrative Elite* (Princeton, N.J.: Princeton University Press, 1973) was very useful.

23. Aberbach et al., *Bureaucrats and Politicians*, Ch. 3; Muramatsu and Krauss, "Bureaucrats and Politicians," pp. 130–131.

24. Kellner and Crowther-Hunt, *The Civil Servants*.

25. Muramatsu and Krauss, "Bureaucrats and Politicians," p. 130.

26. According to the constitution of the Fifth Republic, ministers may not simultaneously be members of Parliament. Such a prohibition is not found in our four other countries.

27. Aberbach et al., *Bureaucrats and Politicians*, p. 97.

28. Muramatsu and Krauss, "Bureaucrats and Politicians," p. 132.

29. Ibid.

30. Spotts and Wieser, *Italy*, pp. 128–136.
31. Yves Meny, "France: The Construction and Reconstruction of the Centre, 1945–86," *West European Politics* 10 (October 1987), 52–69; Steven C. Lewis and Serenella Sferza, "French Socialists between State and Society: From Party-Building to Power," in Ross et al., eds., *The Mitterrand Experiment*, pp. 109–110.
32. Jack Hayward, *The State and the Market Economy: Industrial Patriotism and Economic Intervention in France* (New York: New York University Press, 1986), Ch. 2.
33. Ted Robert Gurr and Desmond King, *The State and the City* (Basingstoke and London: Macmillan, 1987), Ch. 5.
34. Ken Newton, "The Local Financial Crisis in Britain: A Non-Crisis Which Is Neither Local Nor Financial," in L. J. Sharpe, ed., *The Local Fiscal Crisis in Western Europe: Myths and Realities* (London and Beverly Hills: Sage, 1981), pp. 222–225.
35. Gordon Smith, *Politics in Western Europe: A Comparative Analysis*, 4th ed. (New York: Holmes & Meier, 1983), p. 225.
36. Ibid.
37. Joachim Jens Hess, "The Federal Republic of Germany: From Cooperative Federalism to Joint Policy-Making," *West European Politics* 10 (October 1987), 70–87.

CHAPTER 6

# ECONOMIC POLICYMAKING: CASES IN INDUSTRIAL RELATIONS

## *Introduction*

The formal institutions and roles of government are an important indicator of where power is located in Western polyarchies. Presidents, prime ministers, cabinets, civil servants, and parliaments make decisions that have a major impact on the ways in which well-being, respect, and enlightenment are distributed among the populations of polyarchies. The power to make significant decisions is not confined to leaders and agents of government, however. Private citizens and institutions also hold power in countries where a private sector exists together with the public one and where the state does not attempt to control all facets of social life. Two important institutions that hold potential power are private business enterprises, especially the giant corporations; and trade unions, representing workers' interests. The former, through their capacity to determine levels of prices, wages, and investment for an economy, can collectively have a greater impact than can the economic policy decisions of government. The power of private corporations can, of course, be effectively checked by organized trade unions, but only in certain areas, such as the determination of wages. Big business and big labor may even combine their forces to nullify any government efforts to counter inflation through successive wage and price increases.

## *Economic-Sector Interest Groups*

### Farmers' and Business Groups

In the private economic sphere, as distinct from the state administrative and political circles, three types of interest groups play an important part in influencing economic policy in all Western European countries: farmers' associations, business associations, and workers' organizations. All three are regularly consulted by their governments in the making of economic policy and in the determination of each country's position on economic matters within the European Community (EC), of which all four of our Western European countries are members. (See Chapter 7.) In postindustrial societies, economic policymaking has become a central preoccupation of political elites in general. The leaders of the major economic interest groups are therefore an essential element in the power structure of each country. Their advice is solicited when major economic decisions are to be made, and they can often precipitate events that will compel government decision makers to come to grips with unpleasant situations.

*Farmers' associations* carry considerable weight in the economic policymaking process of all First World countries, despite the decreasing size of the farm population. In all five of our countries, independent farmers tend to support the parties in the center and on the right. In France and Italy, the parties on the left have a share of votes of sharecroppers and agricultural workers in the regions where they are numerous, but the leading farm associations in these countries represent independent farmers who produce for the larger market. Thus, the farm associations are not in the best position to bargain between parties on the left and the right. In Great Britain, they are tied closely to the Conservative Party; in Italy and West Germany to the Christian Democrats; and in Japan to the Liberal Democrats. Only in France, where they can shift their votes back and forth between parties of the center and the right, can they exert some leverage through the ballot.

Nevertheless, in all five countries the economic role of the farmers is crucial. Whether the country is relatively self-sufficient in farm products, as France is, or partly dependent on imports, as Great Britain and West Germany are, the agricultural sector has an important impact on the balance of payments. France and Italy earn a substantial part of their foreign currencies through agricultural exports, especially to their Common Market partners. The EC's Common Agricultural Policy (CAP) has been worked out and is continually being adjusted with the interests of the key farm produce sectors of each member country in mind. Farmers' interest groups do a lot of lobbying both in their own national capitals and in Brussels, the headquarters of the EC.

There are three types of *organized business* interests in Western Europe and Japan, as in the United States: large private corporations, trade associations (of firms in the various productive and distributive sectors), and peak employers' confederations. The employers' confederations are the principal spokespersons for employers in national-level conflicts with organized labor, such as wage disputes, disagreement over working conditions, government policy issues (e.g., wage and price controls), and questions of the participation of workers in the management of the firm. In each of our five countries, there is a leading peak confederation: the Confederation of British Industries (CBI), the National Confederation of French Employers (CNPF), the Federation of German Employers (BDA), the General Confederation of Italian Industry (Confindustria), and the Japan Federation of Employers' Associations (Nikkeiren). With the exception of Confindustria, these tend to be dominated by the larger firms, which maintain specialists in employer–employee relations and related matters. Contacts among employers' spokespersons, leading politicians, and high-ranking civil servants tend to be very close, especially in France and Japan, where parties of the center-right have held onto power for a long time and where traditions of administrative neutrality are weaker than in Great Britain and West Germany.

Sector-specific trade associations play an important part in the overall economic planning for growth and modernization and in the development of trade policy nationally and internationally. Trade associations work closely with government experts and officials of the

EC in developing these policies. Their ability to commit an entire industrial or commercial sector makes their cooperation indispensable. The major opponent of a given trade association (for example, that for the West German chemical industry) is the corresponding trade association in a competing country (for example, the British chemical industry's). But in negotiations at the EC level, cooperation may be more important than competition, since promotion and protection of the industry in Western Europe against outside competitors will be emphasized. The interlocking relationships among trade association officials, national political leaders, high-ranking civil servants, and the "Eurocrats" based in Brussels are making it increasingly impossible to view national economic policymaking in isolation.

To further complicate the picture, the major industrial giants—private corporations such as British Petroleum, Fiat, or Siemens—have an impact on both national and European-level economic policymaking, over and beyond that of the trade and employers' associations to which they belong. Political contributions by corporation and their leading officers, private friendships between the latter and leading political figures, and the movement of corporate managers back and forth between employment in the private and public sectors all lead to the conclusion that the corporate directorate in postindustrial countries constitutes an important, if unmeasurable, part of the power elite.

Furthermore, many of the leading private firms in Western Europe are subsidiaries of the gigantic multinational corporations, many of which have headquarters elsewhere, especially in the United States and Japan. This has led to a substantial body of critical literature in Europe, asserting that the multinationals are Trojan horses that enable American interests to substantially influence not only the economics but also the political systems in Western Europe.[1] Much of the discussion in Western Europe has emotional overtones, reflecting resentment over the preeminent economic, political, and military position of the United States since World War II. However, the discussion may be losing some of its urgency as European-based multinationals have reversed the process in the past two decades. It is difficult to assess to what extent parent corporations are able to control the actions of their affiliates abroad. But it cannot be denied that the multinationals make it difficult for Western European governments to regulate these businesses because too harsh a regulatory policy could drive a certain firm out of a country, resulting in considerable hardship for the local economy.

## Trade Unions

Can *organized labor* rival organized business as a political force in Western polyarchies? That business interests have a secure position within the power structure of each country (although varying in degree from country to country) would be difficult to refute. Like the United States and despite a generally larger public sector, Western European countries are, in the final analysis, capitalistic. Although governments as well as the EC can regulate and induce certain behavior on the part of the private sector, their economies are still at the mercy of decisions made by a relatively small number of corporation heads. On the employees' side, there is a potentially similar power in that trade unions can bring economic activity to a standstill through use of the strike weapon. Nevertheless, there is considerable variation among our five countries with respect to how well trade unions are

Striking French medical students lie on a bridge over the River Seine in Paris, blocking traffic. This action in early 1990 was part of an effort to call attention to their working conditions in French hospitals and clinics.

actually equipped to use this weapon to their advantage.

Industrial relations in Western Europe have been in a state of flux since the 1960s.[2] Collective bargaining has not been as well established as it is in the United States. Efforts to institutionalize it more firmly have led to more-or-less formal arrangements at the national level between employers' and employees' organizations. For example, minimum wages may be agreed on by representatives of the two sides of industry at meetings presided over by members of the government and high-ranking civil servants. But the actual level of wages above these minimums will vary from industry to industry and from plant to plant within an industry, depending on the relative bargaining power of the workers and employers at these levels. Often the unions are left out of this process altogether because agreements are worked out in committees that represent management and employees; for this purpose, the employees elect their representatives directly with or without union participation in the election. In France, bargains reached locally with one union will apply to all workers, even though in some cases a majority belong to unions that were not a bargaining party.

However, wildcat strikes may break out, which the national employees' federations cannot control. Local workers, whether members of unions or not, can present their national leadership with *faits accomplis*. Although the latter may oppose such strikes at the outset, they often are obliged to support them to maintain some semblance of union solidarity. Because the national leadership of the unions often has little control over local activity, employers and government may both be at the mercy of worker demands for higher wages. When concessions are made in one industry or even by one firm, it becomes harder to resist parallel demands elsewhere, and so the inflationary spiral continues. In fact, governments may find themselves having to combat not only the trade unions but also the employers whenever they attempt to pass a higher-wage bill on to the consumer in the form of higher prices.

Nevertheless, there is fairly wide variation in the strength of organized labor as it faces both the employers and the state in our five countries. Relatively speaking, until recently at any rate, workers have been in the weaker position in France and Japan, and in the stronger in Great Britain, Italy, and West Germany—for different reasons. Three factors account for these judgments: (1) the unity of the trade union movement nationally, (2) the strength of the unions at the plant level, and (3) the strength of the central government as a potential adversary seeking to frustrate union objectives.

In France, all three factors have worked against the emergence of a strong trade union movement. There are three major national confederations of trade unions in France, each with a different ideological orientation. The Communist-dominated *Confédération Générale du Travail* (CGT) is the oldest and largest, but the long-standing exclusion of the Communist Party from government kept the CGT in an isolated position, not only in its relations with the government but also in its relations with other workers' confederations. Of the two major noncommunist confederations, the largest is the *Confédération Française Démocratique du Travail* (CFDT), an offshoot from a Christian Democratic confederation. The smaller one, *Force Ouvrière* (FO), is centrist in its leanings and is also more anti-Communist than the CFDT, which has sometimes found that cooperation with the CGT is advantageous. The division of French organized labor extends from the national level to the various industrial sectors and even to the plant level, where the unions put up com-

A demonstration in Paris by car workers. The two left-wing French trade unions, CGT and CFDT, are both identified by banners as sponsors of the demonstration.

peting candidates for election to local workers' committees. Wherever more than one union confronts the employer, the latter will be in a position to divide and conquer.

At the national level, the French trade unions face not only a united employers' movement, but also a highly centralized and technically expert government. Trade unions send representatives to the various committees that participate in formulating the five-year plans, but they are usually outclassed by the highly proficient representatives of the trade associations and the appropriate ministries. Moreover, because the right was in power continuously from 1958 until 1981, trade unionists felt that they were dealing with a monolith when it came to national-level decisions on wages, prices, and other issues that are vital to workers' well-being. Business interests were well represented politically in the economic ministries in the persons of Gaullist and Giscardist ministers. The higher civil servants have often had a tour of political duty in the service of the leaders of these political parties, and they may have aspirations of ending their careers in management positions in private corporations. With the left in power in the 1980s, the trade unions were no longer on the outside looking in with respect to economic policymaking. However, their ability to influence government decisions has declined since the first year of the Socialist government, as economic policy has come to accord more with employers' interests. Much the same judgments regarding the second and third source of trade union weakness can be made about the Japanese trade union movement, which, aligned with the left opposition and representing only a modest proportion of the workers, plays a minor role in economic decision making, except when it bears on the few industries where it is strong.[3]

The Italian labor movement is also divided between Communist-leaning and non- or anti-Communist confederations. The largest, the *General Confederation of Italian Labor* (CGIL), is made up of workers who are members of, or tend to support, either the Communist or the Socialist Party. However, the Communists are in the principal leadership positions; and, unlike the case of the CGT in France, they are less isolated politically and can have a greater voice in industrial disputes both nationally and locally. The Christian Democratic trade union confederation, moreover, is allied with the left wing of the DC, which favors closer cooperation with the Communists in policymaking. Thus, the trade unions in Italy speak with a more united voice both nationally and locally than those in France. Trade union strength is further enhanced by the weakness and internal division of the Italian government. Lacking a majority in Parliament, the Christian Democratic governments have had to include the Socialists and to woo the Communists for support. Such support has been gained only by making concessions that benefit the Italian labor movement. Still, employers' interests are well represented in the DC's leadership, which means that the concessions are often passed on to the consumer, as can be attested by the high rate of inflation in Italy.

A mixed image likewise emerges from examining the West German labor movement. Here the movement is not divided. The *German Trade Union Federation* (DGB) has the overwhelming majority of organized industrial workers affiliated with it. But the greatest strength of the West German trade union movement is in the large national federations, organized on an industry basis, such as the metalworkers and chemical workers, both affiliated with the DGB. Until the 1970s, union members were not effectively organized at the plant level because the national federations preferred to negotiate nationally with employers and the government. Although the DGB leadership is heavily Social Democratic, Catholic trade unionists are also affiliated with it, and an effort has been made to maintain harmonious relations with both CDU- and SPD-led governments. A great deal of give-and-take has occurred in negotiations at these levels, and the unions have shown a greater tendency than their counterparts in France, Italy, and Britain to forgo resorting to strikes in return for assurances by the government that the standard of living of the German working class will continue to rise. Since the late 1970s, as recession has deepened, the West German trade unions' national organizations have become more militant, especially since the arrival of the center-right government in 1982.

As in West Germany, organized labor in Great Britain is united under one confederation—the *Trades Union Congress* (TUC). The political links of British trade unions are tighter than is the case in the four other countries. National federations are affiliated directly with the Labour Party, and a portion of the dues that trade union members pay to their federations is automatically turned over to the party, unless members contract out by signing a statement of refusal to have their union dues so used. Because only a small percentage of trade unionists contract out, the majority of British trade union members are indirect members of the Labour Party. Or, to put it another way, approximately five-sixths of the membership of the Labour Party is indirect membership. The same ratio of votes is cast by the trade unions at the annual Labour Party conference as a result of this arrangement, which means that, whenever the unions speak with a united voice, they dominate the party. When this voice is at odds with that of the party's parliamentary leadership, the latter finds itself isolated from its rank and file—a vulnerable position. But such direct conflict between the parliamentary leaders and the trade unions seldom arises. Indeed, since 1981 the trade unions have had a 40 percent share in the election of the party's parliamentary leader. In recent years, the trade union movement and the Labour Party have both been divided internally, with the leadership of the TUC and of the party serving as mediators on divisive issues.

Such close ties between the trade unions and one political party can be disadvantageous whenever that party is out of power and economic policy is being made by the opposite party. Moreover, the unions cannot expect even a Labour government simply to translate their wishes into public policy without significant alterations. Since the period of acute industrial unrest in the late 1960s and early 1970s, the Labour Party has been at pains to convince the voters that trade union self-restraint is more likely to be exercised at the urging of a Labour than of a Conservative government. The claim was sufficiently credible that, after narrowly gaining power in February 1974, Labour was able to strengthen its hold in a second election eight months later. But the claim was no longer credible to British voters five years later. After a series of strikes in the winter of 1978–79, which the Labour government had been unable to prevent, Labour was voted out of power. In the 1980s, the Conservative government was able to claim that, not the Labour party, but rather the Conservatives, are best able to hold the trade unions in check.

What makes British trade unions more powerful than those in France or Japan, if not those in West Germany or Italy? It is certainly not because they speak with a single voice when addressing the government or the employers. In fact, the TUC can only exhort powerful unions, such as the Transport and General Workers' Union or the Amalgamated Engineering Union—both of which have hundreds of thousands of members and both of which sometimes have militant leftists among their leaders. Such giants are free to steer their own courses even if these conflict directly with the policy of the Labour Party and the TUC. Paradoxically, the power of the trade unions since the 1960s has stemmed in considerable part from their disunity or, more specifically, from the inability of national union leaders to control the actions of their rank and file at the local level. A moderate national leadership, attempting to cooperate with the government in a policy of wage restraint, may find that the local branches are electing militant leftists, even Communists, to the key positions of representation at the plant level.[4] Some of these same conditions have developed in continental European countries, but the fact that their unions are weaker at the local level means that the grass roots of organized labor cannot impose awkward situations on national policymakers as well as they can in Great Britain. Still, as we shall see, disunity has become less impressive as a source of strength for the British trade unions in the era of Conservative government under Margaret Thatcher in the 1980s.

## Declining Trade Union Strength

There are reasons to believe that developments in the postindustrial era are working against comprehensive and cohesive working-class organization in Western democracies. In Chapter 2 emphasis was placed on the higher levels of unemployment that have come about in part because of long-range trends rather than, as before, because there are troughs in the business cycle. These trends—technological change and the rise of newly industrialized countries providing competition for the manufactured products traditionally produced by advanced industrial economies—have brought on a decline in demand for the skills of certain kinds of workers who prevailed in an earlier era when they formed the backbone of the trade union movement. The skilled worker (or craftsman) and the assembly line unskilled or semiskilled worker are in numerical decline. Union organization in the large factories of the mid–twentieth century reached peak levels because of the large number of workers performing routine tasks on the assembly line or, as in the case of the trained craftsmen, doing repair work on the machines or precision work on various components that were not amenable to assembly line processing.[5]

Earlier in the century, the growth of the unskilled categories of workers faced the existing trade unions—largely comprising the older crafts and skills—with the dilemma of whether to assimilate the new workers or to protect the distinctions in terms of pay and status between skilled and unskilled workers, thus forcing the unskilled to form their own unions. In some cases the former route was taken, resulting in the formation of large and usually powerful industry-wide comprehensive unions; in other cases the union movement remained highly fragmented, with different unions organizing different segments of the workforce within the same industry and even within the same plant.

Today, the trade union movement, already weakened by (1) the decline in the number of manual workers, (2) disadvantages in trying to organize the growing service sector, and (3) the declining bargaining strength of workers' organizations when unemployment is chronically high, must overcome not only the divisions between skilled, semiskilled, and unskilled workers, but also the tendency of workers of whatever skill level to doubt the relevancy of trade unions to their needs. Such workers see their own interests as tied closely to those of their employers; they view the real threat to their livelihoods as not the capriciousness of the employer, but the threat posed by competition from other workers whose skills may be substituted for their own.

Still another contribution to declining trade union strength is the parallel phenomenon of the growth of small satellite firms making components or providing services for the larger corporations that were once performed within the corporation itself, but are now "farmed out" to save labor costs in a competitive market. The satellite firms are able to survive when the economy is buoyant, but many of them fall by the wayside in harder times. For the most part, they employ unskilled workers, who will return to the status of the unemployed when the firm discontinues operations, and whose earning power when at work is below that of workers in more stable factory employment. These conditions are similar to those found in service-sector jobs that rise and fall on the basis of the ups and downs of the economy: jobs in retailing, fast food, and the tourism sector.

The growth of both satellite manufacturing and marginal parts of the service sector has led to the identification of the "dual economy" phenomenon, or the division between the stable sector and the unstable sector of the economy.[6] In the stable sector many types of jobs are more secure, workers are unionized, and pay is higher. In the unstable sector the opposite conditions prevail. To varying degrees these elements of postindustrial "disorganized capitalism" can be found in all five of our countries. The ways in which it affects the policymaking process depend in part on the traditional relationship between the state, the employers, and the unions in each country.

## *Economic Policymaking*

### Pluralism

The policymaking process in all First World polyarchies features the interaction of major economic interest groups with one another and with the state in a continuous process involving both conflict and cooperation. When contrasted with the policymaking processes of Second and Third World countries, policymaking in the First World roughly corresponds to the *pluralist* model, according to which the conflict between major actors takes place within an agreed-on set of rules of the game. Over the long run, gains by one side are balanced by those of the other, with the government playing a mediating role. Public policies can be understood as the outcomes of contests between the competing groups in which both sides have agreed in advance to comply with these outcomes or to seek to change them through normalized processes. Whether public policy sides with one of the contenders or another, it will be a reflection of the momentary balance of power between the contenders, a balance that the temporarily weaker is free to seek to rectify.

Pluralism is the image of the policymaking process that most interest groups and political parties in First World countries present in seeking to justify their actions. They will say that they have acted according to established procedures and within normal channels or that they have acted to keep such channels open—or, in extreme cases, to reopen them—when others have closed them. They will insist that they respect the rights of their opponents and are merely acting to ensure that their own rights will be respected. On the other hand, they may accuse their opponents of seeking to circumvent legality and to deny legitimate rights. Trade unions may accuse employers of constituting a privileged class interested only in preserving their unjustly large share of the wealth; employers' groups may accuse the unions of trying to divide society into warring classes, thus weakening the nation in the face of economic and international dangers. In all such efforts, the pluralist image is put forth as both normal and desirable. Others are accused of seeking to subvert a system that would work to the advantage of everyone if all would approach it with goodwill.

### Corporatism

Some political scientists have challenged the pluralist image of Western economic policymaking, arguing that it treats the *state*[7] as a neutral reflector of group pressures, when in fact the state has interests of its own that it is all too ready to interject into the policymaking process. Some of these writers have incorporated the state into a Marxist framework, but most are adherents to the corporatist school, that sees *corporatism* as a more viable alternative to pluralism, both as a description of how economic policy actually *is* made and as a prescription of how it *ought to be* made.[8]

Corporatists share the belief that the adverse economic conditions of recent years are attributable to the selfish actions of groups in society that have placed their own particular interests ahead of the interests of all. This can be seen in the inflationary spirals, wherein producer groups sought to pass the burden of price increases on to the consumer, that is, to the economically weak who were not in a favorable position to protect their purchasing power. To combat this tendency, government must intervene to curb the power of the acquisitive. But government is often in too weak a position to do so because its leaders are dependent on the same groups for their power. Elections are seen as a bidding process in which promises of tax cuts, wage indexing, increases in social security benefits, and job-creating spending programs vie with one another for available votes.

The largest share of blame for these problems is usually reserved for the working classes, who are said to undermine economic stability through their excessive demands. The central aim of corporatism has always been to bring wage demands and class conflict under control, subordinating them to what is perceived to be in the general interest. What this means, first and foremost, is the interest of the employer in maintaining profit levels and of the government in maintaining economic stability. Instruments that are used to bring about wage restraint range from coercive strikebreaking actions by government to incentive schemes designed to induce voluntary compliance on the part of wage earners and their organizations. In practice, these can be grouped into two sets, the instruments of what we might call *negative* and *positive* corporatism.[9]

*Negative* corporatism would take the form employed by Fascist Italy and Nazi Germany before World War II, a form in which independent trade unions were dissolved and state-dominated workers' organizations were created in their place. This resulted from a bargain between employers and government, in which state controls over production were accepted by employers in return for the state's guarantee of a compliant labor force. Forced to live on lower wages than a free labor market would otherwise have brought them, the workers could take some consolation, in Germany at least, from the fact that jobs were once again relatively plentiful after the early dark days of the Great Depression. The justification for this exploitative system was the assumption that society was a corporate entity whose functioning parts were intimately interdependent. Action taken on behalf of the employers' interests would be to the benefit of all groups, and action on behalf of the selfish interests of one group would be detrimental to the interests of all. Thus, cooperation in the common effort was both normal and desirable. Conflict was seen as abnormal and counterproductive.

The more *positive* version of corporatism, and the version that is more widely advocated in Western Europe today, has been promoted most consistently by left-of-center Christian Democrats and by right-of-center Democratic Socialists, in other words by occupants of the broad center of the left–right spectrum. (See Chapter 4.) This maintains some of the same assumptions as negative corporatism—that society is an interdependent corporate entity and that cooperation is a more normal mode of behavior than conflict. But it also harbors a more optimistic view of the likelihood that workers and their organizations will voluntarily moderate their claims on society so that all in society will enjoy the benefits of cooperative effort. In this version, workers should be induced to cooperate with employers and with the state through efforts to maintain stable prices. In countries where positive corporatism has been implemented, trade unions and employers' organizations are given representation on consultative bodies with the right to be heard before major economic policy decisions are made by government. Democratic Socialists would go farther and grant workers a legitimate share in the profits and even the management of the firms in which they work as a means of sensitizing them to the large stake they have in the health of the economy and of each of its functioning units.

Advocates of positive corporatism contend that the problems of British economic policymaking stem from failure to carry corporatism farther than it was carried in the 1970s. Citing relatively successful examples of state–industry cooperation in West Germany, Austria, and Sweden, they argue that successes registered in keeping both unemployment and inflation from approaching double figures were due to systems of consultation and mutual restraint in income demands by economic actors that made it possible for goods to be priced at internationally competitive levels. This in turn enabled employment to be maintained at home in sectors that were during the same period in decline in inflation-prone Britain. Countries in which positive corporatism allegedly worked best were those in which cooperative mechanisms had been established shortly after World War II and had thus become ingrained. Cooperation and mutual self-restraint had become habitual by the time the crisis of the 1970s arrived.[10] In Britain, experiments with corporatism had come only after the economic situation had begun to deteriorate, and, when introduced, they were not far-reaching and were ultimately unsuccessful The problems of the British economy were due to uncontrolled pluralism, not excessive corporatism, according to this view.[11]

In broad terms, positive corporatism is found in countries where there exists a combination of two defining characteristics: (1) a *strong state tradition* and (2) a *cohesive trade union movement*. These defining characteristics are especially important when it comes to applying the concepts of pluralism and corporatism to economic policymaking. In countries with strong state traditions, the issue (so prevalent in American debates on economic policy) of whether the state should play a role in the economy is rarely raised. Because the state has historically played an important role in shaping and guiding the private sector, the question tends to be *what* the state should do, not *whether* it should do anything to cope with challenges to economic well-being. In positive corporatism, the state plays a role as partner with the private sector and the trade unions, unlike negative corporatism, where the state helps employers control their workers. The role of the state is more secure in positive corporatism than it is in countries characterized by pluralism, where active, as opposed to passive (reactive), state involvement in the economy has not been universally accepted as legitimate. The state in the pluralist policymaking model is a mediator between interests but is not itself actively engaged until the conflict has matured through a complicated process of sifting of issues that are sufficiently salient to receive public attention.

As already noted, the cohesion of trade unions is also a crucial defining feature of corporatism when it comes to economic policymaking. In positive corporatism, the trade unions play a positive role in helping shape economic policy alongside the state and private business interests. If cohesive trade unions prevail, corporatism is facilitated because bargaining partners can make commitments on behalf of their memberships with the certainty that they will be able to honor them. Corporatist bargaining requires mutual trust between the bargaining partners, trust that no one will attempt to take undue advantage of the willingness of others to make concessions. But in some countries with strong state traditions, notably France and Japan among our countries, what might appear to be corporatist relations between the public and the private sector fall short of positive corporatism in that the unions are too weak, and their role in policymaking is too poorly established, for a balanced triangular relationship between state, employers, and unions to exist. In Japan there are elements of what we have called negative corporatism, where a strong state acts on behalf of the interests of employers to keep the workers' movement weak. In France it seems more the case that a strong state acts autonomously of both employers and trade unions to make economic policy, in what some have called a *statist* policymaking pattern. It is probably most accurate to say that both Japan and France display a mixture of statist and corporatist (both positive and negative) elements, with the mix varying with the type of economic policy and the sector of the economy concerned. But, in general, where trade unions are incohesive, as they are in Britain as well, trade union bargainers will be uncertain of the support of those they represent and will be unable to make firm commitments or to convince those with whom they are bargaining that their commitments are reliable. In the absence of this certainty, pluralist contests of strength or else statist impositions of unbargained, unmediated solutions are what is likely to result.

Pickets in front of the London headquarters of the British Broadcasting Corporation, 1989. These members of the National Union of Journalists are striking over a pay dispute with BBC management.

In our five countries we can observe four kinds of combinations of state traditions and trade union cohesiveness. Japan, West Germany, and France have active state traditions, whereas Italy and Britain do not, although in the Italian case the Fascist experience provides a twenty-year exception. But, whereas trade unions in West Germany are strong, those in France and Japan are weak, providing two cases in which the state and the employers have successfully coalesced to keep workers' organizations at bay. In the case of the passive-state-tradition countries, unions are relatively cohesive in Italy and relatively incohesive in Britain, although this has not always meant union weakness in the latter case or union strength in the former. Our two-way classification of the five countries is shown in figure 6.1.

The West Germany combination has strong elements of corporatism; those of Italy and Britain are essentially pluralistic; the French and

| | | Trade Unions | |
|---|---|---|---|
| | | *Cohesive* | *Incohesive* |
| **State Tradition** | *Active* | Positive corporatism (West Germany) | Statism (Japan, France) |
| | *Passive* | Labor-driven pluralism (Italy and Britain, 1970s) | Capital-driven pluralism (Italy and Britain, 1980s) |

*Figure 6.1* Models of industrial relations.

Japanese cases are primarily statist. However, trade union cohesion in Italy is a fragile phenomenon that may not hold up against the factors that are weakening trade unions in post-industrial society. Also, it would appear that the term *statist* as applied to industrial relations fits the French case better than it does the Japanese.

## *Case Studies in the Politics of Industrial Relations*[12]

These competing models of economic policymaking have been applied in numerous analyses of the way policy is made in advanced industrial countries.[13] A great deal of disagreement exists over how comprehensively a given model applies to any particular country. If positive corporatism seems to fit the way industrial relations disputes are settled in West Germany, for example, is it as applicable when we turn to an examination of the making of West German monetary and fiscal policy? Does any single model extend in any country to such diverse socioeconomic policy realms as housing policy, transport policy, and international trade policy? Obviously, the answer will be different from one country to another and from one policy area to another. However, in certain policy areas it is clearer which of the models best applies to a given country; five case studies follow involving industrial relations policies and the related problem of the unemployment produced by industrial restructuring. The cases involve, first, the setting of wages and prices prior to the advent of deeper recession and higher unemployment in the 1980s, illustrating the tension between the competing approaches to the problem of stagflation. Second, the phenomenon of deindustrialization, which was more apparent in the early to mid-1980s, changed the agenda of industrial relations policymaking, which is also reflected in the cases. The case of West Germany illustrates the fact that the positive corporatist approach, successful in coping with stagflation, has been less successful in dealing with the problems of deindustrialization. The Italian case illustrates that efforts in the 1970s to impose elements of positive corporatism on a pluralist base have given way to a resurgence of what can almost be considered negative corporatism in the 1980s. In both countries deindustrialization has changed some of the environmental conditions affecting policymaking. These more recent developments are touched on briefly in the West German and

Italian cases, then dealt with more fully in the French, Japanese, and British cases, discussed in the sections that follow.

## West Germany and Italy: Industrial Relations When Unions Are Strong

The intervention of the German state in the economy goes back to the German Empire in the nineteenth century, and it continued in each successive regime until the early years of the Bonn Republic. During the first fifteen years of the new regime, the official economic policy stance of the West German government accorded with its overall commitment to what it called the "social market" strategy. This set of economic policies was most closely identified with Christian Democratic Economics Minister Ludwig Erhard, who eventually succeeded Konrad Adenauer as chancellor. The strategy was to permit economic forces as much autonomy as possible to pursue their own interests, a policy guided by the laissez-faire assumption that state interference in the economy would impede natural productive forces, stifling the incentives to innovate and take risks. It also expressed the strong German aversion to inflation, stemming back to the disastrous experiences of the early 1920s. The most intervention the Erhard policy would permit was orthodox monetarist control over the supply of money. Erhard placed his faith in a stable growth in money supply to moderate demand and limit price increases during full-scale economic expansion. Given the seemingly voluntary moderation on the part of employer and employees, the policy attained substantial success, to the mutual satisfaction of the government, the employers' organizations and private corporations, and the trade union leadership.

So long as the Erhard strategy and tactics were working, there was no reason to call into question its basic assumptions that minimized the role of the state in the economy. Yet when West German industrial relations are compared with those of its neighbors, one central fact stands out: the existence of rather elaborate and stringent legal constraints in the employer–employee bargaining process. Unlike the situation in Great Britain, for example, unofficial strikes are illegal in West Germany, meaning that national union leaders, challenged by insurrection on the shop floor, can cloak themselves in a wrap of legality and refuse to support unofficial strikes and their objectives. This serves to reinforce the determination of national union leaders to cooperate with employers in following a policy of wage restraint. It also suggests a somewhat stronger role for the state in practice than the Erhard philosophy allowed in theory. In fact, West German law and the enforcement structure maintained to ensure compliance with the law had a corporatist flavor to it, and, compared with some Western European countries, it gave an advantage to the employers.

That corporatism was the underlying economic outlook of a large share of the West German elite became evident as the recession of 1966–67 took hold. Its almost immediate political impact was to discredit Chancellor Erhard and force him out of office. In December 1966, a new government was formed—the Grand Coalition of Christian Democrats and Social Democrats, led by Kurt Georg Kiesinger, the CDU chancellor, and SPD leader Willy Brandt, as vice-chancellor and foreign minister. Seeking a way out of the recession, the leaders of both partners of the coalition were willing to renounce those aspects of the Erhard policies that restrained the state from intervening in the economy. The new economics minister, Keynesian economist Kurt Schiller of the SPD, developed a new West German economic policy: the policy of "concerted action." It meant that the state would take a more active role in controlling economic fluctuations through fiscal as well as monetary policy, a commitment that had been reached in Great Britain and France more than a decade earlier. But the Grand Coalition went a step farther and announced an income policy that would involve the state in putting forth wage and price guidelines for acceptance by both employers and employees.

The Schiller experiment indicated that there was substantial support among West German elites for some version of positive corporatism involving government leadership. The Brandt government (1969–74) continued to seek employer and trade union cooperation in limiting wage and price increases and in containing industrial unrest. The effort was assisted by the success gained by the national trade unions in establishing their presence at the plant level. Whereas localized disputes previously had been negotiated with the firm by works councils elected by employees, in the early 1970s trade union representatives began to actively seek election to the councils and came to control them in numerous instances.

The Brandt and subsequent Helmut Schmidt coalition governments had the majority of workers supporting their political and economic objectives. National trade union leadership was supportive most of the time, having to withdraw some distance from the government whenever plant-level militancy was at its height. This tended to vary with the fortunes of the West German economy, which was subject to greater fluctuation in the 1970s than in earlier periods, but not, it should be emphasized, when compared with other postindustrial economies in the 1970s.

During the 1970s, the SPD under Brandt and Schmidt sought to secure greater worker support for its policies by advancing the objective of worker participation in management—*Mitbestimmung*, or codetermination. The idea was to elevate the institution of the works council from the plant level to the level of the business firm's corporate headquarters and to give workers representation on the governing boards. To achieve this objective, the SPD leadership was forced to negotiate with the coalition partner, the Free Democrats, a party with considerable financial dependence on business interests. The compromise meant the limitation of codetermination to larger firms and to those corporate policies that directly concern the interests of the workforce, not to decisions of major economic importance, such as pricing policy or industrial mergers. The failure to extend codetermination farther undoubtedly limited its effect as a means of gaining worker acceptance of the corporatist framework.

What distinguished the West German pattern from that in our three other countries in Western Europe was a pair of important characteristics: (1) Industrial conflict was consistently lowest in West Germany, even in periods where it was intense by West German standards; and (2) agreement among West German elites (including trade union leaders) on the efficacy of positive corporatism is not found in Great Britain, Italy, and France, where elites typically diverge in their outlooks on industrial relations. The West German pattern was especially characteristic of the period of coalition government when the SPD was the senior partner, a condition reinforced by electoral victories for the coalition in 1972, 1976, and 1980. With the return to power of the CDU/CSU in 1982 in a new center-right coalition with the FDP, the pattern has changed in a more conflictive, and thus less corporatist, direction. The return of the right to power has taxed the ability and willingness of trade union leaders to withstand the pressures of the militant left within their ranks.

Rising levels of unemployment in the early 1980s, accompanied by declining real wages, brought the value of positive corporatism into question for some West German trade unionists. The pursuit of "positive sum politics" had been accompanied by the greater centralization of national trade unions and a growing distance between the professional union officials at the national level and the membership on the shop floor.[14] Members' jobs were threatened by the twin nemeses of recession and automation, especially in the face of a center-right government that was adding to recessionary trends with its deflationary policies. Neo-Marxists on the Social Democratic and trade union left renewed their demand that the forty-hour workweek in West Germany be reduced to thirty-five hours without reduction in workers' income, so that capitalist employers would be unable to continue to profit through laying off workers. Instead, existing workers' incomes could be maintained, while younger unemployed workers could be added to the workforce to fill the hours opened up by shortened workweeks. Two of the most militant industrial unions, the gigantic metalworkers' union and the printers' union, put forth this proposal in early 1984, but it was rejected by employers and the Kohl government on the grounds that it would raise the cost of producing West German steel and automobiles, making them less competitive internationally, with an adverse effect on the entire West German economy. It would create jobs for Japanese workers, not those at home, it was argued.

In May 1984, the metalworkers and printers began selective strikes, especially affecting production in the automotive and related engineering industries. Employers in those industries retaliated by "lockouts," or temporary closings of the plants not yet hit by the strike. This meant that many thousand more workers were off work than were actually on strike. By late June, 450,000 workers were out of work. Those locked out or laid off were ruled ineligible to receive unemployment benefits, which meant a heavy burden on strike funds used by the unions to support members' families during the strike. But the combined strike and lockout was costly to employers as well. In late June, metal industry management and unions agreed to submit the dispute to mediation. Agreement was reached rather quickly on the general principle of a 38½-hour week, to be interpreted flexibly from firm to firm. The center-right government, which had sided with the employers, was not a party to the agreement. Thus, the framework for resolution of the conflict was pluralist rather than corporatist. Still, the speed with which agreement was reached once mediation began in this, the longest West German strike since 1957, suggests that positive corporatist reflexes were still operant in West Germany.

In contrast to the case of West Germany, where elements of National Socialist negative corporatism were systematically weeded out, the early postwar Italian system of industrial relations was strongly influenced by the two decades of Fascist rule the country had experienced. Benito Mussolini's state had explicitly opted for a system of negative corporatism in which state-controlled trade unions assisted the government and the employers in enforcing labor discipline. Although the constitution and statutory law of the new Italian Republic repudiated the fascist system and removed legal restrictions on both employers and employees, Italian employers did not easily give up the corporatist model to which they had grown accustomed during the Fascist years. The weakness of the trade unions during the 1950s allowed employers to impose a negative corporatist reality on a pluralist legal framework, despite, or perhaps in part because of, the fact that workers' organizations and political parties espoused an intransigent Marxism.

Economic circumstances worked against the success of trade union militancy. Rapid modernization and economic growth occurred in the 1950s in Italy as they did elsewhere in Western Europe, but the early period of underemployment lasted somewhat longer because industrialization was less far advanced and there was an overabundance of semiskilled and unskilled workers, especially in southern Italy. Organizationally, the trade unions in Italy were very nearly the weakest in Western Europe. Their memberships tended to be confined to the minority of skilled workers, and they were notably weak in the semi-industrialized southern regions.

At the national level, the unions did not speak with one voice. The largest, the *General Confederation of Italian Labor* (CGIL), had strong links with the opposition Communist and Socialist parties. The Catholic union, the *Italian Confederation of Workers' Syndicates* (CISL), was linked with the left wing of the ruling Christian Democratic Party. The tactic of divide and conquer worked well for employers throughout most of the 1950s. Finally, at the plant level, what presence the unions had was rendered ineffectual by management's practice of ignoring plant works councils, created immediately after World War II and often containing union members. Although the employers' refusal to negotiate wage agreements with the works councils was illegal, the Christian Democratic governments of the 1950s looked the other way. *Confindustria*, the employers' organization, enjoyed easy access to the Christian Democratic governments and especially to the ministries that administered industrial relations policy. Such access was totally lacking to the CGIL. Thus, Confindustria was able to gain tacit state approval for its negative corporatism.

By the late 1950s, Italian industrialization was in full expansion. The demand for both semiskilled and unskilled labor was growing not only in Italy but also in northern Europe, where industries were attracting immigrant workers from the south. These twin pulls reduced Italian unemployment and improved the bargaining position of the trade unions. The incidence of strikes began to increase. The employers who felt the impact most severely were often the most modern and competitive, those whose market was global. The strikes put them in a disadvantageous position relative to firms in countries where industrial unrest was minimal. In many such cases, the employer was the state. The Italian state sector had been expanding substantially during the growth period in areas where the expansion had been greatest—petrochemicals, for example. But those firms most affected by the strikes included American-based multinational corporations as well as large private Italian corporations, notably Fiat and Olivetti. An additional reason that these public, semipublic, and private giants were the most affected was that the unions were best organized in precisely these same firms.

The influx of southern Italian workers into northern cities provided the Communist Party with an opportunity to increase its base of support. During the 1960s, the Italian Communist Party and the Communist-linked trade unions made a concerted effort to reach the growing number of semiskilled and unskilled workers occupying the lowest-paid jobs, often in smaller firms where union organization was the weakest. The disoriented and estranged workers from the south were a uniquely available target. For them, the Communist Party and the trade union offered a sort of home away from home. The Communists provided assistance in finding housing and recreational facilities. In return, the newly recruited were socialized to accept the communist world view. At the same time, however, that world view was changing. The growing prosperity, the more positive attitude of the government and of many of the northern employers, and the rising electoral support for the PCI were factors that mitigated the communist tendency to see the world exclusively in terms of class conflict. Cooperative arrangements of a semicorporatist nature were being developed between unions and management at the local level during this period, encouraged by local governments under Communist leadership. For the moment, however, in the late 1960s, the consequence of the growing strength of the PCI and the CGIL was an increase in industrial militancy that coincided, as in other countries, with an upturn of the economy.[15] Industrial unrest in Italy between 1968 and 1973 resulted in a number of gains for workers and for the trade union movement. Most important was the achievement of legislation in 1970 that established the right of trade unions to organize workers at the shop level, a right that many employers had successfully denied the unions in the past. From this point, the unions succeeded in gaining control of works councils with which management would have to negotiate concerning wages and conditions of work. The strikes also secured substantial increases in real income for the workers, bolstered by revamped indexing arrangements that promised automatic increases in the future to keep workers' incomes ahead of price inflation, thus serving to exacerbate inflationary tendencies. The PCI played an active role in supporting these demands and in neutralizing the government as a recourse for beleaguered employers. The rising strength of the PCI was verified by substantial gains in the municipal elections of 1975 and the parliamentary elections of 1976. Finally, the 1970s saw the tentative beginnings of a move to merge the CGIL and the CSIL into a single trade union confederation. However, greater progress was made in this direction at the local level than nationally.

In the early 1980s, the position of employers hardened as they perceived the center of political gravity to have shifted back toward the right, away from a conciliatory policy toward the unions. By 1984 the northern industrial triangle of Turin, Milan, and Genoa had fallen on severe times. Rationalization of automobile production methods (Turin) and steel production (Milan) as well as the worldwide decline of shipbuilding (Genoa) had resulted in massive unemployment. The government, led by Socialist Bettino Craxi, reflected the mood of employers, which was to keep real wages in check by reducing the power of trade unions to bargain for increases. Early in the year Craxi proposed that the automatic wage increases for the year, indexed to rise with inflation, be cut by one-third, in order to bring Italian inflation down from its chronic double figures. Employers' groups and the two non-Communist trade unions gave their agreement to the proposal, although the employers argued that it did not go far enough. But the Communist-led CGIL refused its accord. To their surprise, Craxi proceeded to implement the policy by decree.

The Communists and the CGIL, who had staged two massive one-day strikes in response to Craxi's action, complained that the prime minister had broken with the long-standing practice of gaining the approval of all interested parties in wage-level decisions. Actually, this positive corporatist view of the process had been valid only for the previous fifteen years since the unions had gained coequal status with employers' groups at the end of the 1960s. Craxi's ability to defy the unions and the Communist Party suggests at least a temporary return to the negative corporatist pattern of the 1950s and 1960s. When high levels of unemployment have occurred in Italy, it generally has been the case that union solidarity diminishes and government's tendency to support the employers' interests is reestablished. In West Germany, a lack of support from government in 1984 was not enough to prevent union militancy from forcing concessions from employers.

The shift in government policy toward the trade unions in Italy reflects the fact that, at bottom, the Italian policy process is a pluralistic one in which government policies reflect the relative strengths of competing interest groups at any given time. In West Germany, both trade unions and employers are able to successfully insist on their established rights in the bargaining process, secure in the belief that, no matter what economic changes may do to their respective cohesiveness and firmness of purpose, the state will honor their claims to be heard and to maintain their rights. This difference is partly a result of the more established position of the West German than of the Italian state. In West Germany, the state is assured of the acceptance by both trade unions and employers of its decisions as legitimate. Unions may strike against employers and employers may lock out workers, but neither will act in such a militant fashion toward the state. Both may be seeking to influence state policy in their direction, but the role of the state is usually to facilitate negotiation between the industrial parties and to register the agreements they have reached, without playing a decisive role as an actor in its own right. The role that the Italian state will play is less predictable, not because the state itself is in a strong position, but because its temporary leaders are in a weak one. They are able to act in ways that appear decisive, as Craxi did in 1984, only at a time when the prevailing economic situation clearly favors one side over the other—the workers in the late 1960s and early 1970s, and the employers in the 1980s. In pluralistic fashion, they are bending to the prevailing wind. The stronger West German state has an interest in preserving a relative balance between trade unions and employers; if the state intervenes, it will be to preserve that positive corporatist balance rather than to add its weight to further unbalance an already unbalanced situation.

## France and Japan: Strong States and Weak Trade Unions

The French pattern of industrial relations has traditionally exhibited characteristics similar to the situation that prevailed in Italy prior to the 1960s. A divided and restricted trade union movement faced employers (the *patronat*), who believed in maintaining their authority over their employees even at the expense of peaceful industrial relations. They relied, when possible, on economic conditions to give them a superior bargaining position. The French Communist Party (PCF) has always played a role similar to that of the PCI in the 1950s. It has maintained strong links with the largest trade union (the CGT) and has avoided cooperation with the employers and with the state except when able to operate from a position of strength—which was seldom the case in France before the late 1960s. Employers frequently were able to deal with non-Communist trade unions, arriving at settlements to which the state gave its accord.

During the Fourth Republic, the policies of the divided governments tended to be ad hoc and inconsistent. With the return to power of General Charles de Gaulle, certain changes took place that brought the picture into sharp focus.

Through strengthening the executive constitutionally and through his own personal authority, de Gaulle was able to strengthen the hand of the government relative to the competing interest groups. Greater administrative coordination was achieved through the lessened role of the National Assembly as a conduit for group influences toward the bureaucracy and by reason of the fact that loyal Gaullists commanded the ministries relevant to economic policy. These ministries hitherto had been divided among leaders of different political parties. In the Fifth Republic, until 1981, the party in power was a party of the right, more favorably disposed to the propertied classes, whereas the political left, including the non-Communist left, was relegated to protracted opposition. Thus, the trade unions were at a disadvantage with respect to the state, whatever their position with respect to employers might have been at any given time.

In the Gaullist perception of economics, the interest of the state in maintaining a productive and stable economy came first. This proceeded from the commitment of de Gaulle to a strong French posture in international affairs, including his insistence that France be equipped with an effective, credible nuclear deterrent. Considerable state resources were channeled into scientific research and technological development. At the same time, his government sought to cope with growing needs and demands in society for such services as education and health delivery systems.

As the Gaullists saw the situation, the combined demands being put on the state were fraught with inflationary potential, a potential that could threaten the willingness of investors to gamble on the French economic future. Investment capital came second only to the state in the Gaullist system of priorities. Therefore, the government economic policy turned from emphasis on economic growth for its own sake to emphasis on improving productivity through technological development and through joining employers in pressing for greater worker productivity as a prerequisite to satisfaction of wage demands. Deflationary policies in the mid-1960s further weakened the workers' position by building a certain "tolerable" level of unemployment into the economy. Despite a number of days lost to strikes that was high for the time in Western Europe, the lack of unity in the French trade union movement meant that long-term strikes could not be sustained. Thus, bolstered by the moral support of the Gaullist state, employers usually could hold out against wage demands.

The strong showing of the ad hoc coalition of Communists and Socialists in the 1967 legislative elections was a sign that working-class disenchantment was beginning to improve the chances of a solid opposition to Gaullist policy. The explosion of May 1968, in which students protested against the overcrowded and alienating conditions in the system of higher education, led to confrontations with the police and, ultimately, to work stoppages in factories. The latter began as sympathy strikes directed against government antistudent actions, but they soon developed into a general strike of workers all over France who demanded higher wages and changes in industrial organization. The demands and the tactics of the French workers were little different from those arising at about the same time in other countries. What distinguished the French explosion were its dimensions. The general strike was of sufficient scope and intensity to threaten the existence of the Fifth Republic. In retrospect, it is clear that it forced de Gaulle to reorder his domestic and foreign policy priorities and, ultimately, to leave office after unsuccessfully testing his popularity in a referendum he easily could have won a few years earlier.

The governments of the right and center-right headed by Presidents Georges Pompidou and Valery Giscard d'Estaing sought to defuse French industrial relations such that it could not again pose a threat to the regime as it had in 1968. Legislation passed in 1968 had legitimized the presence of trade unions in individual firms and plants for purposes of collective bargaining. Governments in the 1970s encouraged employers to establish dialogues with local trade union branches and to negotiate local agreements on wages and conditions of work. Progress was registered in this direction, especially in the early 1970s before the onset of economic decline following the 1973–74 oil shocks, but recognition of local unions was often confined to the moderate unions rather than to the more militant CGT and CFDT. As the economic situation worsened later in the 1970s, the moderate FO became a particularly favored union for employers to negotiate with, trading off benefits for the unions and their members for union acquiescence in the rationalization of manufacturing, involving the shedding of jobs. Under the law, efforts by the CGT and CFDT to fight such developments were largely futile, whereas membership in FO expanded or held its own while the larger confederations were losing members. In difficult times the workers were interested in the relative security FO could promise, rather than the distant panaceas promised by the more militant unions.

The government of the left that came to power under President François Mitterrand in May 1981 portended a radical reversal in the relative positions of employers' and workers' organizations. The government took office with a list of seven major private corporations to be brought under state ownership along with investment banks and the steel and armaments industries. This was designed to give the state greater control over investment decisions in key sectors of the economy and to enable it to substitute itself for the employers in relations with the trade unions representing the employees in the sectors affected. The government also was pledged to reverse the deflationary policies of the previous right of center government under President Giscard d'Estaing, which, they alleged, had created large-scale unemployment and depressed real wages. The reversal would take the form of a reflationary policy, deliberately countering the deflationary trend in other First World countries, which would bring unemployment down through stimulating demand and investment in import-substituting industries. There was also a strong redistributive thrust to the government's program, designed to end the relatively high French levels of income inequality that cross-national studies had revealed during the 1970s. (See Chapter 2.) This would be effected through increased taxation of the higher-income and -wealth brackets, accompanied by improved social security benefits for lower-income earners. Finally, new industrial relations legislation was introduced and enacted, further extending the rights of unions at the firm and plant levels and making it still more difficult for employers to nullify the unions that were, or were seeking to become, the most representative defenders of their workers' interests.

During most of the first year of the new government, all of those aspects of the program were partially or fully implemented, including most of the promised nationalizations, reflation through deficit financing, imposition of a wealth tax, expansion of social security, shortening of the workweek from forty to thirty-nine hours without loss of income for the workers, and enactment of the industrial relations legislation, the Auroux Laws of 1982. The trade unions, usually left out of the economic policymaking process in the past, now enjoyed access to the governmental decision makers and to the management of state-sector firms. The national coal board, *Charbonnages de France,* was headed by a Communist director, and the newly nationalized firms came under the management of persons sympathetic to the government's aims. However, in the private sector, hostility to the new measures mounted in the months after the left came to power. Private investment declined and representatives of business groups refused to cooperate with the government in bargaining over wages and working hours. As the year wore on, indicators of inflation, the balance of trade, and the value of the French franc vis-à-vis the dollar began to show considerable deterioration, and unemployment refused to come down in response to the reflationary policy. To be sure, the government was unfortunate in coming to power in the midst of worldwide recession, but the combined impact of worsening indicators and employers' refusal of cooperation began strengthening the centrist voices within the government.

During the second year of the Mitterrand government, from spring 1982 to spring 1983, a tortuous process of reassessment of economic policy took place. Faced with continued stagflation at a time when other countries were choosing to attack inflation while letting unemployment rise, the government reluctantly came to the conclusion that it must follow suit. The turn to deflation was designed in part to restore business confidence in the government, so that a tripartite relationship involving government, employers, and trade unions could be established. This would make it possible to effectuate an incomes policy in which both wages and prices could be brought under control. The government counted on the continued support of the trade unions, assuming that, for the unions to undermine a Socialist government, even when it was pursuing policies favorable to the class enemy, the only result could be the loss of that government's capacity to mitigate the adverse effect of the policies on the workers. Although the Communist-led CGT, ironically, gave the government greater support than the Socialist-leaning CFDT, in general trade union support was sufficient to usher in a period of positive corporatism, as employers and employees cooperated in holding the inflationary line. By the summer of 1983, with real wages down and profits up from the year before, inflation was coming back down into single-digit proportions, while unemployment continued at levels only slightly higher than those of the year before Mitterrand came to power.

The policy reversal was beginning to take its toll by mid-1983 in closings in the private sector and in the necessity to subsidize firms in the public sector in order to cover losses. The private-sector development was adding to the unemployment totals, whereas public-sector subsidization was designed to keep unemployment within bounds. Massive subsidies in the coal and steel sectors ran counter to the general austerity thrust of government policies, and, in the fall of 1983, Finance Minister Jacques Delors proposed to cut them substantially in the following year's budget. This brought about the resignation of the Communist director of the coal board and signaled the beginning of a more militant opposition to the new direction of economic policy on the part of the trade unions. The cut in public-sector subsidies coincided with the development of a new approach to industrial policy generally, in which the government would encourage the modernization of declining industries, recognizing that this would bring with it considerable loss of jobs—a projected 200,000 for 1984—through the effect of automation and acceptance of the fact that the industries in question were overmanned. To obtain the support of the trade unions once again, the pill was sweetened by the promise of substantial financial support for the workers concerned, enabling them to find new, subsidized employment, in many cases with government-assisted retraining.

Although the CGT tentatively accepted the new direction, the CFDT, with a larger proportion of lower-paid (especially immigrant) workers, who would experience the heaviest incidence of the job losses, opposed the policy and tested it out in one of the first places of application, the state-owned Talbot (formerly, Peugeot) car plant in Poissy, in the outskirts of Paris. Among the CFDT complaints was the fact that the government had not consulted the unions at Poissy before announcing its policy, which would mean the loss of jobs of 1,900 workers, most of them immigrants. The government had planned to pay the immigrants to return to North Africa, but, in the face of the strike, it promised to make provisions for finding new jobs in France for those who wanted to remain. As the strike ended, it also was announced that the government would provide redundant workers with payment for two years to enable them to train for new jobs or, alternatively, to help them find employment in their own regions (especially the industrial north and Lorraine) where they could employ their own skills. This was in response to pressure from the CGT, whose continued support for government economic policy was becoming increasingly problematic.

Trade union unrest came to a head in March 1984, when a two-day strike of public-sector employees was called by the CGT and other unions in response to a government decision to hold public-sector pay increases to 5 percent at the same time inflation was running at 9 percent. Seemingly in support of the Socialist government, the CFDT did not call its members out on strike, although many of them struck anyway. The CFDT leader, Edmund Maire, claimed that his confederation was dissociating itself from the strike because it was over the false issue of wages, ignoring the real issue of jobs. More concerned than the CGT with those most threatened with job loss in the face of the government's industrial modernization policy, the CFDT was clearly distancing itself from the better-paid and more job-secure workers who were better defended by the other unions. The strike demonstrated once more that, when French worker militancy rises, it can seldom express itself in more than short-term strikes designed to put a point across symbolically, whether the government be of the right or the left. But the increased militancy represented a defeat for the government's efforts to build a positive corporatist consensus behind its economic policies. Thus, the Socialist government found itself in the uncomfortable position of having greater support for the main lines of its economic and industrial policies from employers and the parties of the right than from its own base in the trade unions. At the same time, its popular support generally was declining, a trend that culminated in the Socialists' defeat in the legislative elections of March 1986. It is not too far-fetched to suggest that the temptation of the Socialists to utilize the economic policy tools of a strong state in order to overcome the resistance of their erstwhile trade union allies turned out to be as irresistible as the original urge to use the same state weapons as means of righting the balance between employers and unions that was implemented in Mitterrand's first year.

According to the criteria outlined earlier in this chapter, Japan shares with France the twin qualities of having a strong state and divided trade unions when it comes to industrial relations policy and to economic policy in general. But when we look more closely at the two cases, we find the Japanese state playing a more passive role in industrial relations policy than does the French state, and a more passive role in industrial relations policy than in other economic policy realms, especially that of industrial *development* policy, where the Japanese governments have met with considerable success in avoiding the pitfalls of deindustrialization that the other advanced industrial countries have faced, a record that is looked at in the next chapter. In any event, the fact that the state is regarded as strong by the trade unions in both countries adds to the weakness of both the French and Japanese trade unions when they face employers, not only because the unions are divided among themselves, but also because the state appears in both countries most of the time to be in league with the unions' opposite number in industrial relations: the employers.

The lines of division within the trade union movement are different in Japan from the ideological–partisan divisions in France, although there is a sort of left–right division among Japanese unions as well.[16] Whereas less than 20 percent of French workers belong to unions, the Japanese unions organize about 30 percent of the workers, a figure that itself falls short of the Italian, British, and West German levels, all of which are found between 40 and 50 percent.[17] But a feature of the unionized Japanese workers that distinguishes them from those in these Western European countries is that more than 90 percent of them belong to what are, in the first instance, *company* unions. In both the public and the private sectors, in large firms as well as small, the typical Japanese union member belongs to a union whose membership is confined to the economic unit (private company or government agency) where he or she works. In France and other Western European countries, the worker joins a national union federation which may or may not have a presence in the place of work. In West Germany the federation the worker joins is likely to enjoy a "closed shop" status in the plant or office (i.e., it is the only federation to which the worker may belong), but it is a federation that enjoys similar status in many other plants or offices, and in a given company it may exist alongside another union or other unions whose members fall into different categories of workers (e.g., office workers rather than factory workers, or supervisory personnel rather than machine operators). But in Japan the typical worker does not join a national federation; instead, he or she becomes a member of the local company union along with other workers, of whatever category of job, within the same company. The company union in turn may belong to one of the two largest union confederations, *Sohyo*, a fairly militant union of the left, or *Domei*, a moderate union that is often in sympathy with the policies of Japan's Liberal Democratic government. As in France, the peak confederations are distinguished from one another along ideological lines, but the ideology of the confederation is more remote from the concerns of the Japanese worker who joins a company union than it is for the French worker who consciously joins one union rather than another because it is, say, a CGT rather than a CFDT union.

According to Tadashi Hanami,[18] Japanese workers, after signing on to work for a new firm, will be drawn to the company union in order to become more socially solid with a new "family." The only choice to be made is whether to belong to a union or not; it is not, as in the typical French case, which of two or more possible unions to join. The distant ideological affiliation of the company union is therefore not likely to be an important consideration for the new employee. However, indirect affiliation with Sohyo or with Domei can have consequences in the case of industrial disputes. The more militant Sohyo has been known to get its members into impossible positions in bargaining with the companies in which they work, such that their employers may be able to entice them away from the Sohyo-affiliated union into a breakaway union that may later affiliate with Domei or remain independent. If a majority of workers can be drawn into the new union, it then becomes the official union for the company. Both the workers who made the change and those left behind will be motivated to come back together again, putting behind them all previous antagonisms toward one another and toward the employer.

In a famous study of Japanese society, Chie Nakane argues that in Japan, unlike in many other societies, individuals identify with the social organization, or "frame," to which they belong, rather than the social type, or "attribute," to which an outsider might assign them.[19] Thus, a daughter-in-law becomes an integral part of her husband's family, although born a member of another family, if the couple live in the household of the husband's parents. The same is true of servants living in the household. Both the daughter-in-law and the servant are considered part of the household and consider themselves so, whereas a daughter who has married and goes elsewhere to live with her husband thereby becomes an outsider. Similarly, when a young person becomes an employee of a business firm, he or she becomes a "family member" of the firm. The firm virtually becomes the individual's entire world. Indeed, if a new male employee is single, he may look for a female employee of the same firm to marry, so that the marriage will not be strained by the fact that husband and wife belong to different "families" in their places of employment.

Thus, the Japanese worker identifies with the firm as the frame and not with his or her particular skill category or attribute, and certainly not with other Japanese workers elsewhere who might happen to share certain political beliefs. This is why there will not be more than one union per firm and why, if there is a conflict within that union, loyalty to the firm will force the workers to resolve the conflict so that a one-union firm can be reestablished, or else a *no-union* company will be the result of the conflict.

Paradoxically, when conflicts do occur in the relations between Japanese management and labor, they often assume very emotionally explosive and sometimes even violent proportions. This is because, according to Hanami,[20] within the family the rule of the head of the household may not be challenged. To do so is to risk becoming an outcast. One must, in fact, have taken leave of one's senses to challenge such absolute authority overtly. In the company, employees who challenge the authority of the head of the firm do so in ways that demonstrate a temporarily altered personality state. They change their appearance, discarding the usual dark business suits and behave in bizarre ways far removed from the daily routine. When the conflict is over they return to their former selves, as if to say, "That was not me; it was someone else. I am not to be held accountable." And both employers and employees proceed ahead as if there had not, in fact, been such a confrontation.

Accordingly, Japanese industrial disputes are usually short-lived. They will end either by the employer's giving up just enough of what the employees demand so that "face" is saved on both sides, or by the employer's succeeding in splitting the union, a technique alluded to earlier.

Failing either of those solutions, a state agency will be called on to mediate the dispute. In certain ways this outline is similar to what occurs in France. Strikes break out frequently in France and are usually both angry and short-lived. Management tries to divide the workers and, as in Japan, frequently can succeed. Or the dispute may end fairly amicably by each side making concessions, failing which the state may enter into the action. But there are important differences. Although a Sohyo-led strike in Japan may involve certain ideologically motivated nonnegotiable demands, not unlike those conducted in France under CGT or CDFT auspices, French strikes are often called at the national level; Sohyo, on the other hand, lends its support to strikes that arise within a particular firm. The French strikes are often scheduled to last for only a day or for a specified and brief period of time, the object being more to demonstrate the strength of the union within the workforce than to gain specific benefits for the union's members. Such strikes really do not have measurable outcomes, in the same sense as do industrial disputes in other countries, including Japan. Finally, although the state may become involved in both countries, it is a more active involvement in France than in Japan, and it may be initiated at the highest levels of government. The French state is likely to impose a solution that one or both of the parties to the dispute may be too weak to refuse. The semiautonomous Labour Relations Commission that mediates industrial relations disputes in Japan seldom arbitrates, a process that obliges the parties to the dispute to accept the solution imposed by the arbitrator. Rather, it mediates or conciliates, trying to persuade both parties of their own interest in reaching a decision that only they, as members of the same "family," can achieve. Despite these differences, it still should be noted that the Japanese state retains considerable strength in reserve that it could use in case industrial militancy came to threaten Japanese economic viability. The sympathies of the Liberal Democratic government, like those of the right-of-center governments during most of the Fifth Republic, are, in the final analysis, with the employers. The fact that neither government has had to exercise its latent authority over industrial relations in heavy-handed fashion is perhaps due more to the fact that private-sector employers in both countries have the best of it in arguments with their workers most of the time.[21] In this sense, the more balanced industrial relations of West Germany and Italy find the state acting in ways that either reflect (Italy) or restore (West Germany) the balance when it is threatened; the unbalanced industrial relations of France and Japan are not in balance because of the strong position of the state to make sure, if necessary, that the imbalance remains as it is.

## Great Britain: Unions and the State at the Mercy of Economic Forces

The economic problems that other countries have faced in the past decade were encountered much earlier in Great Britain. The British were early pioneers in the virgin territory of postindustrial stagflation. Throughout the 1950s, the consequences for the working class of Great Britain's worsening economic picture were obscured by rising real incomes. The Conservative government's commitment was to Keynesian economics minus the heavy array of controls the Labour government of 1945–51 had carried over from World War II. Great Britain had evolved too far in the direction of state intervention for a complete return to free-market economics, something many Conservatives had never been enthusiastic about anyway. But the basic underlying philosophy applied to industrial relations was essentially that government intervention in the economy should not extend to employer–employee relations. Rather, the outcome of such contests, it was held, should reflect the relative strengths of the contestants.

Rising purchasing power and living standards reduced the perception of interclass hostility among British workers. In the later 1950s, impressed by the Conservatives' repeated electoral victories, the Labour Party abandoned its commitment to a more socialist Great Britain. On the one hand, the existing mixed economy and welfare state could be improved; on the other hand, perpetuation of a private industrial sector could now be tolerated.

The interventionist pluralism of the Labour Party contained a corporatist potential, which could be stimulated by adverse economic conditions. When the party returned to power in 1964 under Harold Wilson's leadership, it chose an incomes policy of wage and price restraint, banking on the support of the trade unions for a Labour government. But given the perception on the part of union leadership that their bargaining position with the employers was a strong one, union compliance with wage restraint was halfhearted at best, especially as grassroots pressure was intensifying and the incidence of wildcat strikes sharply increasing. In 1968–69, the volume of strike activity reached new postwar highs for periods with the Labour Party in power.

Unlike the West German legal system, British law contained no means by which unofficial strikes could legally be contained. Nor were there regulations allowing for periods of cooling off or for compulsory resort to state-appointed mediators or arbitrators. By the time the Wilson government had concluded that wage restraint was not going to work, a considerable amount of pressure had built up from the Conservatives and from employers' associations for legislation restricting strike activity and (implicitly) restraining employees' bargaining position relative to that of employers. The Wilson government introduced legislation to the House of Commons designed to limit the right to strike by imposing fines on workers engaging in unofficial strikes and on trade unions resorting to strikes before exploring government-induced opportunities to negotiate. Although the legislation also provided for expansion of union rights in gray areas not previously covered by legislation, the unions mounted a campaign against it and, with support from Labour back benchers in the House of Commons, forced the Wilson government to withdraw it and abandon its experiments with corporatist policy instruments.

After the reversal of the Labour policy initiative, it was the Conservatives' turn. Following the Conservative victory in the June 1970 elections, the government of Edward Heath introduced legislation similar to that of the Wilson government, although providing a wider array of countermeasures and antistrike penalties. It was enacted into law as the Industrial Relations Act of 1971. By 1972 it had been rendered ineffective due to noncompliance on the part of trade unions and/or employers.

The Heath government also turned to another instrument designed to curb the power of organized labor to push successfully for inflationary wage claims. In 1972, Heath reversed his government's opposition to wage and price controls and, after failing to gain union support for voluntary wage restraint, instituted a statutory incomes policy. This imposed rigidly enforced limits on wage and price increases, thus abruptly reducing the power of labor in its bargaining relations with management. Although the policy met with relative success in its first year, it fell apart in the wake of the Arab oil embargo that followed the October 1973 Arab–Israeli war. With their bargaining power sud-

The British coal miners' strike of 1984–85 was nowhere more intense than in South Yorkshire. The confrontation between rock throwing miners and police guarding a pit entrance at Barnsley took place in October 1984. Below are Yorkshire miners, still defiant, returning to work at the end of the strike in March 1985.

denly enhanced by the nations' energy shortage, the National Union of Mineworkers called a strike in the coal mines. Heath countered by declaring a state of emergency, which a number of other unions defied by striking in sympathy with the miners. The winter of 1973–74 was made particularly severe through reduction of industrial activity to a three-day week and through numerous work stoppages and shortages of supplies. Finally, Heath called an election for February 1974, stressing the issue of whether the government or the unions were running the country. Although no party won a majority in the election, Labour returned to power as a minority government, having a plurality of seats in the House of Commons. Harold Wilson then proceeded to negotiate a settlement of the miners' strike that was favorable to the miners' demands touched off an inflationary wave of wage settlements.

Thereafter, the Labour governments of Harold Wilson and his successor, James Callaghan, followed an incomes policy that sought voluntary cooperation from the unions as part of a "social contract," with a counterpart element of legislation that strengthened the legal position of the unions, especially restricting employers' ability to interfere with the unions' right to organize and represent employees. Through the mid-1970s, the unions were able to gain rank-and-file acceptance of these policies as the British economy struggled through a period of recession coupled with an inflation rate that at times reached higher than 20 percent. But, as unemployment and inflation figures began to descend to more normal ranges, the disincentive against unofficial strikes lessened and industrial unrest resumed. A series of interconnected strikes in the state sector in early 1979 further undermined a weak Callaghan government, and the Labour Party, after an adverse vote of confidence in the House of Commons, suffered defeat at the hands of Margaret Thatcher and the Conservatives in the general election of May 1979.

Margaret Thatcher had captured the leadership of the Conservative Party when Edward Heath had failed to gain a vote of confidence as Leader of the Opposition from Conservative members of Parliament in early 1975. In addition to two consecutive electoral defeats, Heath had been blamed for the inconsistency of his economic policies during his 1970–74 government. The market-oriented right wing of the Conservative Party, which had felt abandoned by Heath when he turned to a more interventionist policy in 1972, now reasserted itself and elected a leader with whom they felt an ideological affinity. When Mrs. Thatcher came to power, she appointed a monetarist, Sir Geoffrey Howe, as chancellor of the exchequer; and her government committed itself to a policy of allowing market forces a maximum of independence to pursue their own interests free of government controls.

As part of its determination to rid the British economy of inflationary pressures, the Thatcher government committed itself to legislation that would considerably reduce trade union strength. This time the Conservatives preferred to enact their reform legislation in piecemeal fashion, avoiding a single massive assault on the workers' organizations. Unlike the Heath legislation, the Thatcher bills, enacted in 1980, 1982, and 1984, were directed toward the national trade union federations acting in their official capacities, rather than to unauthorized work stoppages arising on the shop floor. Although this appeared at first to be a more cautious approach, cumulatively the measures represented a more formidable assault on union power than that mounted by Heath. They were aided considerably by the rising levels of unemployment in Britain in the early 1980s, partly engendered by the government's deflationary policies. The trade union legislation complemented the government's general economic strategy and was assured of smoother passage through Parliament and acceptance by the electorate as a result of popular sentiment at the time that was highly unfavorable to the union movement.

The new laws had two central purposes regarding industrial relations. The first was to curtail the unions' capacity to engage in "secondary picketing," or attempting to halt work at firms other than the ones employing the picketers. This form of picketing was outlawed unless it could be demonstrated that it directly related to a dispute going on with the picketers' employers involving wages or conditions of work. Suits could be brought against unions authorizing such picketing by the employers affected or other workers prevented from working by the illegal action. Potentially crippling damages could be awarded by courts out of union funds. The second aspect of the legislation involved the phenomenon of the closed shop, whereby the employer agreed not to hire nonunion workers and could legally refuse employment to or could fire workers not belonging to the authorized union. Court action could be brought against employers taking such actions if the closed-shop agreements had not been voted on by at least 80 percent of the employees in the firm. Both of these measures struck at the heart of union power. The first sharply curtailed the unions' ability to magnify the impact of one another's strikes by engaging in supportive strikes in other industries or other firms. The second jeopardized the unions' organizational capacities. During the 1970s, British union membership had been growing to the point where by 1979, it exceeded 50 percent of its potential membership, making it one of the "densest" union movements in Western Europe and, in the eyes of the Conservatives, excessively increasing its bargaining advantage. Whereas Conservatives argued that the measures added up to a restoration of the balance in industrial relations that had tilted in the trade unions' favor before 1979, the Labour Party and its trade union supporters feared that the laws had tilted the balance very much in the opposite direction. Indeed, trade union membership dropped off sharply in the early 1980s, with a loss of about two million members from 1980 to 1986.[22]

Today the Conservatives claim that the purpose of their industrial relations policies is to rid Britain of the creeping corporatism that has been developing at least since the Wilson government of the 1960s, and that was restimulated by the policies of the Heath government and its Labour successors in the 1970s. To the "neoliberals" around Mrs. Thatcher, the "corporate state" is only one step removed from the socialist state. Corporatist consultation of government with economic interest groups in the making of economic policy means that an overwhelmingly large concentration of economic power is arrayed behind the decisions of the state. In order to free the economy of state controls, it is necessary to break the hold of the interest groups—especially the trade unions, but the employers' groups and other special interests as well—on the process by which economic policy decisions are made. Paradoxically, the influence of these groups must be removed so "government will be free to govern," which for the Conservatives means so "the government will be free to remove itself from the economy." The paradox is that, in order to reduce the influence of the unions and even to reduce the size of the state sector, the government must take a number of decisive actions, actions of political will that promise to increase the intensity of confrontation between the state and other forces in society. An illustration of this occurred in the coal strike that began in March 1984.

Throughout the life of the Thatcher government, British industrial decline had been as severe as that occurring in any First World country. Plant closures and sizable layoffs were at least monthly occurrences during the early 1980s. Occasionally the government would engage in a rescue operation, as in the case of the automobile manufacturer British Leylands. But in most cases, the government encouraged industrial rationalization with its inevitable reductions in the size of workforces. This was particularly true in the case of the state-owned British Steel Corporation, which scaled down to a more competitive size while offering steelworkers substantial assistance in the form of handsome "redundancy" (severance) payments and pensions, as well as investment in new industry in areas where steel mills closed down, so that workers losing their jobs could find new employment locally. Where possible, younger workers were relocated to more modern steel plants elsewhere in Great Britain. In late 1983 the man who had presided over the steel rationalization program, Ian MacGregor, took over as head of the National Coal Board (NCB) with the intention of implementing a similar program in the coal industry.

What the Thatcher government and the new coal chairman faced in the coal industry was a trade union federation, the National Union of Miners (NUM), whose leadership under its president Arthur Scargill was much more militantly hostile to the Thatcher-led state than were the leaders of the steelworkers' federation, who had agreed to MacGregor's terms after a brief strike. Shortly after MacGregor took command of the NCB, Scargill announced an overtime ban, whereby miners would confine their workweek to a minimum in order to cut down production of coal, which was already in oversupply with worldwide demand at a low ebb. As later became apparent, this was for the purpose of keeping British coal stocks as low as possible against the time when the full-scale strike that Scargill anticipated should occur. The moment came in March 1984, after MacGregor announced the imminent closing of some twenty coal pits in various parts of Great Britain, entailing the loss of 20,000 miners' jobs. Earlier guarantees of both Labour and Conservative governments that miners not eligible for retirement would be reemployed in nearby pits were not included in MacGregor's package, which resembled what he had offered to steelworkers when he headed the BSC. With the support of Scargill and the Communist head of the Scottish branch of the NUM, Mick McGahey, miners in Scotland, Wales, and parts of northern England voted to strike rather than accept MacGregor's package. But elsewhere, in newer mines not scheduled for closing, where miners earned substantially more through bonus schemes than in the less productive mines, miners refused to vote for a strike, and the mines continued to operate. This was particularly true of Nottinghamshire and several other mining areas in the Midlands. In order to try to force the Nottinghamshire miners to cease working, hundreds of "flying pickets" traveled the short distance from South Yorkshire, where the miners had voted to strike, to persuade them, by threat of violence if necessary, not to deplete the overall national strike effort by continuing to produce coal. This example of secondary picketing, illegal under the Conservative legislation of 1980 and 1982, was met by quickly mobilized police drawn from Nottinghamshire and elsewhere in Britain. Clashes between the pickets and police were very bloody in the early stages of the strike, with one death and hundreds of injuries occurring in the first weeks. Although the police effort was clearly coordinated from the cabinet level, the government attempted to remove itself as much as possible from any appearance of involvement in the conflict. Although this would have seemed the obvious occasion on which to test the legislation against secondary picketing, MacGregor's superior, the energy secretary, restrained him from seeking a court order that could have led to massive fines and perhaps the jailing of NUM leaders, but that would also have escalated the violence.

The strike continued until March 1985. Since the strikers were ineligible for unemployment benefits while on strike, there was a steady movement of returnees to the mines. Scargill and the government (acting by proxy through MacGregor) were engaged in a test of wills, with each apparently bent on destroying the other. But both were flawed by a fundamental weakness that prevented either from delivering the knockout blow. In Scargill's case, it was the absence of either a united NUM or a united British trade union movement behind him. Although about three-quarters of the miners were on strike at the height of the conflict, Scargill was reluctant to ask for a national NUM vote authorizing the strike, since this would have required a 55 percent majority for adoption and he could not be sure that such a large percentage would support in secret the strike that they were supporting by their public action of refusing to work. As for the rest of the trade union movement, although the miners received sporadic support in the transport sector from railway workers and dock workers, who could interfere with the movement of imported coal, Scargill failed to convince the moderate steelworkers' union to boycott imported coal in steel mills that were barely surviving in the face of depressed demand for steel. These factors eventually wore down the miners' enthusiasm for the strike, and the NUM capitulated.

In the case of the Thatcher government, memories of Edward Heath's unsuccessful confrontation with the miners in 1974 and of the downfall of the Callaghan government due to the wave of strikes in 1978–79 provided strong inhibition against taking more direct action to end the coal strike. The official rhetoric was that the state should have no place in the midst of an industrial dispute. But its legislation to curtail strike activity had been little used by firms in the private sector, which preferred to settle conflicts through bargaining rather than to confront unions directly through legal action. In any event, most of the coal mines were in the public sector, and the NCB was headed by a Thatcher appointee. The government was restraining him from taking stronger action while it was simultaneously coordinating the massive police effort to keep the industrial conflict below the threshold of violence and to allow miners wishing to keep working to do so. In the meantime, the Labour Party, embarrassed by the strike, sought to evoke positive corporatist images of reconciliation and mutual interest, which fell on deaf ears among the leaders of the NUM. The British economy felt the effects of the strike in the form of reduced output in the steel and other industries, as well as in a somewhat increased dependence on imports of foreign coal. But the principal losers were the striking miners and their families, for many of whom the benefits offered by the National Coal Board in compensation for loss of jobs began to look more appealing than the continued loss of income and dependence on community and family support.

This British case departs in some ways from the image of pluralism associated with a weak state. During the 1960s and 1970s, governments of both the Labour and the Conservative parties were stymied in their dealings with unions, not because they were facing a unified labor movement, such as that found in West Germany or, until recently at least in Italy, but precisely because the autonomy of individual unions and local branches of unions frustrated efforts of the state and, under Labour governments, of the state and the national trade union leadership to maintain a cooperative system of industrial relations. But by the time Margaret Thatcher assumed the prime ministership, the combined scourges of stagflation and de-industrialization that Britain experienced in the 1970s had weakened the bargaining position even of local union branches and had exhausted the patience of the British public with trade union militancy. Mrs. Thatcher came to power at a time when many voters, including many who had voted for the Labour Party, wanted the state to take a strong hand in industrial relations.

## *Conclusion*

A feature common to the foregoing cases is that there is a certain *rhythm* to industrial relations policy in First World countries, a rhythm that may extend to economic policy in general. The rhythm is associated with the phenomenon of business cycles, which have not been eliminated by the advent of postindustrial society, only elevated in intensity in the phenomenon of stagflation. When the economy is at the productive end of its pendulum swing, workers are in an advantageous position relative to their employers because labor is then a scarce commodity, much in demand. But at times when the pendulum has swung to the opposite extreme and unemployment is high, the advantage shifts to the employer. When workers perceive conditions to be favorable to their demands, they can afford to take risks, and the rank and file become more amenable to the militancy of their left wing. When employers feel the labor market to be in their favor, their negative corporatist instincts come to the fore.

In the 1980s, whether official government rhetoric has been neoliberal (Britain), positive corporatist (West Germany and Japan), socialist (France), or mixed but essentially pluralist (Italy), the tendency of government industrial relations policy has been increasingly to favor the interests of employers over the interests of labor. The reasons for this are by no means to be found exclusively in electoral politics, since the elected Socialist government of France has been moving in the same direction as has the elected Conservative government of Great Britain, although it has not covered as much ground. More to the point have been the interconnected phenomena of slow growth, unemployment, and industrial restructuring that have both weakened trade unions and convinced governments that unions pose a potential obstacle to the changes that must take place if the nation's industry is to regain international competitiveness. Thus, the politics of industrial relations has featured much less tripartite consultation in which the unions enjoy a co-equal status, and more unilateral government policymaking seen by unionists as damaging—as well as more unilateral actions by employers, such as closures, layoffs, and even lockouts that are tolerated and even encouraged by governments. Adding to the weakened position of the unions in advanced industrial countries is the fact that a "postindustrial fault line" has developed within the workers' movement, between those workers on the safe side of postindustrial structural change and those who find their jobs crumbling away. This line of cleavage can cut right through a union, as in the case of the British miners; it can isolate workers from others in the movement, as in the case of automobile workers in West Germany and Italy; it can reinforce already existing divergences between skilled and unskilled (especially immigrant) workers, as in France; and it can enable employers to divide workers from their union, as can occur in Japan. The result has been fertile ground for divide-and-conquer tactics on the part of governments as diverse in basic philosophy as those of Margaret Thatcher and François Mitterrand. In short, it can bring together many of the elements of what we have called negative corporatism.

However, these converging tendencies would seem valid only as long as the underlying economic hard times continue. If governments are successful in strengthening economic structures in time to join in whatever growth the worldwide economic future holds, then slimmed-down union movements may be able to recapture a position of rough equality with slimmed-down industry. This should be true in countries where governments perceive the model of positive corporatism to be the one that works best in most circumstances, an attitude that appears to be true of the governments currently holding power in West Germany, Italy, and probably France and Japan. But the neoliberal model of the Thatcher government in Great Britain appears to have imbedded within it a long-range goal of curtailing union power that may not be within the best British pluralistic traditions, not to mention the aspirations of the positive corporatists in the moderate wings of all of the British political parties, including the Conservative Party itself. In trying to face down the British trade union movement, it is taking on a powerful force in a pluralistic society and risking a confrontation not only with the unions, but also with the long-established consensual instincts and preference for fair play of the British political culture.

## *Suggestions for Further Reading*

**Beer, Samuel H.** *Britain against Itself: The Political Contradictions of Collectivism* (New York and London: Norton, 1982).

**Beyme, Klaus von.** *Challenge to Power: Trade Unions and Industrial Relations in Capitalist Countries*, trans. Eileen Martin (Beverly Hills: Sage, 1980).

**Cerny, Phillip G., and Martin A. Schain,** eds. *French Politics and Public Policy* (New York: Methuen, 1980).

**Crouch, Colin, and Alessandro Pizzorno,** eds. *The Resurgence of Class Conflict in Western Europe since 1968*, 2 vols. (New York: Holmes & Meier, 1978).

**Flanagan, Robert J.**, et al. *Unionism, Economic Stabilization, and Incomes Policies: European Experience* (Washington, D.C.: Brookings, 1983).

**Goldthorpe, John H.**, ed. *Order and Conflict in Contemporary Capitalism: Studies in the Political Economy of Western European Nations* (Oxford: Clarendon Press, 1984).

**Grant, Wyn,** ed. *The Political Economy of Corporatism* (Basingstoke and London: Macmillan, 1985).

**Hanami, Tadashi.** *Labor Relations in Japan Today*, 1st paperback ed. (Tokyo: Kodansha International, 1981).

**Johnson, Chalmers.** *MITI and the Japanese Miracle* (Stanford, Calif.: Stanford University Press, 1982).

**Lehmbruch, Gerhard, and Philippe C. Schmitter,** eds. *Patterns of Corporatist Policy-making* (Beverly Hills: Sage, 1982).

**Offe, Claus.** *Disorganized Capitalism: Contemporary Transformations of Work and Politics* (Cambridge, Mass.: MIT Press, 1985).

**Olson, Mancur.** *The Rise and Decline of Nations: Economic Growth, Stagflation and Social Rigidities* (New Haven, Conn.: Yale University Press, 1982).

**Rose, Richard,** ed. *Challenge to Governance: Studies in Overloaded Polities* (Beverly Hills: Sage, 1980).

**Sabel, Charles F.** *Work and Politics: The Division of Labor in Industry* (Cambridge: Cambridge University Press, 1982).

**Shonfield, Andrew.** *Modern Capitalism: The Changing Balance of Public and Private Power* (New York and London: Oxford University Press, 1965).

**Smith, W. Rand.** *Crisis in the French Labour Movement: A Grassroots' Perspective* (New York: St. Martin's, 1987).

## *Notes*

1. For example, Jean-Jacques Servan-Schreiber, *The American Challenge,* trans. Ronald Steel (New York: Atheneum, 1968); Christopher Tugendhat, *The Multinationals* (New York: Random House, 1972).
2. For a useful overview of industrial relations in the First World, see Klaus von Beyme, *Challenge to Power: Trade Unions and Industrial Relations in Capitalist Countries,* trans. Eileen Martin (Beverly Hills: Sage, 1980).
3. The role of trade unions in Japan is discussed at greater length later in this chapter.
4. For a treatment of these various factors, see Leo Panitch, *Social Democracy and Industrial Militancy: The Labour Party, the Trade Unions and Incomes Policy, 1945–1974* (Cambridge: Cambridge University Press, 1976).
5. This section draws on Charles F. Sabel, *Work and Politics: The Division of Labor in Industry* (Cambridge: Cambridge University Press, 1982).
6. Ibid., Ch. 2.
7. We have left the term *state* rather vague until now, perhaps reflecting a pluralist bias of our own. Pluralism conceives of First World *governments* as being divided into many branches, departments, and subunits that are susceptible to penetration by interest groups that will influence them to take sides in their own conflicts. The corporatist perspective tends to take the state as a unit that pursues its own interests. These interests may be concurrent with certain interests of autonomous groups and in conflict with other interests. For a "state autonomy" argument that runs counter to the pluralist tradition, see Eric A. Nordlinger, *On the Autonomy of the Democratic State* (Cambridge, Mass., and London: Harvard University Press, 1981).
8. See Wyn Grant, "Introduction," in Grant, ed., *The Political Economy of Corporatism* (Basingstoke and London: Macmillan, 1985), pp. 1–31.
9. We prefer these terms to *state* and *societal* corporatism broached by Philippe Schmitter, which imply too much state domination of the private sector in the first form and too small a role for the state in the second to accommodate the principal historical examples, which are probably Fascist Italy under Mussolini for state corpo-

ratism and today's Austria for societal corporatism. As we are concerned here with contemporary relations between the state and economic interest groups, the range of examples to which the term *corporatism* ought to apply is much narrower than Schmitter's terms suggest; hence our terms *negative* and *positive* corporatism. Both imply a role for the state as well as for employers' and workers' organizations, but the state acts in such a way as to give employers the advantage over workers in negative corporatism, whereas more of a balance is struck in the positive variety. The former implies a belief by the various actors in a "fixed- or negative-sum game," the latter a belief in the existence of a "positive-sum game" from which everyone benefits.

10. See the various essays in Gerhard Lehmbruch and Philippe C. Schmitter, eds., *Patterns of Corporatist Policy-making* (Beverly Hills: Sage, 1982), especially Manfred G. Schmidt, "Does Corporatism Matter? Economic Crisis, Politics and Rates of Unemployment in Capitalist Democracies in the 1970s," pp. 273–258.

11. From a somewhat different starting point, this conclusion has likewise been reached by Samuel H. Beer, *Britain against Itself: The Political Contradictions of Collectivism* (New York: Norton, 1982), Part 1: "Pluralistic Stagnation."

12. These case studies draw on, among others, Colin Crouch and Alessandro Pizzorno, eds., *The Resurgence of Class Conflict in Western Europe since 1968*, vol. 1 (New York: Holmes & Meier, 1978); Anthony Carew, *Democracy and Government in European Trade Unions* (London: Allen & Unwin, 1976); Geoffrey K. Ingham, *Strikes and Industrial Conflict: Britain and Scandinavia* (London: Macmillan, 1974); E.C.M. Cullingford, *Trade Unions in West Germany* (Boulder, Colo.: Westview, 1977); Robert J. Flanagan et al., *Unionism, Economic Stabilization, and Incomes Policies: European Experience* (Washington, D.C.: Brookings, 1983); W. Rand Smith, *Crisis in the French Labour Movement: A Grassroots' Perspective* (New York: St. Martin's, 1987); Sabel, *Work and Politics*; and two London newspapers, the *Guardian* and the *Observer*, 1983–84.

13. For example, David Coombes, *Representative Government and Economic Power* (London: Heinemann, 1982); John Zysman, *Governments, Markets, and Growth: Financial Systems and the Politics of Industrial Change* (Ithaca, N.Y.: Cornell University Press, 1983).

14. Wolfgang Streeck, "Organizational Consequences of Neo-Corporatist Cooperation in West German Labour Unions," in Lehmbruch and Schmitter, eds., *Patterns of Corporatist Policy-making*, pp. 74–75.

15. Flanagan et al., *Unionism*, pp. 518–522.

16. Tadashi Hanami, *Labor Relations in Japan Today*, 1st paperback ed. (Tokyo: Kodansha International, 1981), p. 92.

17. Smith, *Crisis in the French Labour Movement*, p. 13; Japan Institute of Labour, *Labour Unions and Labor–Management Relations*, Japanese Industrial Relations Series, no. 2 (Tokyo, Japan Institute of Labour, 1985), p. 9. The French figure for union membership declined during the 1980s and may now be closer to 10 percent than to 20 percent.

18. Hanami, *Labor Relations*, Ch. 1.

19. *Ibid.*

20. *Ibid.*

21. In both France and Japan, trade union strength and militancy are greater in the public than in the private sector. In the public sector the state cannot remain a passive observer of conflict between the two other parties; it is a direct party to the conflict and it may, for political reasons, be less resistant to union demands than are private employers.

22. Dennis Kavanagh, *Thatcherism and British Politics: The End of Consensus?* (Oxford: Oxford University Press, 1987), p. 239.

CHAPTER 7

# THE PERFORMANCE OF POLITICAL SYSTEMS

We come now to an overall evaluation of our five polyarchies as promoters of human dignity. How should we assess the performances of these political systems with respect to our four dimensions—power, well-being, enlightenment, and respect? In the preceding chapters, we have made a number of evaluative statements, but an overall assessment remains for this concluding chapter. We devote principal attention to the value of *well-being*. Although this means an imbalance in our treatment of the four values, we consider that the overwhelming predominance of material issues on the agendas of First World political systems in the late twentieth century justifies giving them predominant consideration. First, we undertake brief assessments of the performances of the five political systems regarding the three other values.

## *Power*

In analyzing First World polyarchies, we have been concerned mainly with how power is distributed within the political system rather than with how much power the political system has been able to mobilize as it faces the outside world. Historically, the larger countries have found it necessary to have a relatively high concentration of power internally in order to be prepared for whatever threat might arise externally. The frequent wars on the continent of Europe have testified to this necessity. Today, the Western European polyarchies no longer threaten one another militarily. Whatever threat exists, whether of Soviet military power or of economic and political domination by the United States, has come from outside the region. Such dangers have seemed real enough (in the recent past, at least) so that certain Western Europeans have wanted a closer association with one another through a regional political organization. Later in the chapter, we take note of the progress that has been made in that direction.

First World political systems have retained enough power in the central organs of government so that each country has been able to speak with one voice in international affairs. This has not meant such a high degree of concentration that ordinary citizens have no access channels to the policymaking process or that the pluralistic nature of highly industrialized and urbanized societies has not been able to express itself through representative political institutions. The Second World countries, even those that are now relatively advanced industrially, have found it necessary until very recently to concentrate power. The Third World countries have often sought to limit free access to policymaking circles although their leaders sometimes find that their resources for implementing policies are limited.

In comparison with the United States, it appears that power is more highly concentrated both horizontally and vertically in Western Europe and Japan. Among the First World countries, power is more dispersed in the United States than elsewhere, both because of the constitutional dispersion on the vertical and horizontal scales and because of the strong political culture bias against allowing power to be too highly concentrated in a few hands. The reaction against an imperial presidency, aroused by the sometimes high-handed tactics of the Lyndon B. Johnson and Richard M. Nixon administrations, was, from a European perspective, a reassertion of intrinsic American values and a renewal of American determination to have these values prevail. In Western Europe and Japan, more reliance is placed on the political leaders' commitment to relatively explicit value systems and on senior government officials' commitment to their professional standards. These political and administrative professionals can be held to their standards by their equally professional colleagues. There may be considerable cynicism in France and Italy as to how much those in power are really acting on behalf of the best interests of the citizenry at large, but people also believe that the system will operate in such a way as to prevent the worst excesses. In Great Britain and West Germany, there is a strong belief that political leaders and public officials will adhere to well-established legal norms and that the opposition will see that they do so in fact. The latter belief is thoroughly entrenched in Great Britain; the relatively orderly course of political events in the Bonn Republic has gradually implanted it in the West German political culture as well. As for Japan, trust in government officials approaches British and West German standards, even though the capacity of opposition parties to keep government incumbents in check is weaker than in any of our Western European countries.

This suggests that political culture acts to restrain the concentration of power less in the polyarchies we are examining than in the United States. In actual performance, it can be said that elites have exercised a considerable amount of self-restraint in ensuring that power will not be concentrated beyond certain well-recognized limits. The notable exception is France. Power has always been rather highly concentrated on the vertical scale in France. Steps toward regional decentralization have been taken haltingly and with obvious reluctance on the part of central power holders until quite recently. Horizontally, the concentration of power has varied considerably from regime to regime. In devising the political institutions of the Fifth Republic, General Charles de Gaulle and his advisers were acutely aware of the debilitative effect that power dispersion at the center had had on the capacity of the Fourth Republic to respond to external challenges. Today, one might suggest that they had overcompensated.

The Fifth Republic established an imperial presidency that was the envy of Richard M. Nixon. Without de Gaulle's imperious personality, the authority of the French president has diminished somewhat, but the president remains the supreme policymaker in the French political system, with no need to answer to Parliament. However, whether French presidents have used their powers to full potential has varied among incumbents, according to personal styles and political circumstances. Since 1986, President François Mitterrand has interpreted it more passively than he did previously or than his predecessors. Even though power is, in principle, more highly concentrated in a parliamentary than in a presidential system, the combination of the presidential and parliamentary features in the Fifth Republic gives the French president the best of both worlds, as explained in Chapter 5. To be sure, power is concentrated in the cabinet in Great Britain, West Germany, Italy, and Japan, and the British prime minister and West German chancellor are in superior positions vis-à-vis their respective colleagues. But prime ministers and chancellors must retain the support of their fellow partisans in parliaments. The political demise of such figures as Anthony Eden and Harold Wilson in Great Britain, of Konrad Adenauer and Helmut Schmidt in West Germany, and of numerous short-term prime ministers in Italy and Japan attests to the uncertain base of personal political support that these parliamentary leaders need. By contrast, the French president is assured of holding office for seven years.

It should be recalled that we are talking about political systems in which, whatever may be the concentration of formal (or government) power, informal (nongovernment) power is generally dispersed. There are a number of political parties that are not quasi-government organs, as they are in Second World and some Third World systems; and each country has strong parties in the opposition. There are also a number of interest groups that contend with one another for scarce resources and counteract the power of one another and of the government itself. Where parties alternate in power, as in Great Britain and West Germany, the advantage one group (such as organized labor) might have is offset by the disadvantage of being too closely tied to the fortunes of one party or coalition. Where one party or coalition has enjoyed power for many years, as in Italy, the advantage that one group (such as an organized business) might have is threatened by the danger that the opposition might come to power and turn that advantage into a disadvantage. What this suggests is that there are built-in adjustive mechanisms in First World polyarchies (although Japan may be an exception) that assure a kind of rough balance between contending political forces over the long run, at least, if not in the short run.

## *Enlightenment*

The goal of providing an adequate education for everyone through the secondary level and of making a college education widely available has long been backed by the U.S. government. In the early 1980s, 6.7 percent of the American gross national product (GNP) was being spent by all levels of government on education, as compared with 5.3 percent for Great Britain, 5.8 percent for France, 4.5 percent for West Germany, and 5.7 percent for Italy and Japan.[1] However, some other First World countries—Sweden, Norway, the Netherlands, and Canada—were exceeding the U.S. commitment in these terms, spending for education between 7 and 8 percent of GNP. The United States leads the First World in expenditure on *higher* education and in percentage of the relevant age group enrolled in higher education, but student–faculty ratios exceed 30 to 1 in American colleges and universities. In Italy and Great Britain they are between 20 and 25 to 1; in France, West Germany, and Japan they are 10 to 1 or even below. In the primary grades the American pupil to teacher ratio looks better than the ratio at the higher education level, standing at 19 to 1, midway between the Japanese rate of 24 to 1 and the Italian rate of 14 to 1.[2]

It is tempting to suggest that, at the higher levels of education, if not at the primary level, the United States has sacrificed educational quality for quantity as compared with most other First World countries. In Chapter 2 we emphasized the role of the secondary schools in Western Europe in sorting out children destined to go on to the university from those who will finish school at the secondary level and go into blue-collar and nonprofessional white-collar occupations. This goes a long way to explain the much larger proportion of American young people who attend colleges and universities because, for the most part, American secondary education is not similarly segregated. The possibility of being able to go on to institutions of higher education is not decided once and for all at age eleven or twelve for the majority of American students as it has been for European students. On the other hand, the quality of secondary education available to the favored European minority is undoubtedly higher than it is for the average American high school student who plans to go on to college. The first two years of college often serve the same function as the last years of secondary school do in Europe in giving the American student the intellectual tools necessary to specialize at higher levels, something the European student begins to do immediately on entering the university. Thus, it can still be said that the American outcome is better quantitatively, but that qualitatively it is somewhat inferior.

Still another perspective is offered by Japan, where the effort of the state to maintain an educational system of high quality is matched by the determination of Japanese parents and their offspring to take fullest opportunity of the possibilities offered. Getting ahead in Japanese society through education has long been a culturally sanctioned commitment, which makes it possible for us to rate the opportunities for upward mobility in that society as higher than in most First World countries. Students work very hard, pursuing goals that have been instilled in them early in life, to pass the rigorous entry examinations for university entry. This desire to achieve is not confined to children from middle-class families as it has been in Europe. Approximately 20 percent of students in Japanese public (not private) universities and colleges come from the 20 percent of families with the lowest incomes. In other words, who enters Japanese public institutions of higher education is "virtually unaffected by parental income"; thus "social factors are probably less important for educational attainment in Japan than in almost any other OECD country."[3] The reasons would seem to be found more in Japanese culture than in the way the system of education is structured. There is evidence that failure can be severely damaging psychologically, but success in entering a university is almost an assurance of a good position in government or in a private corporation, whatever one's social origins. The technical capacity of Japan's industry owes something to its educational system as well. Although the number of degree holders in mathematics and in scientific and technical subjects is not unusually high,[4] the test scores of Japanese elementary and secondary schoolchildren in mathematics are among the highest in the world,[5] which is another indicator not only of the quality of the educational system, but of the built-in drive of the students themselves.

Despite the potential qualitative disadvantages of the American educational system, European countries have been demonstrating their belief in the superiority of something like the American approach by pushing for reform of secondary-level education in the direction of the *comprehensive school,* which brings together students of all intellectual levels and does not prematurely foreclose the possibility of certain youngsters' ever going on to the university. Steps have been taken under the impetus of democratic socialist parties in most Western European countries to reform their educational systems, but progress has been faster in some countries, such as Great Britain, where more than 80 percent of students in secondary education are in comprehensive schools, as a result of the rapid advance of comprehensivization in the later 1970s, and especially Sweden, where the comprehensive principle had been firmly established by 1970.

France and Great Britain are two countries for which educational reform has been high on the policy agenda in the past decade.[6] In the eyes of the Conservative government of Margaret Thatcher, comprehensivization of secondary education had proceeded too fast and too far in the decade before they came to office. For the French Socialists under François Mitterrand, educational reform efforts under their predecessors had not proceeded far enough. Mrs. Thatcher's education secretary, Sir Keith Joseph, sought to put more emphasis on the quality of education and less on the quantity, by concentrating state financial resources on a core curriculum that would ensure that British schoolchildren would learn the basics of English, mathematics, and science. The aspects of concentrating financial resources has probably been more successful than that of improving educational quality. Nor has the Thatcher government been very successful in its effort to rejuvenate private education in the country, thus giving families (most probably middle-class families) an alternative to the comprehensive school for their children.

In France, the Socialist government, favoring state-supported comprehensive education, moved in the opposite direction from the Conservatives in Britain concerning the balance between public and private schools. There has been a centuries'-old conflict in Catholic France regarding the relationship between church and state in the educational sphere. Most private schools in France are what are called parochial church schools in the United States, and since 1959 they have been maintained partially through state subsidization in return for their adhering to certain minimum state-determined standards. Socialists traditionally have opposed state financial involvement in the private schools, and when the new government took office in 1981 it sought to make continued state aid contingent on a much fuller private school conformity to Ministry of Education's standards for the state school curriculum. The Catholic Church, Catholic lay organizations, and conservative political parties mounted a vociferous campaign against the proposed legislation, culminating in a day-long march of more than 1 million demonstrators. The opposition succeeded in forcing the government to revise the legislation, making it less threatening to the autonomy of the Catholic schools. Whereas the French Socialist government, like its Conservative opposite number in Britain, failed in its primary objective in the area of educational reform, it did succeed in diverting substantial public resources in the direction of education and in increasing the size of the state school teaching force at the same time Margaret Thatcher's government was whittling down the size of British teaching staffs. The high budgetary priority the French Socialists assign to education is in no small way connected with the fact that a large proportion of party members and even Socialist deputies in the National Assembly are professional educators.[7]

Enlightenment is available to citizens in all Western European countries in the form of a free press, which is not subject to government censorship or constrained to serve as government's mouthpiece, as is frequently the case in Second and Third World countries. In some Western European countries—Great Britain, for example—government secrecy frustrates efforts by the press to engage in the sort of investigative journalism common in the United States and in the scandal-oriented French, Italian, and West German presses. But the practice of government leakage of information has been developing in Britain of late, especially in defiance of the security-conscious Thatcher government. Journalists in Britain must be careful, however, not to run afoul of the Official Secrets Act of 1911, which provides penalties for writers and publishers who publish classified material. In all four countries a pluralistic press can be found, with readers able to choose among numerous daily and weekly newspapers, many of national circulation (in contrast to the more localized press in the United States) of varying political viewpoints. Like the American press, the bias in Western Europe of most major papers tends to be to the right, but virtually every major political party (left, center, and right) has one or more newspapers with relatively high circulation faithfully supporting its leaders and their policy positions. In each country there are distinguished newspapers that cover government and politics with critical objectivity and provide a forum for a wide range of political viewpoints. Examples are the *Times* and the *Independent* in Great Britain and *Frankfurter Allgemeine Zeitung* in West Germany. But there are also numerous offerings of a less serious nature that cater to appetites for a more sensational rendering of the news, inviting comparison with what one finds at grocery store checkout counters in the United States. More so than in the case of the educational system, what is regarded as the ordinary press in Western Europe may reach both qualitative extremes with greater frequency than in the United States. In Japan, the press tends to be more uniform, politically neutral though critical of the government, and probably of higher average quality than is found in the Western countries we are discussing.

Television and radio broadcasting are subject to a wise variety of structural arrangements throughout Western Europe. Our four European countries differ sharply from the United States, however, in that television is state owned and state controlled. To the extent that private broadcasting exists, as it does in Great Britain alongside of the state-owned but autonomous networks of the British Broadcasting Corporation (BBC), it is in the form of concessions granted by the state and subject to the supervision of a state agency (the Independent Television Authority in Britain). Such limited pluralism can also be found in West German television, where the separate states are responsible for mass media policy and different states operate their different channels, and in Japan, whose public–private mix is similar to the British. Whether pluralism exists as now in France or there is a near-national state monopoly, as in Italy, an effort is made to provide viewers (and listeners) with a choice between serious public affairs programs and lighter fare. It is safe to say that the quality of broadcasting is superior to what it is in the United States, where the privately owned networks are predominant. However, there are frequently heard complaints, especially in France and Italy, of bias in public affairs broadcasting, including straight news programs, in favor of government parties to the detriment of the opposition. But in both countries television broadcasting has been opened to private initiative in recent years. The most frequent complaint in Great Britain and West Germany is that controversy has been contained within limits that are not threatening to the cross-party establishments. Whether or not this claim is true, the intellectual content of what controversy there is appears to be on a higher level than that usually found on the major networks in the United States, not to mention the sports and entertainment networks, which have no counterpart as yet in Western Europe. The arrival of cable television there, still on a relatively modest scale, may change this picture. At best, it will result in a greater variety of offerings to a diversified public without detracting from the level of quality programming.

## *Respect*

Almost by definition, the First World comprises countries in which (at least most of the time) governments are bound by legal norms that restrain them from acting in ways that would violate local concepts of human rights. In a survey of political systems in all parts of the world, it was found that thirty-two countries had high scores for maintaining civil liberties and political rights relatively free of government interference. Of these, sixteen were in Western Europe. Great Britain, France, West Germany, and Italy were all among the sixteen. Japan was one of the countries outside Western Europe to be found in the highest category. Of the countries normally considered to be in Western Europe, only one, Greece, fell into the "second freest" category on a scale from 1 to 7.[8] It should be noted that the study distinguishes between "political" and "individual" freedoms. Whereas all five of our countries were in the highest category regarding political freedoms, only three of them (the United Kingdom, Italy, and Japan) were in the highest category regarding individual freedoms. West Germany and France are placed in the second-highest category, apparently for different reasons. In the case of West Germany, it was because of the 1979 antiterrorist legislation that restricted the rights of certain groups to organize and carry out their activities, whereas, in the case of France, it was because "the political composition of government affects the nature of what is broadcast [by the media] to the advantage of incumbents."[9] Still, despite these exceptions, all five countries are placed in the overall category of "free" countries where basic human freedoms are respected. At least five general reasons can be cited for this favorable record:

**1.** Most First World countries have longstanding legal traditions in which the rights of individuals are clearly defined. In the case of the United States and Great Britain, the common-law traditions handed down from medieval England consist of a body of precedents found in earlier court decisions with a number of legal norms applying to the relationship between the individual and the state. These have been supplemented by acts of the national legislatures in both countries as well as by state legislatures in the United States; such acts are then subject to court interpretation. In a very real sense, judges make law in common-law countries, because they are continually reinterpreting old precedents in the light of modern circumstances. However, British judges use considerably greater self-restraint in preferring to be guided by precedent, whereas American judges are more willing to alter law to fit new situations.

In continental European countries, including France, West Germany, and Italy, systems of code law prevail. These derive from the Roman law tradition. In such legal systems, laws originally enacted by Parliament or promulgated by the sovereign have been codified into complex bodies of categories and subcategories that contain the legal norms that apply in various kinds of cases. The role of the courts is more limited in such countries than it is in Great

Britain and the United States because the codes are specific and thus the courts have limited discretion in handling particular cases. It is up to the legislative bodies in these countries to determine what new laws will apply to new situations not envisaged in the codes. Still, in both kinds of system, bodies of law exist that clearly define rights and obligations, at least in settled areas of the law; institutions exist to ensure that these laws are observed—by itself, this is a greater safeguard for the individual than where the law is uncertain and at the mercy of the whims of those in power. This is also certainly true in the case of the Japanese legal and judicial systems, which represent a twin borrowing—of continental European code law at the time of the Meiji Restoration, and of the American system of legal safeguards for persons accused of crime, incorporated during the MacArthur period.

**2.** In addition to their ordinary role of interpreting and applying the law, courts in First World countries perform the function of restraining the executive (or law enforcement) arm of government. Government actions that go beyond delegated powers or that violate established norms may be revoked by court actions. In common-law countries, the courts may declare executive actions ultra vires, that is, beyond the scope of power granted by the legislature and, therefore, unenforceable. In code law countries, there is a network of administrative tribunals that hear cases brought by individuals against state officials. Although technically part of the bureaucracy, they are noted for standards of impartiality and consistent adherence to precedent. Moreover, in both types of legal system, there are appellate courts at the top of the ordinary court system that can reverse the decisions of the lower courts on the ground that norms protecting individual rights have been violated in the administration of justice.

Finally, there is the power of judicial review, that is, the power to declare legislative actions unconstitutional—in some cases on the ground that they violate rights listed in a country's constitution. In the United States, the U.S. Supreme Court possesses such power, which is emulated by constitutional courts in West Germany and Italy, both of which have been active in insisting that constitutional provisions for human rights be respected. The supreme court of Japan also possesses the power of judicial review, but except in certain cases involving the interpretation of provisions of the constitution relating to human rights, the supreme court has been reluctant to make use of its powers against the more political branches of the government. No such body exists in Great Britain, where, indeed, there is no written constitution and where courts are bound to enforce the Acts of Parliament without applying separate standards to judge their constitutionality. But Parliament itself is expected to exercise self-restraint in its capacity to determine the content of the constitution through its ordinary acts, and by and large it does exercise such restraint.

In France, the Constitutional Council established by the constitution of the French Fifth Republic seemed originally to have quite limited powers to judge the constitutionality of legislation. Until the mid-1970s it could decide on the constitutionality of laws enacted by Parliament only when cases were brought to it by the president of the republic, the prime minister, or the president of one of the two chambers of Parliament. In fact, few laws were referred to it until, after his election as president of the republic in 1974, Valery Giscard d'Estaing sponsored a constitutional amendment that enabled challenges by the opposition parties to parliamentary acts to be brought to the Constitutional Council on the petition of sixty members of either parliamentary chamber. This opened the door for many more challenges, whose number rose modestly during the Giscard presidency but then precipitously between 1981 and 1986 when a Socialist government faced a conservative court appointed largely by its predecessor, much as Franklin Roosevelt faced a conservative Supreme Court in the United States in 1933 when he first took office with his New Deal program of legislation. Changes in the council's composition more recently have brought it more in line with the renewed Socialist government under François Mitterrand and Michel Rocard, but during the 1981–86 period there were thirty-four pieces of Socialist legislation that were revoked either in whole or in part.[10] This puts the French Constitutional Council now in the same class as the constitutional courts of West Germany, Italy, and Japan which, within certain limits, have the power of judicial review enjoyed by the American Supreme Court.

There is also a potential for a sort of *European* judicial review to be exercised by the European Court of Justice (ECJ), an organ of the European Community (EC), which is discussed later in this chapter. The treaties on which the powers of EC governing bodies are based largely deal with economic issues, but they relate in certain ways to what are usually considered human rights matters. In attempting to bring about equal conditions of employment among member countries, for example, they put acts of national parliaments that discriminate on the basis of sex, race, or national origin (if from another EC country) in violation of European Community law. The ECJ can declare acts of national legislative bodies (e.g., the British Parliament) to be in violation of treaty obligations, in effect, unconstitutional in EC terms. It is then up to the courts in the country concerned to refuse to honor a law of its own parliament unless it is changed to conform to treaty obligations. This "split-level" exercise of judicial review is emerging slowly in practice, but it is coming into practice even in countries like Britain, where the courts traditionally have not exercised judicial review of national legislation.

3. In the continental countries and Japan, judges have a status similar to that of higher civil servants. They have security of tenure within their professional ranks, but their promotion from lower to higher courts is politically controlled, at least in part. Therefore, independence of political superiors is not assured, a matter that provoked considerable criticism in France early in the Fifth Republic. American and British judges are politically appointed (unless elected, as is true of the majority of American state and local judges), but also enjoy lifetime tenure. British judges are drawn from the exclusive ranks of the *barristers*, which in effect means they are drawn from a pool of, at most, a few hundred senior, highly educated, well-paid lawyers. Recruitment of American judges is from the legal profession in general, which is not professionally divided in the elite/nonelite way the British profession is. Who will be appointed to the higher benches is much less predictable than it is in Britain or the continental countries, where the range of possibilities is narrower and the leeway of the appointive authority therefore more restricted.

Students of the subject are not in agreement regarding the question of whether the narrow basis of judicial selection in Western Europe makes judges more independent of or more dependent on the political executive than are those in the United States. Security of tenure of U.S. federal judges means that most of them outlast the presidents who appointed them. Thus a court at any given time is unlikely to be peopled only by the appointees of the incumbent president. Western European judges may be independent of executive control while remaining tied to professional norms that restrict their range of judgment. Perhaps these mixtures of discretion and constraint are better than too much of either, at least from the standpoint of respect for human rights. Too much discretion might allow a judiciary to interpret the law in ways that are either too out-of-date or too far in advance of the cultural definitions of human rights and obligations that prevail at a given time. Too little discretion would leave the judges without the flexibility needed to right wrongs whenever they are committed against human dignity by other agents of the state or by their own judicial colleagues.

**4.** Because of the pluralistic nature of the First World's political systems, the role played by the political opposition, and the ready availability of channels of public communication, it is unlikely that gross violations of human rights will go unprotested. These phenomena interact with and reinforce one another. Thus, the greater the level of individual freedom, the more confidence individuals will have in group action, including political opposition and the collective public voicing of dissent. Many political systems in the world attest to the fact that the opposite characteristics form a syndrome as well: repression of voluntary groups, of political opposition, and of public dissent, as well as disdain for the many safeguards for the individual that are taken for granted in Western polyarchies.

**5.** Postindustrial societies are witnessing the emergence of a new agenda of public policy problems. Here, we should include a heightened concern for human rights. Critics of the violations of human rights in the Soviet Union and other Second World countries, many Third World countries, and in the Republic of South Africa have shown an increased unwillingness to allow long-standing abuses to continue simply at the discretion of those countries' leaders. Many of the same critics have also directed attention to the continuing denials of respect in their own countries. Progress has been made in areas such as equal rights for minority groups and for women. The former has especially been a problem in the United States and Great Britain, with their significant populations of racial minorities, as well as in Northern Ireland, with its large Catholic minority. Progress probably has been swifter in the United States (although only after many decades of neglect), where there has been a greater willingness on the part of the dominant racial group to look at the problem and attempt to find solutions to it—a willingness, no doubt, stimulated by the militancy of the minority groups themselves. This was not the case in Northern Ireland, where British troops had to take civil power away from the Ulster Parliament because of blatant discrimination by Protestants against Catholics. Although France, West Germany, Italy, and Japan do not have similar minority groups whose rights are so seriously in jeopardy, these countries have been slower than the United States and Great Britain to promote equal rights for women in areas such as employment opportunities and divorce law. But, in all the cases mentioned, there seems to be a growing awareness of the problem as one of human respect.

Although we can say confidently that First World countries as a group display better human rights records than do the other two groups of countries, it is also the case that the First World is on the cutting edge of technological advance in an era in which changes in technology and the foreseeable (let alone the unforeseeable) consequences of those changes have been truly astounding. Threats to the environment from industrial pollution and efforts by government to protect the environment through regulation can be seen as issues involving the rights of private firms to conduct their businesses free of government regulation, or they can be seen as cases of human rights (i.e., as involving respect for the individuals in society who might be physically harmed by toxic effluents or atmospheric waste).[11]

We are dazzled by the anticipated benefits in the realms of the prolongation of human life, the explosions of knowledge, and the immense increases in productivity. But some of the technological breakthroughs hold forth the danger of depriving individuals of accustomed rights to privacy and to control over their own persons while threatening to concentrate enormous power in the hands of scientists, physicians, and information technology specialists and, through them, to the governments and multinational corporations that employ them. First World legal systems, moving with their traditional professional deliberateness and political caution, cannot keep up with changes that are affecting our daily lives. The extent to which electronic devices have taken over the center of our working and leisure time in the past decade is perhaps the most visible manifestation of these changes for most persons. Information technology can cut both ways: It can not only expand our horizons as thinking and learning humans, but it can also limit and condition that thinking and learning in a variety of subtle ways. What is more sinister, it can be a means of simplifying the process by which information about us is gathered, stored, systematized, and transferred between organizations that are interested in us for reasons with which we may not be in sympathy.

Advances in biotechnology promise to revolutionize the processes of human reproduction and genetic inheritance. At the same time that they are in the process of expanding the options available to parents, they are also bringing about a nightmare of conflicting perceptions of the respective rights of parents and children, fathers and mothers, natural and surrogate parents, pregnant women and embryos, religious and secular authorities, all of which involve the clash of conceptions of human dignity and the rights of various categories of persons to have respect as individuals. Such conflicts ultimately may be sorted out by political processes. It is to be hoped that pluralistic systems of conflict resolution and policymaking will be equal to the task and that superior state power will not force issues to premature closure. Weighted in favor of pluralism are the ever-increasing capacity of the electronic media to expand horizons and the fact that technological know-how is widely dispersed throughout the world at large and not confined to a small conspiratorial elite, which means that the process can be kept open and legal systems constantly adjusted to new realities while older values are not lost from sight.

When compared with their own traditions and established standards, First World countries have not gotten universally high marks in recent years. Thus, student and working-class unrest has been met in some Western European countries, including the four largest, with violent police action or repressive legislation removing legal safeguards for certain groups of citizens. Such actions have been defended as required because of the threat of terrorist attacks, such as assaults on embassies, airliner hijackings, or the kidnapping and assassination of prominent public figures. The dilemma is quite clear, especially for countries with uncertain traditions of political stability. Is it worse to deprive acknowledged enemies of the public order of their individual rights, or to allow them relative freedom they may use to deprive innocent citizens of their freedom and sometimes their lives? This is not an easy question for anyone, but especially not for people with memories of political warfare between strong-armed groups of the left and the right.

Even in the United Kingdom, where the instinct to protect the individual from arbitrary action is probably as strong as it is anywhere in the world and where leadership has been taken in certain human rights areas (such as the rights of homosexuals), traditional rights, such as habeas corpus and the right to a speedy trial, have been suspended—in Northern Ireland, because of the civil strife going on there. As noted in the previous section, tightened interpretations of the Official Secrets Act lately have produced some notable violations of press freedom. Significant lapses in all five countries in the matter of human rights make it difficult to give highest marks to them for the value of respect, especially if we recognize that the basic concern for the value of the individual has grown out of the Western tradition.

## *Well-Being*

### The Record

The economic difficulties experienced by First World countries in the 1970s and early 1980s raised considerable speculation as to the future of postindustrial society. The problem of stagflation was treated in Chapter 2 as a general phenomenon affecting all postindustrial countries. However, when we look at the economic record on a country-by-country basis, we are more impressed by the differences in this record among countries than by the similar fates of postindustrial countries. Let us look at the recent record. In so doing, we compare our five countries with the largest economy in the First World, the United States.

Table 7.1 provides us with an overview of the productive capacities of the six economies and of their growth patterns from 1981 through 1986. Although the American economy is by far the most productive in terms of total output, it is not far ahead of Japan on a per capita basis. West Germany had surpassed the United States in gross domestic product (GDP) per capita briefly in the 1970s, although the United States regained its lead by 1981. France, Great Britain, and Italy are ranged behind these leaders. But an examination of growth rates in the 1980s shows that Japan's economy has grown at a more rapid pace than have the others. West Germany, Italy, and France, all of which in earlier decades had grown at more rapid rates than the United States and Great Britain, had fallen behind those two countries in growth rates by the mid-1980s.

Inspection of Table 7.1 also shows that the American and British growth rates are the only ones that were not at lower levels in 1981–86 than in the preceding five-year period. Reasons for the higher growth rates of Japan, Great Britain, and the United States can be found in the data in the bottom row, where the annual percentage of fixed capital formation is also presented. It can be seen that investment in France was actually negative in the 1980s, whereas that in West Germany and Italy has not been sufficient to assure superior economic growth.

The British investment figures are particularly impressive when it is considered that, for the preceding five-year period, 1976–81, Britain actually disinvested, which helps account for the fact that Britain fell below Italy for the first time in the mid-1980s in GDP per capita. Table 7.1 suggests that Italy's lead may be short-lived. However, it should also be recognized that these official figures do not include the so-called informal economy, or unreported economic activity that eludes the gaze of tax collectors. This is said to be particularly buoyant in Italy, although it undoubtedly plays a not-negligible, if unmeasurable, role in every country. If we

**Table 7.1 Economic Growth in Six Countries**

| | *France* | *West Germany* | *Italy* | *Japan* | *United Kingdom* | United States |
|---|---|---|---|---|---|---|
| GDP per capita (1986) | $13,077 | $14,611 | $10,484 | $16,109 | $9,651 | $17,324 |
| Percentage annual growth (1981–86) | 1.7 | 1.7 | 1.9 | 3.6 | 2.6 | 2.9 |
| Percentage annual growth (1976–81) | 2.3 | 2.5 | 2.6 | 4.6 | 0.5 | 2.8 |
| Capital formation, annual growth (1981–86) | −0.7 | 0.3 | 0.3 | 3.5 | 4.4 | 4.4 |

(*Source*) Organization for Economic Cooperation and Development, *OECD Economic Surveys: United Kingdom* (Paris: OECD, 1988). For percentage of annual growth (1976–81) figures, OECD, *OECD Economic Surveys: Germany* (Paris: OECD, 1984), p. 28.

were in a position to accurately measure the totality of economic activity in each of these countries, it might be that Italy's lead over Britain has existed for considerably longer and that the chances of Britain's recapturing a lead over Italy are slim.

The data in Table 7.2 suggest that the average American enjoys greater material well-being than the average European or Japanese. The greatest gap is found in energy consumption, which includes both domestic use and use by manufacturing, commercial, and administrative units. But the American lead is considerably greater in energy use than in GDP per capita, which suggests a much greater use by consumers than in the other countries. This is further reflected in the long lead of the United States in the number of passenger cars and television sets per capita. When we move from private consumer items to *collective* (or publicly provided) goods, the United States no longer leads the league. The United States is in the middle in the number of doctors per 1,000 population, and, in a measure of the adequacy of national health care delivery systems (infant mortality), the United States has a higher rate at 10.6 infant deaths per 1,000 live births than does Japan (5.9), France (6.9), West Germany (9.1), or Britain (9.4). Only Italy, at 10.9, exceeds the high American rate, of the countries dealt with here. On the other hand, as noted earlier in this chapter, the United States, and to a lesser extent Japan, leads the Western European countries in quantitative measures of education.

The Western European countries are more dependent on world trade than is either the United States or Japan, at least if total trade figures are examined. In Table 7.3, combined 1986 exports and imports are listed as percentages of total GDP. Of the four major Western European countries, Italy and France are relatively self-sufficient, being able to meet most of their food consumption needs with domestic production. This is not the case of West Germany or Great Britain, although food production has been growing in these, as in all First World countries. But some of the smaller Western European countries are even more dependent on foreign trade. Imports and exports approach 60 percent of GDP for Belgium; Irish exports reached 51 percent of GDP in 1986. But, large or small, most Western European countries usually show a negative balance of trade in goods, importing a higher percentage of GDP

**Table 7.2 Indicators of Living Standards in Six Countries**

| | *France* | *West Germany* | *Italy* | *Japan* | *United Kingdom* | United States |
|---|---|---|---|---|---|---|
| Private consumption per capita (1986) | $7,389 | $7,116 | $6,963 | $7,132 | $7,156 | $11,500 |
| Energy consumption per capita (kg of oil equivalent, 1986) | 3640 | 4464 | 2539 | 3186 | 3802 | 7193 |
| Passenger cars per 1,000 population (c. 1984) | 360 | 441 | 355 | 221 | 312 | 473 |
| TV sets per 1,000 population (early 1980s) | 297 | 377 | 244 | 250 | 336 | 621 |
| Doctors per 1,000 population (c. 1983) | 2.1 | 2.5 | 3.6 | 1.3 | 0.5 | 2.3 |

(*Source*) Organization for Economic Cooperation and Development, *OECD Economic Surveys: United Kingdom* (Paris: OECD, 1988), pp. 106–107. For energy consumption, World Bank, *World Development Report 1988* (New York: Oxford University Press, 1988), p. 241.

than they export. The major exception is West Germany, which consistently has shown a healthy positive balance in the 1970s and 1980s. Japan, though not as heavily trade dependent, has also shown positive balances, but not as substantial as those of West Germany. The favorable West German trade record has been a source of complaint for its partners in the European Community (EC) because their own negative balances are in part attributable to West Germany's success—often as their principal trade partner. It should be noted that when trade in services and financial transactions are added, some countries such as Britain and the United States are more likely to show positive balances.

The positive German and Japanese trade balances are both a consequence and a cause of the fact that both have enjoyed relative economic stability in a period when most countries have

**Table 7.3 Foreign Trade in Goods in Six Countries**

| | *France* | *West Germany* | *Italy* | *Japan* | *United Kingdom* | United States |
|---|---|---|---|---|---|---|
| Exports of goods as percentage of GDP (1986) | 16.5 | 27.2 | 16.2 | 10.8 | 19.5 | 5.2 |
| Imports of goods as percentage of GDP (1986) | 17.8 | 21.3 | 16.7 | 6.5 | 23.0 | 8.8 |
| Balance (row 1 minus row 2) | −1.3 | +5.9 | −0.5 | +4.3 | −3.5 | −3.6 |

(*Source*) Organization for Economic Cooperation and Development, *OECD Economic Surveys: United Kingdom* (Paris: OECD, 1988), pp. 106–107.

experienced high levels of unemployment and inflation. The West German record has been more consistent than the Japanese. West Germany has been less successful than Japan in holding down unemployment; but, with respect to price increases, Table 7.4 shows that West Germany has held inflation to modest levels, whereas prices in other economies soared in the 1970s. The Japanese experience in the 1970s was erratic regarding inflation. Japan had double-digit inflation rates similar to those in France during most of the crisis period of the mid- and late 1970s; but it was able to bring price increases under control at the end of the decade, and they have been among the lowest in the First World in the 1980s. As noted in Chapter 2, all six countries have seen unemployment rise in the 1980s. Only in Japan has the rise in unemployment been modest. On the other hand, all but Italy had brought inflation down substantially by the mid-1980s, and Italy was able to do so by 1988.[12]

When one considers unemployment and inflation on a comparative basis, as we are doing here, the relatively good and relatively bad rates stand out and become virtual absolutes. West Germany appears to get very high marks for maintaining economic stability, but in the mid-1970s (at least), the West Germans were not so impressed with their own performance, and the coalition government led by Helmut Schmidt had a lot of explaining to do in the election campaign of 1976. The coalition lost ground to the Christian Democratic opposition that year.

**Table 7.4 Indicators of Economic Instability in Six Countries**

| | *France* | *West Germany* | *Italy* | *Japan* | *United Kingdom* | United States |
|---|---|---|---|---|---|---|
| *Unemployment* | | | | | | |
| Average unemployment rate, | | | | | | |
| 1964–73 | 2.2 | 0.7 | 5.5 | 1.2 | 3.1 | 4.4 |
| 1974–79 | 4.5 | 3.2 | 6.6 | 1.9 | 5.1 | 6.6 |
| 1983 | 8.4 | 8.2 | 9.7 | 2.6 | 11.6 | 9.6 |
| Unemployment rate, late 1988 | 10.2 | 8.5 | 16.5 | 2.5 | 7.7 | 5.4 |
| *Inflation* | | | | | | |
| Average annual percentage change in consumer prices, | | | | | | |
| 1961–70 | 4.0 | 2.7 | 3.9 | 5.8 | 4.1 | 2.8 |
| 1971–80 | 9.0 | 5.9 | 12.2 | 11.1 | 13.6 | 6.6 |
| 1980–86 | 8.8 | 3.0 | 13.2 | 1.6 | 6.0 | 4.4 |
| 1988 | 3.0 | 1.6 | 5.3 | 1.1 | 6.4 | 4.2 |

(*Source*) For unemployment: Organization for Economic Cooperation and Development, *Economic Outlook* 35 (Paris: OECD, 1984), 43; *The Economist*, December 17, 1988, p. 109. For inflation: Organization for Economic Cooperation and Development, *Economic Outlook* 35 (Paris: OECD, 1984), 51; World Bank, *World Development Report 1988* (New York: Oxford University Press, 1988), p. 271; *The Economist*, December 17, 1988, p. 109.

By the 1980 elections, however, with West German unemployment and inflation figures remaining approximately where they had been four years before, the coalition regained most of its lost ground. Then, in 1983, with the higher levels of unemployment a more salient matter than the lower inflation, Schmidt's Social Democrats lost substantial electoral support to the new center-right coalition and to the emergent Green Party on its left. In the meantime, a British government had been voted out of office and Italian governments had struggled through a period in which there had been a real possibility that the Communists would gain a share of power. During the same election years in which the West German coalition twice survived challenges, two incumbent American presidents were defeated at the polls. Seven months after the second Schmidt victory, the French president was repudiated by the majority of French voters amid rising unemployment figures and continued double-digit inflation. In Japan, on the other hand, the turning around of the inflation rate preceded a surprising recovery in the 1980 election for the governing party, which had experienced several years marked by scandals, internal dissidence, and seeming voter disaffection. More recently, governing parties in Britain and the United States have twice been reelected amid signs of economic recovery, preceded by a substantial reduction in the inflation rate. It would be difficult to refute the proposition that electoral success for incumbents in postindustrial political systems is closely tied to the recent economic record and especially to the indicators of economic stability.

## Structural Adjustment Policies

The foregoing indicators of comparative levels of well-being among our countries relate to what are usually called *macroeconomic policy* objectives. Governments attempt to attain objectives concerning economic growth, consumption levels, energy conservation, trade balances, and levels of unemployment and inflation through the manipulation of broad economic policy levers, particularly fiscal policies involving budget balances between revenue and expenditure and monetary policies involving control of the money supply. (See Chapter 2). But governments have found that these instruments of macroeconomic manipulation are inadequate to solve the problems of sectors of their economies that are becoming less competitive in the face of technological change and competition from countries able to produce the same goods or supply the same services at lower cost. Economists have come increasingly to argue that macroeconomic policy should be systematically supplemented by what is called *microeconomic policy*. This involves gaining greater control over the factors that go into the *supply* of goods and services for a country's domestic markets and for international markets. Countries that are successful in maintaining positive trade balances, it is said, are those that are most successful in finding the appropriate mix of microeconomic policies; in other words, their governments have been the most astute in dealing with the problems of *structural adjustment*.

An example of the difference of emphasis that is involved when we look at structural adjustment as a microeconomic, rather than a macroeconomic, problem is the shift in our focus from overall levels of *unemployment* besetting a country's economy to the levels of *employment* found in different sectors of the economy and how these are changing over time. Table 7.5 provides a breakdown of some representative sectors of the six economies examined in the previous section. Percentages in the table are of gains or losses in employment for the period 1973–83. The sectors are placed roughly into

**Table 7.5 Employment Adjustments in Selected Economic Sectors for Six Countries, 1973–83**

| | *France* | *West Germany* | *Italy* | *Japan* | *United Kingdom* | United States |
|---|---|---|---|---|---|---|
| *Traditional sectors* | | | | | | |
| Agriculture | −3.0 | −3.2 | −2.6 | −2.4 | −1.4 | −0.6 |
| Basic metals | −2.1 | −2.4 | +0.5 | −1.9 | −5.0 | −4.2 |
| Textiles | −4.0 | −5.4 | −0.7 | −3.6 | −5.8 | −2.5 |
| *Modern industrial sectors* | | | | | | |
| Chemicals | −1.2 | −0.8 | −1.0 | −1.9 | −2.7 | +0.3 |
| Motor vehicles | −1.5 | −1.4 | +0.3 | +0.2 | −3.2 | −1.2 |
| Electricity, gas, water | +0.4 | +0.6 | +1.2 | +1.3 | −0.4 | +1.7 |
| Food | −0.4 | −1.2 | +0.0 | −0.1 | −2.1 | −0.7 |
| *Service sectors* | | | | | | |
| Transportation | +1.1 | −0.6 | +1.4 | +0.3 | −0.9 | +0.8 |
| Retailing | +0.8 | −0.2 | +2.0 | +1.5 | n.a. | +2.2 |
| Financial services | +2.2 | +1.2 | +3.8 | +3.2 | +2.6 | +3.4 |

(*Source*) Organization for Economic Cooperation and Development, *Structural Adjustment and Economic Performance* (Paris: OECD, 1987), p. 163.

three categories: traditional economic sectors (agriculture, basic metals, textiles), modern industrial sectors (chemicals, motor vehicles, food, and electricity/gas/water), and service sectors (transportation, retailing, and financial services). It is clear that the service sectors have shown gains in employment in all countries, and the traditional industries have shown universal losses. Financial services have shown the largest job gains in all six countries; textiles have shown the greatest losses in all but Italy (exceeded by agriculture and chemicals) and the United States (exceeded by basic metals). Differences between countries are striking. Thus, we see that Italy, Japan, the United States, and France have shown employment losses only in manufacturing industries, whereas West Germany and Britain have experienced losses of jobs in some of the service sectors as well. Indeed, financial services is the only sector in which Britain has shown job gains.

In postindustrial society, we expect employment to decline in manufacturing and to increase in the service sector. Within manufacturing, the traditional heavy industries that once were labor-intensive have become more capital-intensive, and the same has been true in the chemical and automobile industries. Thus, the fact that Italy and Japan actually showed employment gains in motor vehicles, and the fact that Britain and West Germany showed job losses in transportation, and West Germany in retailing, appear counterintuitive from the standpoint of the concept of postindustrial society. Of course, this could be because Italy and Japan are not taking advantage of labor-saving opportunities in the production of cars, or that Britain and West Germany have been auto-

**Table 7.6 Value Added in Selected Economic Sectors for Six Countries, 1973–83**

| | *France* | *West Germany* | *Italy* | *Japan* | *United Kingdom* | United States |
|---|---|---|---|---|---|---|
| *Traditional sectors* | | | | | | |
| Agriculture | +0.5 | +1.0 | +2.0 | −1.3 | +1.9 | +0.3 |
| Basic metals | −0.2 | −0.8 | +0.9 | +0.1 | −3.9 | −4.8 |
| Textiles | −1.5 | −1.7 | +1.1 | +2.9 | −3.5 | +1.0 |
| *Modern industrial sectors* | | | | | | |
| Chemicals | +2.8 | +1.2 | +2.8 | +5.1 | +0.1 | +1.4 |
| Motor vehicles | +0.8 | −1.5 | +1.6 | +3.3 | −3.7 | +0.5 |
| Electricity, gas, water | +2.8 | +2.9 | +0.0 | +4.7 | +1.5 | +1.8 |
| Food | +2.6 | +1.4 | +2.6 | +1.6 | +0.4 | +0.4 |
| *Service sectors* | | | | | | |
| Transportation | +2.6 | +3.3 | +3.1 | +2.4 | +0.9 | +2.7 |
| Retailing | +2.1 | +1.3 | +2.3 | +5.9 | −0.3 | +2.3 |
| Financial services | +2.9 | +3.7 | +2.8 | +4.4 | +3.9 | +2.3 |

(*Source*) Organization for Economic Cooperation and Development, *Structural Adjustment and Economic Performance* (Paris: OECD, 1987), p. 163.

mating their transportation sectors. Table 7.6 shows the annual growth rates of *value added* in the production of these categories of goods and services. When we compare individual countries across the manufacturing/service sector divide, we see that West Germany and Britain have shown increases in value per unit in the transportation sector, but that they have shown losses in the vulnerable industrial sectors of basic metals, textiles, and motor vehicles, compared to gains in all three of these fields by Italy and Japan, in two of them (textiles and motor vehicles) by the United States, and in one of them (motor vehicles) by France. In other words, some countries have been able to continue increasing their output of goods. This has meant shedding the labor needed to produce these goods in some cases. In other cases the expansion in production has been great enough that there have been employment gains as well. These countries clearly have found the technology and work organization necessary to produce more efficiently in order to meet international competition successfully. Others have not been able to make up for job losses with productivity gains that enable them at least to retain their market shares.

The reasons for these differences are many. They relate to the factors that go into the production of goods and the provision of services: labor, capital, and technology.

**Labor.** We have earlier noted that the Japanese and American educational systems produce higher percentages of academically oriented students prepared to go on to college or university than do those of our European countries. One measure of this is the percentage of seventeen-year-olds in general education, as opposed to the percentage in vocational training or already in the workforce. In 1984 it was 81 percent in the United States and 63 percent in Japan; the other countries ranged from 32 percent in West Germany to 18 percent in Britain. However, when those seventeen-year-olds who are in some form of school-delivered vocational training are added to those in general education, the Japanese percentage rises above the American, to 90 percent. The French, West German, and Italian also rise fairly steeply, to 63 percent, 50 percent, and 47 percent, respectively, whereas the British rises only to 30 percent.[13] This was before the introduction in Britain of the Youth Training Scheme, which today takes many of the remaining 70 percent of seventeen-year-olds out of the job market and seeks to prepare them more adequately for jobs than the regular educational system did. Still, we may here see one reason why Britain between 1973 and 1983 experienced declines in both jobs and output in many industrial sectors: The educated or otherwise trained labor force was not available on the scale it was in other advanced industrial countries.

In Chapter 6 we saw that the relationships between organized labor, employers, and the state vary substantially among our countries. In general terms, in those countries where labor is most accommodative to the claims of both management and the state for greater productivity and lower per-unit wage costs, we would expect industry to have the greatest competitive advantage. We saw that the institutional arrangements for industrial relations in Japan and France give employers a distinct advantage over labor, particularly in Japan, whereas the opposite has been the case in Britain and Italy, at least until lately. In West Germany the two appear roughly even in strength, but the relationship is cooperative, rather than conflictual. Table 7.7 gives some indication of how the six countries rank with respect to the accommodation of industrial relations to economic realities.

The percentages, all less than 1.0, represent the extent to which wages respond to increases in unemployment. The relatively low percentages for the United Kingdom and West Germany represent relatively sluggish responses, sug-

**Table 7.7 Decrease in Nominal Wage Growth Resulting from a One-Percentage-Point Increase in the Unemployment Rate (sample period in the 1980s)**

| *Country* | *Percentage* |
|---|---|
| Japan | 0.88 |
| United States | 0.60 |
| Italy | 0.60 |
| France | 0.33 |
| United Kingdom | 0.15 |
| West Germany | 0.14 |

(*Source*) Organization for Economic Cooperation and Development, *Structural Adjustment and Economic Performance* (Paris: OECD, 1987), p. 133.

**Table 7.8 Measures of Labor Market Flexibility**

| *Country* | *1979 Industry Wage Differentials* | *Regional Movers—1980 Percentage of Total Population* |
|---|---|---|
| Japan | 34.0 | 2.6 |
| United States | 26.8 | 3.3 |
| France | 23.9 | 1.3 |
| West Germany | — | 1.3 |
| United Kingdom | 20.4 | 1.1 (England and Wales) |

(*Source*) Organization for Economic Cooperation and Development, *Structural Adjustment and Economic Performance* (Paris: OECD, 1987), pp. 135–136.

gesting that organized labor is better able in those two countries than in the others to resist the pressure against nominal wage increases that unfavorable labor market conditions (as reflected in unemployment increases) are likely to entail. The order of countries is not what we might expect from the review of industrial relations in the preceding chapter. Italian unions appear less able to deliver wage-level stability to their members than we might have expected, whereas West German unions appear better able to do so. But it should be noted that the ordering of the countries is close to what we might expect when we look at the employment and output losses to de-industrialization shown in Tables 7.5 and 7.6. Greater wage flexibility in Japan, the United States, and Italy may help account for the greater buoyancy of industrial sectors in those countries that are in deeper trouble in the three other countries.

Two other measures of labor market flexibility produce approximately the same orderings of countries as the one in Table 7.7 (Italian figures unavailable). In Table 7.8 we see coefficients for four of the countries concerning variation in wage levels within manufacturing industries. This gives some idea of the extent to which firms anticipating growth can attract skilled workers with substantially higher pay, whereas firms in trouble can keep their labor costs within bounds by paying lower wages. In 1979 Japan showed the greatest variation in this respect, followed by the United States, France, and the United Kingdom, in that order.

The second measure in Table 7.8 involves geographical mobility within a national labor market for five of the six countries. Here the United States shows a population with a greater capacity than elsewhere to "move to the jobs" wherever they are available, thus reducing market "friction," or the lag that occurs between the creation and filling of job vacancies. Japan is second on this scale, well ahead of the other three—France, West Germany, and England/Wales. The ordering in Table 7.8 is again quite close to the ordering for structural adaptability of economies as displayed in Table 7.5 and 7.6.

**Capital and Technology.** Aside from the education indicators, the above measures pertaining to the quality of the *labor* input into the supply of goods and services in a country reflect only very indirectly the efforts its government makes to influence the competitive standing of national industry. Governments have policies designed to affect wage levels and geographical mobility, but they can be thwarted by institutional and cultural factors beyond government's control. Government can also influence the allocation of *capital* to industry by programs designed to steer industrial activity in more promising directions in the light of technological and world market trends. Government aid to industry includes subsidies that may or may not have the effect of stimulating investment into new products or new technology for more efficient production. In general terms, the United States, Japan, and West Germany are countries that avoid heavy subsidization of industry, whereas France, Britain, and Italy have engaged in subsidies ranging from 3.5 to 4 percent of industrial value added in recent years.[14] This ordering provides little reason to judge subsidization as being conducive, in general terms at least, to successful industrial restructuring, as the more successful countries have, for the most part, been those low on the subsidization scale.

When we take a more qualitative look at industrial investment expenditures to see whether resources are being devoted toward research in and development of new technologies (R&D), we find much the same ordering of countries as we do for government subsidization (i.e., the countries whose governments subsidize industry most heavily are also the countries in which the overall commitment to R&D is the weakest). This can be seen in Table 7.9, which also indicates that the countries with the greatest overall commitment to R&D are the countries in which the government's share of R&D funding is the smallest. Finally, the table also shows that the countries with the greatest R&D commitment are those with the greatest per capita output of the information technology sector, which might be considered a measure of the extent to which the Second Industrial Revolution has taken hold. It would appear that the governments of Japan and, to a lesser extent, the United States and West Germany, instead of intervening financially in their industries for whatever purpose, have sought to maintain the proper climate for private-sector adaptation to the technological and market changes that have been occurring. It should also be noted that the state sectors in the three other countries are

**Table 7.9 Indicators of National Commitment to Research and Development**

| | *R&D per Capita in $ (1983)* | *Share of Public Funding in National R&D (1983)* | *Output of Information Technology Industries as Percentage of GNP (1984)* |
|---|---|---|---|
| United States | $379 | 49.2% | 1.4% |
| *Japan* | 257 | 24.0 | 2.3 |
| *West Germany* | 272 | 39.4 | 1.3 |
| *France* | 223 | 54.0 | 1.1 |
| *United Kingdom* | 218 | 50.2 | 0.9 |
| *Italy* | 94 | 52.4 | 0.9 |

(*Source*) Organization for Economic Cooperation and Development, *Structural Adjustment and Economic Performance* (Paris: OECD, 1987), pp. 95, 104, 254.

larger than they are in Japan, the United States, or West Germany. This has tended to mean government assistance to state-owned industries, keeping them operating at a greater capacity for a longer period than otherwise might have occurred had they been in private hands. Governments have found it harder to escape political responsibility for job losses in state-owned than in privately owned industry and have acted to keep them in existence for a longer period of time, postponing the inevitable day of reckoning.[15]

It is possible that one should look more to the micro- than to the macroeconomic level for an understanding of the recent reversals of economic fortunes by macroeconomic measures experienced by the United States and Great Britain. Conservative governments under Ronald Reagan and Margaret Thatcher have taken credit for, first, the reduction of inflation and, then, the reduction of unemployment (which has gone farther in the United States than in Britain), arguing that their macroeconomic strategies known as "Reaganomics" and Thatcherism" have been responsible for these records of relative success. However, Reagan's "supply-side" economics with its emphasis on tax reductions and Mrs. Thatcher's monetarism with its commitment to a stable money supply produced undesirable macroeconomic side effects; budgetary deficits in the United States and, initially at least, higher unemployment in Great Britain. It is possible that what has begun to turn manufacturing and productivity levels around in the two economies has been a renewed confidence placed by government leaders in the capacity of private industry to regenerate itself and the withdrawal of assurance that the state will step in to rescue firms that cannot keep up with the times. It took a while for the message to sink in, especially in Britain where the habits of reliance on the state were stronger, and it is still too early to know if in the long run, these experiments will prove to have been successful.

As for Japan, one could argue that this is a case of both macro- and microeconomic success accompanying a more interventionist approach, thus casting the above "North Atlantic" examples into doubt as generalizable to the rest of the world. Two answers might be given to this argument. In the first place, the Japanese state has gradually withdrawn from the process of detailed planning of national economic development, leaving this more and more in the hands of the leaders of large multinational corporations. Second, when, in the postwar period, the Ministry for International Trade and Industry (MITI) played a stronger role, it was in a period that included postwar reconstruction designed to help the Japanese economy catch up rapidly with the advanced Western industrial countries and, later, to enable Japanese industries not to persist without change in the face of international competition, but to adapt to new technologies and market conditions. Once the adaptive habit had been thoroughly learned by private industry, the state could retire to a less-obtrusive position, ready to step in to help in dire emergencies, but relatively confident that industry would exhibit the astuteness necessary to make such emergencies rare occurrences.

## *Human Dignity and the European Community*

We cannot conclude our discussion of the performance of the leading First World polyarchies without mentioning an effort that some of them have made *collectively* to enhance human dignity on at least certain dimensions. The European Community, as it has developed over the years, has probably performed best on the dimension of well-being, because the principal steps taken toward European integration have been economic ones. The members of the European twelve are currently France, West Germany, Italy, Belgium, the Netherlands, and Luxembourg (the original six), as well as Great Britain, Denmark, Greece, Ireland, Spain, and Portugal (the six that have entered the EC since 1973). Clearly, the outstanding accomplishment of the EC has been the establishment of a common market among the twelve countries for industrial and agricultural products, which has meant the removal of tariff barriers among them and the establishment of joint restrictions on the importation of products from nonmember countries.

For the six original countries, at any rate, the Common Market served as an additional stimulus to economic growth during the 1960s. For the later entrants, this has not been so obvious. The 1973 entry of Great Britain, Denmark, and Ireland coincided with the energy crisis and with the concomitant reversal in the general economic fortunes of the Western polyarchies. The EC could not prevent the member countries from responding separately to the energy crisis. The addition of Greece, Spain, and Portugal in the 1980s has intensified the division between affluent northern European countries on the one hand, and poorer Mediterranean countries that have more serious economic problems that now must be shared in certain respects with the others. Nevertheless, it should be noted that achievements of the EC in the economic sphere have been remarkable if measured against original expectations. Given the history of protectionism and economic warfare before World War II (and even stretching back into the nineteenth century), such developments as the pooling of coal and steel production in the 1950s and agreement on a Common Agricultural Policy (CAP) in the 1960s are truly remarkable.

It is possible to view the EC from a standpoint that is not idealistic, but eminently practical. For the countries that first formed the Common Market, at least, the new organization became an *instrument* of their economic policies—an extension of other instruments employed at the domestic level. Each member government, from this standpoint, saw the EC as meeting a particular need in its own efforts to deal with economic problems. For the French, the CAP has been, among other things, a means by which a large, inefficient agricultural sector could be assured of sheltered markets in the partner countries while time was bought for a policy of encouraging consolidation and mechanization of French farms. This has been accomplished (to a considerable extent) through the EC policy of imposing levies on farm commodities imported into the EC from non-EC countries. The levies are collected by member governments and the proceeds distributed to farmers in the member countries. This involves the payment of large sums by the governments of food-importing countries, especially Great Britain and West Germany, through the medium of the European Commission, to the governments of food-exporting countries, which, in turn, disburse the funds to their farmers. Because the French farm sector is the largest of the twelve countries, it has been the main beneficiary of the policy along with the French state, whose burden of farm subsidization has greatly been eased.

There have been considerable advantages for the other original member countries as well. West Germany and the Benelux countries are heavily dependent on foreign trade, and the Common Market represents an assurance of a high volume of such trade. In fact, trade among the member countries increased rapidly after 1958, adding substantially to the factors promoting rapid economic growth in these countries. More specifically, it meant for West German manufacturers the opening up of the large French market that previously had been guarded behind relatively high tariff barriers. For Italy, the advantages have included the availability of additional sources of development funds for the southern region and sympathetic partners when credits are needed to keep the weak lira viable, features that later attracted Ireland, Greece, Spain, and Portugal to membership. Industry in the modern north of Italy has also benefited from the expanded market, just as has industry in the other original member countries. In addition, the more efficient of the Italian farmers share in the benefits of the CAP.

The CAP has also been an attraction for Danish, Irish, Greek, and Iberian farmers as well as for their governments. In the case of Great Britain, whose farm sector is a very small portion of its economy but whose farmers generally are highly efficient, the CAP is viewed (not by the farmers themselves) as a negative feature of the EC, involving high British contributions to the EC budget through the levy system, most of which goes to farmers across the Channel. Nor do many Britons perceive great advantages to the industrial and commercial sectors of their economy resulting from EC membership. By the time Great Britain entered the EC in 1973, her economy was lagging far behind those of her new partners, who had enjoyed the full benefits of the earlier boom period. But the boom was over, and membership in the EC no longer could provide the stimulus to British manufacturers to modernize and become more competitive, as it had done for French and Italian manufacturers fifteen years earlier. Although Prime Minister Thatcher and her Conservative government wish Great Britain to remain within the fold, they are determined to bring about a reform of the CAP that will make the EC less burdensome to British consumers and taxpayers.

In 1985 the twelve heads of governments of the EC agreed on an elaborate set of measures, labeled "Project 1992," designed (1) to finally remove all restrictions to trade between member countries that previously had existed in the form of regulations and mutually agreed quotas that had the same effect as tariff barriers, and (2) to complete steps that had been begun toward creating a common market for transportation and other services (e.g., banking and professional certification). These have been prime objectives of the British government under Margaret Thatcher, which is committed to the principle of freedom of trade and has especially pushed for a common market for financial services, with respect to which Britain should have a comparative advantage. However, in other ways the agreements are less the object of British enthusiasm. The completion of a barrier-free market within Europe is likely to be accompanied by the erection of common EC barriers against goods and services of non-EC countries, a prospect that Western European countries such as Sweden and Switzerland as well as the United States and Japan are viewing with some apprehension. Also, the trade measures have been accompanied by a loss of the British veto power and a modest boost in the powers of the European Parliament (discussed later), which represented concessions on the part of a British government jealous of its sovereignty.

On the other hand, the EC has accomplished very little in getting the member countries to coordinate their policies in other sectors. Thus, it has had relatively little effect on redistributive policies, on educational policies, or on upholding human rights. These are areas in which the performance of the member countries is uneven and often falls short of their own aspirations. However, it should be added that the *prospect* of membership in the EC may have played a role in hastening the democratization of Greece,

The European Summit in Madrid, in June 1989. In the front row are the Presidents and Heads of Government of the twelve European Community memberstates. Behind them are their twelve foreign ministers.

Spain, and Portugal, which were governed autocratically before the mid-1970s. Democratization of countries in Eastern Europe may well qualify Poland, Hungary, and Czechoslovakia (and perhaps others) for associate status, a sort of half-way house to membership. As for East Germany, when reunification with West Germany takes place, the eastern part of the enlarged Germany will simply become a region of an existing EC member-state.

It might be expected that experience in dealing with common problems within a common decision-making framework would encourage national political elites to transfer certain elements of national sovereignty to EC executive and legislative bodies and that some sort of European parliamentary system would emerge, gradually taking on a shape somewhat like what prevails in most of the member countries. In fact, the institutions that could assume such roles already exist. There is a community executive in the form of the European Commission, which consists of seventeen commissioners who are appointed by the member governments. If this body were to become truly responsible to the rudimentary legislative body—the European Parliament—the dominant role of the national governments, as currently exercised in another body—the Council of Ministers—might diminish over time.

The European Parliament consists of members directly elected by the voters in their countries. The first direct elections to the Parliament took place in June 1979 and since then have occurred at five-year intervals. It is the hope of committed Europeans that a popular base will enable the European Parliament to be more assertive in EC affairs, even to the extent of encouraging the European Commission to form an alliance with it and promote policies that may be unacceptable to some of the member governments, thus defying the Council of Ministers. The European Commission had adopted a very cautious stance toward the Council ever since its knuckles were rapped by General de Gaulle in the mid-1960s, but the decisions of 1985 have signaled a resurgence of Commission confidence and assertiveness. If carried too far, such an alliance of European organs would be contrary to long-standing government policies of the three most powerful member states—West Germany, France, and Great Britain—which seem to view the EC as a useful vehicle for intergovernmental cooperation and the occasional coordination of their foreign policies toward the rest of the world, especially the United States and the Soviet Union.[16] These governments are themselves responsible to their own parliaments or, as in the case of the French president, directly to the electorate. Opponents of greater European integration can argue that abandoning national sovereignty would actually be giving up well-established national systems of democratic control for a yet-to-be-tested system at the EC level.

Clearly, arguments can be made on either side from the standpoint of our set of value commitments. In principle, the EC could be an admirable vehicle for the integration of national policies that would enhance well-being, enlightenment, and respect for the peoples of Western Europe. Democratization of the EC would mean effective popular control over what is potentially a formidable concentration of power to produce good or evil. But a very real question is whether such democratization could actually be made to work and whether officials of the EC with the power to make decisions affecting human lives would not be so remote from those people as to render the latter powerless. As we have seen, many valid questions can be raised along these lines when we look at the way contemporary postindustrial societies are governed within existing national units.

## *Postscript (Germany 1990) and Conclusion*

In the spring of 1990, the near certainty that East and West Germany will soon be reunited into a new German state is riveting the attention of observers of the Western European as well as the Eastern European scenes. Elsewhere in the First World, events such as the survival of Liberal Democratic party rule in Japan following the February 1990 Diet elections, and the eruption of violence in Britain in the wake of the poll tax introduced by the Margaret Thatcher government in April 1990, have had to fight for media attention alongside East German and Hungarian elections and the struggle of Lithuania for independence from the Soviet Union. In fact, the events in Central and Eastern Europe are bound to have a profound impact on all five of the political systems that have been the concern of the past seven chapters. The most profound impact, of course is that upon West Germany, which will cease to be *West* Germany upon reunification, although it may still bear the name Federal German Republic.

The swift succession of dramatic events that are leading to the outcome of reunification began in the early fall of 1989, when, one after the other, the Communist governments of Hungary and Czechoslovakia decided to permit East Germans who had crossed into their countries to emigrate to Austria and West Germany. The East German government attempted to stop the flow of emigrants, many of whom were young, educated people, with good prospects of jobs in West Germany at considerably higher pay than those available in East Germany. This resulted in a spontaneous outburst of protest demonstrations in Leipzig, East Berlin and other cities that forced the removal from power of President Erich Honecker. On November 9, a hastily formed replacement government of lesser known Communists attempted to quell the uprising by removing the ban against emigration, or, in symbolic terms, by opening the Berlin Wall that had for nearly thirty years prevented free movement between East and West Berlin. This opened up the floodgates for a massive migration of East Germans into West Germany that averaged over 2,000 persons per day by the first months of 1990. In the wake of what was, in effect, a popular vote of non-confidence, the harderline Communists gave way to a reform-minded government, which made it clear that its principal objective was to achieve a true democracy in East Germany and to move toward reunification with West Germany.

Very quickly, the West German government echoed the call for reunification, and in early December 1989, Chancellor Helmut Kohl alarmed his NATO allies/European Community partners, as well as the Soviet government, by outlining a plan for a confederation of the two German states that would be a step toward an eventual federation. The four powers that had occupied Germany after World War II then moved to gain some control over the fast-moving process and, in a conference at Ottawa, Canada, attended by foreign ministers of both German governments (the "two"), and of the United States, the Soviet Union, Britain and France (the "four"), the so-called "two plus four" plan was agreed upon, whereby these six governments would work out the agreements that would lead to a unified Germany under conditions acceptable to all six. Eventually the agreements would be submitted to a larger body of all European states, East and West, for their accord. The acceptance of this plan by the Soviet Union removed any serious doubt that reunification would occur. From that point it became a question of how soon it would happen.

In the early months of 1990, a new political process came into being in East Germany, as elections for a new parliament were scheduled for mid-March, and West German political leaders, including Kohl for the Christian Democrats (CDU), Foreign Minister Hans-Dietrich Genscher for the Free Democrats (FDP), and former Chancellor Willy Brandt for the Social Democrats (SPD), crisscrossed the DDR (German Democratic Republic) in search of votes for their counterpart parties in the East. Most observers expected the SPD to win fairly handily, given their historic strength in the Berlin area and the industrial region of Silesia, and there were suggestions that Brandt would become the first President of the newly united Germany. But this was to reckon without the strategic advantage held by Kohl, who was able to focus East Germans' attention upon his call for economic concessions to East Germany and for the speediest possible reunification. Social Democratic leaders were more circumspect, believing that East Germany should not be railroaded into joining the Federal Republic, but that the new German regime should be the result of negotiation between more nearly equal partners. Election of a Social Democratic government in East Germany would ensure that Kohl's views could not easily prevail. Meanwhile, the existing communist government, headed by reform-

East German citizens are applauded by West Berliners as they drive through Checkpoint Charlie after the historic opening of the Berlin Wall by the East German government, November 1989.

minded Communist Hans Modrow, although resigned to the fact that it would not remain in power beyond the election, was campaigning on the demand that a future East German government should put the needs of East Germans first. Trailing far behind all of the above in the polls were various New Left, indeed post-materialist, parties resembling the West German Greens, that could justifiably claim credit for starting the stunningly successful protests of the previous fall, but which were unable to mobilize the support of most voters, who had themselves stayed on the sidelines in the fall events until it was clear which way things were going. In the March 18, 1990, East German elections most voters were to prove themselves decidedly materialistic. As an electoral force, the Green movement proved itself to be essentially a Western phenomenon.

The big winner in the March 18 elections was the East German version of the Christian Democratic Union of Helmut Kohl. The coalition of the Christian Democrats and two smaller conservative parties gained 48 percent of the popular vote and the same percentage of seats in the parliament. Although it was the second largest single party to emerge from the elections, the Social Democrats gained a very disappointing 22 percent of both votes and seats. The Communist party of Hans Modrow obtained 16 percent of both and the Liberals 5 percent. However, the Liberals were once again, as almost always in the Bonn Republic, in a position to hold the balance of power between left and right, as their 21 seats were enough to put the Christian Democratic-led coalition over the 50 percent mark.

But, for a variety of reasons, Christian Democratic leader Lothar de Maizière preferred to negotiate the formation of a Grand Coalition of his own three-party alliance with the Liberals and the Social Democrats. He reasoned that, in view of the momentous nature of the decisions to be reached, it would be best to associate all of the parties with West German counterparts in the responsibility for making them. Moreover, the constitution of the DDR specifies that amendments to it may pass only with a two-thirds majority, which would be assured only if the Social Democrats were added to the coalition. The formation of a Grand Coalition government in early April meant that the Bonn coalition of CDU/CSU and FDP would not face its exact mirror image in East Berlin and raised the possibility that reunification negotiations between the two German governments would have important issues to resolve.

Probably the issue gaining the most public attention at the time the new government was formed was the question of the conversion rate between West German and East German currencies—the Deutschemark (DM) and the Ostmark (OM). Although Kohl and Genscher had campaigned on the promise of a one-to-one conversion rate, voices within the Bonn government argued that this would put too severe a strain on the West German economy, with inflationary implications that might necessitate an unpopular tax increase before the December 1990 Bundestag elections. The suggestion of a one-to-two conversion rate (i.e., one DM would cost East Germans two OM) gave rise to howls of protest and renewed demonstrations in East Berlin at the opening of the newly elected Parliament. The conversion rate issue is part of a larger complex of issues involving the question of how much of their superior living standards West Germans can be expected to sacrifice, at least in the short run, in order to upgrade the material conditions of their Eastern brethren. The more equal the currency exchange rate, the more purchasing power East Germans would gain, which would mean upward pressure on West German prices. But to impose a conversion rate closer to the true market rate, which, depending on the definition, might be somewhere between one-to-five and one-to-ten, would be to condemn East Germans, at least in the short run, to a continuation of their much lower standard of living at a time when West German technological efficiency is taking over sectors of the East German economy and producing unemployment.

Although a compromise on the monetary issues was worked out over time, it has become clear from the sudden media spotlighting of East German economic conditions that the vaunted German capacity for hard work and efficient production has been much truer of West Germans than of East Germans. The massive influx of less educated and less skilled East Germans into West Germany in early 1990 brought attention to the lack of effective incentives toward hard work and career self-propulsion in the East than are found in the West. Integration of the two economies in *sociocultural* terms may prove to be a long-term process, indeed. Added to the problems of economic performance, and likewise attributable to the wrong kind of incentive system, are the dismaying disparities in pollution control between East and West that are so great as to have momentarily silenced Green protests against the *relatively* innocuous sins of West German industry. In industrial regions such as those around Halle and Leipzig in southern East Germany, industrial pollution has reduced the life expectancy average prevailing elsewhere in the country by as much as five years. To modernize East German industry in order to bring it up to Western technological standards of productivity, safety, and cleanliness will require a massive private and public investment at a time when the West German taxpayer will be asked to shoulder some of the burden of a welfare system designed to go much further than that in the West to make material conditions within society more equal. In West Germany the social market economy means that the ability to survive in competition determines one's place in society with the state smoothing out the rough edges. In East Germany individuals have been sheltered to a much greater extent from economic competition and assured of a modest, but safe, niche in society. Somehow these two opposed value commitments must be reconciled.

We can visualize the problem of amalgamating East and West Germany as involving the confrontation of two separate political cultures that have evolved from what was once a single, although certainly variegated one. Recalling our definition of political culture from Chapter 3, it is a statistical distribution within a given population of orientations toward politically relevant objects. When a population is split apart, the processes of political socialization and generational change can produce over time two separate distributions of political orientations. If an attempt is made, two generations later, to put those two subpopulations back together again, the best that one can hope for over the first decade or so, would be two very distinct political *sub*cultures with an overlay of agreement on basic objectives among political elites. The two subcultures can be expected to harbor quite different distributions of orientations regarding some, and maybe all, of our four basic values reviewed in the present chapter, adding up to quite different concepts of human dignity.

Clearly, the West German concept of human dignity is much more *individualistic* in tendency than is the East German concept. In East Germany, the underlying Marxist-Leninist philosophy of the long-ruling Communist party puts the collectivity ahead of the individual. Individuals advance along the four value dimensions that make up human dignity in so far as the society as a whole advances. Values are seen in class-collective terms: that is, the *power* of the working class collectively to advance its objectives against class enemies; the *respect* that workers and other formally undervalued groups should be accorded by those in society who have been more privileged; the advances in *well-being* to be gained by society as a whole as a result of the solidarity shown by workers engaged in building a more abundant economy; and the gains in mass *enlightenment* through the equalization of educational opportunities for the masses. Ordinary citizens in Eastern European countries appear to have become alienated from the regimes that have promoted those values and cynical toward the values themselves. It can even be said that the mass egress in 1989–90 of more than a million ethnic Germans from East to West represents a reassertion of the individual through an unwillingness any longer to share in collective misery and to seek improvement in well-being for oneself and one's family by an act that diminishes the human resources available to the collectivity to which one formerly belonged.

But this is a very negative sort of individualism, to the extent that it is not accompanied by a commitment to the relevant features of the competing value system represented by the part of Germany into which the hundreds of thousands are immigrating. There, individualism, even in a strictly materialistic sense, is accompanied by an acceptance of the competitive system of capitalism, where material advancement is, to a greater extent, dependent upon one's acquiring skills that are in demand, the rewards for which will depend upon supply and demand conditions in the open market. Many East Germans interviewed by Western media as the prospect of reunification looms have expressed reservations about such an economic system, seeing it as a potentially dehumanizing system where materialistic values supercede all others. What attracts them to the West is apparently the style of life enjoyed by Westerners when they are at their leisure, or else when they are working in the headier atmosphere of the young professionals depicted in Western films and televised dramas. The West represents variety and excitement in place of the drabness and boredom of life in the East. But one wonders how it will appear to those for whom it will also come to represent longer hours of boring work.

There is another aspect of human dignity, which we have touched on in Chapter 2, that is also getting a good deal of attention in connection with the prospective reunification of Germany. This involves the question of the *respect* Germans hold for other peoples. This is usually phrased in terms of respect of Germans for non-Germans, but, it is worth noting as well that the greater the cultural disparities between West Germans and East Germans, the greater the possibility that each subculture will deny the "other Germans" the respect that Germans on each side ordinarily give one another. But, setting that possibility aside, it remains the case that Germans as a people do not have a lustrous historical record when it comes to according respect to people inside or outside their country who are not themselves Germans. Instances from pre-1945 German history when some Germans did reveal a sense of identification with humankind at large, have been seriously obscured by the record of Germany during the Nazi regime, and especially during World War II.

Much of the discussion of a potential resurgence of German ethnocentrism that might be unleashed by reunification has centered on the experience of the Holocaust, when 6 million Jews were exterminated by the Nazis while the "Aryan" German population looked away. Incidents of West German intolerance toward Turkish *Gastarbeiter* today provide evidence to support the argument that even the more outward looking West Germans have not changed fundamentally, and that, once the details of reunification have been worked out, the government of a new Germany will feel strong enough to ignore the displeasure of the rest of the world and seek to remove non-German minorities from the country. The questions raised by the Kohl government about the postwar territorial settlement, and whether the border between East Germany and Poland should be regarded as legally fixed, added fuel to speculation about a renewed German nationalism. Further misgivings have been stimulated by the rise in 1989 of a right-wing, nationalist and anti-immigrant party, the *Republikaner*, which has demanded the restoration of Germany's pre-1937 boundaries as well as the expulsion of Turks and other non-German minorities. Although it is recognized that such manifestations attract overt support from only a small percentage of the West German population, the fear is that they express only the tip of the iceberg. And it is further believed that the iceberg is greater in East Germany than in West Germany, especially the anti-Semitic iceberg, for the schools and the media in Communist East Germany had systematically denied what their counterparts in West Germany had come in recent years to acknowledge: the responsibility of their own part of Germany for the Holocaust. In East Germany the regime had taken the stance that Nazi crimes against humanity were an artifact of the capitalist system, which still prevailed in the West, not the East. Hence, later generations in the West should feel guilt over what their forebearers had done, but not those in the East. Lacking a feeling of guilt regarding the consequences of anti-Semitism, East Germans were free to indulge themselves in the old-style feelings of ethnic hatred without any sense of *déjà vu*.

In fact, the framework we have employed in this text precludes an analysis which suggests that certain value commitments, however pleasant or unpleasant they may appear to us, are *inherited* traits of people of one nation more than of another. Our framework suggests that differences in value systems, while historically conditioned, are primarily a consequence of differences in the life experiences of present generations. If there is reason to think that East Germans may be less tolerant of non-Germans than are West Germans, we would suggest it is not because the former have not had their "Germanness" knocked out of them, but because their life experiences, particularly those of a socioeconomic nature, have been quite different. In terms of the value of respect, as well as that of well-being discussed above, East Germans appear to be more materialistic than West Germans. Tolerance of others is not likely to be a well-developed quality for people whose lives have given them little occasion to elevate their self-images and aspirations. Just as Ronald Inglehart's studies show that postmaterialism is found in higher amounts among educated persons from middle-class families than among working-class offspring of working-class parents, similar studies would undoubtedly find that a greater incidence of the latter type of person in East Germany would yield a more materialistic value system than that found in West Germany. Intolerance manifests itself among East Germans vis-à-vis Jews, Poles, and Vietnamese immigrants among others; but perhaps no more so than it does among Russians toward Lithuanians, or among Serbs toward Croats, or, for that matter, among Israelis toward Palestinians (and vice versa in all three examples).

If it is true that the cultural patterns of East and West Germany are dissimilar in certain politically relevant respects, then it may also turn out over time that the political party system of West Germany will not be exactly reproduced in East Germany. In March 1990, Chancellor Kohl may have succeeded in reaching a materialistic core of the East German political culture by appealing to German nationalism and the desire for economic betterment. His West German Social Democratic Opposition had incorporated too much of the postmaterialist value system into their public image to convince a large portion of East Germans that the Social Democrats were in tune with their basic preoccupations. But in time, the commitment of Kohl and other West German conservatives to a capitalistic, individualistic version of materialism may leave many East Germans longing for the socioeconomic safety net the old regime provided. At that point a Communist party with a reformed public image might reemerge as an indigenous regional party supported by many East Germans.

Whatever the mistakes and sins committed in its application, Marxism, as a pure value system, remains attractive to many of the world's underprivileged. It can not readily be classified in materialist versus postmaterialist terms, because, while it sees economics as the underlying driving force of all human activity, it profoundly condemns a social and political order that rewards and reinforces successful acts of human acquisitiveness. In this sense, Marxism is altruistic, or *other*-oriented, whereas capitalism is self-oriented, regarding selfishness as a good thing, at least in the abstract. Although they are rejecting a system that has failed to deliver on its more materialistic promises, many East Germans may not be prepared to embrace the underlying premises of the alternatives the West German political parties are offering.

In conclusion, it seems appropriate to remind ourselves that the Western value system that lies at the heart of the concepts employed in this text, like any value system, contains a set of ideals that are nowhere realized, or even approximated, in practice. One clash of systems and ideals that has been going on since the Bolshevik Revolution, indeed, since Karl Marx wrote, appears to have been resolved in favor of the *current* manifestations of Western values, at the expense of its *current* leading challenger, Marxism–Leninism. But the clash of values, and, happily, the reconciliation of values, will go on into the next century.

In the present century, democracy provided, after World War II, the context that facilitated a reconciliation between some of the promises and programs offered as alternatives by capitalist and socialist value systems. But inequality and poverty continue to be found even in the economically most advanced countries of the world, as well as ignorance and impatience with unpopular ideas. These consequences of the imperfect realization of our ideals will have to be met by a rededication to those ideals. The problem of preserving the natural environment against the onslaught of modern science and industry will be brought under control only when modern science and industry are more intensively directed toward environmental protection and recovery. If one system of ideas has proven itself unworkable in practice, it does not follow that an alternative system, that to which First World states formally adhere, has proven itself eminently workable. The exploration of alternatives requires a pragmatic application of the comparative method of analysis, akin to the scientific method of experimentation. By this method we can reject certain propositions that experience shows us to be false; but, likewise, we can not take as proven propositions that only a handful of cases tell us have not been falsified. If capitalist democracies appear to have worked better at an advanced stage of industrialization than have single-party socialist regimes, we can not say it has been proven that capitalist democracy is superior to any other conceivable form of regime. Such a conclusion would be based on too narrow a set of observations, nor would it give us an answer to the question: Which, if either, is responsible for those successes First World societies *have* registered, capitalism or democracy?

## *Suggestions for Further Reading*

**Alt, James E., and K. Alec Chrystal.** *Political Economics* (Brighton, England: Wheatsheaf Books, 1983).

**Andrain, Charles F.** *Politics and Economic Policy in Western Democracies* (North Scituate, Mass.: Duxbury, 1980).

**Ardagh, John.** *Germany and the Germans: An Anatomy of Society Today* (New York: Harper & Row, 1987).

**Ehrmann, Henry L.** *Comparative Legal Cultures* (Englewood Cliffs, N.J.: Prentice-Hall, 1976).

**Eulau, Heinz, and Michael Lewis-Beck,** eds. *Economic Conditions and Electoral Outcomes: The United States and Western Europe* (New York: Agathon, 1985).

**Gamble, Andrew.** *Britain in Decline: Economic Policy, Political Strategy and the British State,* 2nd ed. (Basingstoke: Macmillan, 1985).

**Gastil, Raymond D.** *Freedom in the World: 1986–1987* (Westport, Conn.: Greenwood Press, 1987).

**George, Stephen.** *Politics and Policy in the European Community* (Oxford: Clarendon Press, 1985).

**Heidenheimer, Arnold J.,** et al. *Comparative Public Policy: The Politics of Social Choice in Europe and America,* 2nd ed. (New York: St. Martin's Press, 1983).

**Hibbs, Douglas, Jr.** *The Political Economy of Industrial Democracies* (Cambridge, Mass., and London: Harvard University Press, 1987).

**Lincoln, Edward J.** *Japan: Facing Economic Maturity* (Washington, D.C.: Brookings, 1988).

**Lindberg, Leon N., and Charles S. Maier,** eds. *The Politics of Inflation and Economic Stagnation: Theoretical Approaches and International Case Studies* (Washington, D.C.: Brookings, 1985).

**Riddell, Peter.** *The Thatcher Government* (Oxford: Martin Robertson, 1983).

**Ross, George,** et al., eds. *The Mitterrand Experiment: Continuity and Change in Modern France* (Cambridge: Polity Press, 1987).

**Sassoon, Donald.** *Contemporary Italy: Politics, Economics and Society since 1945* (London and New York: Longman, 1986).

**Tufte, Edward D.** *Political Control of the Economy* (Princeton, N.J.: Princeton University Press, 1978).

**Wallace, Helen,** et al., eds. *Policy-Making in the European Community,* 2nd ed. (New York: Wiley, 1983).

## Notes

1. United Nations Educational, Scientific and Cultural Organization, *UNESCO Statistical Digest, 1986* (Paris: UNESCO, 1986), passim.
2. Ibid.
3. Organization for Economic Cooperation and Development, *Structural Adjustment and Economic Performance* (Paris: OECD, 1987), p. 76.
4. *UNESCO Statistical Digest*, p. 207.
5. R. A. Garden, "The Second IEA Mathematics Study," *Comparative Education Review* 30 (February 1987), 47–68.
6. The following comparison is based on a study by John S. Ambler, "Constraints on Policy Innovation in Education: Thatcher's Britain and Mitterrand's France," *Comparative Politics* 20 (October 1987), 85–105.
7. Ibid., p. 99.
8. Raymond D. Gastil, *Freedom in the World: 1986–1987* (Westport, Conn.: Greenwood Press, 1987), pp. 40–41.
9. Ibid., p. 18.
10. John T. S. Keeler and Alec Stone, "Judicial–Political Confrontation in Mitterrand's France: The Emergence of the Constitutional Council as a Major Actor in the Policy-Making Process," in George Ross et al., eds., *The Mitterrand Experiment: Continuity and Change in Modern France* (Cambridge: Polity Press, 1987), p. 167.

11. This is an area in which the Japanese Supreme Court has taken leadership away from the Japanese government in protecting a new category of human rights. Edwin O. Reischauer, *The Japanese* (Cambridge, Mass., and London: Harvard University Press, 1977), p. 264.
12. "The Flawed Renaissance: A Survey of the Italian Economy," *The Economist* (February 27, 1988), special section, p. 4.
13. OECD, *Structural Adjustment*, p. 72.
14. Ibid., p. 229.
15. Although it is true that West German industry does not appear by the measures displayed in Tables 7.4 and 7.5 to be making structural adjustments as effectively as those of Japan, the United States, and Italy, it will be recalled that West German trade figures are the most favorable of our six countries. Perhaps there is a *qualitative* element to West German manufacturing that stems from effective capital investment and R&D targeting as well as accumulated skills and know-how that maintain an exporting edge even for industries that exhibit relative decline by other indicators.
16. It should be noted, however, that in 1990 the governments of West Germany and France promoted a review of options for an Economic and Monetary Union and even a Political Union. The former might lead to a single currency for EC countries and to a central banking system; the latter might involve a democratization of EC institutions. The British government is resisting these steps, which the German and French governments see as essential if Project 1992 is to be successful in stimulating economic integration and regeneration in Western Europe.

# PHOTO CREDITS

**Chapter 2**
Page 46: Fritz Henle/Photo Researchers. Page 50: (top) Tom Hollyman/Photo Researchers; (bottom) Rapelye/Editorial PhotoColor Archives (Art Resource). Page 57: Niepce/Rapho-Photo Researchers.

**Chapter 4**
Page 102: Daniel Simon/Gamma-Liaison. Page 109: Derek Hudson/Sygma. Page 119: Stuart Franklin/Sygma.

**Chapter 5**
Page 131: Art Resource. Page 136: German Information Center. Page 138: Gilbert Uzan/Gamma-Liaison.

**Chapter 6**
Page 165: AP/Wide World Photos. Page 167: Hubert Raguet/Gamma-Liaison. Page 174: AP/Wide World Photos. Page 190: (top) Alain Nogues/Sygma; (bottom) Stuart Franklin/Sygma.

**Chapter 7**
Page 223: D. Aubert/Sygma. Page 226: AP/Wide World Photos.

# INDEX

# Index

# Index

# Index

# Index



## R



## S

# Index